G000168538

# WHEELS OF LIGHT

For Peggy Fitzgibbon

Kindest regards

fr. Con Buckley

# WHEELS OF LIGHT

Introductions, Homilies, Prayers of the Faithful, and Reflections for each Sunday of the Three-Year Liturgical Cycle, with extra Material for Special Feast Days.

Fr. Con Buckley

authorHOUSE®

*AuthorHouse™ UK*
*1663 Liberty Drive*
*Bloomington, IN 47403 USA*
*www.authorhouse.co.uk*
*Phone: 0800.197.4150*

© *2015 Fr. Con Buckley. All rights reserved.*

*No part of this book may be reproduced, stored in a retrieval system, or transmitted by any means without the written permission of the author.*

*Published by AuthorHouse 2/2/2015*

*ISBN: 978-1-4969-8410-4 (sc)*
*ISBN: 978-1-4969-8409-8 (hc)*
*ISBN: 978-1-4969-8411-1 (e)*

*Any people depicted in stock imagery provided by Thinkstock are models, and such images are being used for illustrative purposes only. Certain stock imagery © Thinkstock.*

*This book is printed on acid-free paper.*

*Because of the dynamic nature of the Internet, any web addresses or links contained in this book may have changed since publication and may no longer be valid. The views expressed in this work are solely those of the author and do not necessarily reflect the views of the publisher, and the publisher hereby disclaims any responsibility for them.*

*Bible quotes in this book are taken from:*

*The Jerusalem Bible, for this is the text used in the Catholic liturgy. (London: Darton, Longman and Todd, 1966, 1967, and 1968).*

# Preface

My parishioners down the years have praised my sermons, the fruits of many hours of preparation, and they have asked repeatedly, "Why don't you publish them?". On the Internet, published as *A Priest Reflects*, they have already proved popular. I am publishing them in this book so that readers can access them in the flesh also, as it were.

Orthodox theologians say that the liturgy is the educator of the faithful. So priests who bemoan the lack of good adult Christian education have a sure remedy at hand. Sunday scriptures, homilies, prayers, reflections, and feasts comprise an awesome faith dynamic. This is especially true if ministers use their instructional and inspirational power well, if they light up the Sunday Word by their preaching, so as to instruct and energize the faithful, and send them out with a powerful sense of the faith's depth and greatness.

These introductions, homilies, reflections, and prayers should help the presiding minister in that task, so that his people will go out on fire to live the immense riches in Christ embodied in the Sunday mass's scriptural themes, to live it in and for our times.

Let me outline my methodology in this process. It is a new and more coherent "seamless robe" approach. The main theme or themes of the scripture of the day, or of the feast, are developed throughout in an ongoing lively way. Thus the introductions offer a brief summary of the day's Word, identifying the link between the Old Testament and the gospel, and noting anything the second reading adds. So that, when the scriptural texts are read, people, alert to the central themes, will listen more profitably.

The homilies elaborate on the scriptural or feast themes and relate them to life now, with stories, anecdotes, newspaper headlines, and references to recent events. The aim is that the Word light up our experience today; for scripture is forever old and forever new. My doxology, repeated at the end of each homily, is scriptural. Apart from the fact that when people hear it they'll know the homily is ending and doubtless breathe a sigh of relief, it emphasizes that the Word of God is life for this world as well as the next.

The creed introduction and prayers of the faithful echo the homily themes in petitions for Church leaders, civil authorities, youth, the sick, the dead, and private intentions. I feel we should be praying on Sunday for youth, so that the gaps in our congregations there will be bridged. The presiding priest should add topical intentions on local or international issues.

My reflections after Holy Communion are brief, not the homily all over again. They reinforce the overall message and leave people with something memorable to take home.

All in all, then, I hope this book will help all who celebrate mass or services of prayer, to make their input gospel based, inspirational, relevant to life, and to the point. The homilies last about five minutes, people's normal attention span. I hope people get as much enjoyment from reading and using the material, as I got in its composition.

Fr. Con Buckley.

These liturgies, continued, are on line at www.apriestreflects.com, or at www. conbuckleyssunday sermons.com. Or search Google for "Fr. Con Buckley sermons"

# PART I

# Liturgical Cycle, Year A

# The First Sunday of Advent A

## *Introduction*

We start a new Church year by preparing for Christ's birth. Isaiah anticipates his Advent in the first reading, and the gospel tells us to be ready when he comes. Let's light the candle on the wreath to begin our preparation. And before our first Advent mass, let's confess any sins that block his coming in our lives.

## *Homily*

What was the most moving event in your life? Doubtless for a lot of you, it was the cry of your first or recently born baby. For each child is freshness, innocence, wonder. A new unique being has entered our world, with our help, in God's ongoing creation. Its cry offers hope for the future, new love for our hearts. It's with similar hope that the Church, after ending its year with remembrance of the dead, calls us in its new year to prepare for a birth. For if each child is a miracle, how much more so is the birth of the Christ child? For us that birth is not a one-off. It occurs constantly in the miracle of the Church year.

We prepare well when a child is expected, attending meetings with the doctor, buying baby clothes, setting up a nursery, making sure the expectant mother eats nothing that might harm the baby. So also the Church asks us to prepare well for Christmas with fresh inner life and belief. Having lit the candle on Advent wreath, let's resolve to do just that. During Advent let's cast off inner darkness, shine up our souls, as it were, as we do our shoes. For this baby calls us to renewed faith, prayer, and charity.

Christ describes this as staying spiritually awake should he come at any time. The night of death always threatens. So we need mornings of renewal to rise from the dark sleep of sin, so that when our soul is required of us, we'll be ready to stand proudly before the Lord, as he stands in judgment (Lk.21:27-28, JB). The world is a testing ground and a vale of soul-making. Advent furthers that process; it enables a new morning for the soul. We're given a time to rise from any sleep or death in the joy of Jesus's birthday. In this dark time of year, when light is scarce, his Second Coming is a warm beacon that shows the way to leave our inner winter, and experience a new spring.

And we always need that renewal. I was at a school once explaining about Holy Communion, and a child put it very well. I said, "Without this food we grow weak." "Yes," said the child, "and we fall down." he was right. Without God's life within, Satan drags us down until we risk being lost altogether. We need times of prayer, confession, and charitable outreach to redress any drift in our life. Christ's baby cry invites us to such renewal now so that we'll be bright stars at Christmas. "Cast out our sin and enter in, be born in us today," the carol says. And if Christ is reborn in us at Advent, there will be new light also for the Church, and the whole world to which we're mysteriously connected.

But Advent is a preparation not only for his birth, but also his Second Coming at the end of time. We cleanse our hearts now so that we'll be ready to go out to meet him with the saints at last, and he'll say, "Well done, good and faithful servant" (Matthew 25:23, JB). For a new heaven and new earth will come about then, but we must help to shape it now. And we're wise to do so for everyone's good. For the godless values of which Satan is lord pass away at last and leave us empty before eternity, but Christ is Lord of love, glory, and peace for our deeper happiness in this world and forever and ever. Amen.

So, as the people of God called to renew our inner life this Advent to be ready for Christ's coming at Christmas, at our death, and at the end of time, let's affirm our faith.


### Prayers of the Faithful

And as God's people preparing for Christ's birth at Christmas, let's ask our Father for the things we need this Advent.

For our Holy Father the Pope and all church pastors, that through their efforts the the saving light of the Christ child will renew the face of the earth.

For civil leaders, that they may contribute to the welfare of all their people by the laws they pass this new year, and govern us especially in the interests of peace, and for the special benefit of the poor and most vulnerable in our society.

For youth, that, inspired by Christ's birth this Christmas, they may make a new commitment to him and his Church for their deeper happiness in this world, and the final salvation of their souls, so that they'll go out to meet him with all the saints at last.

For ourselves in our families, that, through this Advent of prayer, fasting, and alms giving, we may be freed from sin and renewed within, to face the new year with fresh minds and hearts, and enlightened souls.

For all the fathers and mothers preparing for a birth this holy season, that it may bring immense happiness and joy to them.

For the sick, the lonely, the aged, and the poor, that they may be freed, healed, and comforted by the coming of the Christ child. May our care and love bring Christ to them this Christmas, especially to those in need within our own families.

For the dead, especially those who have died recently, that they may be reborn to a new life and come home to God, their gentle and loving Father and Mother in heaven.

And we ask all these our prayers through Christ, born for us this holy season in overflowing peace, grace and joy. Amen.

## Reflection

There are three ways to approach Christmas. The consumer way: buy, buy, and end with a hangover and bad bank balance. The Dickens way: good will, roaring fires, snowy scenes. And Christ's way, which adds faith, love, and inner peace. By balancing the three, we celebrate Christmas fully. For feasts, reunions and familial good will are as vital to the season as prayer. Let's ask Mary for a glorious Christmas in every way. Hail Mary.

# Second Sunday of Advent

## Introduction

As we light a new candle, let's reflect on how Advent renewal is going. In the first reading we've a vision of the new earth the Christ child brings—the wolf lying down with the lamb. Like John in our gospel, we can help shape this paradise by making straight the way of the Lord in our hearts and world. Let's confess any ways we fail to do so.

## Homily

If there's a patron saint of Advent its John the Baptist. He was the first herald of Christ's birth. The word *John* means "the Lord has shown favor." He responded to God's favor generously. So the Church puts him before us as a faith model today. A cousin of Jesus, born late to Zechariah and Elizabeth, from birth he worked to prepare for Jesus, and fulfill scripture: "Prepare a way for the Lord, make his paths straight" (Mark 1:3, JB).

We can to do the same now. For we were anointed as Christ's prophets at Baptism, and vowed to love God and others with all our heart, soul, and mind. John did that with total generosity, giving his life for the truth; because he'd grown steadily in grace from youth when he went into the wilderness to find God and begin a great mission to bring people to God, and his Christ. We can do the same in our small way.

Indeed, we vowed to do so at Baptism and Confirmation. Let's confirm those vows by witnessing to him before the world and by holy lives. Like John, rather than straws in the wind of worldly values, let's be people of God—people of faith, integrity, and love. He called people to God and right in a violent immoral age. Yet was it so different from our world. It too needs to be called from skepticism, immorality, and materialism to faith, love, and goodness. John was heroic in opposing of the corruption of the day; so must we.

But John didn't just preach; he lived the faith. And he finally gave way to Christ. He wasn't focused on his own fame, power, or glory, only on the truth. In our age too, we should stand for all that's true, good, and holy, even if it means standing out, or suffering. And having done our duty, let's have John's humility also, accepting our limitations and humbly placing ourselves in the Lord's hands, saying, "I am nothing special. I am just doing my duty." Not all of us can be great prophets like John, but we can light up the earth by living our Baptismal vows, and helping to redeem the fallen aspects of our world.

Our homes especially can be lights of love, honesty, and integrity, and above all fun. For people need Christian joy now as never before. So gathered here in faith, let's vow to do just that in the spirit of John. Let's love our children and spouses. Let's lead them in happy homes, and accompany them to joyful Advent and Christmas masses. Let's work in our community for peace and justice for the poor. Let's make this Christmas a special time for lonely, sick, or old people who need our care in whatever small way we can. But above all, let's celebrate this great gift of God and his Son with every good cheer, even to excess. So that, like John, we'll be raised up when Our Savior comes. For the crooked ways of the world distort and destroy the soul, but in Christ we can make all of that straight, make a difference by shining lives. For Christ is Lord of love, goodness, peace, beauty, and truth both for happiness in this world and forever and ever. Amen.

So, baptized to be modern prophets for Christ, for all that's true and good and joyful in life, let's profess our precious faith anew.


## Prayers of the Faithful

As the people of God we pray now to our heavenly Father for all that we need to be his loving hands this Advent and Christmas.

For our Holy Father, the bishops, and Church pastors, that, like John, they will make straight in our confused and broken world a highway of faith, peace, and goodness for God and his Christ.

For civil leaders, that they may listen to the voice of God and the people, not just their own interests and worldly ideology.

For youth, that they may find the true youth of their hearts and souls in following Christ and his Church faithfully to inner joy here and hereafter.

For ourselves, that this Advent we may live out our prophetic Baptismal role; may we witness to Christ and all that's life giving and gracious in our homes, workplaces, and wider world.

For the sick and needy of our parish and world, that through our generous sharing of our time with them we may help shape a more pleasant, more enjoyable, and more loving Christmas for all.

For the dead, may they enter the heavenly home reserved for them from the foundation of the world, helped by our communal prayers.

And we ask all these prayers through Christ Our Lord, the source of all goodness, grace, and peace forever and ever. Amen.

## Reflection

There is a story told of a man, also called John, who heralded Christ in today's world. He used to call into the Church each day to say hello to Jesus. People noticed that he became kinder and happier as a result. "What do you do in the church?" they asked him. "Oh," he said, "I just say hello to the Lord, and he says hello to me. We get closer as time goes on." That, dear people, is the prayer we're all called to this Advent—to get closer and closer to the Lord and so be more amiable and life-giving to all around us. Let us pray that our mother Mary will help us do that. Hail Mary.

# Third Sunday of Advent

## *Introduction*

This is Gaudete Sunday—the third Sunday of Advent—and we light a pink candle to show our joy in the Lord. "He will exult with joy over you," the first reading says (Zeph. 3:17, JB). Paul tells us to be happy, for the Lord is coming; and Christ says that they're happy who don't lose faith in him. Let's call to mind ways we fail to laugh with the world.

## *Homily*

The great joy in life is to be close to someone we love. I saw on TV once, teenage girls at a boy band show. One of the girls was in tears and said words like: "O my God! I can't believe I'm close to him!, he actually spoke to me!". I smiled that a pop star could evoke such adoration and ecstasy. It seemed out of proportion. Then I thought, *No!* We all need someone larger than life in our hearts and imaginations to love, worship, and look up to. Of course in this, the ultimate object of our devotion, God, brings us most joy.

That's what we celebrate this Gaudete Sunday. The Lord is near, so we experience joy like that of our teenager. Saint Paul says: "let your tolerance be evident to everyone, the Lord is very near" (Phil. 4:5, JB). Already we have the joy of Christ with us in Word and Communion every Sunday. Let's pray that he'll come even closer to us at Christmas, stay with us for the New Year, and never let us down, until he takes us home at last.

But reflecting further on Advent and Christmas joy, I thought curiously of Christ's passion. We don't usually think of the passion as joyful, but watching scenes from Gibson's film, *The Passion of the Christ,* brought home to me the extent of Christ's love, and I made a link with his birth. There was joy in Christ's heart, though he was born in a cold stable and died on a cross. For true happiness is more than skin deep, more than facile satisfaction. Its freedom to achieve our aims and enjoy our lives at the deepest level. And that's difficult without self-giving love of God and others. There's no happiness without loving and being loved. And we mustn't equate love with sex. It's important, but it's more satisfying and enduring when built on personal love. We tire of pleasures, but never of love. And finally, only God fulfills our dreams in the eternal love of his heavenly home.

Like the girls at the Westlife event, we seek someone to adore. In God's presence we find lasting joy: "No eye has seen, no ear heard, things beyond the mind of man, all that God has prepared for those who love him," Paul says (1 Corinthians 2:9, JB). Isaiah says the same to the people; "Cry out for joy and gladness, you dwellers in Zion, for great in the midst of you, is the Holy One of Israel" (Isaiah 12:6, JB). We are united with Christ in Communion, and he is with us at Christmas, throughout the year, and always. So as the second reading says, our Christian joy should be boundless and timeless, and light up our souls unto eternity. But like that girl at that particular event, overcome and crying, our joy should overflows more at this time of year, for Christ is close in the flesh.

Our Christmas blaze of lights, feasting, peace on earth, and good will all exist because of this nearness. Let's make no apology for extravagantly celebrating his birthday. For as our scripture says, his love drives out all fear, and transcends even pain and the dreariness of winter. For its joy is deeper than anything the world can give. Rejoice, Paul says, because God "guards your hearts and your thoughts, in Christ Jesus" (Phil. 4:7, JB). Certainly all else palls, but he is Lord of beauty, truth, goodness, peace, and salvation for happiness in this world and forever and ever. Amen.

So as the people of God gathered in expectation of the Lord's imminent coming in this happiest of seasons and at the end of time, our final liberation, we make our profession of faith, in the joy of Christ's timeless presence.

## *Prayers of the Faithful*

Let not your hearts be troubled for the Lord is near. Christians, natural optimists, we make our prayers for the things that we need, material and spiritual.

For our Holy Father and all Church leaders, that joy and confidence in the Lord may always inspire their witness; in that joy, to bring his fullness to all, may they promote good standards of living, and inner spiritual riches for all the nations of the earth.

For civil leaders, that by their wise rule they may bring joy into all their people's lives this Christmas and throughout the new year, especially to those most deprived of the fullness of life and joy through poverty, sickness or mental depression.

For youth, that this Advent they may find more and time for the Lord in their lives and so experience a lasting joy the world cannot give.

For our own personal happiness in our homes and communities, that we may we have plenty of everything: enjoyment of life's pleasures, love given and returned, and God's grace in our souls this Advent and Christmas.

For the sick and needy in our midst this Advent and Christmas, that finding time for them may be part of our renewed prayer, penance, and generous giving in the spirit of Our Lord's birthday.

For our dead, especially those who have died recently, that they may enjoy ultimate enjoyment and happiness in the presence of the Lord, and their loved ones who went before them in faith.

And we ask all these things through Christ the salvation of the world and our loving Lord, through him may we enjoy a full life in this world and happiness forever. Amen.

## *Reflection*

"I want you to be happy, always happy in the Lord," (Philippians 4:4, JB). This time of year, there's no value in long faces. The smile is the key to life, and its full enjoyment. It brings riches and joy to those around us. So let's smile now and always, even if sometimes through tears. For God guards our hearts and minds in Christ Jesus Our Lord, and Mary is our mother forever. We pray to her for smiling faces and hearts to light up the world around us this Advent, Christmas, and New Year. Hail Mary.

# Fourth Sunday of Advent

## Introduction

The first reading reminds us today that God the Father sent us Jesus to recreate us as his family. This is the good news Paul describes, his closeness to us. As fathers, mothers, or general caregivers, let's do the same for all, and confess where we fail in this.

## Homily

One day I was visiting a home. A little girl was on the floor in the sitting room; her father was in the kitchen preparing lunch. She said. "Shh, don't call Dad. I'm preparing a present for him." She took an empty matchbox, wrapped it in colored paper, so that it seemed a gorgeous present, took it into the kitchen, and gave it to him. He understood, kissed her, and said, "Thanks, baby." That matchbox wasn't empty; it was full, full of love. The father's kiss was love returned. Mutual love is what parents and children need most.

A popular country and western song by Tammy Wynette, called *No Charge*, about a mother and son, makes the point. A son gives a piece of paper to his mother. Roughly paraphrased: for mowing the lawn he asks for five dollars, for making his own bed he asks for two dollars, for going to the shop for groceries he asks for five cents, and for playing with his little brother while she went shopping, he asks for twenty-five cents.

The mother turns over the page and writes – I roughly paraphrase her answer: for the nine months I carried you, no charge; for the nights I sat up with you when you were sick, no charge; for all the prayers I said for you when you were in trouble, no charge. She goes in that vein for some time while the son gets more and more embarrassed.

Eventually, realizing his ingratitude, and what he owes his mother, he embraces her.

We're sometimes like that with parents, and with God. Far from appreciating all he's done for us, we make endless demands. God might write: For the world and the pleasures of life I gave you, no charge; for still loving you when you turned away to follow violent selfish ways; for sending Jesus to bring you and the world back to happiness and innocence; for the agonies of the cross he suffered for you; for giving you my risen Son to be with you forever as Savior; for the victory he won over sin and death for you; for the holy Church he gave you to be your spiritual home; for the heaven he opened for you where you can be happy forever after your life and work in this life is done—no charge. The cost of God's love is no charge. Let's give him due return without charge also.

And let's love the parents he gave us. Not just the mothers but fathers too, for they seem an endangered species now. Is militant feminism making them more sidelined? In any case, I say to fathers who are caring for their families, take heart. We are with you. God is with you, in your work to create a life for your family. Let's all pray for dads hanging in there, overworked and unappreciated, and give them a hug this week.

For good mothers and fathers alike, are the salt of the earth. God is the perfect Father and Mother. We're not just his people, but his family. In Christ he made us his adopted sons and daughters, but even before that for all eternity he loved us individually. That's what life's about, love. We come to Church to say to God, "We love you." For Jesus's prayer, the Our Father, tells us to call God "Daddy."

But there's a third father we sometimes forget. We call priests "father" and say they should marry. But we forget they already have a family in their parishioners, and witness to transcendent values by their celibate life style, as Christ did. They need love and support too, as their spiritual children. For though imperfect, they do their best to bring us to our heavenly home. They teach that all else passes, but Christ is Lord of grace and peace for our happiness in this world and forever and ever. Amen.

So as God's family, called to faithful love in our homes and in the Church, let's profess the faith anew at this time of the fatherhood and motherhood of God.

## *Prayers of the Faithful*

We pray for our Holy Father and all leaders of God's family the Church, that the Lord may lead them in loving parental care for their Christian family and all earth's people.

For state authorities, that they may care for all in love, justice, and fairness, and be especially mindful of their needy children, the poor and oppressed in body, mind, or soul.

For our youth, that they may find time for their heavenly Father and his home, the Church, knowing that that's where lasting happiness lies for this world and the next.

For ourselves in our homes, that as parents we may keep our families happy, loved, well fed, clothed, housed, and faithful to the faith of their larger family, the Church, this Christmas and always.

For senior citizens, sick, lonely and needy relatives this Christmas, that through our care for them in body and soul—visiting, feeding, clothing, and comforting them in love—they may know the gentle love of Christ.

For all our beloved dead, especially parents and grandparents who have passed away, that they may receive the reward of their care and love from their heavenly Father in his eternally enjoyable and happy heavenly home, which is full of all good things.

And we ask all these prayers through Christ Our Lord, in the power of the Holy, to God the Father who cares for us all with infinite love as our heavenly Father. Amen.

## Reflection

At Christmas we often forget Jesus's earthly father, Saint Joseph. We couldn't have a better model for parents and all carers. He saved Mary from being stoned to death. And he saved the infant Jesus by fleeing across the desert into Egypt. He spent his whole life working as a carpenter to keep Jesus and Mary in comfort; Jesus loved Mary and Joseph so much he spent thirty of his short thirty-three years on earth with them. So we pray now the prayer we all learned to Joseph, his Son, and wife that they will watch over us and our families. Jesus, Mary, and Joseph, I give you my heart and my soul etc.

# The Birth of Our Lord Jesus Christ

## *Introduction*

Tonight our joy overflows at Christ's birth and saving love. All was dark before God sent him, but after his coming, as Isaiah says: "The people that walked in darkness have seen a great light" (Isaiah 9:2, JB). So, as Paul says, we live good, holy lives as we await his Second Coming. The angels and shepherds proclaimed peace, good will on earth. Now and always, let's banish hatred, and bring peace and love to all around us.

## *Homily*

What event in life brought you most joy? Your first kiss? Your wedding day? Your first child? Such events sustain us in dark times. The birth we celebrate tonight is similar. Before Christ's birth, all was dark; after it, all was glorious. He came to a lost world as a helpless baby, and humanity was reborn. For that frail child was God's love made flesh. Hymns like *Silent Night* but faintly capture that miracle of that love, born in a stable. We can't thank him enough for the gift of his Son. For we live since as divine children.

We gather tonight to celebrate that; God loved us so, he was born in a manger. Our carols only faintly capture that mystery. A child is born for us; a son is given to us who is Christ the Lord. Mary gave Jesus the first kiss for us; for he came in humble love in the cold of Herod's winter, and all our deepest dreams came true.

That should shake up even today's hard secular world. God broke the veil between creature and creator in the form of a crying child. Mary's wrinkled baby should soften even the hardest heart into faith, life, and peace. And it should inspire all of us to treat those around us with great respect. For to harm a human being now—a brother or sister in Christ—is blasphemy. Our family is everyone, especially the old, sick, poor, and lonely.

The need to celebrate all these blessings adequately explains why we go mad at Christmas. The Word became flesh in an excess of God's love, and his birthday should be celebrated with excess. For in becoming man, Christ made material things holy too. Any effort to divide the material and the spiritual is perverse. Christmas means food and drink as much as prayer; indeed, it deserves twelve days of feasting. For the human body and God are one in this baby. He didn't come as an angel, but eating and drinking, and feeling cold and pain, and loving and being loved in the flesh like us.

Because this is true joy, the angels rightly got worked up: "Today in the town of David a savior has been born to you, he is Christ the Lord. Glory to God in the highest heaven, and peace to men who enjoy his favor." (Luke 2:11-12 and 2:14, JB). Let's take to heart this message in an earth of war, suffering, and hate, lets be his favored ones. John Lennon in one of his songs complained that even in the holy season people don't seem to know its Christmas; the killing continues in a mockery of its message of peace. Refuse to be part of that, lets work actively for peace at Christmas and always. Like a popular seasonal song by Roy Wood says, lets make it Christmas every day.

Mary gave Jesus his first kiss on behalf of us all. Our good works of peace and love are the kisses we give him in return. For we're commissioned by his birth to spread peace, love, goodness, and happiness to those around us, now and in the New Year. For, though the cruel warring world mocks his message from God, to that frail child belongs the kingdom, the power, and the glory forever and ever. All else is dross by comparison; it passes away to dust and ashes at last, but he is Lord of love goodness, peace, and joy both for human happiness this world and forever and ever. Amen.

So as God's people rejoicing at his birth and working to bring his peace, love, and justice to all earth's peoples this Christmas and in the New Year, we profess our faith.

## Prayers of the Faithful

We pray for our Holy Father the Pope and all Church leaders, that they may be ambassadors of peace and world equality, and so bring Christ's saving presence to the whole world at this holy time, and for all time.

For civil leaders here and throughout the world, that they may live the Christmas message of peace and goodwill to all.

For our wonderful youth, that this holy time may see them safe in the bosom of their families, the eternal arms of Christ, and ever true to holy mother Church.

For ourselves, that where there's darkness in our lives we may dispel it with the light of God. May we bring peace, love, grace, and happiness to our spouses, families, and all at this holy time.

For the sick the old the lonely and the depressed, that through our love and care they may know the love, comfort, and healing of Christ this Christmas time and always.

For all those who have died in the peace of Christ, especially the relatives and friends who can't be with us this Christmas, that God may lead them safely to the heavenly home where we will be reunited with them one day.

And we make all these prayers with confidence on this holiest of nights, through Christ Our Lord born for us in a stable of love. Amen.

## Reflection

The Christmas Truce during the first world war, illustrates the theme sung by the angels at the first Christmas; peace on earth, good will among men. The soldiers on their own bat crossed the dividing lines between them, shook hands, exchanged gifts, and even played games together. This proves that the ordinary man knows what Christmas means—peace; they know what Christ represents—peace; they know what the Christian faith represents—peace. It also shows the "good will" to peace is there in each heart if we only respond, if we're strong enough to do it regardless of politicians, if we heed the Our Father phrase, "thy will be done on earth as it is in heaven". For, as the Christmas song by John Lennon says, peace is there "if we want it", an end to hunger is there "if we want it". Sadly the soldiers went back to doing the will of man the following day, to power and dominance of others that is part of our sad fallen nature. If we really "wanted it" there would have been peace on earth on earth long ago. justice on earth long ago. The key to peace then is each human heart, each human will, redeemed and enabled by the grace of God. Lets pray to Mary that she'll help us achieve that universal peace and good will in God and his Christ which is the final redemption of humankind. Hail Mary.

# The Holy Family of Jesus, Mary, and Joseph

## *Introduction*

The family is under siege today, with breakdown common. So we might listen to the wise advice for parents and children in the first reading to practice mutual respect, love, and kindness. As Paul says, "let the message of Christ, in all its richness, find a home with you" (Col 3:16, JB). Like the Holy family, may we endure all hardship and be bonded in unbreakable love. And in this season, let's confess any failure to heal family divisions.

## *Homily*

Last Christmas calls about abused children and battered wives flooded help lines. Violence, abuse, and loneliness were the dominant themes; alcohol was a major factor in many cases. Not a good ad for our family life, or sense of what matters at Christmas—peace and good will. Add to this a huge increase in family breakdown in our society, and the picture seems depressing.

So is there any point in the Holy Family feast? Certainly not, if our image of Jesus, Mary, and Joseph is of a no-problem family. But that's far from true. They were poor. After traveling to Bethlehem, they were shut out of the inn. Jesus was born in a stable. They fled from Herod across the desert with scant food and danger everywhere. Then they were refugees in a strange land, threatened, excluded.

Nor is Luke's account of the teenage Jesus free from rebellion. When his parents found him in the temple, he said, perhaps petulantly: "Do you not know that I must be busy with my Father's affairs." (Luke 2:49,

JB). Yet he submitted to them and grew in age and grace before God and man.

Indeed, Jesus spent 90 percent of his life eking out a living with Joseph and Mary in an obscure village. Could God have affirmed the value of family life more? And if that family had plenty of trials, it brought them closer, rather than pushed them apart. And that's the message of the feast. They're the family who hangs in there, prays together, stays together, defying all difficulty, building home life in the love of God and each other. For love is a conscious decision to keep loving, no matter what.

That's more difficult today, but it's doable. A huge number of families still get it right: by the grace of God remaining true to Christian principles of love, faithfulness, and non-violence; sacrificing the pub and personal ambition to be together; and working for each other and their children in an atmosphere of affection, trust, and peace. It's not easy building such a family, but the alternative is unthinkable—social disintegration, reversion to irresponsible selfish individualism. The ones who usually suffer most in that scenario are the most precious beings of society, children. They deserve the love and security a caring father or mother, preferably both, can only give. They need a warm home so that they too can grow "in wisdom, in stature, and in favor with God and men" (Luke 2:52, JB).

The Holy Family was a real family. They stayed together through adversity. No less is expected of families today—to create loving, caring, stable homes where children can grow in age and grace. For worldly lust passes, but Jesus is the Lord of faithful, enduring love and care both for our happiness in this world and forever and ever. Amen.

So gathered here as God's family the Church, and praying for all our precious families before our Father and the holy family in heaven, we make our profession of faith.

## *Prayers of the Faithful*

For the Pope, the Father of God's family, that he and all bishops and fathers who pastor God's familial Church may do so with the love, care, and diligence of Christ himself.

For our leaders in public life and government, that they may promote and support family life by their laws and rule, and so bring about a healthy and nurturing society.

For our youth, that they may enjoy good, life-giving family life and also be happy members of their larger family in God, the Church.

For ourselves in our own families and homes, that we may love and nurture equally all our family, and that we may feed, clothe, nurse, educate, and bring them up in age and grace and truth before God and man.

For husbands and wives, especially those in endangered marriages, that they may continue to grow in the love that first brought them together until they're one forever in their final heavenly home.

For our aged sick or lonely relatives, friends, and neighbors, that we may reach out to them in familial love and care and so bring to them the love of God.

For the dead members of our families, that they may, with our prayers, come to their heavenly home where we will be reunited with them one day.

And we ask all these prayers through Christ Our Lord who spent most of his life in a humble family home in an obscure village.

## *Reflection*

That there is no place like home, is a common saying. So is the wise observation that a good home is where the heart is. Love flourishes there and is nourished every day; no one lacks a hug, a kiss, or a shoulder to cry on. Let's pray to our Mother Mary, who was the perfect mother, and Joseph the most caring of fathers, that they may fill our homes with such nurturing peace and love, for that is where the heart will always find rest. Hail Mary.

# Solemnity of Mary, Mother of God

## Introduction

We sometimes forget that we've both a mother on earth, and a mother in heaven. Christ gave Mary to be our mother on the cross (Jn.19:26-27). We pray to that Holy Mother today for all mothers, and we express our sorrow for any failure in parental care.

## Homily

William Ross Wallace's poem proclaims what has become a general saying, that the hand that rocks the cradle is the hand that rules the world. Certainly, a good mother is priceless. And today's feast of Mary, mother of God and our mother, gives us a model for parents. God chose for Jesus a real down-to-earth authentic lady. "He has looked upon his lowly handmaid" (Luke 1:48, JB), she says. She also drew a moral from God's choice: "he has pulled down princes from their thrones and exalted the lowly" (Luke 1:52, JB).

That is, God's choice of Mary upsets worldly values. It says the really important people are not the legends in their own eyes but unpretentious, gentle, humble, and loving people often laughed at by the world: saintly nuns, kind carers, good fathers and mothers, faithful parishioners, dedicated nurses and doctors, and so on.

At the time of Jesus's conception there were plenty of the opposite sort of woman—rich, powerful, self-serving women such as Herod's wife. But God didn't ask her to be his mother or invite her to worship his son. It was humble shepherds who came to his son in a manger. And it was a poor, obscure village woman who suckled him. Our salvation was in her acceptance of that role. But she could do no less.

For it expressed God's will, and all her life she had put that will before her own.

And that's the message for us today, as the worldly towers of Babel crumble around us. To cop ourselves on. For our sense that we're here to serve God and fellow humans can fade if we're enslaved by money, or total lust for fame, or other worldly pursuits that leave us no time for our families, deeper relationships, or God. Even at Christmas we can lose ourselves in this way. I remember that, when I was abroad being shocked by Christmas commercialism; the day was a success if sales were up. On Boxing Day decorations came down and it was straight into the sales. Many of us still celebrate the Twelve days of Christmas with family gathering, midnight mass, presents, visiting the crib and so on. Surely, for Christians that should not change?.

I hope it will not, for real happiness is in the Christmas message— to be faithful to God's humane, wise, and gentle Christmas values as represented by Mary. I'm sure 90 percent of us are doing precisely that; seeing beyond the vain glitter, to the ideal of family togetherness. I do not at all agree with the pessimists. They show lack of faith in the Lord and his Holy Spirit. In many modern-day Bethlehems, overlooked by the world, God is even now inspiring the Marys of our world—people with humble, generous souls who answer his call, and forge the real future of society by means of real caring hearts and homes.

Look at the difference Mary's yes made. Because of it we're assured of the long-term victory of goodness. We make a similar difference if we hang in there faithfully in love no matter what the world throws at us. That word *faithful* is a wonderful word, and it is just what Mary was. We should be like her. Our faith and goodness should light up our world as it lit up hers. In homes, parishes, and work places, through prayer, social work, collecting for Vincent De Paul, caring for the elderly, and working in parish pastoral teams we can make a difference. Good priests, nuns, and saintly lay people—they're the Marys of our day. For only humble, faithful Christians can birth Jesus in a world as troubled, violent, and lost as it was in Mary's time.

"Behold the handmaid of the Lord" (Luke 1:38, KJV). Let's say and mean that. For cruel worldly values fade to dust at last, but Christ is

Lord of love, goodness, grace, and glory both for this world and forever and ever. Amen.

So as God's people, called to serve him and others with humble hearts, like Mary, in an often dark and troubled world that needs our faith and care, let's profess our faith.

## *Prayers of the Faithful*

For the Pope, and all church leaders, that they may serve God and his people with humble care and love, like that of Mary toward her family, and all of us her new family.

For all those who govern us, that they may not lord it over the people but give humble, honest, and equal service to all.

For our great youth, that they see that true and enduring value is in Christ and Mother Church and find rest for their souls there.

For ourselves in our trials and difficulties, that we may turn to Mary our Mother, and Mother of the Church, at all times, and ask for her healing and loving care for us all.

For the sick, the old, the lonely, and the oppressed, that through our love and care they may experience the love of Christ.

For the dead, that they may come to their heavenly home in peace light and glory.

And we ask all these prayers through Christ, the son of Mary, amen.

## *Reflection*

The story of Lourdes gives us a good image of Mary. There she came to a poor frail girl, Bernadette, and addressed her with great gentle love:

"Would you do me the kindness to come here". Bernadette said that she was very beautiful but also young and humble and radiant with light, not at all overbearing, or full of herself. That's our gentle mother, and each of us is her beloved child as brothers and sisters of Christ. Confident of her gentle love and care, we commend ourselves and our families to her. Hail Mary.

# Second Sunday after Christmas

## *Introduction*

Today we're reminded that God became flesh and dwelt among us. Any view that he is remote from us eating, sleeping, working humans is gone. Jesus reveals a God who, sharing our joys and suffering, shows us how to live good, fulfilled lives in this world and with him forever in heaven. So let's confess any ways we fail to appreciate his love.

## *Homily*

You may have heard or read Oscar Wilde's children's story known as *The Happy Prince*. It has become a parable for our time. The prince's gold statue dominated a famous city. One day a swallow, resting on him, was surprised to see a tear run down his golden face. "Why are you crying?" the bird asked. "Because I see all the misery in the city around me," the Prince replied. "Please, swallow," he added, "pluck some gold from my body and give it to the starving family over there." It was late in the year, and the swallow should be flying to warmer climes, but he stayed, feeding the poor by stripping the prince of his gold. Then, too late to go south, he snuggled into the prince's heart and died. The city lords, seeing the prince's dull and tarnished frame, pulled it down to make way for a military monument. The prince, and the dead bird in his heart, were thrown on the scrap heap.

That's the story of the gospel. For our prince is Christ, who, as today's gospel says, became flesh and dwelt among us. He cast off his golden clothes to suffer and die for us, ending up on the scrap heap of the cross. Loving us and crying over our misery, he came down from heaven to heal us.

We, his followers, are called to be that swallow, servants of a prince of love. We're to make the same choice as Christ, do something about human need, and get our hands dirty in the process. Sure scaling down our own interests to do his work usually means sacrifice, but true love always involves suffering.

That's the long-term meaning of Christmas for the drab year ahead. For as the tinsel fades, we face again the reality of the world. But Christmas celebrations tell us that we're not alone. God's with us in the flesh, walking in our shoes, sharing our joys, weeping our tears, rejoiced in our successes. And from him we get our Christian identity. The prince who stripped himself of glory for our sake, wants us to be his hands now. As the swallow experienced, it may cost us a lot to serve him, but it will be worthwhile.

For by loving and serving Christ, we will fulfill our humanity, the purpose of our existence, which is to do some good as we pass along. To give glory to God by incarnating his love in our fallen yet beautiful world. The world may throw us on the scrap heap as a result, but God will raise us up. Christian love means going down there like Christ into the gutter: meeting the violence and suffering of our world; doing what we can to redeem it where we are; making his love, justice, truth, and goodness real in our own homes, marketplaces, factories, shops, and TV stations. For though we're flawed and human, he needs our hands. Like the swallow, each of us can be his heart to the world.

God raised Jesus from the scrap heap of the cross and made him Lord. We should proudly serve that golden Savior, and be his hands in a life of love and service. For the things of this worlds pass away, but to Christ, the golden prince who stripped himself of glory for us, belongs the kingdom, the power, and the glory forever and ever. Amen.

So as God's people serving our Prince, and each other, with his love, gentleness, and faithfulness, let's profess our faith.

## *Prayers of the Faithful*

For our Holy Father, and all church leaders, that they may be humble servants of God; spreading light, love, peace, faith and good standards of living to all the earth.

For civic leaders, that they may serve all the people under their care, free from corruption, favoritism, and lust for unaccountable power.

For our wonderful youth, that, like the swallow serving the Prince, they may serve Christ and his Church with ever more generous hearts.

For ourselves, that in every aspect of our lives we may be gentle servants of God and others and so help to redeem our needy world.

For the sick, the aged, the lonely, and poor of the world, that we may be the hands of Christ reaching out to them with love and care.

For the dead, that through our continuing love and charitable prayers they may come to their heavenly rest.

And we ask all these prayers through Christ our Golden Prince of love and care both for this world and forever and ever. Amen.

## *Reflection*

A perfect example of caring for all as the hands of Christ is Mother Teresa of Calcutta. But she tells us that it is not enough to serve people's bodily needs; we must love them as people and as God loves us, individually and intimately. She notes that it's no use loving or serving in theory, solving all the world's problems in grand talk, while the poor are dying at our very gates. We pray that our charity may be more than fine words, but real help for the needy on our doorstep. Hail Mary.

# The Epiphany of the Lord

## *Introduction*

Today we finish the Christmas period of feasting with the feast of the Epiphany, or little Christmas as we knew it once. On that day, women who'd done the work over Christmas were supposed to sit down; men were supposed to do the serving for a change. We pray that we'll help in this way, and we ask forgiveness for gender discrimination.

## *Homily*

That the wise men came from the east is a timely reminder. As the sun rises in the east and gives life everywhere, the coming of the wise men from the east denotes that Christ's salvation is for all. The Old Testament said so too, that when the Messiah came, God's salvation would reach earth's ends. All would be reconciled with God by his Christ.

In effect, all people are our brothers and sisters in Christ now; because saved by him, regardless of race or religion or nation. The tsunami in Indonesia a few years ago brought that home to me, as we all pitched in to help. The unity of humanity there prefigures the Christian vision of the new heaven and the new earth that must come in God's plan. The great debate the tsunami disaster also threw up, however, was the reality of suffering in the world still, despite the Lord's coming. Why does God allow such things? One answer is that God doesn't ordinarily interfere with nature's functioning; if he did, we'd be manipulated puppets, not free human beings. World redemption must be our free choice too, and we are moving in that direction, with the early prediction of disasters and so on.

But if, due to our freedom, God cannot force the solution to all our problems on us, it doesn't follow that he doesn't care. Christ didn't accept sickness or disease, but worked to heal the afflicted everywhere. Affliction, he said, was from the evil one, part of the fallen world he came to redeem. And he shared our sufferings on the cross to show God loves us and cares, and is with us in the task of healing all his children everywhere in the world. For though suffering's inescapable in a free fallen world, it can be alleviated by active human love and care. Christ came to be with us in that work. The wise men came to him from afar; our task is to bring salvation to all, those near and far away alike.

So I'm sure he's proud when we respond generously to world disasters. For he wants us to be his healing hands now, helping all afflicted by tragedy. Modern medicine is one aspect of this practical redemption. So is science, which can foretell natural disasters such as earthquakes for early evacuation. And technology—helicopters and such—can get help quickly to the needy. This is God's work, and we must support it wholeheartedly.

But in an increasingly global village, rich countries must give more. That's the larger lesson of disasters. A United Nations representative said on TV the other night; we rush to help tsunami victims, but ignore problems in the Congo and other war-torn regions. Christian aid agencies work tirelessly in these areas; we must pressure the European Economic Community and other world powers to do likewise. For its God's will that prosperity and peace should come to all peoples. The earth's resources, reports the United Nations, could feed thirty-five times our present world population. The problem is unequal distribution of wealth—the first world gobbles up so much there's little for the rest. For every euro given to poor nations, we take out nine in payments to first-world banks.

The wise men who came to Christ were doctors. They and we must share the medicine, education, and prosperity that we have. For the mission given to us by Christ is to heal a broken world. It was for that he was born and died, to show that God cares about human suffering. And spiritual poverty. The wise men represent all earth's children coming to his saving grace too. We work so that all will come to salvation in body and soul; God's universal Kingdom come. For this world passes, but he is Lord of life, goodness, truth, and salvation for our happiness in this world forever and ever. Amen.

As God's own, blessed to be so and praying for the practical and spiritual redemption of the whole world, as Christ's hands on earth now, we profess our faith.

## *Prayers of the Faithful*

For our Holy Father and the leaders of the Churches; may they reach out to all people with a message of healing, both for this world's ills and their eternal salvation.

For our civil leaders, that they may help the practical and spiritual welfare of all the citizens and reach out generously with what aid they can to those in need abroad.

For wonderful young people, that beyond personal wealth, power, or fame, they may be conscious of a larger responsibility to God, neighbors, and people everywhere.

For the sick, the aged, the depressed, the lonely, and those without faith, that through our care of body and soul, they may come to fullness of life here and hereafter.

For ourselves, that we may be conscious of welcoming all people as our brothers and sisters, and deepen our own faith, hope, and charity for the good of our children.

For the dead who have passed from the cares of this world, that they may come safely to their heavenly home, especially all our loved ones and all our sisters and brothers in the parish who have passed away recently or whose anniversaries occur at this time.

And we ask all these our prayers through Christ, who is universal Savior and Lord in every way, forever and ever. Amen.

## *Reflection*

A good example of the saving grace of Christ, is the story of the leper priest Father Damian. He went to live with a leper colony on the isolated island of Moloka'i, Hawai'i, when no one would care for, or pastor that flock. One morning, washing his feet in hot water, he realized he could feel nothing. He had become a leper. He went out onto the altar and prayed, referring to "we lepers." He lived Christ's practical and spiritual mission to the needy, as all of us should. We pray to Mother Mary for similar courage. Hail Mary

# The Baptism of the Lord

## *Introduction*

Our gospel today features Christ's Baptism. It should remind us of our own Baptism, and how precious it was. For then we became God's children. We received the Holy Spirit and became part of his local and universal Church. Let's give thanks for that, and confess ways we have failed to live out our Baptismal promises.

## *Homily*

What a wonderful thing Baptism is. Our tiny son or daughter is made a child of God and freed from evil and death. Today's gospel emphasizes this in Christ's own Baptism. When I was in Palestine, a group of us relived that Jordan experience. In the midst of the desert, off with shoes and into the cool water, knobby knees, varicose veins, and all. As water poured over me I imagined the rough figure of John, the crowds waiting to be baptized, and the youthful Christ up to his knees in the water. A dove swoops. The Father shouts, "This is my beloved Son." Yet our Baptism is as glorious. God says the same to each of us at Baptism: this is my beloved son, this is my beloved daughter.

For when he ascended to heaven, Jesus made us all God's babies, and the Father dotes over us as he doted over Jesus. And we in turn should rejoice to be his children, his best creation, given a new innocence and heavenly destiny as water is poured over us.

That destiny is mainly to be holy as our heavenly Father is. Farmers, shopkeepers, nurses, street cleaners, unemployed, whatever, it makes no difference. For as Vatican II says, at Baptism we're all made equal children of God, each empowered to bring God's goodness into the world. As children of our blessed Lord, we should do that joyfully.

But being holy is different from being perfect, we'll never be that. It means serving all that's good and best, living out our Baptismal calling to be priests and prophets for Christ, despite our weaknesses. We're to renew the face of the earth in the power of the spirit we receive. Young or old, sick or well, working or pensioners, we never retire from that calling, to be holy as our heavenly Father is. We're to live a life of prayer and love all life long, to light up our world. At each stage of life, we're to be faithful to his Church. For we are saved not as individuals but as part of a community of faith, worship, and charity.

That's why I say to people at confession, stop listing the same old faults. Think instead of how well you live you Baptismal calling to work for Christ, his Church, and the world's good. As the New Year dawns, let that be our resolution, despite our frailty and sinfulness to struggle toward ever-fuller service of God, his Church, and humanity. Old or young, sick or well, working or retired, we can do that because of the spirit we received at Baptism. Whether president of America or a helpless invalid, we can all do great work. I hate modern talk about quality of life, as if only young, shiny, healthy-haired ones of TV ads count. We're all precious from the first to the last breath, vital to God's plan. Our main task is to be faithful and serve humanity, so that when Christ comes again, as the Baptismal prayer says, we'll to go to meet him with all the saints, and inherit the kingdom that he has prepared for us since the Creation. For all else fades to ashes at last but Christ is Lord of love, goodness, peace, happiness, and salvation forever and ever. Amen.

So as God's people baptized into, and serving Christ in the world as faithful members of his Church, let's profess our faith anew.

### Prayers of the Faithful

As people reborn by water and the Spirit let's pray for our needs.

For the Pope and all Church leaders; true to their Baptismal and priestly calling may lead the faithful in humble service of God, and the needy people of the world to justice.

For civil leaders, that they may serve their people's needs in body and soul, and be especially mindful of the poor and vulnerable in society.

For our wonderful youth, that they may keep their Baptismal and Confirmation vows to be faithful to Christ and his Church, and to work for his just universal kingdom come.

For ourselves, that in our homes, communities, and local Church we may serve Christ faithfully and live out our Baptism in goodness and holiness in daily life, so as to be examples to our children who need our guidance, inspiration and love.

For all our children who were baptized or who have received First Holy Communion or Confirmation, that they will live out their Christian calling to be holy, worship every Sunday as faithful members of his holy Church, and witness to Christ in daily life.

For the sick, the aged, the lonely, and the depressed, that consciousness of their dignity as precious children of God through Baptism, we may help them to come to know the love of God their Father through our care.

For the dead who wore the white robe of Christ's resurrection at Baptism, that they may enter into the fullness of eternal life promised then, come into their heavenly home.

And we ask these prayers through Christ of the heavenly Father for he is Lord forever and ever. Amen.

## Reflection

Baptizing fifteen adults of various nations once reminded me of the universal nature of the Church, and that Christ's command is being ever more fully fulfilled: "Go, therefore, make disciples of all the nations;

baptize them in the name of the Father, and of the Son, and of the Holy Spirit" (Matthew 28:19, JB). I asked one of those who had just been baptized how she felt, and she said that for the first time she felt real peace within. We who were baptized as infants missed that kind of adult commitment to Christ. So we might make that mature commitment to Christ and the Church anew today in our hearts, and ask Mother Mary to help us live it every day, in purity of heart. Hail Mary.

# Ash Wednesday

## *Introduction*

Today we start Lent's prayer, fasting, and almsgiving to prepare for Easter. Let's do so as if it was our last Lent. For we know not the hour when our souls will be required of us. Conscious of a constant need for repentant renewal of faith, we confess our sins.

## *Homily*

Lent's prayer, fasting, and almsgiving follow a great tradition. Christ prayed and fasted for forty days and tells us it's the way to overcome evil. Our Lady of Medjugorje says prayer can change our violent world, and the saints say that fasting makes prayer a thousand times more effective. Our ancestors often prayed and ate nothing but bread and water for Ash Wednesday; it was a means to inner cleansing. My father told me that his parents took only black tea and dry bread on Good Friday.

If fasting is so spiritually healing, why is it so hard to sell now? Maybe because a consumer society encourages excess in sex, food, and drink. Recently, parents in a local town refused to let children take the pioneer pin for Confirmation. Do we want children drinking at the age of twelve? Restraint seems foolish in today's world, but we Christians are more than citizens of the world. Fasting is our calling, in imitation of Christ who prepared for public life in this way. It enabled him to resist Satan's temptation to make power and wealth his God. We can also achieve much self-denial; God's people too, it nourishes our souls, frees us from sin, and helps us transcend the world's evils.

Ashes symbolize all that. You know the story of Jonah: God told him to preach repentance to Nineveh, the immoral city. When he did so, the king and people prayed, fasted, put on ashes, and were saved. Similarly our Lenten penances signify repentance and turning back to God. And with this goes alms giving; notably, if what we save in fasting goes to help the deprived of this world. Our fasting to give to world charities can help, in some small way, to right the scandalous imbalance between the rich and poor.

And in these three aspects of Easter preparation – fasting, prayer, and charitable giving- nothing extraordinary is expected of us. We can just give up luxuries such as alcohol, sweets, or smoking, which are bad for us anyway, and pray more, morning and evening, and give of our excess to the poor. All this ensures that our hearts will be cleansed to welcome our Easter Lord. He gave all for us on the cross. We give something back by Lenten disciplines and we store up riches in heaven. For this world passes, but he is Lord of life, love, goodness and salvation forever and ever. Amen.

So as God's people committing ourselves in this time to fresh prayer, fasting, and charity so as to welcome the Risen Lord with renewed hearts, we make our profession of faith.

## Prayers of the Faithful

For our Holy Father the Pope and all the pastors of the Church, that they may lead the people of God and all the world's people to the fullness of faith this Lent and Easter.

For civil leaders, that they may put no obstacle in the way of the renewed faith of the people this Lent, but also promote people's spiritual welfare for a balanced society.

For our wonderful youth, that Lent may be a time of commitment to Christ and the Church, especially those who have drifted from the faith. May our prayer and fasting help them to come home.

For ourselves, that this time of Lent may be a time of grace, peace, and inner growth for us as we devote ourselves to self-denial, prayer, and alms giving in imitation of Our Divine Lord.

For those of our world who reject God, that they may heed the call of Christ to repent and believe, and so find rest and happiness and salvation for their souls.

For the sick, the aged, the lonely and oppressed, that through our care this Easter they may know the healing presence of God's love

For the dead, especially those who need our prayers to come to the fullness of light and life, that this season of grace may be a final liberation for them and especially for those holy souls who have no one to pray for them.

And we ask these our prayers in this grace-filled time of Lent when the ashes on our heads symbolize the rekindling of grace and holiness in our hearts, through Christ Our Lord. Amen.

## Reflection

Most Catholic visionaries of recent centuries, from Our Lady of Fatima, to Bernadette of Lourdes, to the modern-day apparition at Medjugorje, give us a message of prayer and penance for the conversion of sinners. They see this as urgent, and related to peace and justice in the world. We pray for that tonight as we embark on our Lent of holy disciplines, that we may obey the Lord's command to repent and believe and so bring others to new life in God. And we ask Mother Mary to help is in this. Hail Mary

# First Sunday of Lent

## *Introduction*

This Sunday features the desert temptations. Satan urged Christ to serve his own wealth and power rather than God and others unto the cross. It's the temptation we all face, and one the Church has failed over and over in its history with its grand palaces and pompous prelates. Let's fortify ourselves against that by Lenten practice and confession.

## *Homily*

Christ tells us in today's gospel that man doesn't live on bread alone. It's a message for our time that requires us to realize that we need faith to give deeper value to our lives. Some Christians sent to the salt mines in Russia during the secular communist era illustrate this: "Others there were stronger and had more bread than I," several of them say, "but they died and I lived; it wasn't that I kept the faith, but that the faith kept me." Modern science bears this out, saying evolution favors those of faith; they are the fittest who survive. Yet many foolishly close themselves off from belief. Like dictators such as Stalin, some politicians would enforce this approach now by banning Catholic schools. The thin end of a secularist wedge? The European treaty doesn't mention God. But undue worldliness robs us of the faith that sustained us down the ages, and is our final salvation.

And that's what Christ tells Satan in the desert. Man doesn't live on bread alone. During the economic boom, that wisdom cut little ice; money, cars, big houses, foreign apartments were everything. As wealth increased, faith declined. Who needs God? Money is enough. Satan's voice echoes in our world: "I will give You all these (the kingdoms of worldly power), if You fall at my feet and worship me" (Matthew 4:9,

JB). No wonder the first commandment is the first. Not that worldly goods aren't to be enjoyed; God made them for us. But "alone" is the key word in Christ's reply to Satan: "Man does not live on bread *alone*."(Lk.4:4, JB). When we make material things all, our souls shrivel. Does a mother care for baby's physical wants only? Christ saw through Satan's ruse; so must we.

But the devil didn't give up; he turned the screw tighter: Come on, you're God's Son! Use magic for your gain. Forget the stupid scriptural role of being the suffering servant. Serve yourself and trample on anyone in your way! Satan would make Christ in his own image, a power-hungry fanatic like Hitler smashing enemies, riding to glory on the blood of fellow humans. Our modern world is full of such people who kick pensioners to death for a few euros, or drug lords who destroy our youth for pads in some seaside idyll. Christ chose suffering love rather than ruthless greed and fame, and became Lord of all.

But first he faced another key temptation, to put God to the test. The temple caper is like someone today saying: "God, give me a lotto win, or else." Like a spoiled child, we'd have God dance to our every tune. He doesn't ordinarily ignore natural laws. If he did, our freedom would be out the window. Christ tells Satan that real faith is in trusting God through suffering, when the easy way out isn't given. It's the test Christ passed on the cross. He cried, "My God, my God, why have you deserted me?" (Mt 27:47, JB), but he was quoting a psalm whose finale saw the Christ triumph *precisely through his suffering*. For worldly trials test us and pass, but Christ on the cross is Lord of love, goodness, glory, and happiness for our deeper happiness in this world, the nourishing of our immortal souls forever and ever. Amen.

So as God's people, seeing through the blind pursuit of worldly power and greed that can strip us of faith and self-giving love of God and fellow human beings, leaving us desolate on the shore of eternity, let's profess our faith anew.

## *Prayers of the Faithful*

Craving more than bread or money or self-glory, let's ask for all we need.

For our Holy Father the Pope and all leaders of the Church, that they may convince us of our need for God as well as the things of the world, the value of self-giving charity, and steadfast faith as our true lasting riches amid life's ups and downs.

For civil leaders, that they may help, by their laws and practices, to nourish the spiritual as well as the material well-being of all their citizens.

For ourselves, in homes and work places may we practice self-giving love, faith, and trust in God through all trials, sufferings, and difficulties, and so gain the crown of life.

For our wonderful young people, that they may not be so caught up in the pursuit of wealth, power, fame, and pleasure at all costs so as to neglect the humble service of God and others that is salvation for their souls and their main reason for being on earth.

For the sick, that they may see value in unavoidable suffering and offer it up like Christ for the salvation of the world.

For the dead, especially those whom we have loved, that through the prayers and masses we offer for them they may come to their heavenly home.

We ask these prayers of Christ who intercedes for us before the Father, amen.

## Reflection

In recent times the Church often put wealth and power before humble service of God and its people. This self-centered and unaccountable power is surely the reason it is brought low now, by its sins against the vulnerable. Christ's words, "Man does not live on bread alone" (Matthew 4:4, JB), should convince us that vulgar shows of pomp, power, and wealth are far from the apex of our Christian existence. Christ stressed that Christian leaders should never lord it over people, like the worldly do, but be humble servants of the servants of God. Christ himself lived that life of service even unto the cross. Thankfully, the present Pope Francis is heeding his words; he lives in a simple apartment. Christ washed the feet of his disciples and had nowhere to lay his head. As a Church we pray to our lowly Mother that we may learn that worldly glory passes but it is in imitating our humble servant Lord that we gain real riches. Hail Mary

# Second Sunday of Lent

## Introduction

Scripture today features faithfulness to God despite the suffering that involves. Abraham left family and country for God. Paul says, "bear the hardships for the sake of the good news."(2Tim.1:8, JB). Christ came down from the mountain to face the cross, for it was God's will. Let's confess times we shun hardships in serving God and the Church.

## Homily

> She walks in beauty like the night
> Of cloudless climes and starry skies,
> And all that's best of dark and bright
> Meet in her aspect and her eyes.

You know Byron's poem about a woman at a dance. It wasn't her physical beauty that attracted him, but the beauty of an innocent soul. Real beauty is within. People flocked to Jesus because he radiated goodness. Yet the powerful crucified him. God's light shining through his humanity showed up their darkness. That divine beauty, revealed on Tabor, dazzled the apostles. Peter wanted to stay there forever; it was heaven on earth.

Yet coming down the mountain Christ's talks of the cross. A British Baptist preacher, Charles Spurgeon, said, "There are no crown wearers in heaven who were not cross bearers on earth." We have periods of joy in God, but our faith is proved amid life's trials. Just as the everyday struggle to make marriage work must follow wedding-day bliss, Jesus came down the mountain to live the cost of total love unto the cross.

So must we. Life's luminous moments of faith can anticipate the radiance of heaven. But to achieve that we must, as in Lent, prove ourselves by prayer, fasting, and charity. We must cling to God through all sufferings. We must struggle up the mountain of sickness and death at last with the cross, before heavenly bliss. Because of human freedom, God doesn't take away suffering; if he did so we'd be manipulated puppets. Yet being his suffering faithful brings joy no worldly gain can give. I see that when I visit hospitals. I see illness, but also faith that enables people to transcend pain by inner strength in God; so many say, "Without faith and prayer, I'd never get through this pain."

Ads would convince us that beauty is about costly makeup. But closeness to God is what makes us most beautiful. And such inner grace grows rather than diminishes with age and suffering. Look at Mother Teresa. She was small, old, ugly, and wrinkled, yet her inner peace was contagious. A person who worked with her in Calcutta told me that, when she entered any room, everyone lit up. It was like that with Jesus. And we too can achieve a beauty that's more than skin deep by prayer, mass, and living the gospel. In Christ we can achieve a glory that draws others to our light, and flowers finally into eternal life.

In times of loss and pain, or whenever we're put to the test, such faith should enable us to endure and overcome all. That's what we should shout from the rooftops that Jesus who showed his divinity on Tabor is everyone's light for this world as well as the next. Each of us is beautiful in some way, but more so when one in Christ. That's why we can say of his Church, and all those who belong to it, despite her human faults and theirs, that they walk in beauty and light, even in the darkest worldly phases of their lives here. Our beauty in union with the Risen Lord can overcome all life's darkness, sin, and suffering. For though the world is to be enjoyed fully as a great gift from God, it fades to ashes at last, but Christ is Lord of life, truth, beauty, and grace both for our fuller happiness in this world and forever and ever. Amen.

So as God's people, following Christ through all the trials and sufferings of life so as to rise with him to untold glory forever, let's profess our faith.

## *Prayers of the Faithful*

As God's people secure in his dazzling light as Risen Lord we make our prayers through him with confidence to our Father.

For the Church throughout the world, especially our Holy Father the Pope and all its leaders, that shining with the Lord's light it may dazzle the world into faith and goodness.

For ourselves, that in our homes and work places, during this holy time, we may be a light of faith and love to all those around us.

For good civic leaders, that they may lead us out of every gloom and recession, and further our spiritual as well as material well-being in any way they can.

For our young people, that they may come to fullness of life and light through the disciplines of Lent and the joy and glory of meeting the Risen Lord this Easter within his great and holy Church community.

For the sick, the lonely, the aged, and the depressed, that they may come to peace through our love and care for them. May the grace of God comfort and enable them to link their suffering to Christ's sacrifice on the cross, and so help save the world.

For the dead; may they come to that glorious risen state Christ prefigured on Tabor.

And we ask all these our prayers through the same Lord of glory, amen.

## *Reflection*

Some people have charisma. I remember an audience with John Paul II. He radiated warmth. Yet that wasn't won easily. He suffered under fascism and communism in Poland. Later as pope, he was shot. And finally we watched him, an ill pontiff, struggling to speak to the crowd in Saint Peter's square. No wonder he was canonized recently; he earned his ascent to holiness in the crucible of suffering faithfulness to Christ and his holy church. Like him we too can attain through life's crosses the radiant glory of the blessed. May Mother Mary, who suffered with Christ, lead us also to his glory. Hail Mary.

# Fourth Sunday of Lent

## *Introduction*

"I once was lost but now I'm found, was blind but now I see." John Newton's *Amazing Grace* lyrics remind us that Christ cures all spiritual blindness. In our gospel, we see him opening the eyes of the blind man. Yet the Pharisees refused to accept his light. Unlike them, let's keep our eyes open to his light, in faith and goodness. Let's open our eyes and hearts to his grace and confess any sins that close us off from God and others.

## *Homily*

Close your eyes. Imagine going around in a perpetual night. That was the hell from which Jesus delivered the blind man. But he didn't stop there. He brought the man's soul into light too. The blind man believed in Jesus and became his witness, preaching even to the Pharisees. But, hard of heart, they wouldn't accept his witness, or its focus, the Christ. Corrupted by riches and power, they refused to see, lest they have to change their ways.

This is a warning for our time. At birth we're spiritually blind. Baptism brings us into the God's light and enables us to walk in it always. But the path of God is more difficult to walk now. Many, taking the Pharisees' role, bombard us with darkness. So pause again. This time imagine your soul in darkness. Now let Jesus lead us out of that night to the dawn of God's paradise, free from any lingering spiritual blindness or moral hardness of heart. For its easy in our world to pursue self and pleasure regardless of God or others, to abandon life-giving basics of right and wrong, to close our eyes to the crying needs of those around us, and to tailor our conscience to whatever the world dictates. A world where, as the gospel says, the blind lead the blind into the ditch.

Much of the world, of course, rejects that way too. As children of light in Christ we must especially resist that way, and help others to do so. We must hold to the high morality and idealism that Christ offers, and which is summed up in two simple commands: love God, and love one another. They seem simple, but in fact involve a self-giving that is quite demanding—a suffering commitment to justice, peace, goodness, and love. God's ten commandments were not a burden, but were given to free the Israelites from spiritual slavery. Jesus gave us eight beatitudes to lead us to similar freedom. But, like the Pharisees, we can choose hardhearted worldly blindness instead, not only spiritually and morally but also socially; for example, when we don't heed the cries of the poor.

Again close your eyes. Imagine you're in a council house with three children trying to live on social welfare, with the loan shark at your door. Imagine you're a single mother living on a meager allowance, trapped in poverty. Imagine you're a lonely pensioner in a cold house, sick, dying. Now open your eyes to such needs and help alleviate them in whatever way you can. Even in difficult times we can all help in some way.

Jesus came to heal all such blindness, to lead the world to freedom, justice, goodness, and happiness. Souls lit up with his presence, seeing and living in the light and so illuminating the world as well. Rather than loving the darkness or hardening our hearts, let's embrace his light. For the blind worldly way leads but to dust and ashes, and at last to perpetual darkness. But he is Lord of love, goodness, happiness, and light both for our freedom and happiness in this world and forever and ever. Let us too say, like the blind man, "I once was lost but now I'm found, was blind but now I see." Amen.

So as God's people, opening our eyes spiritually, morally and socially to what's right and true in Christ, let's profess our faith.

## Prayers of the Faithful

For the Church throughout the world, especially the Pope and all its leaders, that they may lead the flock and the whole world out of blindness and darkness into Christ's glorious light of faith, love, peace, justice and goodness.

For ourselves, that free from the blindness of sin and hardness of heart, we may bring faith, kindness, and love to all around us at home or at work, and especially to our children.

For civil authorities, that unlike the authorities of Christ's day, they may open their eyes, not close them to faith, as the real welfare of the people they serve.

For our wonderful youth, that they may be lights of faith to illuminate the future of the Church and of society.

For those who suffer from incurable blindness or deafness or any other ailment that curtails their life, that they may find comfort in Christ their loving Lord and in our care for them as his healing hands now on earth.

For the dead, that they may not be trapped in everlasting darkness, but may come into the full light of God and his Christ with the help of our prayers.

And we ask all these prayers through Christ Our Lord why is forever the healing and saving light of the world. Amen

## Reflection

Early in life, Saint Francis was rich and spoiled, blind to his own soul's darkness and the spiritual decay of his day. Then God appeared to him and said: "Francis, rebuild my church." He went around restoring churches. Then he opened his eyes to the wider spiritual and social ruin around. Wearing rough clothes, he begged to give to the poor and called hosts of other young men to the work of renewing the church. Soon 10,000 of these, tired of worldliness, flocked to his order. Francises of our age, we ask Mother Mary to open our eyes to serving Christ and his Church in whatever way we can. Hail Mary.

# Fifth Sunday of Lent

## Introduction

Sometimes we downplay Christ's humanity. The most humane of men, he felt things deeply. He cried at the death of Lazarus, over Jerusalem, and for Martha and Mary. May we similarly feel with those in sorrow, and let's confess any ways we fail in this.

## Homily

I was at a funeral recently of a relative killed in a car crash. As the coffin was closed, his wife and daughters had to be supported, they were so bent with grief. Christ understands such sorrow. In today's gospel, when Jesus was told of Lazarus's death, he was so distressed a sigh came from his heart, and he burst into tears. He was no plaster saint. He wept so much, all said "See how he loved him!" (John 11:36, JB).

Our most human aspects are our feelings. They're easily hurt. Christ the most human of men felt inner and outer pain deeply, and feels our human pain with us. At the crucifixion he faced the ultimate anguish of being rejected and killed by his own. He did everything in his power to reach them, yet they rejected him. As Isaiah foresaw thousands of years before: he was "a thing despised and rejected by men; a man of sorrows, and familiar with suffering" (Isaiah 53:3, JB). Even the raising of Lazarus didn't work. He loved Martha and Mary and wanted to ease their pain, and he hoped that raising Lazarus would convince everyone that God sent him. How painful was their persistent unbelief.

Let's not add to his pain, but console his heart and accept the saving love of God that he represents. For today too, in pride and arrogance, many still spurn the gentle Savior, like a child spurning a mother's arms. Visionaries nowadays talk of statues of Christ weeping blood. I'm not surprised. He wept blood in Gethsemane because his people scorned and killed him. It's no different now, for even in heaven he has a human heart.

Nietzsche, the philosopher of fascism and modern secularism, said we must kill God and follow our own will, regardless of higher law. We must exercise power beyond traditional Christian standards of good and evil. But what did this lead to? The Holocaust. Stalinist and other genocidal secular systems followed suit; also rejecting and crucifying Christ, in the form of the weak. In his day, Paul talks about the powers that be fighting against God and his Christ, and that many, though they see the light, prefer darkness.

Man against God is a curious creature. Like the Pharisees at the resurrection of Lazarus, no matter what God does, its no use; hearts and minds are closed and determined to remain so. We Christians should make up for that by our love. As many turn their backs on Christ for cruel godless worldly ideologies of which Satan is Lord, our role is be faithful, to be the faithful, steadfast followers though thick and thin.

For what hurt Jesus most was hardheartedness: "If only you would listen to him today, do not harden your hearts", scripture says (Psalm 95:7–8, JB). Let's open our hearts to the Lord and work for him and his Church until his gentle grace-filled reign has come in the whole world, a paradise indeed. For he came not to be served, but to serve and to give his life as a ransom for many.

That's the model for us: To build his gentle kingdom in a broken world. To serve God, community, parish, diocese, and people in sufffering faithfulness. We may say, I'm too busy. I've no talent. But Christ has no hands now but ours. We have to be his light. For people need to realize in every age that worldly self-centered hardheartedness and arrogance, of which Satan is lord, are a delusion and a snare. They fade to dust and ashes at last and leave us empty before eternity, our lives having been wasted in useless pursuits. But Christ is Lord of love, truth, and happiness for our joyful and deeper living in this world and our happiness with the Lord of all real life forever and ever. Amen.

So as Christ's faithful consolers, let's make our profession of faith.

## *Prayers of the Faithful*

And as God's own, lets pray for what we need.

For church leaders in the world, especially our Holy Father the Pope, that, convinced that God has sent Christ, they may convince all searching for meaning and love.

For civic leaders, that, unlike the Pharisees and Romans, they may not put obstacles in the way of God's Church, and Christ's all-enriching message for society.

For our wonderful youth, that they may discover their full peace and humanity in the Church of Christ, who is Lord of life forever.

For ourselves, that in our hearts and homes we may accept Jesus as Our Lord and Savior sent by our loving Father in heaven, and nurture that same faith and love in those under our care, furthering their full life and happiness both here and hereafter.

For those who have lost loved ones, that, like Martha and Mary, they may be comforted by God, and their loved ones raised up to heavenly happiness.

For the sick, that they may keep faith in the Lord and find his healing presence in our love, care, and prayers for them.

For the dead, that they may be raised up like Lazarus at death and on the last day when Christ will come to raise us in body and soul.

We ask all these prayers through the same Christ who raised Lazarus and never fails to raise us up too. Amen

## Reflection

I often listen to *The Messiah*. I find especially moving that Isaiah phrase, "he was despised and rejected; a man of sorrows, and acquainted with grief" (Isaiah 53:3, KJV). In beautiful melody it reminds us of all Christ suffered for us and how he bore the burdens of all who suffer, and identified with all good people who suffer for their goodness. As we prepare to share Christ's sorrows during Holy Week, we ask Mother Mary to give us true devoted hearts, to enter into the spirit of Christ crucified and risen. Hail Mary.

# Palm Sunday

## *Introduction*

We begin the most solemn week of the Church year. We follow Christ's entry into Jerusalem, his institution of the Eucharist, his suffering on the cross, and his resurrection. To prepare for this holiest time of the Christian year, let us confess our sins.

## *Homily*

People are fickle. One minute they're all about you. Then they hear a malicious whisper, and they'd cut your throat. That was Jesus's lot. He raised Lazarus. The crowd hailed him as Messiah, laid down palms, and welcomed him to Jerusalem. They shouted, "Blessings on him who comes in the name of Yahweh" (Psalm 118:26, JB). But a whisper from the Pharisees and all that turned to jeers of "Crucify him" (Mk 15:13, JB).

That cut Christ to the heart, but we can be as cruel. How fickle we are sometimes in his service, abandoning Christian commitments when challenged by the world. Peter did so, but repented. Let it be the same with us, for nothing should separate us from the love of God in Christ Our Lord, who though betrayed, denied, abandoned, loved us to the end.

Close your eyes and imagine Christ's desolation hanging there, and think of times when you felt likewise. I can imagine seriously ill people in hospital crying, "My God, my God, why have you deserted me?" (Mt. 27:47, JB). But they should remember that God didn't abandon Jesus, but raised him up. He'll do the same for us, and our trials in this world will be over. If we walk with him, he'll raise us up. No one bypasses Calvary, but we can triumph by taking up the cross and following Jesus.

Holy Week gives us the chance to do that. It brings our hearts and minds into harmony with Jesus as he goes from Golgotha to Easter. So let's attend the ceremonies devotedly this week, the high point of our Christian worship. Let's be with Christ at the Last Supper. Let's listen to the Passion and kiss the cross. Let's celebrate his rising with joyful alleluias. For we're in those mysteries still. He's still betrayed for money. His face is still scarred by violence. Many still refuse the life he offers. And there are shades of ourselves in those who added to his pain—Peter, Judas, Pilate, the high priests. Abuse scandals show how even priests crucified him in the form of vulnerable youth, in our time.

In Holy Week, let's reject all such evil within ourselves. Let's go to confession and achieve inner peace. For no one can follow Jesus through Holy Week without the truth dawning that, despite our faults, God loves us. Let's not thrust the spear deeper into his side. Rather, let's be apostles at his supper, Mary at his cross, Veronica wiping his face, Magdalene at his tomb. For the world's cruelty fades to dust, but Christ is Lord of love, goodness, peace, and salvation; he suffered every torment on the cross for our happiness in this world and forever and ever. Amen.

So walking faithfully with Christ this week through all the events of our redemption, let's make our profession of faith.

## *Prayers of the Faithful*

As God's people committed to him in suffering faith and walking with him through suffering and death to glory, we make our prayers to our caring Lord for all that we need.

For the leaders of the Church throughout the world, that this Holy Week may see them committed anew to spreading his peace, love, and salvation to the whole world.

For state leaders, that unlike Pilate they may not crucify Christ by persecuting him and his Church or neglecting to serve his holy people, the poor, and underprivileged.

For young people, that this Holy Week may lead to a new flowering of faith, hope, and charity in their lives.

For ourselves in our hearts and homes, that this Holy Week may be a pilgrimage time of renewed love for our great Lord and Savior in his time of suffering, death, and resurrection for us.

For the sick, the aged, the lonely, and the depressed, that as they share in the suffering of Christ now so they may find healing, comfort, grace, and peace through their own resurrection.

For the dead who have passed through the suffering of death like Christ, that they may also share his resurrection.

And we ask all these prayers with confidence to God through Christ whose wounds constantly plead before the father for us. Amen.

## *Reflection*

Mel Gibson's film, *The Passion Of The Christ,* is one of my favorite films. I was especially struck by the scene in which Christ gives up the Ghost. A tear of God falls to the ground, thunder and lightning strikes, and his accusers slink away on their donkeys, completely deflated. Moreover, Satan, who had been gloating in the background, is suddenly plummeted back to hell. This is final victory not death. Then the film shifts beautifully to the Last Supper, and Christ giving his body to the disciples and us for all time (Luke 22:19). It reminds us of the key link between the Passion and the mass. It is his body given up for us anew every Sunday, and given to us at every mass as our bread of life and salvation. Let's cherish that great last gift of his, available to sustain us through life, and the pledge of our final resurrection. Hail Mary.

# Holy Thursday

## *Introduction*

As a meal unites a family, Christ's supper binds us to him and each other. Gathered for that supper, we remember first holy communicants and Eucharistic ministers being commissioned, and we confess failures to live the weekly communion we celebrate.

## *Homily*

An evening meal is a great gathering for most families; when the parents return from work and the children from school. The meal creates a bond no other activity can replicate. That was also true of Christ with his apostolic family; especially since it was the Paschal meal they were celebrating, the liberation of God's people from slavery. Our Last Supper with the Lord, each mass, has both those dimensions; we gather as his family to be united with him and each other, and our great liberation in Christ's cross is re-enacted.

For the Last Supper was the first mass. There Christ gave us the source of our unity and salvation for all time. So it's the heart of our reality as the people of God; binding us together as his people. No wonder our great ancestors cherished it. My mother told me how, long before cars, they walked to mass barefoot over puddle-filled roads on the back of the ditches with shoes tossed over their shoulders. They put their shoes back on when they reached the Church. Going to mass was an essential for their life.

This fits with its name, which comes from the Latin, *ite missa est*, the mass is ended go in peace. As faithful mass goers we find the fullness of life and peace in this growing communion with Christ whereby the life of God flowers in us. Those who question going to mass should realize that Christians are essentially a Eucharistic people; as Christ says, "if you do not eat the flesh of the Son and drink his blood, you will not have life in you" (Jn. 6:53, JB). Mass and Communion are as vital to our soul's health and growth as eating is to our bodily life. So we can't thank him enough for this great going away gift.

Indeed, the word *Eucharist* means thanksgiving. In it we give thanks to Jesus for his Last Supper going away present. For it raises us up and guarantees our salvation. Christ promises: "Anyone who does eat my flesh and drink my blood has eternal life, and I shall raise him up at the last day" (John 6:54, JB). In effect, and this is amazing news, through our mass and communion we are already part of eternal life here below, and are guaranteed to flower into an eternity with God at death, and on the last day.

For, as it was with the apostles, each mass is his life shared with us. After the resurrection the disciples recognized Jesus at the breaking of bread. It's the same with us. It's at this Eucharistic meal, and the sharing of the Word and prayer together, that we come to know him and share his life. Hence, after his ascension, the apostles shared this amazing news; through our mass and communion we are already part of eternal life here below and are guaranteed to flower into an eternity with God at death and on the last day. It has the same essential function today. If we didn't have our daily dinner, we'd be malnourished; regular Sunday mass ensures our life-long spiritual nourishment. And in it we offer ourselves to the Lord as a fragrant offering, even as he offers himself to us.

So another word often used for the mass is *offering*. Its Christ's sacrifice on the cross offered on the altar. Our loves, trials, and sufferings are joined with his and made holy. So the attendance of each of us is as vital as the attendance of the priest. Each of us at mass, is like an apostle at the Last Supper. But its not a selfish act. It is given so that we might be enriched to be apostles for Christ in the world too; that is, as it did them, it should inspire us to go out to change the world.

Christ washed his disciples' feet before the first mass. The message is clear. Attending mass is useless unless we serve God and others, humbly, totally, unselfishly. He tells us not to lord it over people in any way, but to love and serve. The Church in palaces often forgot this. So did abusing priests; they fell into the trap of serving their own power and perverted pleasure rather than the loving service of others in God; what a perversion of the priestly role. So on the night when Christ washed the feet of the apostles—the first priests—before giving them the Eucharist, let's also wash each others feet. As an example of humble love and service, let me now wash his children's feet to make up for the Church's failures in the past, and to show how we should really treat each other as humble, loving people of self-giving service and peace (washing of the feet).

## Prayers of the Faithful

And as the people of God at Christ's Supper let's ask for what we need.

For our Holy Father the Pope and all leaders of Churches, that they may follow the example of Christ and be humble servants of the faithful, and God's children worldwide.

For our civil leaders, that their public life may not be one of corrupt self-interest, but of dedicated service to all the electorate, especially the poor and deprived.

For our youth, that they may make the weekly Eucharist the center of the their lives and their growing relationship with Christ so that by his grace they may help transform the broken world into his kingdom of unity, peace, and love.

For ourselves, that, faithful to the weekly supper of the Lord, we may go out from that table to serve others at home or in our workplaces with the caring humility of Christ.

For the sick, the lonely, the depressed, and the needy, that through our kindness they may know that Christ loves them.

For the dead, that they may come to the final banquet of eternal life, which they have already anticipated in the Lord's supper.

## *Reflection*

They asked Napoleon, when he was dying, what was his happiest moment. Was it when he took the crown of Europe? No, he said, it was his first Holy Communion. At last he realized what the greatest thing in this world was: the Lord's Supper, where we're one with him in an infinite glory no earthly fame can match. Let's pray that we'll always cherish this gift, and come to his table every Sunday with grateful and joyful hearts. Hail Mary.

# Good Friday

## Introduction

"Then Jesus said to his disciples, 'If anyone wants to be a follower of mine, let him renounce himself and take up his cross and follow me'" (Matthew 16:24, JB). As we gather around Christ's cross this "good" Friday, let's kiss and adore it with deep love for Our Lord who suffered for us, and follow him in bearing our own crosses for God's sake.

## Homily

I don't won't keep you, the ceremony is long, but as we gather today may Christ's sufferings change us. A man in the United States confessed to a murder after seeing Gibson's film, *The Passion of the Christ*. A young person in New York coming out from the theater admitted that it was difficult not to pray after seeing it. We should also respond to the passion with a change of heart, with awe at this testimony of his total love for us.

For as Christ died in intense mental and physical pain, God hadn't abandoned him. Gibson's film again makes that point. As Christ dies, a single tear of the Father splashes on the ground. Suddenly all is changed. His worldly accusers slink away on their donkeys and Satan, who was triumphantly enjoying the show, is cast back to hell. Gibson switches to the Last Supper: "This is my body which will be given for you" (Luke 22:19, JB).

God won the victory through this defeat. He raised Christ up and gave him all power in heaven and on earth. So if you think anti-God forces are stronger, think again. God's still in charge, and he has handed over all authority to his Christ, who has in turn entrusted it to the Church. How privileged we are to be part of that. So let's be his faithful no matter what the world throws at us; let's return love for love to console his heart.

Let's be his suffering servants unto death. For all else passes, but he is our king of love on Calvary, forever. Amen.

So as the crucified Lord's own, in the end-times of his kingdom, let us pray that a kingdom so painfully won, may come today. (We'll now have the special intercessions).

# Easter Sunday

## Introduction

Last night (tonight) we lit the holy fire symbolizing Christ as light of the world. For as the candle inscription says, we celebrate "Christ yesterday, today and forever; the Alpha and the Omega, the beginning and the end of all." In the light of that Risen Lord of the universe with us here, let's confess any sins by which we may have offended him.

## Homily

"Praise the Lord, I saw the Light," the Hank Williams song says. Close your eyes imagine living in darkness. Now open them to a Church ablaze with Easter light. The coming of electricity, when we were young, was like that. Before that the faint light of oil lamps, for us kids doing our homework, was a strain on the eyes. As it was for our mother doing her sewing. Then all lit up at the touch of a switch. Today is like that. The Risen Christ suddenly dazzles a dark, fallen world, restoring it to the full light of God. Electricity fails sometimes, but the light that illuminated the world that first Easter will never go out. It will continue to grow ever brighter until the whole world is bathed in glory. Sadly, Paul says, some prefer darkness or are too caught up in the world to live in that light.

Watching a priest at midnight mass I was shocked by his matter-of-fact tone. *Come on*, I thought, *show some joy!* For Easter *is* joy. We're in the end time of the Risen Lord. The dream longed for two thousand years by the prophets has come true. Indifference to that is criminal. Like the disciples, we should race from the tomb shouting: "he has risen" (Mark 16:6, JB). From the cross of shame came God's stunning victory. The dark that oppressed humans since Adam—sin, suffering, violence, death—is gone forever.

For when God raised Jesus, made him Lord and Savior, he also banished human emptiness and hopelessness forever. Now we often proclaim or sing as an acclamation after the mass consecration: "he is Lord, he is Lord. He is risen from the dead and he is Lord, every knee shall bow every tongue confess that Jesus Christ is Lord." That was a key creed statement of the early Church. It must be out's too, for accepting this Risen Lord as personal Lord and Savior is the heart of our faith. Its what energizes our bringing of the good news to the world with its materialism, violence, cynicism, drugs, and youth despair. For once one accepts the Risen Christ as Savior, a happiness the world cannot give flowers like spring in the heart. We see, as Tolstoy is said to have said, that others threw light on human existence, but Christ illuminated it beyond measure forever.

That's the resting place of every restless heart. Even for this world that news contains untold inner riches. We have vital work to do here, and we should enjoy the good things of the world given us by God. But they're only fully enjoyed and meaningful in that dazzling light, that glorious and timeless intervention of God on our behalf that destroyed all sin and death's power over us forever. And not only does this light up our lives in this world and make them infinitely rich in every way, but when the world eventually passes away we have infinite riches in the Risen Christ forever. *Our* final victory here below and forever was guaranteed by *his* resurrection. We're on a winning side for all time. For all else passes, but he's now Lord of light, love, goodness, happiness, and salvation both for our deepest fullest life in this world and with him forever and ever. Amen.

So as God's people reborn into light on this night of his risen glory let us live and rejoice in the faith we now profess.

## Prayers of the Faithful

And gathered on this holiest of days, the high point of our Christian life and worship, let's pray confidently to the Father through the glorious Risen Christ for the things that we need.

For the Pope, the bishops of the Church, and all its leaders throughout the world, that they may bring to all the joyful liberating message of the Risen Christ at this time and always.

For ourselves, that this Easter mass of light and joy may lighten our own hearts into a grand spring and summer to come.

For our youth, that the Easter message may be more than cliche holiday cheer. May it penetrate their hearts and bring them to a satisfying personal commitment to the Risen Lord and his Church.

For the old people in our midst, that their lives of faith and goodness and service may bring them the Lord's rewards of happiness and peace, and may God love come to them through us.

For the sick, that they may know that the Lord is with them in their suffering and experience the care of the Risen Christ.

For the dead, that they come to their own resurrection prefigured this night in the resurrection of their Lord and Savior who, when he rose, raised all of us to glory.

And we ask all these our prayers through Christ our Risen Lord and Savior, who is close to his people and brings them the salvation and light of God forever and ever. Amen

## *Reflection*

African people who came to me for Baptism explained to me once how great a light the Christian faith was. Burdened by pagan fears and witch doctors, they'd lived in a twilight world of dark gods. It was great news to them that Christ died and rose, that God loved them and was there for them forever in Christ. They found an eternal dignity, value, and freedom in that vision. Yet today many Westerners, who've enjoyed that light for centuries, would take us back into pagan darkness. On TV, tarot cards are okay, but preaching the faith isn't. Let's make up for that by appreciating how Christ set us free, by renewing the great gift we have received in our spoiled West also, and let's pray to his mother and our mother, as his brothers and sisters in faith, to help us in this. Hail Mary.

# Second Sunday of Easter

## Introduction

We're still in the happy time of Easter, and scripture recounts the glories and suffering of the early Church, bathed in the love of the Risen Lord. Two thousand years later so do we. Let's confess any ways we may have failed to return that love.

## Homily

"The candid scholar, the unselfish priest, the uncomplaining mothers of many." Louis MacNeice's poem, *The Kingdom*, lists those who remain part of a secret kingdom of goodness among us. In Christian terms that is all who believe, and put their belief into practice in daily life. That's what Christ tells us all to do in today's gospel. Faced by Thomas's skepticism, he tells us to "doubt no longer but believe" (John 20:28, JB).

And how we need that now. A negativity in relation to faith and Christian morality makes me scream every time I turn on TV. The trend seems to be to make ourselves God, wealth our truth, and unfettered desire our morality. God, the Church, or the Pope must be wrong if they don't say what suits fashionable trends. So we become pseudo -Christians, the TV DJ our real Christ, the media our real scripture.

But that is a grave mistake. For deep down vain worldly values are illusory freedom; the don't give life in the long run. And they threaten to destroy our inner life, religious heritage, and moral sense, and the ground of God we stand on. Its no wonder that many young people flounder in this no man's land, neither believing nor actively agnostic, just plain indifferent. The earth of faith, truth, and meaning that sustained our ancestors taken from under them, they drown in nothingness, in a meaningless sea of hype. Maybe that's why many people give up on life, or go on shooting sprees, or join extreme cults. Despair is inevitable when man becomes his own earth-bound law without higher hope or ideals to satisfy the divine within, screaming for expression. For the passing world isn't enough, we are such things as dreams are made of; our souls need real food.

Recently, in this respect, I was inspired by the testimony of a wealthy engineer who joined the priesthood in America. When they asked him why, he said that he had it all, money sex, pleasure without restraint but his heart was empty; he said surely there must be more to human life than that; he found it in selfless priestly service of God and others.

The Risen Lord, by conquering evil, brought a hope and a belief that the forces of the cold self-centered world, of which Satan is lord, cannot defeat in the long run. At Easter, Christ says to our age, as he said to Thomas, "Stop doubting and believe." He opened the scriptures to show God's plan for our deeper happiness in this world, and our eternal salvation, fulfilled in his risen glory and its apotheosis, the church.

Though some in a faithless generation, like the rich man in the Dives story (Luke 16:19–31), won't believe though he is risen from the dead, his rising ensured God's final triumph. Sure, if Christ came among us now, some still wouldn't still believe or change their lifestyle. They'd just have a tribunal of inquiry that would end up with a million-page document and no conclusion. But more would welcome and heed his call to doubt no longer but believe. As American economist and engineer Stuart Chase wrote: "For those who believe, no proof is necessary. For those who don't believe, no proof is possible."

Affluence today seems to be producing more and more such hard unbelief. Our forefathers, through war, famine, and persecution, believed. Yet what made them great is considered foolishness to a wealthier age. But our forefathers will have the last laugh at the side of the Risen Christ in glory. Doubt no longer but believe. It's not money but faith that enriches the world. It's ordinary, hopeful, trusting, believing, good people who prevent it from disintegrating into chaos. It's to their side, not that of skeptical self-servers that we're called. For only by standing by his side will we triumph over the world's dark Lord and gain the kingdom, the power, and the glory forever and ever. Amen.

So as God's own, raised by Christ to untold dignity and grace for this life and the next, his glorious living practicing saints, we profess our faith with overflowing Easter joy.

## Prayers of the Faithful

As God's people, proving our faith by our presence here, we offer our prayers through the Risen Christ to our heavenly Father.

For the Church in the world, especially the Pope and bishops, that their luminous faith may draw all to rise to glory and a new and happier and fuller way of life in Christ.

For civil leaders, that they may not put stumbling blocks in the way of faith, but realize that we need the City of God to complete the circle of life and eternity.

For youth, that they may see beyond the emptiness and darkness of unbelief to the infinite glory of faith, and its living life of virtue and truth within God's holy Church.

For ourselves, that in homes and workplaces we'll have the courage to stand up for and nurture the healing faith that our children need for a full life in this world and the next.

For the old, the lonely, the sick, and the depressed, that they may find in the caring Lord the source of strength to journey in faith and hope to the glory of the resurrection.

For the dead who've passed from this life to the next, that by our prayers, they may come to the fullness of glory in the heavenly home Christ enabled for all by his rising.

And we ask all these prayers through Christ our risen Lord, amen.

## Reflection

Johnny Cash, the singer, once gave up on life. He crawled into a cave to die. But God spoke to him, dispelled his despair, and restored his faith. After that he dedicated his talent to gospel songs, and once even recorded the whole New Testament in the Holy Land. He often said that without the Lord he'd never have survived or found inner peace. The greatest of psychiatrists Jung said the same, that the death of God is the death of man. Even modern science agrees. A recent study shows that evolution favors those of faith. So Christ's words are life in every way. We pray to Mary that we, and our wonderful youth, will be wise and practice the faith so vital for their life even here below. Hail Mary.

# Third Sunday of Easter

## Introduction

They knew him in the breaking of bread. That's also how we come to know the Lord, in receiving the Eucharist, listening to his Word, and praying as one. As we prepare to break bread, read his word, and pray together, lets confess ways we fail Christ.

## Homily

Once I baptized adults of various ages and nationalities at the Easter vigil. Beforehand I asked an English adult what she looked forward to. She said, "Really receiving the body of Christ." After her Baptism and Communion I asked how she felt. "For the first time I feel real peace within," she said. Today's gospel says the same thing.

The apostles were in despair before they broke bread with Christ. But in Communion and his opening of the scriptures, their Christian optimism was restored. Going to mass routinely we can forget how great a boost it is. Each mass is a journey to Emmaus with the Lord, and if we celebrate it well, we leave with our hearts burning within us. For we've received the Word and Bread of life from the lips and heart of God himself.

Indeed, it's only through communing with Christ here that we're filled with a faith and hope that carries us into and through every ensuing week of joys and sorrows. Life is full of problems. Weekly Communion with the Lord and his word gives us the spiritual depth to bear all, in the seven days in the busy world that follows. For here at Sunday mass we share in his final victory over sin, suffering, and death. Here with our brothers and sisters in Christ, we grow in the life of God, are united with the saints in glory, and become one with the local and universal Church. So immersed in Christ, we can endure all things and overcome all things. For we are part of his living risen body.

When we go up to Communion, the minister says "the body of Christ" and we answer "Amen." We affirm the host as his body, and that we *are his body* gathered as one. So the mass is Christian life in essence, and it's best celebrated on Sunday, the day he rose from the dead; the Sunday mass is *the* mass.

We need to meet every Sunday to be and receive his body. Regardless of our work and responsibilities, let's find time for attending the weekly Eucharist. Work is important; we must live in this world, earn our bread, and support our families. But when we've all that done, we mustn't let excessive worldliness rob us of our larger destiny—the salvation of our souls. The deepest happiness for this life comes from union with God, and that's best achieved at mass. If we didn't eat physically we'd die. In the same way, without regular Holy Communion we'd grow thin within, easy prey to Satan's wiles.

Irish mass-going ancestors realized this. They worshiped at mass rocks or walked over ditches barefoot to mass; they endured every hardship and persecution to be with the Lord; he was there for them; they wanted to be there for him. (Mass rocks were rocks used as altars in mid-seventeenth century Ireland when Catholicism was banned). They knew that the Lord's living presence in the breaking of bread, in scripture, and in communal prayer was irreplaceable; without them, they were Christians in name only. And the faith was bound to fade away in their hearts in the long run.

They felt what Christ said: "if you do not eat the flesh of the Son of man ... you will not have life in you" (John 6:53, JB). But when we do eat it we are already part of eternal life here and sure to be raised up when he comes again at last. Imagine that! Through the Eucharist we are already part of eternity in this world; until we flower into its fullness at last. That's Christ's promise. Though our work in this world is important, and each of us has something special to do here—that's why we're in the world—all that eventually fades, but Christ in the Eucharist and the Word is Lord of love, peace, happiness, and salvation both for our deeper glory and dignity and happiness in this world, and forever and ever. Amen.

So as Christ's body gathered here, breaking bread and listening to his word every Sunday as our ongoing life, peace, and salvation, let's make our profession of faith.

## Prayers of the Faithful

And as a glorious Eucharistic people we pray confidently for our needs.

We pray for our Holy Father the Pope and all the leaders of the Church, that they may lead all to a rich appreciation of the presence of the Lord in the Breaking of Bread.

For civic leaders, that they may serve the people well, especially the vulnerable.

For ourselves, that we may never drift from meeting the Lord in our weekly Eucharist, but cherish that union more than life itself.

For our youth, that realizing their need for regular Communion with the Lord and his body each Sunday, they may hearken to Christ's words and realize that its as essential for them as it was for their great ancestors.

For the sick, the aged, and the housebound, that, through our bringing of Holy Communion to them they may know our care and that of Christ, present in the Eucharist.

For the dead, that, having broken the Bread of Life and the Word here, they may achieve all that they signify in eternal happiness.

And we ask all these prayers through the Risen Christ who constantly pleads for us before the throne of God.

## Reflection

I read recently about believers incarcerated in Nazi concentration camps. They hoarded bits of bread and drops of wine for weekly mass, though starving. For them the Eucharist nourished them more than any food in that bleak secular Nazi hell. They didn't just survive through union with the Lord, but transcended all that man-made secular hell could throw at them. They were the ones alive in that camp; their captors were the ones who were dying, for to be dead inside is death indeed. Let's all appreciate the Eucharist as they did and pray to our mother Mary for weekly faithfulness. Hail Mary.

# Fourth Sun of Easter

## Introduction

On this Vocation Sunday we gather under the care of Christ the Good Shepherd. As his faithful flock we pray for more active lay people, religious, and priests to win a great harvest of souls for God. Let's confess any ways we fail in this key work of salvation.

## Homily

When I was in the Holy Land. I saw shepherds chatting on hillsides, their sheep all mixed in together. *They'll never sort out that lot*, I thought. But each shepherd would call, his own sheep would disentangle themselves and trot after their master. That's Christian life. Christ, the good shepherd, calls, and we follow freely to green pastures.

This Vocation Sunday we are reminded that each of us have special roles in life. Our main Christian one is holiness. But we also have worldly roles. For most it's marriage. It's a sacrament, because great grace is needed for a life of love, faithfulness, and family care. Some don't marry. There's no sacrament for that, there may be in the future.

Then again we all have vocational tasks in life—as nurses, teachers, shopkeepers, and so on. Each of us makes a contribution to the building up of this world as part of God's plan for a balanced and productive society. Christian witness is shown in such ordinary family and worldly work too. And in some ways worldly work, married life, and care of the young is more important than religious life. What keeps the world from chaos is loving Christian people and homes, what Vatican II describes as the "domestic Church."

That said, this Sunday we pray specially for priestly and religious vocations. For scarcity in this area is worrying. The laity's new prominence in the Church is a must, but priests are still needed to preside at the Eucharist and shepherd the flock. Without that the Christian community would be impaired. Also without monks, sisters, and brothers and their service and prayer, the Church would be less. Religious Consecration enriches life beyond measure.

"A crisis in ministry," a press headline said recently. "Only ten nuns joined this year." The vocation crisis is real. At this time we need prayer, Eucharistic adoration, and active promotion of vocations. And there are practical steps we can take: suggest a priestly or religious vocation to children, share our vocation story, serve in parish ministry and encourage our youth to do so, support those interested in a priestly or religious life.

And we should affirm the priests and religious we have with friendship and prayer. For they are shell shocked by an increasingly secular and irreligious age. Media attacks on the Church have left many demoralized. In the last few years four young priests left the ministry in my diocese. Sure, priests have disgraced the cloth, and some religious have abused positions of trust; we must beat our breasts. But there are a vast number of blameless consecrated people still that we must support, lest we soon have none.

Maybe it's God's will that we have fewer priests and religious so that the laity can come into their own, as Vatican II wished they would. And maybe this crisis is God's way of bringing down harsh hierarchical structures. But even in this scenario we should pray for new vocations within a more humanely structured Church that is being shaped now, and Pope Francis is heralding. But Christ needs more such shepherds for his flock. Let's pray for good consecrated people in a revitalized Church, so that today Christ can lead the world to God. For all else fades, but he is Lord of love, peace, happiness, and salvation, both for this world and forever and ever. Amen.

So as God's people living out our various vocations in love and by prayer and practical means shaping a new flowering of consecrated and priestly life, let's profess our faith with new hope.

## Prayers of the Faithful

For our Holy Father the Pope and Church leaders throughout the world, that they may promote good vocations and form and nurture them for a fruitful new apostolate in our ever-more spiritually needy age.

For ourselves, that we may be active in promoting, supporting, and encouraging vocations to the priestly and religious life so that our Church may grow and thrive as it did in the past.

For our wonderful young people, that they may find Christ in the priestly and religious service of God's people, and never turn away when the Lord calls them to such devoted service.

For civil leaders, that they may promote a spiritual culture that helps the flowering of good vocations in every walk of life.

For the sick, that through medically and spiritually caring vocational people they may find the healing hand of God.

For the dead, their work in this world done, that they may reap the rewards of their goodness in the life to come.

And we ask all these prayers through Christ the Good Shepherd, who never neglects the flock in their need. Amen

## Reflection

The story of Sister Brid McKenna O.S.C., the miracle-working sister, is inspiring. As a young religious, riddled with arthritis, she could scarcely walk. One day, praying in Church for help, she heard God saying that she was healed and should go and heal others. She stood up perfectly well, to head an apostolate of healing to the world. Her mission is especially to priests and religious, for, as she says, they're under special attack from Satan today; because they're in the front line of God's struggle for souls. The many spiritual and physical miracles Brid saw, especially when people were blessed by the Monstrance, are described in her book, *Miracles Do Happen. God Can Do The Impossible.* We pray that we may answer God's call to vocational mission as generously. Hail Mary.

# Fifth Sunday of Easter

## *Introduction*

Trust in God is a key Biblical theme. Christ asks the same of us today: "Do not let your hearts be troubled. Trust in God still; and trust in me (John 14:1, JB). No matter our trials in life, let's not lose that trust, and let's confess if we fail or doubt God's loving care.

## *Homily*

"I feel awful. I wish someone would shoot me. I can't go on living." That's what someone said to me recently. It shocked me to the core. I can't conceive of anyone ever giving up on life; it is so precious. But maybe I shouldn't be so shocked. Despite so-called progress, many in society are in despair. Look at the numbers of people ringing the Samaritans and help lines. We all go through rough patches, but there seem to be more problems nowadays. When difficulties pile up, we're tempted to lose hope. Don't! Instead listen to Jesus: "Do not let your hearts be troubled. Trust in God still; and trust in me."

Indeed, that's what the gospel is about, Christ's care for us. He will heal us if we let him. Indeed, he alone can lift us up in our darkest hours and lighten our burdens. Scripture says: "unload all your worries on him, since he is looking after you" (1 Peter 5:7, JB). And Jesus in today's gospel says that by trusting in him, the Way, the Truth, and the Life, we can endure all things. To avail of his healing love, all we have to do is to trust.

The late John Paul II is a good example of someone who did just that. His motto was Christ's words: "Be not afraid for I am with you." That's how he endured communist and fascist oppression, a bullet in the stomach, and a terrible last illness. Through it all he smiled at the world.

At one time young people were putting his motto on wrist bands. We should wear it on our hearts, for then we'll be wise. Trust in God will carry us past all obstacles. For God is not a luxury; he is as necessary to us as the air we breathe.

Without him life's empty and meaningless and it's easy to give up. But with him we get past troubles. This is a proven fact. A psychological study in hospitals has shown that those with faith are more likely to recover from illness and recover more quickly. The story of Pierce Brosnan, the James Bond star, is another example of the effectiveness of turning to God for help. He went through a deep crisis recently, and he commented to friends that if it hadn't been for his Catholic faith, he'd never have survived.

What makes us, God's people, so strong in adversity is the certainty that we're not alone. God is with us and lifts us up from every abyss of pain. Indeed, if we trust and pray, he turns all our weaknesses into strengths. Christ spent most of his time caring for those who were sick, or scorned by society. He was down there among the so-called "rabble" because he cared; they were his precious children too, indeed more so. He still does that today, and so it must hurt him deeply when people spurn his outstretched arms.

He knocks at the door to offer every sort of healing, but we won't let him in. Then when things get rough, we have no sure ground left to stand on. We shouldn't make that mistake. By accepting God as our hope for this world and the next, we find a deep peace and strength that the hard commercial world cannot give. For all else fades to dust at last, but Christ is Lord of healing, love, and grace for this world and forever and ever. Amen.

So as God's people putting our trust in God and his Christ in every crisis small or great, and so winning through, let's profess our faith.

## Prayers of the Faithful

As God's own people in Christ let's make our prayers to the Father of all our deepest needs with supreme confidence.

For the Church throughout the world, that trust in the Risen Christ may illumine its life and bring others to God's arms.

For civil leaders, that they may win the trust of the people by wise, honest, and all-embracing policies, policies that include people's spiritual welfare.

For our youth, that trusting in the Lord and remaining faithful to his Church, they may come to deeper inner happiness and strength in this life, and to fullness of life forever and ever.

For ourselves in our homes and communities, that we may live the words of the psalm: "Lord, in trouble I invoke you, and you answer my prayer" (Ps. 86:7).

"The righteous man will live by faith," scripture says (heb. 10:38, JB). We pray for the sick, that they may never lose faith or trust in the Lord, and through our care they may know the loving care of Christ in their every distress.

For the dead, that they may win the reward of their faith and trust by coming safely to the kingdom prepared for them from the beginning of the world.

And we ask all these prayers with confidence from the father, through Christ who constantly intercedes for us and the Holy Spirit who is the Advocate.

## Reflection

There's a story told about Saint Teresa of Ávila. An evil man was about to be hanged. She prayed that he'd find salvation. Up to the time of his death, he cursed and blasphemed, but suddenly at the gibbet, to everyone's astonishment, he kissed the cross. Teresa gave thanks; she felt her prayer and trust brought about his salvation. It's the same with us. If we trust in the Lord, all will be well. We pray to Mother Mary who believed, even as her son died on the cross, that we'll come to a deep trusting faith. Hail Mary.

# Sixth Sunday of Easter

## *Introduction*

Our readings this week tell us that faith must be lived out in everyday life. It's no use saying we believe if we go out and live the opposite. Let's pray for a living active faith and confess any ways we may have failed to live out our Christian calling.

## *Homily*

What's the most important part of the mass? Of course, the Communion. But after that the dismissal: "Go … to love and serve the Lord." How is that so important? The point is that the mass is of no use if we don't live it in our daily lives. God says to us at mass, go and *live* the grace and love you've celebrated; otherwise, you celebrate a lie.

Christ says the same in our gospel: "If you love me, you will keep my commandments" (John 14:15, JB). You know the story in the Bible of the sons. When the father tells one to go into the vineyard, he says OK, but he doesn't go. When the father tells his other son to go into the vineyard, he answers that he won't, but he does go because he loves his father. He knows the grapes are ripe and must be picked, and it will hurt his father if they rot. So the second son shows his love not by words, but by action.

It's the same with us. It's useless professing faith if we don't live it. Only by following Christ and his Church's laws faithfully in everyday life, worshiping every Sunday, and being his missionaries in the world, do we prove our love. Of course there's human weakness: we want to obey God but err through weakness. God understands this. That's why he sent us the Holy Spirit to help and strengthen us and the Church in our every weakness. When we fail to obey the father's commands, his healing forgiveness is there for us. Christ died and rose so that, as the gospel says: "Repentance for the forgiveness of sins should be preached to all the nations" (Luke 24:47, JB). We all break God's commands at times. But availing of his forgiveness in confession, we pick ourselves up constantly. We do our best, and leave the rest to God's mercy.

For Christian holiness is not in being perfect; none of us will be that. Rather, its a constant effort to be as good as we can. We persist in trying to obey God because we know he loves us and doesn't command us because he's a policeman, but because he wants what's good for us. Just as the ten commandments were given as part of the Israelites' liberation from slavery, obeying Christ is our peace, happiness, and freedom. For freedom is not in license but in doing what's right. License leads to slavery; bad habits take us over and can lead to death in body and soul, harming us and undermining society.

So in living God's commands we're loving ourselves, society, and the world. And we're building Christ's kingdom of love, peace, justice, and truth. We're redeeming a fallen world from what makes it unhappy, and we're living according to our deeper dignity and glory. Keeping God's law we achieve happiness both for here and for hereafter. And we help bring about what Christ died and rose for: to deliver the world from evil.

"If you love me, you will keep my commandments." Above all, keeping his commands shows that we really love God, for otherwise any profession of love is empty, like faith is without good works. For as Christ says, not everyone who says to him Lord, Lord, will enter the Kingdom or heaven but those who do the will of his Father in heaven. And he makes it clear that it is by our acts of practical charity, feeding hungry etc, that we will be judged at last. Let's remember that as we're dismissed at mass. Let's go out to love and serve the Lord in everyday acts of living faith, integrity and witness. For this world's cold values of which Satan is lord leave us empty for this world and fade to ashes at last and leave us empty before eternity, but Christ is Lord of goodness, happiness, peace, freedom, and glory both for our fuller life in this world and forever and ever. Amen.

As God's own showing our love by action as well as word, we profess our faith.

## *Prayers of the Faithful*

As the people of God gathered here let's pray for our Holy Father and the other leaders of the Churches, that they may lead us and all people in the freeing way, in the truth and life that is Christ, by the living example of their lives as well as their preaching.

For our leaders in society, that they may place no obstacles in the way of the Church, in its fulfilling of its mission to bring all people to the fullness of faith and life.

For ourselves, that in our homes and workplaces we may not only profess but all live the commands of God and his Christ, and so help bring all around us to freedom, happiness, and salvation.

For our young people, that they may not be deluded by the values of the world of which Satan is lord, but come to see the value of professing and living the faith as their true fullness of life, glory, and liberation both for this world and forever and ever.

For the aged, the sick, the lonely, and the poor in body or soul, that the message of Christ that they carry from this table may lead them to freedom, healing and oneness with God, and through our care for them may they know the love of God in their lives.

For our beloved dead, that their work in this world done, they may reap the rewards of their faithfulness to Christ in the home he has prepared for them in heaven.

And we ask all these prayers through the same Christ, Our Lord, who leads us forever out of the darkness into glorious light. Amen

## *Reflection*

The Story of Vincent de Paul is one of the most inspiring in the history of the church. The society that still bears his name is a light to the poor and downtrodden all over the world. For he wore himself out in charitable activity. He is the very epitome of the man who not only lives a holy way of life, but also brings the holiness and healing of Christ to others. I am always inspired when I go to see his preserved body in a Paris church. What we see there is a small dapper man, but one big in heart. Lets pray that we will have similar zeal in the service of God, his church, and his beloved poor. Hail Mary.

# The Ascension of the Lord

## Introduction

We end our Easter celebrations with the Ascension of the Lord. He had to go so as to send the Spirit and begin the Church. But he is with us still as Risen Lord in our midst ensuring the Church's triumph over evil until he comes again at the end of the world. Let's confess any ways we may have failed our great Lord.

## Homily

Nowadays the Church is in turmoil—scandals, dwindling mass attendance, growing atheism, defections from its ranks. We who love Christ and his Church could easily lose heart. But we shouldn't. Christ's ascension is the perfect antidote to pessimism. It guarantees the Church's faith and its bright future. For Christ ascended to the father not to abandon us but to be with us forever. From God's right hand he orchestrates the world's and his Church's inevitable final triumph. He sent us his followers out at the ascension to teach all nations and bring his salvation to the ends of the earth.

In effect, he trusted us to finish the work he began. But knowing our weakness, he sent his Holy Spirit to help us forever, and he himself is with us as Risen Lord: "I am with you always, yes to the end of time" (Matthew 28:20, JB). What consoling words; we are already on a winning side. Let's not fear then, however bleak life seems. God gave dominion to his Christ to rule the world in the Spirit, and gain the final victory for God.

So the world's salvation is assured, whether it realizes it or not. True, evil remains—wars, abortion, kidnappings, decadence, greed—but as scripture says, "however great the number of sins committed, grace was even greater" (Romans 5:20, JB). Even in recent revelations of the institutional Church's failings, the Holy Spirit is present. I believe he is using this to renew and reform the Church. And I see his work in the holy people I meet every day; their steadfast perseverance in faith and goodness, despite negative publicity, is not my doing but that of the Spirit. Though Church leaders can be a stumbling block at times, Christ still rules the Church in the Spirit. Remember the apostles tried to stop him going to the Father. But he had to go so that the spirit would come, the Church would be born, and its mission succeed.

Every Easter, the church's Baptism of huge numbers from various countries reminds us that the church's success is on-going and secure. And that in the Spirit it will survive today's troubles and atheism as it survived thousands of political and ideological systems since its foundation. For at its heart is not human ideas or systems, but the ascendent Lord. If it was a human system it would have died long ago, like all its opposing ideologies have. Indeed from thousands of crises during history its actually emerged stronger. You know the Star Wars slogan "the force will be with you." The Risen Christ's force is with the holy church, ensuring that it won't be defeated, now or ever.

But does that mean we can sit back and let it happen? No, Christ needs our help. We must be his saving hands in that work. We were baptized for that purpose. He ascended to God and sent his Spirit so that *we could finish his redemptive work*. The Church was born at the Ascension and Pentecost. That work of Christ must continue until the end of time through us, so that when he comes again he'll gather a vast number of the saved into the eternal Kingdom of God.

Let's play our part in that victory by actively spreading and defending the faith now and so glorify God and fulfill our Baptismal and Confirmation vows. Having done that, we'll ascend to the Father, for the corrupt world of which Satan is lord turns to dust and ashes at last and leaves us empty inside for this world and the next, dry as a bone before eternity, but the ascendant Christ is the eternal Lord of life, goodness, peace, and salvation for this world and forever and ever. Amen.

So as God's people empowered for mission by his glorious ascension and resplendent presence with us forever as risen ascendent Lord, let's reaffirm our faith.

## Prayers of the Faithful

We pray for Pope Francis and the Church throughout the world, that it may never lose heart but grow and thrive in the power of its risen and ascendant Lord.

For ourselves, that we may never be just passive Christians but active builders of his integral kingdom of saving love in our homes, in our work places and wherever we are.

For all who govern us, that they may promote the values of faith and life and not just the values of worldly power, greed, and narrow self-interest.

For our fine young people, that they may be inspired to become priests, religious, and lay workers for Christ and his Church. May they be the glorious new apostles of our age, going out in the power and grace of the risen and ascendant Lord to enlighten the world.

For those suffering due to sickness, old age, or poverty, that they may be helped by our generosity and love.

For the dead, that the ascension of the Lord may bring them all to the heavenly mansion prepared for them from the foundation of the world. Amen

And we ask all these prayers through the ascendant Lord who always listens to his people's pleas and raises them up to his glory.

## *Reflection*

There's a story told of Saint Teresa of Ávila, who lived in the sixteenth century. One sister stole into the Church to watch her at prayer. Suddenly Saint Teresa's body actually left the floor and was lifted up into the air. She was so caught up in God, she transcended the laws of the natural world. We may not achieve that intense contemplation, but even our simplest prayers raise us up to the throne of God where Christ sits at the his right hand. Lets always live in the ascendent glory of our blessed Lord. Hail Mary.

# The Solemnity of Pentecost

## *Introduction*

Today we celebrate the Spirit's coming to begin the Church. We pray that we will all go out like the apostles from reception of that Spirit at Baptism and Confirmation to work fervently to bring the world to Christ. We ask forgiveness for any indifference to that call.

## *Homily*

Today is the Spirit's age. Once a ghostly figure, we now see him as the key to all that's good in the Church and the world. Indeed, we feel his presence, or the opposite, when we encounter a person, a home, or nation. For he's what's good and holy in each person. Once at an audience with John Paul II, I felt his Spirit envelope us like a warm glow. That's true of people we meet each day: they radiate humane goodness. That's the Spirit—what's individual, humane, special, and divine in people everywhere. But a contrary spirit can rule us too. I hope I'm wrong. Is there a colder, more cynical spirit abroad now?

I hope that is not the case. For the Holy Spirit, as Paul says in all his writings, is always positive, creative, and kindly, building up rather than pulling down. God forbid that a contrary, worldly, heartless spirit, of which Satan is Lord, should rule us as we become more materialistic and irreligious. With mass attendance and vocations falling, sometimes the church in the west now seems under siege on all sides from increasingly triumphant and aggressive worldly forces. Should we give up too in this climate?

No! Our feast snaps us out of any tendency to be disheartened. Its message is of joy and hope. Christ ascended to the Father to become universal Lord. From his throne he sent his Spirit to bring his saving grace to all nations. That Spirit is now the dominant force in the world, ensuring the final victory for God and his Christ. Let's put aside fear then. The Spirit's eternal presence means contrary negative forces are always transitory.

For God's Spirit is always more powerful than the destructive spirit of that part of the world of which Satan is lord, the spirit of unbelief, war, disunity, greed, and harsh unaccountable power that crushes the weak. But that is not to say that living in the Spirit is easy, only that the victory belongs to God and his Risen Christ in the long run; we have to live God's spirit in the mess and pain of the here and now, strive for all that's good and beautiful and true, despite the suffering that will bring.

The early Church, despite persecution, knew this; the apostles went out in the Spirit's power to face sufferings, and so birth the Church. They were brokenhearted when Christ left, but knew he had to go, so that the Spirit could come, the Church be born, and his power liberate all from the kingdom of despair and death. So if the faith is under attack now, we must remember that it has gone through worse crises, and come out stronger.

Our task is to promote in our lives, families, societies, and countries that Spirit of love received at Baptism and Confirmation. It's as such faithful servants of the church born at Pentecost, in its real and mystical dimension (the secret church of all good men, of whatever religion or none), that we'll be raised to glory. For the hard, corrupt world's spirit of which Satan is lord fades to dust and ashes at last, but Christ's Spirit is life, goodness, peace, faith, hope, beauty, and salvation for all people's deeper happiness in this world and forever and ever. Amen.

So as God's own reflecting the Holy Spirit of faith, hope and love in our lives so as to redeem our broken world, let's profess our faith.

## *Prayers of the Faithful*

And as the people of God gathered in the grace of the Holy Spirit, let us pray for the things that we need with confidence to our heavenly

Father who always listens to his people, as we pray from his Spirit present in us.

For our Holy Father and all leaders of the Churches throughout the world, that they may respond to the Holy Spirit in their own lives and be his holy presence to the world at large, and link with his presence there in other religions and the church of all good people.

For civic leaders, that they may serve the spiritual as well as the material needs of the people they rule, and serve the poor with generosity and love.

For our wonderful young people, that reflecting God's good spirit, they may serve generously in the Church. We pray especially for First Communion and Confirmation children, that they will keep their vows to be faithful practicing Christians.

For ourselves in our homes, that we may reflect the Spirit of God that we received at Baptism and Confirmation, and so be lights of faith and goodness to our families and community.

For all those in need around us—the sick, the aged, the lonely, and the poor, that we may respond to them with generous love and care and so bring the healing Spirit of Christ to all.

For the dead, especially those for whom we now pray, that they may be raised up to the throne of God in the Spirit forever.

And we ask all these prayers through Christ in the Spirit to the Father, who always heeds such ardent prayers. Amen.

## Reflection

God is seen in scripture as a perfect parent. Christ describes him as "Abba," or "Daddy." All of us can address God in similar terms, for the Church is a family, and we're his children. Mary, our Mother, completes the family. So to dads and mums out there, struggling to bring up families in love, hang in there; you are doing the work of the Spirit. You are the domestic Church. You're special, and your reward will be great in heaven. Indeed, let's pray for all wonderful parents in the parish, mothers and fathers, to our Mother in heaven that the warm, loving spirit of God may rule in our homes. Hail Mary.

# The Most Holy Trinity

## *Introduction*

The Trinity is the great mystery of faith, what the Celtic Church called the three in one and one in three. Our readings describe each person of the Trinity in turn. The first charts the Father's immense majesty. The second the power of the Spirit in us, and the third describes the Risen Christ as Lord of all. Let's confess ways we fail the triune God.

## *Homily*

"The world is charged with the grandeur of God," wrote Gerard Manley Hopkins, a nineteenth-century Jesuit priest, who influenced so many poets of the modern era. That grandeur, he shows, comes from the Trinity, which isn't a remote mystery, but the dynamic behind all goodness, beauty, and truth on earth. Indeed, the earth teems with sacred threesomes that reflect that triune God—sun, moon, and stars; earth, sky, and sea; father, mother, and child. It's even why we're male and female. Scripture says, "In the image of God he created him; male and female he created them" (Genesis 1:27, JB).

How does sexuality make us like God? The love union of man and woman begets a third, the child. As God is three in the heavenly home, so it is in the earthly home. What a wise plan of God, that each person conceived on earth should come from a loving union like that of the Trinity. Is that why everything is male and female and produces offspring? Clearly, we're all sacred; our human rights come from being outpourings of the triune God.

Sadly today we often ignore that centrality of the Trinity in our faith. Our forefathers can teach us a lot in this. Early church prayers invoked the three in one and one in three; depth of earth, height of heaven, deep of ocean. For our ancestors, the triune God wasn't an abstract idea, but all around us. Legend says Saint Patrick used the humble three-leaved shamrock to explain that mystery. It has three leaves, but is only one plant. Whether Patrick actually did this is irrelevant. Throughout his ministry, he Christianized the natural sense of God in Celtic culture, so its just what he would have done. A good example is the Celtic cross; it unites the cross and the sun, Christ and nature.

The Trinity also permeates the sacraments, the earthly mediations of God's grace. We baptize in the name of the Father, Son, and the Holy Spirit; we absolve from sins in the name of the Father, Son, and the Holy Spirit; we confirm in the name of the Father, Son, and the Holy Spirit. And our mass prayers are trinitarian. We pray all the prayers through Christ to the Father in the Spirit. But the simplest greatest trinitarian prayer is the blessing of ourselves. We impose the Trinity and the cross on our very bodies.

Why then is the Trinity sometimes played down? Maybe the culprit was the reformation which overstressed Christ, Christolatry. As today's gospel makes clear, this fails to recognize that everything Christ did came from his union with the Father in the Spirit. Also reform fundamentalists tend to overstress the Bible: Bibliolatry. Our faith is not a matter of a book. Its center is the person of the Risen Christ, always in intimate relation with the Father and the Spirit. For everything he did on earth came from that union.

So also God's presence among us is trinitarian. It's in the power of the Trinity that we live and move and have our being. And at last we'll be swept up by Christ in the Spirit into the Father's kingdom of love. With our loved ones we'll share the life of God in a heaven of love and unity powered by the Trinity. For the divisive values of this world of which Satan is lord fade to ashes at last, but Christ, one with the Father and the Spirit in a unity of love, is Lord of love and life forever and ever. Amen.

So as people of a trinitarian faith, let us say the creed now in a new way noting its trinitarian format: the first part deals with the Father, the second with Christ, and the third with the Spirit, which is linked to the Church, his outpouring to the world.

## Prayers of the Faithful

As the people of God rooted in the mystery of God as Father, Son and Spirit let's pray for what we need to our triune God.

For church leaders, especially our Pope and the bishops, that they may reach out to other faith and all people of good will, in the power of God as Father, Son, and Spirit and so bring the world to unity in diversity.

For civil leaders, that they may promote the unity and peace of the people, north and south, and so image the Trinity of peace.

For our wonderful youth, that, as the Trinity makes all things sacred, they may believe in and worship that triune God with all their hearts within the Church, the concrete emblem of the Spirit in its mystical and holy aspects.

For ourselves, that as we bless ourselves at home and bless our children with holy water, we may become ever more aware of the Trinity's presence in us, above us, and around us in caring love.

For the sick and all those suffering in mind or body, that the three persons in one God may raise them up to new life.

For the dead, that they may enter through Christ (the door) in the Spirit (the key) to the eternal House of God the Father.

And we ask all these prayers through the same Christ, in the Spirit to the eternal Father of us all forever and ever. Amen

## *Reflection*

A common prayer invokes Christ beside us, before us, and behind me, king of our heart. Again in this ancient ancestral prayer the triple nature of God's presence is invoked. We pray that Mother Mary, part of the trinity that was the home at Nazareth, may keep us all in a living relationship with the triune God. Hail Mary.

# Corpus Christi

## *Introduction*

Today's readings remind us that the Eucharist feeds us as the Israelites were fed in the desert. Paul, in the second reading, says it unites us with and makes us the body of Christ. And Christ tells us that through it we're part of eternal life here. Let's confess ways we fail to appreciate how vital for our faith the Eucharist is.

## *Homily*

Since Renaissance Platonism and the Reformation, we've played up the soul and played down the body, but that's not Christianity. Even today's feast stresses the united bodily and spiritual presence of Christ in the Eucharist. It's as real as someone entering our house. You know when great people come into a room, we feel their charisma. It was like that with Christ. His great presence made people flock to him and hang on his words. You may say, "I wish I'd been there." But we are "there" every Sunday. He comes to us in Communion in as real a way. The substance of the bread and wine is changed into his body and blood; it may look like bread and wine, but it's really his body and blood, soul and divinity. Through it, he comes to us in body and soul; if you don't believe me believe Christ: "For my flesh is real food and my blood is real drink" (John 6:55, JB). When people walked away from Christ because of these explicit words, he didn't call them back.

For the Real Presence follows from the incarnation; the Word became flesh, and it's in that unity that he comes to us in Communion; he's hardly going to divide himself there. It's not like a person talking to you who is miles away. Jesus in Communion is intimately present to us, enabling faith, hope, and charity to bloom, making us Christian to the core of our being, nourishing our souls like good eating does our bodies. This strengthens us for life's journey, furthers our growth in God's life, binds us to his body the Church, and strengthens us to witness to him in the world. Finally it empowers us to defeat sin, suffering, and death. We become what we eat, and what we eat here is the living Lord.

But priceless blessings come to us from visits to his sacramental presence in the Church too. He is present for us at all times in the tabernacle. If you knew Jesus was visiting your area in the flesh, you'd rush to meet him. But he's in the Church all the time. Benediction and exposition are great reminders of that fact.

All in all, then, we can't overemphasize how precious a gift of God the Eucharist is. Our wise forefathers knew this, in making mass such a part of life. Jesus was there for them, they were there for him. Let's continue to let this gift mold and transform our lives in graceful living, bringing us ever closer to God, the Church, and each other, so that when we see Our Lord face to face we won't be strangers. But don't take my word for it. Christ himself says that unless we eat his flesh and drink his blood, which is real food and drink, we won't have life in us; he goes onto to say: "Anyone who does eat my flesh and drink my blood has eternal life, and I shall raise him up on the last day" (John 6:54, NIV).

Imagine that! Through Communion, we're already growing in eternal life in this world, until we flower into eternal glory. We're already part of eternal life in each mass and Communion. To know that is wisdom. For this world passes to dust and ashes at last, but Christ in Communion is really united with us, body and soul, as he is Lord of life both for our deepest happiness here below, and forever and ever in heaven. Amen.

So conscious that we are an infinitely blessed and glorious Eucharistic people, blessed with Christ's real presence among us, let's profess our faith with new enthusiasm.

## Prayers of the Faithful

As God's people communing with Our Lord's presence to and for us here in body and soul, let's pray confidently for what we need.

For Church leaders, especially our Holy Father, that they may enthusiastically encourage the world's peoples to receive and be the living Body of Christ so that all may grow in his love, and thereby flower into eternal glory.

For civil leaders, that they may by just and integral law and rule bring all the people to their highest dignity and happiness in body and soul.

For our glorious youth, that heeding Christ's words: "If you do not eat the flesh of the Son of Man and drink his blood, you will not have life in you" (John 6:53, JB), they may come faithfully every Sunday to the table of the Lord.

For ourselves, that we may never fail to come every Sunday to be nourished at the table of the Lord and go to spread his loving and healing presence to our homes and precious children.

For the sick, the old, the lonely, and housebound, that through monthly reception of the Eucharist on First Fridays, they may participate in the body of Christ and be raised up.

For the dead, that having shared in the banquet of eternal life here through the Eucharist they may enjoy it forever in heaven.

And we ask all these prayers through the same Christ Our Lord here present with us, his holy Eucharistic people. Amen.

## Reflection

This week we had the feasts of Corpus Christi and The Sacred Heart, which remind us of Christ's Real Presence. The first was requested by God when he appeared to Saint Juliana in a private vision. He said he wanted a feast set aside in honor of his Real Presence. For as the Church went on, faith would diminish to the point where it would need a feast day to remind people of his Real Presence. For the same reason he asked Saint Margaret to help institute the Sacred heart feast in the octave of Corpus Christi. For the Eucharist is his heart beating for us and united with us in love. Let's ask Mother Mary to give us the grace to cherish this real and greatest of gifts from God given to us, his only begotten Son. Hail Mary.

# Second Sunday in Ordinary Time

## *Introduction*

"Look there is the Lamb of God" (John 1:29, JB). This week we might open our eyes in a fresh way to Christ and follow him faithfully. For, as an anonymous witty Christian said, most of us, instead of following him along the way, are more often by the way, or in the way. Let's confess any ways we hinder, or are indifferent in following him.

## *Homily*

Recently, the killing of a honeymoon girl abroad for a few dollars appalled me. If we continue to abandon Christ for worldliness, will more of this happen? Already the news is full of drug killings. Wrecking lives seems to mean nothing; yet what use to drug barons are pads in the Bahamas if they can't sleep at night? "'There is no happiness,' says the Lord, 'for the wicked'" (Isaiah 48:22, JB). Money brings no joy if faith, neighborliness, and what's right is sacrificed to it. Wealth, cars, exotic holidays, pleasurable sex were given by God to enjoy. But, if gained by destroying our souls or our frailer fellow humans, they're useless. To hell with God, the old, the weak, the needy—enjoy yourself at all costs! Is that where we are now? Progressing technologically, but regressing fast spiritually and humanely, to a self-centered hedonism? A youth said recently on radio, "My New Year's resolutions are three: put myself first, put myself first, put myself first."

Sure, we should love ourselves, but not at the expense of shutting out God, others, and what's right in doing so. Not long ago, when on my way to visit an estate where a person had died, I asked directions. A young woman said, "The house you want is over there somewhere." I went around and came back and found that the person who'd died lived next door. She didn't know her neighbor, much less that he'd died. People make excuses: "twas worse in the old days." It wasn't. We were poor but all in the same boat. No heads in the air, we helped neighbors, gave God his due, and were happier.

Which brings me to happier news: a report in the media of an increase in England, United States, and the continent in people becoming priests. They interviewed one, an engineer. I don't have the exact source or words but I paraphrase roughly what he said: "I went through it all, money, sex, pleasure, the blind pursuit of all I wanted without restraint, but my heart was empty. Then I said, surely there's more to life." He discovered that meaning in serving God. "Okay, priestly celibacy's foolishness to the world," he said, "but that's its witness value." Our readings echo that view. Paul tells us to honor our bodies as temples of the Spirit, and Samuel says: "Speak, Lord, your servant is listening" (1 Sam, 3:10, JB). That engineer listened to God present in his heart's deepest aspirations, and decided to give his all to the service of God and others, to fill his empty heart.

One Christmas, I was called to a flat in a large town. I found a young girl dead in her vomit from drugs. The sight haunts me still. What a waste! Instead of self-destruction, if only she'd found the joy of Christ. Instead of giving her life to drug dealers, if only she'd given it to God like that engineer, she might have lived longer and happier and made a difference by her life. And that's a lesson for us: To cherish our neighbors. To be joyful children of God, not victims of soul-destroying values. For the hard self-serving world fades to dust and ashes at last and leaves us empty both for this world and on eternity's shore, but Christ is Lord of life, love, happiness, beauty, truth, peace, and salvation both for our lasting joy in this world and forever and ever. Amen.

So as God's own called to follow Christ and his Church on the right way, and to care for others as ourselves, let's profess our faith.

### Prayers of the Faithful

And as the people of God gathered here, let's pray with confidence to our heavenly Father for our own needs and that of the world.

Let's pray for the Churches throughout the world, especially the pope and bishops, that they may be beacons of faith, charity, and vital inner riches to a needy troubled world.

For civil leaders, that they may set aside all corrupt self-interest and serve all the people with integrity and justice.

For youth, that, like that young seminarian, they may see the vanity of total worldly pursuits, and open their eyes like the blind man in the gospel and follow Christ along the way to real lasting joy, peace, happiness, and salvation for their souls.

For ourselves, that in our homes and nations we may testify not to greedy selfishness but to loving faith and care and so help lead all around us, especially our children, from darkness to light.

For vocations; that young people may not be so blinded by the world and pursuit of money, pleasure, and self as to neglect the call to selfless service of God and others.

For the needy aged, lonely, sick, or poverty stricken, that through our help and care they may experience the love and care of God.

For the dead, may they come to the fullness of life anticipated in the Eucharist.

We ask all these prayers through Christ Our Lord of love forever and ever. Amen

## Reflection

During John Paul II's life, during the Nazi Polish occupation, many urged him to resort to violence. But he kept reiterating that instead they would overcome by love. He organized people in a peaceful victory over both this tyranny and the later communist one. And, as pope, he overcame the hate of the person who shot him by visiting and forgiving him. And his final sickness was a perfect example to those caught up in unavoidable suffering; he struggled to bless people in Saint Peter's Square a few days before he died, though practically dead on his feet. He did this because his love of Christ enabled him to endure all things, and overcome all suffering in faith. Let's do the same. Hail Mary.

# Third Sunday in Ordinary Time

## *Introduction*

"They left everything and followed him" we hear of the apostles (Lk. 5:11 JB). Our liturgy this Sunday calls us also to follow him faithfully through all the trials and suffering of life and so win the crown of life. Conscious of ways we fail him, let's call to mind our sins.

## *Homily*

I never tire of telling Saint Francis of Assisi's story. In the thirteenth century, after seeing a vision of a ruined Church and hearing Christ's voice telling him to "rebuild my Church," he spent himself restoring corrupt Church institutions and serving the poor. One day in chapel, his rich father angrily ordered him to return family property that he had given away. Francis took off his clothes and walked naked from the Church saying, "Father, take back everything. I go empty handed to serve Christ." After that he clothed himself in a rough robe tied with a chord and begged from the rich to give to the poor. Though he lived a poor, simple life, 10,000 young men left all to follow in his footsteps. Tired of worldly ways, they wanted to give all in following Christ and serving humanity.

In the same way in our gospel Christ calls the apostles and us to abandon everything and follow him in overflowing faith and charity. We may not be asked to be as radical as the apostles or Francis, but we can follow Christ in our way, and shape our world and Church in his gentle, caring image. True, that's harder today when worldly ways are more vigorously promoted and faith is attacked. Yet to be faithful to Christ and all that's good and true is a greater and more lasting way to glory.

Francis inspired millions during his life, and has continued to inspire billions since his death - even the present Pope took his name - but his rich, self-serving father left nothing to posterity but a record of his greed. Evil and worldly ways attract in the short term, but in the long run they leave us empty. Billions adored Hitler and Stalin as they turned Churches into museums and sent believers to concentration camps. But where are Hitler and Stalin now, and what is their legacy? A trail of totalitarian evil and genocide.

Vital choices face each of us every day: to follow God's way in Christ or to abandon him for the corrupt ways of the world of which Satan is lord. It's a hard choice, for the power of evil has a curious attraction and has its prophets too. But its satisfactions are short lived; as the Bible says, godless ways are like something we eat that seems sweet at first but eventually turns sour in the stomach. By contrast goodness seems sour at first but turns to pure sweetness in the stomach at last.

Its in that sense that the gospel says we can't serve two masters. We must make the choice for money or God. There's no such thing as an ideological vacuum. If we're not serving one master, we're serving another, and there are always worldly ideologies that browbeat believers into following transient philosophies. Yet thousands of these have come and gone, but the Church goes on forever, because its enduring wisdom.

Let's cling to it and be wise too. For its the road to happiness in this world as well as the next. Even secular scholars are realizing this. A noted psychologist on the radio said recently that we should believe, even if just for psychological well-being. And a scientific study I read recently said that evolution favors those of faith. If we need faith for inner depth, long-term happiness, and our very survival, then, abandoning it is foolish.

Yet even the best, at times, are fooled by the lure of worldly power and glory into persecuting the good and true. Francis was exiled, the apostles were killed, and Christ was crucified. Yet they won in the long run. They knew the ways of the world fade to ashes at last and leave us empty before eternity, but God is love, truth, beauty, grace, inner peace, and salvation, God cannot be defeated in the long run for he is man's deeper happiness for this life, and our soul's salvation forever and ever. Amen.

So as God's own following Christ faithfully in love and freedom to redeem our times, despite attack from the envious world and its values, let's profess our faith.

## Prayers of the Faithful

And as God's people, loving him with all our hearts and souls, let's pray to this caring heavenly Father for all our needs.

For church leaders, especially our Holy Father, that they may lead the faithful and all the world in the wise following of Christ, and so redeem our troubled times.

For civil leaders, that they may not promote secular agendas that deprive us of our great faith heritage, which is still the true riches of our people and especially our youth.

For ourselves, that in our homes and communities we may stand up for Christ and his Church, and so go out to meet him when he comes at last as one of his faithful saints.

For our great young people, that they may not be so caught up in the ways of the world as to neglect the deeper values of life and the salvation of their immortal souls.

For the sick and needy in our society, that they may find their comfort in the Lord and that we may never fail to treat them with the love, care, and gentle patience of Christ.

For the dead, that having remained faithful to Christ in this life they may come to the fullness of heavenly glory.

And we ask all these our prayers through the same Christ, our ever-caring and loving Lord of life. Amen.

## Reflection

There's a story told of the early martyrs. Those who abandoned Christ and worshiped idols were spared death and given money. One man accepted this money and cursed Christ. As he watched the others going to the lions, a bystander said to him, "How lucky you are. You're alive and wealthy while they're all dead meat." "No," he replied, "they are the ones who are alive. I am the one who is dead." He had sold his soul for sordid gain and knew he'd made a very bad bargain indeed. Let's pray we won't make that mistake. Hail Mary.

# Fourth Sun in Ordinary Time

## Introduction

This Sunday begins a series of gospels on the Sermon on the Mount, Christ's new commandments. They're wholly positive, and not really laws, but inner ways to blessedness for this world, that leads on to the next. Let's confess any ways we've failed in these key Christian areas of mercy, peace, love, and purity of heart.

## Homily

"I have a dream!" You know Martin Luther King's famous speech. It envisages an equal USA for all, achieved not by violence, but by new attitudes in men's hearts. Today's gospel is Christ's "I have a dream" speech—a plea for a world where all are equal, and all are God's free and blessed children. For Christ's eight beatitudes are not laws, but keys to changing the human heart, and thereby changing the world into God's perfect kingdom.

As such they contain no "thou shalt nots." They're wholly positive, geared to change people inside. Law is useless, Christ says, and I summarize the Beatitudes, unless we have mercy, love, peace, purity, generosity, and a thirst for right deep within us. That's the key to blessedness in this world and the next. No wonder even non-Christian saints like Gandhi found them so beautiful. Through non-violent protest he followed a blessed way to an independent peaceful India. He proved that Christ's way can change a violent world into God's peaceful one. For if men's hearts are peaceful, so is the world around them.

In effect, the Beatitudes are Christ's blueprint for a peaceful and blessed new world. As such they override the old Ten Commandments. He keeps saying: "It was said to you in the past, but I say this to you."

(Mt. 5-6, JB). I won't deal with all the Beatitudes here; I'd keep you all day. But even one of them, if practiced by everybody, would bring heaven on earth. For example, take the first: "how happy are the poor in spirit."(Mt. 5:3, JB). Christ is not saying it's good to be poor; rather he means that the key to universal equality and justice is to be poor "in spirit." If each person freed his heart from greed and possessiveness, then injustice would disappear. There would be universal sharing of earth's resources, an unfailing way to solve society's ills, and make all happy.

But Christ is also a realist. Detachment from riches and worldly greed will make us happy, free us within and win us untold friends. But it will make the world hate us. We'll expose how useless and unsatisfying its greedy, materialistic, violent and selfish values are. So the world will seek revenge. That's why he says those are blessed when the world hates and reviles them for following his advice. They must be doing what's right. So we shouldn't let worldly propaganda change our focus. As a holy man put it, the test of how well we're following Christ is how much we're made to suffer. Christ, the holiest man who ever lived, was crucified. His crime was challenging the wealth, power, and corruption of Jewish and Roman lords. They thought killing him would kill his vision.

The world tries to kill God in the same way in every age so that it can give full reign to its greed and power lust. But we who love God—his blessed people—must continue to follow Christ's gentle way. For he calls us to freedom from greed, overflowing love, purity of heart, and generosity of Spirit to redeem the world. And bring us full happiness here as well as hereafter. If we're free and pure within then we'll be wise and happy, free from worldly ways that manipulate and destroy. For the world's values of which Satan is lord fade to ashes and leave the soul high and dry both in this world and before eternity, but Christ is Lord of love, goodness, peace, and truth both for our deeper happiness in this world and forever and ever. Amen.

So as God's people called to live the Beatitudes and so transform a corrupt, violent, and unjust world into Christ's graceful, peaceful, truthful, and glorious kingdom, let's profess our faith.

## *Prayer of the Faithful*

As the people of God, blessed children of the Beatitudes, let's pray for the things that we need.

For Church leaders throughout the world, that they may witness to Christ's poverty, not palaces of wealth and power, and so help transform the world into God's just Kingdom.

For our civil leaders, that they may serve the good of all, especially the weak and vulnerable, not just their own wealth, power and privilege.

For ourselves, in our homes, communities, and nations, that we may witness to Christ's blessed way of peace, love, mercy, goodness, purity of heart, faith, and beauty, and so redeem the world.

For the sick in our community, that through our care they may know the blessed love of God and his Christ.

For the dead, that they may enter into the glory of the Blessed after following Christ's faithfully in this world.

And we ask all these prayers through the same Christ who is Lord of love, truth, and beauty forever and ever. Amen

## *Reflection*

The film *Gandhi* tells the story of the holy man who led India to independence. In it, there's a wonderful scene. A Christian who was working with him asked him to abandon his way of peaceful protest. But Gandhi reminded him that Christ said to turn the other cheek. The Christian adviser's answer was that that shouldn't be taken literally. The world is in the mess it is because we don't take Christ literally, for the Beatitudes are a perfect recipe for a perfect world. Gandhi proved that; when civil war broke out, he fasted and prayed until they stopped fighting. We pray that we too will follow Christ's way, which is also a universal recipe for peace, justice, and happiness, and so come to fullness of life here and hereafter, under the glorious banner of the Beatitudes. Hail Mary.

# Fifth Sunday in Ordinary Time

## Introduction

A person I know says, "I'm a non-believer. I don't harm anyone, and that's enough." But surely, I protested, we're here not just to avoid harm, but to do as much good as we can. We're to be the salt of the earth and the light of the world, as our gospel says. Let's confess ways we fail Christ, not just by sin, but also by not doing all the good we can.

## Homily

In the James Bond film *Quantum of Solace*, the hero seeks peace within himself. Though Bond is light years away from Christian life, inner peace is also our objective. The word used for this in the Bible is *shalom*, which is more than absence of war. Its means inner completeness, health, and integrity. It is the state of one who lives in harmony with himself, his neighbor, nature, and God. That's what Christ calls is to, to be the salt of the earth and the light of the world, to inspire those around us, to create a shalom world.

But that's hard work, and we're frail, so we need God's grace in Christ to help us. Without that grace, we're lost, because as Paul says, there's another law in us; that of the flesh, the law of the unredeemed, the law of satanic darkness that threatens to swallow up our soul's deep aspirations. Our task, achievable by God's grace and Church sacraments, is to free ourselves and others from all such soul-destroying inner and outer darkness.

That's what Christ means when he says we must be the salt of the earth and light of the world. We must live uprightly, pure in motive and action, helping the oppressed, knowing our need of God, active for universal goodness and peace. All this, of course, is the opposite of the corrupt world, which inevitably hits back.

That's why the image of the just man who suffers as result of his goodness fills the scriptures. He persists in godly ways despite attack and persecution from the corrupt and envious world. The ultimate example of this servant of God who, though persecuted, redeems the world is Christ, our model and inspiration. He takes our part when we're attacked for doing what's right, and his grace enables our victory in the long run.

That's why the saints were joyful even in persecution. Ultimately they did what was right for Christ, to bring themselves and others into his kingdom of light, love, peace, and graceful living. Similarly we shouldn't work for passing fame and wealth alone, but also for the recreation of the world in God's image, his kingdom come.

All that is summed up in our gospel. We're to be the salt of the earth and the light of the world. Lost in darkness, narrow self-interest, cruelty, war, injustice, and godless pride, the world needs our lamps to guide it out of the morass where it lies trapped by Satan. We're to be Christ's redeeming light, powered by inner batteries of faith and good works. That is, there must be an active outgoing as well as inner dimension to our faith.

One understands why Luther worried about this gospel; "your light must shine in the sight of men, so that, seeing your good works, they may give the praise to your Father in heaven" (Matthew 5:16, JB). It's Matthew's response to the doctrine of salvation by faith alone. In Christ, one is first transformed within, and then transforms the world by radical goodness in action; hence also Christ's parable of the end of the world where we will be judged by the nature of our active charity. Ultimately God's glory and the world's redemption are the aim of our good deeds. For the corrupt values of this world pass away, but Christ is Lord of light, life, goodness, love, truth and peace for this world and forever and ever. Amen.

So as God's own, safe in his light as we spread it to others by word and action, we profess our faith.

## Prayers of the Faithful

And as the people of God, living in the light of Christ, we pray confidently for what we need to be his proud witnesses.

For Church leaders, especially our Holy Father and all pastors of Churches, that they may be real beacons for Christ to our world, drawing all people to the saving light of God.

For civil leaders, that they too may bring God's light to the world by just laws and allowing the faith to flower in the land.

For ourselves, that we may be the salt of the earth and the light of the world at home, at work, and everywhere, radiating God's grace by word, good works, and faith, especially to our children.

For our wonderful, bright young people, that they may never abandon the light of faith or drift back into the meaningless darkness and hopelessness that Christ suffered so much to deliver us from.

For the sick, the lonely, the aged and the oppressed, that by our good works on their behalf they may know the infinite love and comfort of their caring Lord.

For the dead, that they may come fully into the light of Christ in heaven, if they have not already done so, by our prayers which are a true good work on their behalf.

And we ask all these our prayers through the same Christ Our Lord who is forever the light of the world. Amen

## Reflection

Saint James also says good works must underpin faith. He points out that is useless telling a person in need to stay fed, warm, or housed, if we do nothing to help. Our words are empty; our faith vain posturing. Hence Christ himself says, "your light must shine in the sight of men, that seeing your good works, they may give the praise to your Father in heaven" (Matthew 5:16, JB). Even Lutherans agree; they signed a joint document with Catholics recently saying that Christianity means faith lived in love. We pray to Mary to help us live our faith in good works of active charity. Hail Mary.

# Sixth Sunday in Ordinary Time

## Introduction

We have glorious gospels at this time, taken from Christ's Sermon on the Mount, his new commandments for his new people. Called to live this blessed way to happiness, let's confess any ways we fail in mercy, peace, justice or any other of the Beatitudes.

## Homily

Our gospel today continues the Sermon on the Mount, which, the key to Christian moral life, gives a new set of commandments, centering not on law but inner goodness, the clean heart. The Sermon restores the commandments' spirit, ruined by the external righteousness of the religious authorities: "if your virtue goes no deeper than that of the scribes and Pharisees, you will never enter the kingdom of heaven" (Matthew 5:20, JB).

In this, Christ is often presented as liberal against conservative; that's only partly true. He both revises the old law, and yet makes it more demanding for his new people. For example, of the fifth commandment he says: "You have learnt how it was said to our ancestors; 'you must not kill, and if anyone does kill he must answer for it before the court'. But I say to you, anyone who is angry with his brother will answer for it before the court" (Matthew 5:21–22, JB). This higher standard addresses the attitudes within that cause murder; if we don't heal the violence within, outer law is a deterrent, not a cure.

Even more radical is the fact that, revising the law in this way, he claims a greater authority than Moses. And what he says makes more sense. It *is* useless saying "You shall not kill" (Exodus 20:13, JB) if we have murder in our hearts. Law, he says, won't correct the problem of violence in the world. We must first heal the inner attitudes that spark violence: anger, hatred, insults, resentment, feuds, legal wrangles etc. Our higher aim, he says, "is to be perfect, just as your heavenly Father is perfect" (Mt. 5:48, JB).

Another law he revises in the same way is the sixth commandment about sexual relations. The old law is: "You shall not commit adultery" (Ex. 20:14, JB). But he says we must first right the attitudes of heart that lead to adultery: dangerous out-of-control lusts that we harbor in our hearts. Only purity within, and enduring love, can cure this evil.

It's in that spirit also that he tackles issues of marriage, divorce, and women's rights. He situates an interior basis for true marriage and family faithfulness in self-giving, faithful love. Some Jewish laws allowed divorce, but he shows that this undermines the life-long commitment of love and faithfulness that gives marriage its deepest dignity.

This may not resonate with liberals. But his aim is to set an ideal for the new people of God of true, enduring, and faithful love that reflects God's love for us. True marriages are made in heaven and "what God has joined, man must not divide" (Mark 10:9, JB). He restores Genesis's spirit as against the "hardness of heart" of lawmakers in Israel who revised it; life-long marriage is vital to his new Kingdom of God righteousness.

But the larger lesson for us today, in this, and other key areas of human life, is that we must tackle the root causes of evil and create a truly righteous law in the heart that leads to integral life and love. Not to restrict us but to make us truly happy. True, this is a huge challenge for our "anything goes" world. But for the sake of our integrity and that of the world, we must do our best to live up to his ideal. We must try to be the salt and light of the earth in suffering marriage faithfulness, in peacefulness within, in deep compassion from the heart. Those who find this too difficult have his merciful forgiveness to fall back on. But we must at least try to live up to his ideals, for our good and that of the world. For the values of the world that are other than God's pass and leave us empty at last, but Christ is Lord of faithful enduring love, truth, and graceful living forever and ever. Amen.

So as God's people doing our best to uphold right inner attitudes of love and faithfulness in marriage, and peace and integrity in life, and yet trusting in his infinite forgiveness when we fail through human weakness, we profess our faith.

## Prayers of the Faithful

As citizens of Christ's kingdom lets pray for our deepest needs.

For church leaders, especially the Holy Father, that they may witness to the Beatitudes as the universal way of freedom, peace, truth, salvation, and enduring love.

For civil leaders, that they may move away from violence as the solution to issues that divide us and continue to follow Christ's way of peace and reconciliation.

For our loving youth, that following Christ's blessed way, may they gain happiness here and help redeem the world around them.

For ourselves, that in our homes and marriages we may try to live up to Christ's ideal of life long caring love and faithfulness.

For all those in need, that free from greed, we may reach out to them and share our resources freely with them.

For the dead, that, through our prayers, they may be freed from darkness due to sin and attain the blessed Kingdom of God

And we ask all these our prayers through the same Christ Our Lord who teaches us in the Beatitudes the way of life.

## Reflection

*"Gloine ár gcroi, is neart ár mhuini, is beart de reir ár mbriathar."* Purity of heart, strength of mind, and acting on one's word was the

motto of the Fianna, the legendary warriors of the ancient Celtic poetic sagas in the Irish language. This motto shows the universal nature of Christ's beatitudes. The Sermon also upholds total trustworthiness in verbal relations; if we don't really mean it, we shouldn't swear at all, Christ says (Mt. 5:17, JB). Only by lives free of falsehood in word and act can we uphold community. Here Jesus is moral liberator; one's life and community shouldn't be based on lies, but on truth, honesty and integrity. Let's pray for truthful pure hearts in his service. Hail Mary.

# Seventh Sunday in Ordinary Time

## Introduction

We continue the outlines of Christ's new beatitude morality. Today he shows the uselessness of violence. He asks us to be peaceful within. Let's confess if we fail in this.

## Homily

The life of Nelson Mandela is a wonderful example for us today, and very much in the spirit of the Beatitudes, though he himself followed native religion. He was very much the person Christ describes as the epitome of the blessed one, the just man persecuted in the cause of right. Like Gandhi, who was a more overt fan of the Sermon on the Mount through his correspondence with Tolstoy, he worked peacefully to break the apartheid system, not returning violence for violence. The same could be said of Martin Luther King's work in America. Which all proves the universal nature of Christ's truths in the Sermon; they are what all good men believe in their hearts, and practice in their lives.

In effect the Beatitudes, and more so the Sermon as a whole, are a blueprint for the transformation of the world into God's just kingdom, which Christ, as he constantly affirms, came to establish. The first words of his public ministry are "The Kingdom of God is close at hand. Repent and believe the Good News". He says each human heart must be pure, if peace and justice is to come to a world remade in the image of its Creator.

That's the witness Christ asks of us in today's gospel, the witness of a grace-filled, just and peaceful heart. We must be the opposite of the violence that permeates the world and makes it into a hell rather than a heaven. Christ says violence only begets more violence, and our only hope is to break that vicious circle. He said to Peter: "All who draw the sword will die by the sword" (Matthew 26:52, JB). The way of the sword has meant endless wars between peoples from the year dot. Christ challenges us, his new redeemed people, to a better way. He points out that the only way we can change things is by not returning evil for evil, for then we become as bad as those we oppose. We must stop the vicious cycle, turn people's hearts to peace by example, like he did, by not returning violence for violence on the cross. This sure way is for all, not just Christians. It has been proved again and again in our modern world, from the message of the anti-Vietnam war activists, to peaceful protest movements everywhere.

Jesus tells us to break the cycle of violence by returning good for evil, for peace begins in each human heart. This view is behind a whole series of blessed ways in the Sermon: going the extra mile, lending without interest, forgiving our enemies, avoiding revenge etc. All these defuse conflict. They may involve some pain, but its worth it if they break the warring way that has plagued humankind from the year dot. But Christ not only preached but also lived this way of peace; on the cross he forgave those crucifying him.

And this illustrates another key part of the Sermon, that of loving one's enemies, doing good to those who hate us, and praying for those who persecute us. In this we're asked to be children of an all-forgiving God. His sun shines equally on the wicked and the just. His loving forgiveness must be the norm if perpetual war is to cease. What should distinguish the Christian, is warmhearted unconditional peace and love. For this is the way in which we discover our true identity and become perfect, as our heavenly Father is perfect. For this world's violent selfish values pass and leave the soul empty at last. And if we die with hating unforgiving hearts, we may live like that for all eternity. But if we follow the way of Christ, we will be free within at death, we will have achieved peaceful, gracious and free living here, transformed the world around us, and we will be one with the Prince of Peace at last forever and ever. Amen.

So as Christ's people, members of his new kingdom, living that generous love and peace that makes us children of God, we make our profession of faith.

## Prayers of the Faithful

And as the people of God, gathered here in his presence with us as eternal Lord of love, we ask for the grace we need to be his peaceful and just lights to the world.

For our Holy Father and all leaders of the Churches, that they may be lights of peace, of nonviolent ways of resolving conflicts, to the various areas of war in our world.

For all countries torn by war, that civil leaders may pursue the path of peace and reconciliation, and all of us may help in healing processes, and pray for their success.

For ourselves, in our homes, communities, and workplaces, that we may not harbor grudges, but may forgive family or community members who hurt us, and reach out hands of warm love and forgiveness to all, especially teaching our children peaceful loving ways.

For the sick, the old, the lonely, and the oppressed, that through our help and care they may know the love and care of God.

For the dead, that any grudges and hatreds they harbored in this life may be absolved by our prayers; may we hasten them to the heaven where all are one in peace.

And we ask these prayers through the all-loving Christ who prayed for his enemies on the cross and heals all our divisions. Amen.

## Reflection

The Sermon on the Mount is summed up in the last phrase: "You must therefore be perfect, just as your heavenly Father is perfect" (Mt. 5:48, JB). This is our aspiration, even as persistent weaknesses dog us through life we can an achieve an amazing degree of perfection by God's grace in Christ, as the saints proved. But we will never be paragons; even the saints had faults. Indeed, it's in humbly recognizing our frailty that we see our need for God. Even Paul mentions a sting in the flesh that kept him humble. But we mustn't settle for mediocre Christianity all the same. We must keep up a heroic *effort* to transcend our sins, to get up when we fall, to maintain our best intentions. May Mary help us in this life-long struggle within the Church's bosom to be saintly lights to the world, with the immense rewards that entails. Hail Mary.

# Eighth Sunday in Ordinary Time

## *Introduction*

We cannot serve God and money, Christ's warns us. Greed and worldliness can take us over and become false and useless gods, leading us to soul destruction now and forever. Conscious of this, let's confess any ways we let greed oppress our lives.

## *Homily*

A scene in Graham Green's novel, *The Power and the Glory*, reminds me of our gospel. The book is set during the communist revolution in Mexico when regime opponents were hunted and killed. You know the famous photo taken at the time of priests hung from lampposts. Finally only a whiskey priest remains. They lure him to his death by telling him that a dying person needs confession. As they execute him, the commandant says: "We'll finish God and create a perfect secular Marxist state." The priest says, "Ah, but you forget about sin." As the communist kills the priest, a boy who is watching spits on the revolver.

Marx's mistake was to make man's material condition his whole focus, and impose the classless society by force. So materialistic ideology became a God that excluded all higher values of morality or spirituality and reduced man to the level of the beast. Stalin, historians estimate, killed 40 million Russians in ideological zeal. At the same time he was closing down churches, and sending priest to the salt mines. Yet even on the material level he left people, if anything, much worse off. Just as Kim in North Korea, a Stalinist state, builds nuclear bombs now, while his people starve. That's one part of our age's history—secular materialistic totalitarianism: the one party state, the secret police, the great leader, the little books of materialistic utopianism that produced hell after hell. We forget that Hitler's National Socialism was similar, and had its little book, *Mein Kampf.*

But is the opposite Western aspect of this worship of mammon any better—capitalistic worship of money as the be-all. Even during the recent boom the gap between the rich and poor widened considerably and even more so in the aftermath of austerity. Now in the EU we take from old-age pensioners to give to rich bondholders; all are sacrificed to the god, economy, and the interests of the rich are always served. That fetish even demands human sacrifice. Those who don't make it are losers, so alienated young people go on shooting sprees. Must human value be defined by our bank balance?.

Christ offers a better way to the rich young man who comes to him asking how to attain to eternal life. That way is to be poor in heart, the first beatitude, detached from all greed and materialism, satisfied with enough, sharing earth's resources equally, rising above all rabid possessiveness, cherishing everyone as of value in themselves, seeking ultimate lasting riches in God. For human life is more than money; it cannot give us our earthly and higher spiritual value, meaning, and dignity. I think that's what Christ warns us about in today's gospel. We all need enough and should work for a good standard of living and the freedom money brings, but we mustn't turn this into a fetish to which we sacrifice our souls, and trample on people, and God, and justice in the process.

Moreover, even when we gain the world it isn't enough, money isn't enough, pleasure isn't enough, power isn't enough, fame isn't enough. If they become our gods, they just eat us away inside. It was to save us from such worldly emptiness, restore our higher eternal dignity, and yet to show the world how to create a true materialistic utopia, in detachment and sharing, the best of both worlds, that Christ came. He knew false worldly gods fade to ashes at last leaving us wrecked in body and soul. But he is true love, goodness, peace, and ultimate detachment from greed, justice for the poor, and all that's for our deeper happiness and freedom within, both for our happiness in this world, and forever and ever. Amen.

So as God's own working to heal a broken world that can only be redeemed by godly detachment, being happy with enough, sharing with those less well off, free from soulless money obsessions, and loving God and others selflessly, we profess our faith.

## Prayers of the Faithful

And as the people of God, putting our trust in his all-holy Christ, we pray for the things we need in body and soul, with a due sense of balancing both.

For Church leaders, that they may lead all from worship of false materialistic gods to detached sharing, justice, and equality for all, especially the world's excluded masses.

For civic leaders, that they may not be so caught up in the gods of economics and its ruthless money ideology so as to stifle the ordinary people's welfare in body and soul.

For our great youth, that they may find the way to true happiness and hope for the world in God's truly humane detached values, and those of his all-holy Christ.

For ourselves, that we may not be so caught up in getting and spending money as to neglect the deeper road to real happiness, peace, truth, and saving grace in Christ and his Church; the better way of sharing, love and cherishing all equally as God's children.

For the lonely, the aged, the sick, and the oppressed, that they may find in God and our Christian care and love the comfort and hope and love that they need.

For the dead, who carry nothing of this world into the grave where all are equal, that through our prayers they may come to their larger and more enduring heavenly riches.

And we ask all these our prayers through Christ the only Lord of life here below and real salvation forever and ever. Amen.

## *Reflection*

The Faust story illustrates the gospel. He rejected God and sold his soul to the devil for twenty-four years of pleasure, wealth, and power. Years flew by, and he realized that he'd made a poor bargain; riches didn't even make him happy, he could only eat a certain amount, sleep in one bed, and pleasure soon palled. He had sold his soul for useless passing things, and as Satan approached to take his soul, it was too late to change. Let's pray that we won't fall into that materialistic trap. Hail Mary.

# Ninth Sunday in Ordinary Time

## Introduction

This Sunday we are reminded of the great news that the Risen Lord is with us forever. We need not be afraid of anything in his light; we can trust in him. Indeed, all else is building on sand. Let's confess any ways we failed to trust in God and his Christ.

## Homily

We Christians should be joyful. Jesus's risen presence with us forever is great news. The well known story of the Russian poetess Irina Ratushinskaya illustrates this. She spent years in a labor camp in Siberia for being Christian. There she developed liver and kidney trouble, but she survived while strong men died, because she tells us that faith prevented her psychological life from being damaged by hatred and bitterness, it taught her to be happy in any circumstance. Christ lit up her life even in that godless hell.

In that sense, faith's not a luxury but life itself. Even science proves this. A famous psychiatrist interviewed on radio recently said that belief promotes mental health. And the great psychologist Carl Jung says, in his works, that if God didn't exist we'd have to invent him, that the death of God is the death of man. Certainly, the death of God, the creed of fascism and modern secularism, is the demise of man in all his deepest aspects.

But nowadays the flabby devils of middle-class materialism, pleasure, and pride would lure us from the faith that is life. They'd drag us back into the hopeless darkness from which the Risen Lord saved us. They would condemn our children to godless schools and so on. We'd be up in arms if they forced us to give up something vital for our health, but secular enforcements do just that; no society that refuses to foster, or give money for its citizen's spiritual welfare will ever be a complete or happy society. Even common sense should tell us that. When we know suffering or loss, the uncaring commercial world has nothing to offer. But trust in God always raises us up, and he is always there for us. Having triumphed for us over suffering, in life's storms he gives us the safe harbor and comforts of his holy Church.

Despite its faults, one of Christ's great legacies to us is the Church. At Baptism it brings us into a family he is with until the end of time. The authority in heaven and earth given to Christ at the resurrection, he passed to his Church at the ascension. Our house is built on a rock. Let's remember that when many make a football of the Church, attacking its moral teaching. Petrine authority, apostolic unity of belief and truth, is a great gift.

And never was it more needed now when we face constant efforts to water it down. Multitudes of self-appointed popes on TV and radio would replace the Rock as our mentors. Giving in to that would bring spiritual chaos. Christ gave us holy Mother Church for unity and fullness of faith. As Cardinal Newman noted in nineteenth century England, churches that split from it, have split again and again since. Now anyone can set up a church and call it God's church. And churches that have gone worldly haven't thrived; indeed, the opposite. Let's be wise then and stay with the one true church founded on the rock, maintaining Christ's truth in season and out. For it is based not on the babble of arbitrary men, but on the Word and the eternal apostolic faith passed on from Christ.

Even the pope is just a servant of this. He can't snap his fingers and allow what he wishes; he's prisoner not a master of the gospel and what has come down from Christ. Let's be wise and keep to that timeless truth. For worldly ideology passes, straws in every wind, but Christ in his Church is Lord of ageless truth, happiness and salvation both for this world and forever and ever. Amen.

As God's own showered with the timeless truths of Christ as mediated by his Church from its apostolic roots, let's profess our faith.

## Prayers of the Faithful

And as the people of God, we make our prayers with confidence to the Father.

For the Church, our Pope and the bishops in the apostolic succession, and all the other fine mainstream churches, that each in their own way, may continue to hold to the truth of the gospel and tradition and so be a house built on the rock of Christ.

For civil leaders, that they may respect the autonomy of the Church and its institutions and allow it to freely teach the eternal truths that it has received from God.

For ourselves in our homes, communities, and countries, that we may trust in Christ and the faith that our ancestors kept through every persecution and so be lights of faith and hope to our world.

For our youth, that they may trust in the Lord present in authentic Church teaching, so that it will bring them to happiness here and hereafter.

For the sick and all those who need our care, that we may reach out to them with the healing love and care of Christ.

For our dead, that free from all the burdens of sin and darkness they may come through our prayers to their heavenly home.

And we ask all these prayers through Christ, who is Lord of life and intercedes for us before the father forever and ever. Amen

## Reflection

There's a plaque in the rose garden in Tralee, County Kerry, Ireland, and on it are words of Rose Fitzgerald Kennedy, mother of Jack and

Bobby: "I find it interesting to reflect on what has made my life, even with its moments of pain, an essentially happy one. I have come to the conclusion that the most important element in human life is faith." She attended mass daily, and that enabled her to transcend all her troubles and find healing and peace. Let's all share that wisdom. Let's pray to Mary, mother of the Church, that we too will build our house on the rock of faith within the holy Church. May it enable us to withstand life's storms and pain, and come safely to our heavenly home. Hail Mary.

# Tenth Sunday in Ordinary Time

## Introduction

Matthew's call in our gospel is one of the most consoling Bible stories. For it says that we don't have to be perfect to follow Christ. He loves and calls us as we are. So let's confess any ways we may have thought ourselves rejected by him due to our sins.

## Homily

God calls unlikely people to serve him; Matthew's call is a good example. Tax collectors were the despised in Jesus's day; they collected taxes for the Romans and kept part of the money for themselves. Today, too, those called to ministry aren't necessarily paragons. Jesus reminds us in the gospel that he came to call not the virtuous, but sinners. If you'd like to be a priest, don't say, "I'm too flawed." God calls us warts and all. He called Peter; and after the latter denied him, made him pope.

Indeed, following Christ, even while recognizing our weaknesses, is the first step to holiness; the proud self-righteous are a pain in the neck, even to God. I am so happy to be a priest, ordained and content in my present parish. But I don't see myself as any holier than any of you in the congregation; on the contrary, I'm sure most of you are holier and doing a better jobs as parents, or whatever. Indeed, I'm a late vocation to the priesthood, like Matthew, and so conscious of my shortcomings.

Yet at the age of nine, I said to my parents that I wanted to be a priest. Though the calling is difficult—things like celibacy, loneliness, pressure of the work, makes one want out—I know deep down that if I wasn't serving God, I'd be empty inside. Matthew left everything and followed Christ. To me, as it was with Jeremiah or the prophets, my vocation is everything. But I know some young people don't see it that way.

A young person I met recently challenged me. This person didn't believe in God and said, "Why all this faith business? If I do no harm to anyone, that's enough." It made me think. Surely it's not enough to avoid evil. Our deeper Christian calling—indeed, the reason any of us is here in this world, is to do as much good as we can, to make a difference by our lives. I know I do that as a priest, for I witness to the deeper things of the soul and help many achieve their greatest goal, salvation. Also, hopefully, I help bring people to a saving and enriching relationship with God. So that young man made me sad.

The world's secular minimalist ethic is so impoverishing. For, whether we like it or not, we're spiritual beings. God gives a dimension to our lives that's priceless. That's why our ancestors prized the relationship between the world and eternity. Since Christ, we've had one foot on earth and the other in the larger world that makes it tick. And despite secular propaganda, we need both; people in every culture have proved that.

Indeed, perhaps the great failure of the modern world is the inability to grasp this truth, that we have to look after the inner man or woman too. As a result, people lose out badly on their deeper dignity and destiny. So ultimately, as I see it, the role of priests and religious is to witness to people that they are children of God, made in his image, and destined for eternal life. For this is a universal truth.

Buddhist or Hindu monks and nuns, also celibate, remind people too that the world's not enough, that our soul is our riches when all else loses its gloss. My own mother knew this instinctively. She'd often quote hebrews: "for there is no eternal city for us in this life" (hebrews 13:14, JB). If we invest everything in the world we'll be disappointed, but giving all for Christ, like Matthew, we'll sprout wings. For all else passes and leaves us empty, but he is Lord of goodness, peace, beauty, and truth for our happiness in this world and forever and ever. Amen.

So as the people of God, serving God in our larger calling to be his holy people and nurturing vocations to the priesthood and religious life for everyone's sake, let's profess our faith.

## Prayers of the Faithful

As the people of God gathered in the presence of the Risen Lord who is our life, we pray with joyful hearts for all that we need.

For the Pope, bishops, priests and lay ministers, that they may be true to their calling and lead the people of God and the whole world to deeper life in God.

For our wonderful youth, that they may never let their sins prevent them from offering themselves for the priestly or religious life, but answer God's call generously.

For civil leaders, that they may be wise and see that the Church's spiritual service of the people is a great civic enrichment too.

For ourselves, that we may promote vocations to ministry by prayer, giving of our time to church ministries, and practical efforts to nurture vocations among our children.

For the sick, the old, the lonely, and the poor, that, by our kindness and care as ministering angels, they may know God's love.

For the dead, that their life's work over and their witness to the faith complete, they may come safely to their heavenly home. And we pray in particular for those who have died recently in the parish, and also those whose anniversaries occur at this time.

We ask these our prayers through Christ our Risen Lord and Savior who constantly intercedes for us before the father. Amen.

## Reflection

Saint Thérèse of Lisieux so longed to be a nun they allowed her to do so at a very young age. The same is true of Saint Brigid of Ireland.

Her father wanted to marry her to a rich man, so that she would not enter the convent. But legend has it that warts broke out on her face, until she was allowed into the monastery. The minute she entered, she was beautiful again. Let's pray to Mary that she will make us realize how beautiful a vocation is, and how it blesses us all, not just those who are called. Hail Mary.

# Eleventh Sunday in Ordinary Time

## *Introduction*

Today Christ asks for laborers for his vineyard, the work of salvation. The work was never more urgent. Let's pray for that and confess any ways we may have failed in promoting more shepherds for the precious flock, and the Church's urgent mission.

## *Homily*

They were like sheep without a shepherd. How apt for our time. But if many now leave the Church's green pastures for a spiritual desert, this is not new. In Christ's day, he often found himself up against a stone wall in his preaching. Indeed, conscious of the difficulty of the task, he sent out many helpers to call people back to God.

Sending laborers to gather his harvest is as urgent today. Now also he asks us to work and pray for shepherds who'll save the flock from the wolves of unbelief. In our age, too, the flock is scattered relentlessly by worldly philosophy, consumerism, and materialism. Indeed, perhaps the most serious aspect of our era is the trivialization of the human soul, the world's facilitation of the Evil One's efforts to wrest us away from Christ, our soul's green pasture. "I will raise up shepherds to look after them and pasture them" (Jer. 23:4, JB). Let's pray for good priests, bishops, and lay apostles to keep God's lambs safe now.

Christ attacked religious leaders of his own day for failing to do their duty in that respect. Criticism of bad shepherds, whether in newspapers or TV is as vital now. For the constant temptation of religious leaders is to put their own interests and power before the flock. Recent clerical scandals are cases in point. That's why Christ not only preached, but lived the life of a good shepherd, washing feet and saying "The greatest among you must be your servant" (Matthew 23:11, JB). The role of lay apostles, priests, bishops, even the pope is to be "servants of the servants of God," imitating Christ, the good Shepherd.

Of course since the Church is human as well divine, it will never be perfect. But Christ must constantly renew his Church, creating fresh prophets and leaders when the old fail. And of course both Church and civil government must ultimately answer not only to God, but to the people. God's judgment always faces bad shepherds of Church and state. He constantly brings down the mighty and exalts the lowly. So I see Providence's hand in recent revelations of priestly abuse. The exploitation of the weak and the innocent is a crime God can't let go unpunished. Maybe in that sense his prophets today are the media. In any case, as Scripture makes clear, there is always a divine process by which, as Christ says, "Anyone who exalts himself will be humbled" (Matthew 23:12, JB). We priests need a dose of humility to bring us down to humbler service, after the example of Christ.

Such service is so needed now. There's a vast flock are out there, crying for spiritual guidance. Many are destitute, humanely and spiritually. So today's shepherds at home or in the Church can't afford to be lax. Every day we read of people beating up the old for a few euros, or killing the innocent. Their sense of what's right and God's law gone, they've nothing to guide them in a jungle world. The challenge for us is to be good shepherds to such, Christ's hands guiding them back to integrity. If we make any effort in this, he'll do the rest. For he is our victorious Savior, and to him at all times belongs the kingdom, the power, and the glory for our happiness here and forever and ever. Amen.

So as God's people called to be shepherds of souls, witnesses for Christ for the world's enrichment, and praying for good shepherds for the flock, we profess our faith.

## Prayers of the Faithful

And as God's people gathered in his risen presence, we pray in the power of the Spirit for what we need to be good shepherds.

For the Church throughout the world, that by imitating Christ in humble service of God and others, it may be a light to draw all people back to faith, truth, and integral living.

For our young people, that they may answer the call to be shepherds of the flock today.

For ourselves in the Church, the home, and the workplace, that we may be true shepherds and spiritual guides, especially for our children.

For the sick, the old, the lonely, and the materially and spiritually poor, that through our care, they may come to know the love of God.

For the dead, their work in the world over, that they may come safely to their heavenly home. We pray especially for those who died recently or whose anniversaries are at this time.

And we ask these our prayers through Christ, the Good Shepherd who constantly intercedes for us before the heavenly Father. Amen.

## *Reflection*

Saint Patrick, they say, heard in a dream the Irish people calling him to preach the gospel among them. He responded, and came and preached the good news through every hardship. For at that time, the people he came to, were like sheep without a shepherd. Since then the Irish, in turn, have sent many believers and missionaries abroad. Saint Patrick's cathedral in New York was partly built by the pennies of poor emigrant believers. We pray to Mother Mary that our present generation will also bring the light of Christ to the whole world, and show it how to be faithful in his service. Hail Mary.

# Twelfth Sunday in Ordinary Time

## Introduction

Our liturgy this week calls us to serve God in action, not just words. To live our faith and so be lights to a needy world is our Baptismal call. Let's confess ways we fail in this.

## Homily

Once a person approached a famous professor about a young man and said: "They say he was one of your students." The professor replied, "he did indeed attend my lectures, but believe me, he was never a student of mine." There's another story about a person visiting a monastery containing numerous monks. Amazed, the man asked the abbot how many disciples he had. "Two or three," he replied. Christ also distinguished between camp followers and true disciples. Many today, too, though called to follow him along the true way, are more often in the way, or by the way.

This is because the serious demands he makes causes many to shy away from full commitment. For example, many rich people pay no heed to his command to help the needy until it hurts. Also, many today shy away from key aspects of practice like Sunday mass, attending the sacraments, or standing up for Christian values. Or they heed secular ideology rather than Church teaching. Such mediocre following is no use to the Lord. As God says in the Bible, "Since you are ... lukewarm, I will spit you out of my mouth" (Rv. 3:16, JB). To remain true disciples, despite every storm, is the spiritual test we must pass.

A story of the early Church shows how falling away can happen to even to the best. Christians were being persecuted for their faith. Those who renounced Christ and worshiped the emperor as a God were given large amounts of money. One Christian who had been very prominent in the Church accepted the money and burnt incense to the emperor as his lord. As he watched fellow Christians going to die, a soldier mentioned how lucky he was to be alive and wealthy while his colleagues were dead meat. He replied that they were the ones who were alive, he was the one who was dead. He had sold his soul for passing wealth, false worldly gods, and knew it was a poor choice.

Let's not do that, but keep up the effort to live our faith despite weaknesses and doubts. And in this we can take courage from the example of the apostles. They struggled at every point to follow him, even running away from his cross. Yet he didn't write them off. And eventually they did serve him unto death. No less is expected of us. Lifelong service of Christ and his Church through thick and thin is the Christian call in every age.

When we were growing up, that was easier. Everyone went to church services and followed a code of life that was broadly Christian. Now, as this erodes, we have to really stand up and be counted; especially young people who have the added problem of peer pressure. Add to that our human failings and recurrent sins, and all are tempted to give up. But like the apostles, we must live our faith faithfully despite all these temptations to lapse. Remember when the people left Jesus because of his teaching on the Eucharist as real food, he said to the apostles: "do you want to go away too." Peter answered: "Lord who shall we go to? You have the message of eternal life."(Jn.6:67-68, JB). That's the answer we must give today too. For all else fades to dust and ashes, but he is Lord of love, truth, beauty, goodness, and salvation for this world and forever and ever. Amen.

So as God's own called to steadfast discipleship, to faithful suffering following of Christ and the Church, let's profess our faith.

## Prayers of the Faithful

And as the people of God, his disciples on the way of life with him and his Church, we pray for the strength to be the faithful.

For our Holy Father the Pope and all the leaders of the Church, that they may by word and examples bring the whole world to true godly discipleship and eternal salvation in Christ.

For civil leaders, that they may not put any obstacles in the way of Christians trying to nurture their children's faith.

For young people, that they may light up the world by living the vows they made at Confirmation, to follow Christ and practice the faith faithfully within the Holy Catholic Church all life long.

For ourselves, that in homes, workplaces, and countries we may have the courage to stand up for Christ and be his living presence to our children and loved ones in particular.

For the sick, the lonely, the aged, and the needy in body or soul, that through our love and witness they may know the love of God.

For the dead, that, their lives over, the faith kept, and their work in this world done, they may come to the reward of life and light in the heavenly home with God. May our prayers light them home. We pray especially for those who died recently in the parish and those whose anniversaries occur at this time.

And we ask all these our prayers through the only Lord of love, peace, and happiness, Our Lord Jesus Christ, who constantly intercedes for us before his Father in heaven. Amen

## Reflection

A great example of faithful following of Christ is Saint Stephen, the first martyr. He was a deacon who preached Christ in the early church. He was brought before the opponents of the church and warned under threat to his life to stop. But he kept on preaching all the same, so he was captured and sentenced to death. As he was stoned to death, his face shone with light and he cried out, "Lord do not hold this sin against them" (Ac. 6:60, JB). We pray that we will have the same courage against more subtle attacks on the faith today. Hail Mary.

# Thirteenth Sunday in Ordinary Time

## *Introduction*

Hospitality is something Christians are famed for. Let's not let that tradition lapse, for as Christ says, even a cup of cold water given in his name will have its reward. Conscious of that, let's confess any ways we have failed to open hearts and homes.

## *Homily*

There's a fine scene in Alice Taylor's novel, *The Woman Of The House.* Kate comes home from abroad to attend her parents' funeral. Coming to the house where she was reared, she finds the door bolted. When she was young, that door was always open; people came to drink tea and chat. But now there's a new woman of the house. Her door is closed, the door of her heart. Kate longs for a time when love will fill that house again.

And that's what the gospel is about today, loving open hearts. Christ says giving even a cup of water to a neighbor in need will win a reward. Christian hospitality is famous. Mats in front of our houses proclaim, "welcome." Are our homes still as open? Do we still value our neighbor in an increasingly secular materialist society? Recently, on a sick call, I asked directions to the person's house. "It's the other side of town," the person I asked said. I drove round and came back to find that the sick man lived next door to the person who'd given me directions. She didn't know her neighbor, let alone that he was in need. That's hard to believe, but not uncommon now. Not long ago, we had the case of an aged woman who was seven days dead before she was found.

This life Sunday we're asked not to let such things happen. We are asked to care for our neighbors in Christian love, and to nurture and support especially the weak and vulnerable around us. We're to guard the innocent child in the womb, to cherish those with disabilities, to let the aged live out their life in comfort. For all people, of whatever age or state, are infinitely valuable to God, and are our brothers and sisters in Christ. Let's think in such Christian terms, not cold, worldly ones of people's usefulness or otherwise.

Obviously by gathering here to pray, you show you're not like that. You value being together at the ultimate celebration of life, the mass. Indeed without your presence Christ couldn't be here to bless our community. And in Christ we are real sisters and brothers to each other. Our ancestors knew this; their doors were always open to faith and neighbor, and everyone turned up at funerals to console the bereaved. Now the vulnerable and the needy are shut out of our grand pristine condominiums. How sad and how misguided, for the things of the world pass away and at last our souls are what will be required of us.

So I ask you to pray for those who make wealth their God, who have every luxury but neglect what really matters in life—people, loving hearts, honoring God, nurturing our immortal souls. For the hard values of the world of which Satan is lord fade to dust at last and leave us empty before eternity. But Christ is Lord of grace, love, truth, beauty, and life both for this world and forever and ever. Amen.

So as God's people, called to real neighborliness, faith, and respect for life at every stage as sacred, we profess our faith.


## Prayers of the Faithful

For the Pope, the bishops and all pastors of the Churches, that their overflowing generosity of spirit and infinite respect for life in all its forms may light up our world and turn it to God.

For civic leaders, that they may respect life from the cradle to the grave and serve the people selflessly, especially the needy.

For our young people, that they may not be so caught up in the values of the godless world as to neglect the values that endure forever, and are from God.

For ourselves, that we may be dedicated witnesses in our homes and in our communities to all that is from God, all that is good, true, just and life affirming, especially with our children.

For the sick, the old, the lonely, and the impoverished, that through our care for them they may know the love and care of God.

For the dead, that they may come quickly to their heavenly inheritance through our powerful personal and communal prayers. We pray especially for those who have died recently in the parish and those whose anniversaries occur at this time.

And we ask all these our prayers through our all-generous and loving Lord, who constantly intercedes for us before his Father. Amen

## Reflection

There's a story told about Mother Teresa of Calcutta. People were saying to her, "Why all these unwanted babies? Support abortion." "No," she said, "if you don't want these babies, give them to me. I'll look after them and love them as the precious children of God that they are." Sometimes we're persuaded in the modern world, and in our ads, that only the young, shiny-haired ones who wear costly makeup, count. Let's affirm, like Teresa, that people of whatever stage or age in life are God's precious children. Let's affirm all life in love, and nurture it at every stage of its existence. Hail Mary.

# Fourteenth Sunday in Ordinary Time

## Introduction

"Come to me, all you who labor and are overburdened, and I will give you rest," Christ says to us today (Mt. 11:28, JB). And as we come to be united with him intimately in Communion, where he comes to us as the great lover, let's confess any ways we may have failed to bring rest to those who labor and are overburdened in body or soul.

## Homily

Recently we had the feasts of Corpus Christi and the Sacred heart. Both remind us of the Risen Christ's presence among us. The feast of Corpus Christi was requested by God himself in his appearance to Saint Juliana in the thirteenth century when he said that he wanted a special feast set aside in honor of his Real Presence. For as the Church went on, faith in his Real Presence would diminish to the point where it would need a feast day to remind us that he's really with us in the Eucharist, body and blood, soul and divinity. For the same reason he requested Saint Margaret Mary in the seventeenth century to ask the Church to institute the feast of the Sacred heart in the octave of Corpus Christi. He wanted to emphasize that the Blessed Sacrament is his heart beating for us, his loving Presence in our midst as Risen Lord.

The gospel today says: "Come to me, all you who labor and are overburdened, and I will give you rest." That's what he does in Communion. And that's also the gospel for the feast of the Sacred Heart, for that is Eucharistic as well. Let's reaffirm our faith, then, in the timeless embrace of his personal love reaching out to us from the altar. For when we receive we become one with that loving Lord in an intimate way. As the twentieth-century visionary, Saint Padre Pio, used to put it, in Communion Jesus kisses us all over. We are like two candles that melt together and are no longer distinguishable. And as we leave the Church, we're a living monstrance; since we carry the living Lord within us.

This is such a glorious mystery we need to bring home its importance to young people especially. For they can be very ignorant in relation to the greatness of this sacrament. I remember visiting a school once, and I asked what we receive in the Communion. "Holy bread," a child said. He didn't realize that it is more than bread—it is the real Presence of Christ. No wonder then John Paul II said, in one of his works oft quoted, that priests, religious, and lay people should redouble their efforts to teach the younger generations the meaning and value of Eucharistic devotion. He asks, how will young people be able to know the Lord if they're not introduced to the mystery of his Real Presence in the Eucharist? And he says that in one day the Eucharist will make us produce more for the glory of God than a whole lifetime without it, and even Mary carries out a perpetual mission of adoration in the presence of the most holy and adorable Eucharist, pleading for the salvation of the world.

How privileged we are then at this mass. And let's celebrate joyfully, not only our union with God in Communion, but also plead for the union of the whole world with him, and especially those young people lost without God today. Indeed I ask every person here to pray before the Eucharist every day for our youth. For we can't even imagine what power there is in Eucharistic prayer. When we go to the Church and pray in Christ's presence and receive him, then our prayers are one with his and reach the very height of heaven. All else is dust by comparison. For the world of which Satan is lord fades to ashes at last, but in the Eucharist we're one with the Lord of love, goodness, peace, happiness, beauty, and salvation for our untold happiness in the world and forever and ever. Amen.

So as God's own, growing in the very life of God himself through every mass and Communion, until we blossom thereby at last into eternal joy, let's profess our faith.

## *Prayers of the Faithful*

As God's family, gathered here in the power and glory of the Eucharistic people, which we are, we pray in the grace of the Risen Lord for our and the world's needs.

For our Holy Father the Pope and all the leaders of the Churches, that they may bring all who labor under burdens to freedom, to rest, happiness, and glory in Christ.

For our civic leaders, that they may not place undue burdens on those they govern but lift up all their people, especially the poor, the weak, the lonely, and the oppressed.

For ourselves and our communities, that, making the Eucharist the center of our lives each Sunday, we may grow in the eternal peace of Christ here below and pass that great legacy to our children.

For our young people, that, appreciating the greatness and essential nature of the mass and Eucharistic for their spiritual health and peace in this world, they may be faithful to it each Sunday and flower through it into eternal glory even in this world.

For those burdened with sickness, that through regular or First Friday Communion and our loving care and prayers, they may experience the strength, healing and peace of Christ in their suffering.

For the dead, that throwing off the burdens of sin and punishment, they may enter into the rest of Christ.

And we ask all these prayers in the living presence of the Risen Lord, who constantly intercedes for us and in us to his father.

## Reflection

Saint Padre Pio's reverence for the Eucharist and Christ's real presence was legendary. He'd spend ages at the consecration. Yet no one said his mass was too long. Indeed millions asked for the privilege of being at it, for that was his greatness—not all the miracles he supposedly worked. Let's pray that, like him, we'll celebrate mass and receive Communion so devoutly we'll go out with radiant faith to those around us. Hail Mary.

# Fifteenth Sunday in Ordinary Time

## *Introduction*

Today we have the beautiful parable of the sower. Let's pray that the seed of God's word that is sown among us, as we listen devoutly to our readings, may bear fruit in abundance in our lives. And let's confess any ways we neglect the scriptures.

## *Homily*

Today's parable reminds me of sowing potatoes when I was young. We cut them into seed sections, each seed had to have one eye. Then we opened drills—rows—lined them with farmyard manure, and placed the seeds three feet apart. It was hard work, but worth it. In the summer the new potatoes tasted like heaven, eaten with fresh new cabbage and bacon. Christ must have been thinking of such experiences when he told the parable of the sower. No doubt he had sown and reaped many crops with his relatives. He preached among country people whose lives were a round of sowing and harvesting.

Nowadays people get new potatoes from abroad, in supermarkets. But many still keep flower gardens and lawns and see the fruits of their sowing. Christ was talking of a different harvest, however. His seed was God's Word, the message of salvation he preached. Each of us hears that still in scripture read here, and we need that spiritual nourishment for, like crops, our salvation is a growing plant. We receive its seed at Baptism and the water and sun of the Holy Spirit to nourish it. But the manure that makes it bear abundant fruit is a combination of Christ's Word, Communion, mass, sacrament, prayer, and living charity. And the harvest is a holiness of life, until we gain the greatest harvest of all, union with Christ and with all the saints on the last day.

But there's a warning for us in the parable. Despite the work of priests, teachers, and parents in preparing the soil and sowing the seed of faith it may not to bear fruit in all. Ravenous birds of secularism and worldliness may pick it out of many hearts before it flowers. Paul complains about the worldly destroyers of the faith in his day, who fought against God and his Christ. But that's true in every age. Satan has his prophets who try to to remove the seed of eternal life from our hearts, so that we'll come before God at judgment empty and those around us without faith. For our harvest is for others too.

I'm reminded of a story about a man who abandoned the faith after he left his country. Later in life he came back to the Church. The priest receiving him pointed out the damage he'd done in the meantime. Because of him, his children, their spouses and children, and descendants for generations may have no faith. So keeping the faith alive in our hearts is vital for future generations too; its passed on not by angels but by people. And we won't keep it or leave it as a legacy to our descendants unless we water its roots constantly by prayer, the mass, the sacraments, and living charity. People who say that they believe but don't need church worship and practice, are deluding themselves.

In less than a generation unpracticed, or less deeply rooted faith will wither like neglected seeds on stony ground. Without the nourishment of the Eucharistic sun, the water of the Word, and the manure of prayer, it will surely die. Lacking depth, it will inevitably be blown away by the Evil One's storms, or choked by the cares, worries, pleasures, and riches of the world.

So the parable is a warning for today. The seed of God in us must be even more carefully nourished now, when faith is more under attack. We must work all the harder to build up our souls in an increasingly secular world if we're to be with the saints marching in at last to enjoy the final harvest, the great hundredfold. For on the last day all else will fade to dust and ashes, but the faithful will be one with Christ, the only Lord of goodness, happiness, peace, and salvation for this world and forever and ever. Amen.

So as God's people nourishing and deepening our faith in order to yield a hundredfold for God, ourselves, and others unto an eternal reward, we profess our faith.

## *Prayers of the Faithful*

As God's people, nourishing the seed of faith by our worship, we pray for our faithfulness, and that of all the baptized.

For our Church leaders, that they may nourish the seed of faith in those in their care, and spread the saving Word and Eucharistic Presence of Christ unto a rich harvest.

For civic leaders, may they promote or place no obstacles in the way of people's growth in faith, lest they have to face God's judgment at last for their stewardship.

For ourselves, that we may not be so caught up in the cares of life and pursuit of wealth as to neglect to nourish the seed of faith within our hearts, the life of our souls.

For youth; cherishing God's voice and that of his Christ rather than the voices of the world, the flesh, and the devil, may they nourish their souls unto the great final harvest.

For the sick, that through our love and care they may know and experience the deep love and care of God and his Christ.

For the dead, through our powerful communal prayers here, that they may come quickly to the glorious harvest of eternal life.

And we ask this through Christ who constantly intercedes for us in heaven, amen.

## *Reflection*

When young we learned the folk story of *The Reaping Race*, about three teams of husband and wife, reaping a section of corn, the women gathering and tying the sheaves. The first couple start too fast and cannot keep up the pace. The second couple, a small man and a strong heavy woman, also falter due to the uneven nature of their team. The ones who win the race are a balanced couple who keep up an even pace all through the day, even stopping for refreshments. Our faith is like a reaping race and we must keep steadily along the course, taking the nourishment we require from the church, and with our partner winning the prize, our eternal salvation. Lets pray that we'll do that. Hail Mary.

# Sixteenth Sunday in Ordinary Time A

## Introduction

Faith is a wonderful thing; it can move mountains. That's the message of scripture; Christ compares it to tiny mustard seed that becomes a great tree nurturing life of every kind. Let's appreciate our faith and confess any neglect in its practice.

## Homily

There's a fine scene in the movie *Star Wars*. Luke, training as a Jedi, is asked to use "the force" to raise a spaceship from a swamp. He makes an effort, but fails. Then the tiny Yoda concentrates and lifts the ship. Luke says, "I don't believe it!"; Yoda answers, "That is why you failed." This echoes Christ's words that faith gives us untold power.

Such faith is needed today when there's no shortage of skeptics. There's place for healthy doubt; it deepens faith. But its not good to keep nothing sacred, or make ourselves God, or morality a plaything of desire. There's no greatness in deserting God and ignoring his Word, to make the glib DJ on TV our Christ, the superficial world our scripture.

That's not to say that all is negative now. There's so much good today too, and so much faith, and great progress in science, technology, and medicine. But every age has its downside. Militant secularism may be our's, and we must guard against it, for there is no true civilization without spirituality and moral depth. Yet faith is more authentic now; its no longer social conformism. People must hold to faith against trends that play it down.

So that, as a book I read recently said, we risk producing technological savages now, versed in technology, but spiritually and morally regressive. Be that as it may, there are powerful militant, secular, and libertine elements today who would strip us of our great religious heritage and Christian moral idealism. We must be on guard lest we sacrifice the faith to such trends, so that when crises come we'll have no deep inner life to sustain us. Once the earth of faith slips from under our feet, only meaninglessness, nothingness, and despair remain. By contrast, Christ said, "I have come so that they may have life, and have it to the full" (John 10:10, JB).

So let's wake up and be wise. Worldly values pass and don't satisfy the soul. Where have twentieth-century secular prophets led us? To hell after hell. Vast numbers of human lives were lost and even more oppressed by our era's godless ideologues: Stalin, Mao Zedong, Pol Pot, Saddam Hussein, Gaddafi, the list is endless. So is their legacy: the one-party state, the great leader replacing God, the secret police, the suppression of opposition, the vast military machines that march on while people starve and their human rights are ignored. Twentieth- and twenty-first-century militant agnosticism is far from enlightened, as Pope Benedict reminded opponents when he visited Britain. That type of agnosticism continues today in places like North Korea and Syria, and more subtly in the developed world. By contrast, Christ offers us God's way of peace, truth, happiness, and inner integrity. Sure, fundamentalists distort that, but they don't reflect the true Christ.

Many are realizing this in a postmodern era. They are seeing beyond the dead end of the faithless mind, and man-made distortions of faith, to the gentle, all-wise, and all-holy message of Christ. Certainly in many countries, such real faith still survives and sustains millions despite more subtle modern-day persecutions. As one wise person said, we in the truly Christian areas of the West, have always lived with one foot in this world and one in the next. It has made us great and enabled us to rise above everything.

Let's maintain that enriching faith, heeding Christ's words that faith is the world's lasting hope. Only believing people loyal to God through worldly attacks and religious aberration will triumph as Christ did on the cross of love and forgiveness. For all else fades to dust, but to the gentle Son of God belongs the kingdom, power, and glory for this world and forever and ever. Amen.

So for God's people building our house on the solid, grace-filled foundation of the all-holy Christ, that no cruel passing worldly storm can shake, let's profess our faith.

## Prayers of the Faithful

For Church leaders throughout the world, that guarding the riches and fullness of faith in Christ, they may bring not only the faithful but the whole world to peace and grace.

For civic leaders, that they may welcome and support authentic faith, our heritage of light, and not be lured into imposing empty passing worldly values like the awful secular dictators of our age did.

For our young people, that holding to the faith that raises them up to glory in both this life and the next, they may achieve their full potential here and flower into eternity at last.

For ourselves, in our homes, workplaces, and communities, that we may stand for the faith that is happiness, peace, greatness, and glory for ourselves, and especially for our children.

For the sick, the aged, the lonely, and the oppressed, that they may never lose hope but trust in Christ and through our love and care know his love, comfort, and healing.

And we ask all these prayers through our infinitely caring Lord whose wounds intercede for us constantly before the Father. Amen.

## Reflection

There's a fine scene in Clint Eastwood's film, *Pale Rider*. Miners are being forced off their claims by a rich man who wants to make money more quickly by blast mining. Then a Christian minister comes to help the miners. The rich man had been away, and when he learns the news he gives out to his henchmen, saying that it was stupid of them to let a preacher into the canyon. Before he left the spirits of the miners were nearly broken, but with an ounce of faith, he was of the opinion, that they'd soon be dug in deeper than ticks on a hound dog. He, the ultimate man of the world, knew the power of faith to lift people. Let's be wise and keep and live the precious faith we received to make us great and strong before the storms of life, fit for eternal glory. Hail Mary.

# Seventeenth Sunday in Ordinary Time A

## Introduction

Today Christ tells us the importance of both keeping the faith, and spreading it to others. We are to be his missionaries to save a needy world in body and soul. Let's confess ways we fail in cherishing the living faith and witnessing to it before the world.

## Homily

I never tire repeating Oscar Wilde's children's story known as *The Happy Prince*. So I hope you'll forgive for telling the story again. A prince's gold statue overlooks a city. One day a swallow resting on him was amazed to see a tear in his eye. "Why are you crying?" he said. "Because I see misery in my city," the prince said. "Please, swallow" he said, "pluck the gold from my body and give it to poor families." It was late in the year and the swallow should be flying to warm climes, but he stayed, feeding the poor with the prince's gold. Then, too late to go south he nestled into the space of the prince's heart and died. The city lords seeing the tarnished prince, pulled him down to erect a shopping center. He and the bird in his heart finished on the scrap heap.

That's the gospel story. Our prince is Christ who stripped himself of glory to save and feed us in the desert of a fallen world. We are the pearl of great price he cast off his golden clothes for. He suffered and died, ending up on the scrap heap of the cross, to bring us, the spiritually poor and lost, the food and clothes of saving faith. Loving us and crying over our misery, he came down from heaven to feed us with the bread of life and the Word. We, his followers, are called to be like that swallow, serving this Prince. For we face the same choice as he, to stay aloof before people's needs or to get our hands dirty. Like the swallow, we can fly to our own interests or help Christ save others. The latter choice means sacrifice, but there's no humane Christian love without some death to self.

That's the deep meaning of the gospel. We must be prepared to sell everything to gain the pearl of great price, committed faith, which is our great treasure for this world and the next. We can spend another week in self-giving Christian love or self-serving worldliness. But if we choose the giving Christian way, we're never alone. He's with us, feeding us with his body, sharing our joys, weeping our tears, suffering our pain, applauding our accomplishments. For we're his family. And God's prince who divested himself of glory for our sake begs us to be his hands to all in need.

As it did the swallow, it may cost us, but it'll be worth it. For loving and serving others and Christ we'll fulfill our humanity, the purpose of our existence. We'll gain what purely worldly pursuits can never give. We'll do untold good, fulfill the reason that we're here on earth to make a difference for good, and help incarnate God in our fallen yet beautiful material world. And that must be done in the flesh as well as the spirit. Don't believe those who'd divide the two.

Our Prince Christ teaches us to serve people in body too. He went around healing what the Pharisees saw as the dregs of society. Good standards of living for all are important. Christ said, "I have come that they may have life, and have it to the full" (John 10:10, JB). So we should set aside some earthly ambitions and pleasures to bring the poor some of what we enjoy. Christian love is going down like Christ into the squalor, violence, and suffering of the world. It's being Christ's hands of both charitable and spiritual nourishment. For as that swallow helped the prince, Christ needs our hands and hearts to save the world in body and soul.

Sure this may lead to us to be cast on the scrap heap by the world. But our reward will be immense. For the world of which Satan is lord fades to dust at last, but to Christ, the Prince of love, belongs the kingdom, the power, and the glory forever and ever. Amen.

So as Christ's swallows, as it were, distributing his golden legacy of faith, truth and charity to a needy world, we profess our faith.

## Prayers of the Faithful

For church leaders, that they may be Christ's hands helping the world to fullness of material and spiritual life.

For our civic leaders, that they may not concentrate on their own worldly progress and glory, but fulfill the needs of the people they serve, especially the poor.

For our wonderful youth, that, like the swallow in the story, they may be the healing hands of Christ to all those around them in faith and love, and so rest at last in his heart.

For ourselves, that in our homes we may be the special caring hands and heart of Christ to our spouses and children so that, like Christ, they may grow in age and grace before God and men.

For the sick, the aged, the lonely, the oppressed, and the neglected in our families and society, that through our love and care they may know the love of God.

For the dead whose faith is known to God alone, that through our prayers, a great act of charity on their behalf because in the next world they cannot always help themselves, they may come to the fullness of life and eternal glory.

And we ask all these prayers through Christ our Prince of Love and care forever and ever. Amen.

## Reflection

You may know the story of the Curé of Ars. He came to the town of Ars in France in the nineteenth century as parish priest, and found the church in ruins and the congregation gone. But gradually, attracted by his life of prayer and goodness, people restored the church and came back to mass, Baptism, and the life of the Church. Not only that, but his holiness became so legendary that millions flocked to him from all over the world for confession, for he had the gift of seeing into people's souls to find where they needed deep healing. We can be like that in some way, lights of faith and love and spiritual healing to others. Let's ask Mary to help us in this. Hail Mary.

# Eighteenth Sunday in Ordinary Time

## Introduction

Christ fed the crowd in the wilderness. He still feeds us with the Eucharist in today's wilderness. Let's confess ways we've fail to appreciate our Communion with him.

## Homily

Once at Easter I asked an adult about to be baptized what becoming a Christian meant. "Being united with Christ," she said. After her Baptism and first Communion I asked how she felt. "I feel real peace for the first time," she said. Christ feeds the crowds in John's gospel. He still feeds us, his people, at each mass, and we're satisfied in body and soul. Let's remember how great a gift that is, for receiving every Sunday, we can take the Eucharist for granted. So today as we see Christ giving the crowds living bread in the wilderness, let's remember that we gather here to share the same living bread. Let's renew our love for communion, which unites us so intimately with Our Lord. And let's reaffirm his real presence for us in the host, and in the Tabernacle of the Church.

I sometimes think that he gets lonely waiting for people to come to Communion or speak to him in the Tabernacle. That's why perpetual adoration is wonderful. It gives us a chance to be with the Lord and make up for people's indifference. For Eucharistic Communion is the kisses of our relationship. There's a story of a man who'd go to Church each evening on the way home from work and just say, "hello, Jesus, it's me, Tom." he'd built such a personal relationship with Jesus it was like two pals meeting after work.

Our meeting with Jesus in weekly Communion, and visiting him here, should be as personal and close. For that's what faith is all about;

building up a relationship with God. And the great way to do that is through this sacrament. For he promises: "Whoever eats my flesh and drinks my blood has eternal life, and I will raise him up at the last day" (John 6:54, JB). Imagine, we become more and more part of eternal life each time we receive Jesus and adore him in this sacrament. We join him in his heavenly home, eat with him, and share his glory, and are guaranteed his help for our earthly struggles.

For the Christ we receive is not remote or uncaring. He died for us, and God raised him and made him Lord, gave him all authority in heaven and on earth. In the Eucharist, whether receiving Jesus or adoring the Blessed Sacrament, we're totally united with this glorious Lord who conquered sin, suffering, and death for us. In Communion he makes us part of his glory, bears our burdens, and enriches our lives for this world's joys and sufferings. Indeed, by sharing this bread we're little less than gods, as Paul says. For we share God's life, commune with the saints in glory, and are one with the universal Church.

That's why Sunday mass is so vital, and why it has to be on Sunday. For Christ rose on Sunday, and that's when he raises his people with the bread of life. So that, as scripture says, we can live a life worthy of our calling in complete selflessness, gentleness and charity. For as Christ feeds us, we should feed the needy around us in body and soul.

He washed the disciples' feet at the first mass. Our Communion with him should lead to humble service of God and others in daily life, helping him to build the world into a Eucharistic community of service. Here he makes us part of eternal life and asks us to bring that life to the world. For all else fades to ashes, but he is Lord of life, love, peace, and salvation for the happiness of all people in this life and forever and ever. Amen.

So as God's people sharing in his bread of life and bringing its fruits to others in overflowing love, we profess our faith.

## *Prayers of the Faithful*

For our Holy Father the Pope and bishops of the Church, that they may feed the people of God by preaching the Word well, encouraging all to reach out to help the poor, and leading us as a Eucharistic community to happiness and eternal life.

For our civil leaders, that they may serve the people under their care well, especially the poor and most vulnerable in society.

For our young people, that they may come every Sunday to the table of the Word and the Eucharist, to be fed by Christ unto greatness of life for this world and the next.

For ourselves, that we may go from the table of the Lord to carry his faith, love, peace, and grace to our children, our workmates, and our community, and so enrich the lives of all we touch.

For the sick, that through regular or First Friday reception of the Eucharist they may know the comfort, care, and healing of Christ the Good Shepherd.

For the dead, that having received Christ regularly here below they may come to the promised final resurrection and to the highest heaven through our prayers and masses.

And we ask all these prayers through Christ who is Lord of us his Eucharistic people of all the living forever and ever. Amen.

## Reflection

There's a famous place in Italy where wine is supposed to have turned into the Lord's blood during the mass of a priest who doubted Christ's real presence in the Eucharist. Be that as it may, the purpose of the story is to bring home to us the real bodily presence of Christ to us in communion. Let's pray to Mother Mary, who gave birth to Christ in the body, that we'll always appreciate his total living presence with us in the Eucharist, for there we are fed with the real Lord himself, body and blood, soul and divinity. Hail Mary.

# Nineteenth Sunday in Ordinary Time

## Introduction

Trust in God is the key to faith. When Peter sinks in the waves, Christ lifts him up and says: "man of little faith … why did you doubt" (Mt.14:32, JB). God also says to his people in the Old Testament: "do not be afraid, for I am with you" (Isaiah 41:10, JB). It was the motto of John Paul II, recently canonized. Let's confess our failure to trust in God.

## Homily

"I feel just awful. I wish someone would shoot me. I feel I can't go on living." That's what someone said to me recently. It shocked me to the core, for to me life is precious. I can't conceive of anyone ever giving up on the joy of life. But maybe I shouldn't be so shocked; despite modern progress many in society are in despair. Look at the ever-increasing numbers ringing the Samaritan help lines. We all go through rough patches in our lives. Problems and difficulties pile up, and we're tempted to lose hope. In that situation we should listen to the words of God: "So do not be afraid, for I am with you."

Peter lost faith and began to sink, but Jesus rebuked him, lifted him up and calmed the storm. That's what the gospel is about. He will heal us if we let him; indeed, he alone can lift us up in our darkest hours and lighten our burdens. Scripture says, "unload your burdens onto the Lord, and he will support you" (Psalm 55:22, JB). And Jesus in today's gospel says that with trust in him we can even walk upon water. All we have to do to gain his help is to believe, and put our hand confidently so that he can lift us up.

One who did that wholeheartedly was the late John Paul II. His motto was "Do not be afraid, for I am with you." And look what he achieved, saintly holiness and world fame. Once, inspired by John Paul, many young people were putting that phrase on wrist bands. Good! We should not only wear it on our wrists, but on our hearts. For then, like John Paul, we'll be wise and dynamic people. Faith and trust in God will carry us past all obstacles. In that sense God is not a luxury, but vital as the air we breathe.

Without him, life's empty and meaningless. This is a proven fact. A new psychological study in hospitals has shown that those with faith are more likely to recover from illness and recover quicker. And so many people point to the value of their faith when they experience trouble. I read about Pierce Brosnan, the James Bond star, who seems so self-assured, that recently he went through a terrible crisis in life. Only his Catholic faith, he says, enabled him to survive. And that's the consolation of all the people of God; we're are not alone, and God is closest to us in dark times. But we have to seek his help. Because of our free will, he can't do anything until we ask. But if we trust in him and pray, he'll not only help, but in the long run turn our weakness into strength.

Christ, while on earth, spent most of his public life caring for people especially those who were sick, poor, or scorned by society. He was down there among them because he cared; and all were precious to him. We must remember that. We're children of a loving God, who sent his Christ to us, and who doesn't judge by worldly standards. His favorites are all those oppressed by the world. And he wants to lead all on his sure way out of life's darknesses. So we're wise to seek his help, with trusting hearts.

Indeed, it must hurt God deeply when we refuse to do so. Jesus, the very embodiment of God, wept over Jerusalem, because he longed to gather his people under his wing like a hen her chicks, but they would not; he could do nothing for them against their will, because of human freedom. Let's be wise and always seek his help in crises, lest when things get rough, we're doomed to wander in a wilderness without end, even while Christ waits to lead us to green pastures. For when all else fades to dust and ashes, he is Lord of love, peace, glory, beauty, and truth for our happiness in this world and forever and ever. Amen.

So as God's people trusting in him to save, heal, and lead us throughout our lives, let's profess our faith with a new sense of his caring love in our lives and in the world.

## Prayer of the Faithful

For our Holy Father the Pope and all the leaders of the Church, that trusting wholly in God, they may bring all to the same life-giving faith and trust.

For our civic leaders, that they may respect God, his Church, and servants, and serve the whole community with selfless dedication

For our great youth, that like those who, during John Paul II's life, put the phrase on their wristband "Do not be afraid, for I am with you," they may trust in Christ's love and so find strength, peace, grace, and depth for their lives, unto eternal happiness in God's arms.

For ourselves in our homes, workplaces, and communities, that our faith and trust in Christ may rub off and be a light to others also, especially our children.

For the sick, that through trust in the Lord they may find in Christ the comfort, hope, and peace for difficult times.

For the dead, that, their work in this life done, they may, through our prayers and continuing love, come to the arms of the Lord in the heavenly home prepared for them.

And we ask all these prayers with the same trust in Christ our loving Lord and savior that we bring to our faith.

## *Reflection*

A sense of trust in God, no matter what, fills the psalms: "I have faith even when I say, I am completely crushed." (Ps.116:10, JB). At times people let us down. It's when we're in trouble, they say, that we know who our real friends are. And certainly, in that respect, Jesus, as many songs say, is our special friend for all seasons. Let's pray that trust in him may characterize our lives, and make us truly great. Hail Mary.

# Twentieth Sunday in Ordinary Time A

## Introduction

They say if you put a number of people in a room, before long they'd form into rival groups. Tribalism is deep in us and despite the veneer of progress, it remains. Christ asks us to redeem its violent aspects by being peacemakers, loving our enemies, reaching out to the opposite tribe we'd exclude. In our gospel, he gives us an example by ministering to the non-Jewish Canaanite woman. Let's confess any tribal hatred in our lives.

## Homily

A joke about the Protestant-Catholic division in Northern Ireland, shows how much we need to break down Christian divisions. A member of Ian Paisley's Free Presbyterian Church, at death's door, converted to Catholicism. There was uproar among his friends who pleaded: "Don't do it. We wouldn't mind you joining any other church, but a Papist!" "Well," he said, "to tell the truth, I'm dying of cancer, I figured it was better for one of them to die rather than one of us." The same might be said of the "other side."

Joking apart, senseless divisions cast a shadow over all faiths. Narrow tribalism was a temptation Christ himself faced. The apostles urged him to minister only to Israelites and exclude the Canaanite woman. Though he tested her faith, he had no intention of doing so. In the early church we're told, "the whole group of believers were united heart and soul." (Acts. 4:32, JB). Can we say the same now, as Christians tear each other apart?

I watched once a famous match in Belfast a few World Cups ago. The Republic went up there needing a draw to qualify. Some of the

Republic's players described the hatred they met on going onto the pitch; fans abused them as Fenian bastards, bloody papists, and said that their team would make sure the Republic wouldn't go to the world cup. Most of the Republic's team, though of Irish origin, had been born in England. They were totally bewildered; they couldn't understand what all the fuss was about.

Doubtless, if one tried to explain the cause of division among Christians in Northern Ireland, the roots would be found in politics as much as religious history. But if the churches contributed in any way, they must repent and now is the time to do so in an EU and Vatican II world. For until we're peacemakers, excluding no one, we're not Christian.

Our scripture makes that clear; God says his house is a house of prayer for all peoples. Paul, in the second reading, talks of his pride in his mission to embrace the whole world in Christ. And Jesus extends his healing to the alien Canaanite woman. Our Christian calling is to promote unity among people of every race, church, and nation, for Christ came to unite a divided world. "May they all be one, Father, may they be one in us" he prayed at last (John 17:21, JB). Our key Christian mission is to promote that unity.

It's not better that one of "them" should die rather than one of "us." We should all walk hand in hand to the larger soccer World Cup in heaven. For that's the true destiny of our world: to live united and equal in God's unqualified all-embracing love. And this our love should not be a matter of feeling, but a conscious decision to reach out even to our enemies. As Christ opened his arms to all on the cross, we must be a sign to the whole earth that it is not a "them and us" world, that the divisions of a violent, war-torn world belong to the evil one's kingdom. But our Christian duty is to help Christ redeem the great human evil of divisive hatred. For that leaves us empty and blood soaked on the shore of eternity, but he is Lord of all-inclusive love, goodness, peace, unity, and happy togetherness, both for this world, and forever and ever. Amen.

So as God's people called to heal and redeem our broken, fallen, hating, and divided world in Christ, let's profess our faith.

## *Prayers of the Faithful*

For our Holy Father the Pope and all leaders of Christendom and other faiths and philosophies, that they may rise above all narrow violent divisions and reach mutual understanding and fellowship, as children of God on a beautiful peaceful earth.

For civil leaders across our borders, that they may continue to come together in reconciliation, understanding, and mutual affirmation and so continue the peace process.

For our young people, that, free from prejudice based on race, color, nation, or creed, they may promote unity and help to heal our divided world in the Spirit of God.

For ourselves, in our homes and communities, that we may be channels of peace, love, and unity, especially toward our children, teaching them tolerance and acceptance of difference.

For the sick, the aged, the lonely, and the depressed, that they may know God's comfort and healing care through our reaching out to them in love.

For the dead, that they may come to the unity, happiness, and peace of the heavenly mansions through our prayers for them here.

And we ask all these our prayers through Christ, the Prince of Peace, amen.

## *Reflection*

There is a story told of a rabbi in Auschwitz who saved a Nazi guard from being killed by inmates after the camp was liberated. He said that to kill him, they would have to pass over his dead body. He showed that forgiveness and forbearance that is the mark of all true men of God, from whatever faith. For as Our Lady of Medjugorje constantly repeats in her messages to the world, peace must start with peace in each human heart. Let's start that process in our own hearts now as we pray to Mary, Queen of Peace. Hail Mary.

# Twenty-First Sunday in Ordinary Time A

## Introduction

Jesus was given all authority in heaven and on earth when God raised him up. Before his ascension, he passed that authority on to the Church: "Whatever you bind on earth shall be considered bound in heaven" (Matthew 18:18, JB). He gave the keys of the kingdom to Peter, the first Pope. Let's confess any ways we disrespect Church authority.

## Homily

All seemed doom and gloom after the collapse of the economic boom; we seemed to face endless recession, new wars, unemployment, lost prosperity. Yet, though the sky seems falling down, we Christians must be optimists. Jesus is risen; life now is always one of hope. I read once about a priest who spent twenty years in a Chinese labor camp who survived because of such optimism; he became Christ's gentle face even to his tormentors.

Nothing should cause us to lose heart either. For Jesus says, "I'm with you always, yes to the end of time" (Mt, 28:20, JB). He triumphed over the world's storms, and set up a safe harbor for us, the Church: "you are Peter, and on this rock I will build my church, and the gates of the underworld can never hold out against it" (Matthew 16:18, JB).

One enduring legacy of Christ's resurrection is apostolic authority. We enter a haven of salvation at Baptism, a community Christ promised to be with until the end of time. He says the gates of hell, the underworld, can never hold out against it, for he has already won the victory. That's why I laugh when worldly people talk of the Church's demise; they've done so many times before; it's always risen from the ashes. Even modern-day devils of materialism and indifference are passing. But our Church is timeless, and ever young, and ever new, in its Risen Lord's glorious timeless light.

For the Risen Lord is not only with his Church forever, but gave the keys of the kingdom to Peter. God gave the Risen Christ all authority, and at his ascension he passed it on to his Church, and Peter its pope. So our house is built on a rock no worldly storm can destroy. As Christ says: "everyone who listens to these words of mine and acts on them will be like a sensible man who built his house on rock. Rains came down, floods rose, gales blew and hurled themselves against that house, and it did not fall, it was founded on rock" (Mt. 7:24-26, JB). Let's remember that when people make a football of the Church. Christ gave us it, and guaranteed its faith forever, on the rock of Peter.

Never was that authority more needed than today when we're tempted to water down the faith. Self-appointed authorities on TV or radio would replace the rock as our masters. Giving in to that would bring spiritual chaos. We need the sane, unifying rock, which is Peter, to keep us firm in every storm. Cardinal Newman noted in the nineteenth century, that churches that split from Rome have split again and again. So that's why we must cling to the one true, Catholic Church founded on the rock, maintaining the truth in season and out of season; and proved by the spiritual depth of the billions of saints its produced.

So lets listen to its voice, rather than myriads of self-appointed popes. For that Church is not the disordered babble of arbitrary men twisting the truth to suit themselves, but a building founded on gospel and apostolic tradition maintained by right authority for two thousand years. Only a divinely guaranteed institution could have survived for so long.

And in this, paradoxically, much stems not from the Pope's power but his lack of it. When people ask him to change doctrines to suit new trends, his answer is, "I've no authority to do so." he is a prisoner of timeless truth, not a puppet of the world's shifting sands. For worldly values fade, but Christ is Lord of love, truth, peace, and salvation for this world and forever and ever. Amen.

So as God's people, given timeless gifts in the Lord and in right Church authority that has stood the test of time and produced innumerable saints, we profess our faith.

## Prayers of the Faithful

And as God's people whose house is set firmly on the rock, we pray for our needs.

For church leaders founded on the rock of the apostles and Peter their head, that they may never forget that they are servants not masters of Christ's teachings.

For civil leaders, that they may respect the authority of the Church in its spiritual sphere and give it every assistance in carrying out its mission for the good of society.

For young people, that they may hold to the rock which is the Church, and the saving truth of Christ, amid the shifting sands of transitory worldly ideologies.

For ourselves; may we listen to Christ's elected servants and bring his saving truth, love, goodness, and faith into our homes for our children's happiness here and hereafter.

For the sick, the lonely, the aged, and those suffering in body or mind, that in Christ and his holy Church they may cling to the faith that heals the brokenhearted.

For the dead, that, faithful to Christ and his Church in life, they may remain part of it after life in the timeless Communion of the Saints that is heavenly bliss.

And we ask all these prayers through Christ, our Risen Lord forever. Amen

### Reflection

You may have seen that fine film, *A Man For All Seasons*. It's about Thomas Moore, the chancellor under Henry VIII of England. The king asks him to renounce papal allegiance and accept him as Church head, but Moore answers that he loves the king but must obey God and his vicar on earth first. Henry had Moore executed, yet all still recognize him as a great saint. Let's as bravely obey the Church's timeless divinely conferred authority in matters of faith and morals, against all invasive power-hungry attacks today too. Hail Mary.

# Twenty-Second Sunday
# in Ordinary Time A

## *Introduction*

The cross is our faith, Christ is king on Calvary; his victory over evil on our behalf redeems all suffering, and when God raised Jesus, he raised our sufferings to glory too. Let's be faithful through life's sufferings and confess if we fail to carry our cross with him.

## *Homily*

Do you remember the old stations of the cross? They were full of sweat and blood. They missed the fact that the crucifixion is not just blood and pain, but God's triumph over evil. They did, however, have a point at another level. For the cross shows us God as humble, suffering love, redeeming human cruelty. Which is how Isaiah describes the Christ: "I offered my back to those who struck me, my cheeks to those who tore at my beard" (Isaiah 50:6, JB). That's the mystery of our faith—Christ, though Lord, suffered without retaliation. He perfectly imaged God's humble suffering love on Calvary.

The apostles found this image of God hard to accept. Even after proclaiming Jesus as the Christ, Peter tries to stop him going to Jerusalem to die. Jesus rebukes him saying; "Get behind me, Satan!" (Mt. 16:23, JB). For Peter was like Satan in the desert, asking Christ to serve his own interests rather than God and humanity. The apostles also wanted Jesus to be a Hitler Messiah, riding to glory on the blood of fellow humans, and they wanted to serve as top dogs by his side, serving a Messiah who crushed all opposition by arms. They couldn't understand his choice of being a humble, suffering servant of God and us in love. He made that choice, foreseen by scripture, in the desert. After Pentecost the apostles saw its wisdom.

So must we. We must also choose to be suffering servants of God and others to redeem a divided hating world, where power is Lord and the weak are crushed. Christ gave to the last drop of his blood to change all that into a world of peace and justice and love, and he passed on that baton to us: "Love one another, just as I have loved you" (Jn. 13:34, JB). He showed us how to love by giving up everything, even his soul at last. Sadly the Church and Christians through the ages have more often followed the opposite way—Satan's way of pride, greed, and crushing of the weak. Hence, Church scandals. God needs to topple the power of a wealth-mad worldly Church every so often from its unchristian throne. For the main temptation the Church and its members face, is to reject the cross of love for passing worldly gain and power. Look at the many who walk away from the challenge of faith today to slavishly obey a world that would avoid the cross of faithful churchgoing, of moral living, of priestly celibacy, of religious poverty and obedience, of humble lay service, of marriage faithfulness, of charitable giving until it hurts, and so on.

Live it up! Serve yourself at all cost! Crush everyone who stands in your way! Use people for your pleasure! These are Satan's worldly soul-destroying illusions. Pursuit of possessions, sex, and self-satisfaction at all costs might bring temporary pleasure, but it fails to nurture the soul, and it all turns to dust and ashes at last. Following that way, we risk being left with just our own hard selves and an empty soul for all eternity, for as a man lives so shall he die. Christ on the cross, by contrast, would have us follow the way of giving love, suffering faithfulness, greatness of heart.

Sadly, even simple sacrifices for God such as getting up on Sunday to go to mass seem beyond many today. But Jesus, the Lord of Calvary, is our model. He says in today's second reading that real love is in giving until it hurts. Sure, his way seems hard, but it is sweetness and light in the long run; it flowers eventually into happiness here, and eternal glory. Those who suffer with Christ for humanity's sake will be raised to the highest heaven. For the things of this world of which Satan is Lord fade to ashes at last, but Christ is Lord of truth, beauty, goodness, and love forever and ever. Amen.

So as God's people called to faithful suffering service of God and others in real humane love to redeem the world, let's profess our faith.

## Prayers of the Faithful

And as God's people let's pray for what we need.

For our Holy Father, and all leaders of the Church, that they may not be afraid, as Paul says, to preach Christ and him crucified.

For civic leaders, that they may choose the humble service of those they lead rather than self-serving pride and corruption.

For our great youth, that they may not shy away from the sacrifices involved in true faith and charity, but in generous giving may be born to deeper happiness here and eternal glory hereafter.

For ourselves in our homes, that serving our spouses and families faithfully in self-emptying and cross-carrying love, we may gain the greater crown of life in God's arms at last.

For the sick, suffering in body or mind, that, carrying their unavoidable crosses bravely, they may turn them into gold for their own salvation and that of others, making up in their bodies, as Paul says, for what's lacking in Christ's sufferings.

For the dead, Christ's faithful amid the trials and crosses of life, that, helped by our prayers to rise above sins or failings that need atonement, they may come to heavenly peace.

And we ask all these prayers through Christ our Risen Lord whose wounds intercede for us before the Father forever. Amen.

## *Reflection*

The famous prayer of Saint Francis has a great ending: "its in giving that we receive and in dying that we're born to eternal life." Let's pray to Mary, who suffered at the foot of the cross, to help us die to self every day so as to really live. Hail Mary.

# Twenty-Third Sunday in Ordinary Time A

## Introduction

Hospitality is universally celebrated and very Christian. Christ says in our gospel that even a cup of cold water given in his name will be rewarded. Christians should be famous for their open houses. Behind today's bolted doors, let's confess any failure in this.

## Homily

One of the great things I remember about our house when I was young was it openness; everyone, neighbor, friend or acquaintance could ramble in, without a prior invitation and feel at home. Even the rambling travelers, with their pots and pans and squads of children were not turned away, but always received something. And of course we had what were called the rambling houses, well known houses where people met for story telling, music and dancing and general chat. The Stations (house masses harkening back to penal times), were special occasions when, after the priest had left, all sat down to a good meal, and afterward knocked sparks off the floor with set dances.

This sort of openness is difficult today; I'm always shocked to find, on my visiting rounds now, every door firmly locked. Anxious faces peer out at me from behind fearful curtains, saying "who is it?". Yet we talk of progress. I wish we could progress humanely as well as technologically for that is our Christian calling, open homes and hearts.

That's what I wish for us this Sunday, that our homes will always be open. For the essence of faith is the open heart and hand, and it's God who inspires that in our souls. Indeed, we're here at the surest sign of open warm self-giving, the Eucharist. It's Christ's body and blood given to us from the self-giving heart of God. Thereby Christ, the Lord of Love and Prince of Peace, shapes us into caring sisters and brothers to each other.

In monasteries, religious address each other as "brother" or "sister." That's what we all are as children of God in Christ. And since we're his family, he promises in our gospel that where we gather in his name he's there in our midst. With him comes love, unity, and peace. Our ancestors knew this; their doors were always open to faith and neighbors. And when people entered houses, the greeting was "God be with you" or "Peace be to this house." Everyone was offered a cup of tea or something stronger. This same sharing was seen in the way everyone turned up at funerals, to support and console sisters and brothers in grief. In wake houses, lavish hospitality was showered on sympathizers. People were all in the same boat of poverty at that time; there was no room for heads in the air.

And that is what Christ meant when he told the parable of the Good Samaritan. For in a true Christian community, we're never alone in life, in trouble, or in death. We're a communion of human and Christian solidarity that includes the living and the dead, for the Church transcends time. So as we gather here in this love and faith, the gospel reminds us of the key aspect of our fellowship, simple humane kindness. Our calling is to build a community of such kindness, for as John Donne eloquently put it, "No man is an island."

Yet some today seem to think they are. It's so sad nowadays to see so many in big houses, behind electronic gates, shutting neighbors out. Are the hard values of money, pride, and arrogance destroying the humane Christian warmth that's our heritage? I hope not, for only by supporting each other can we survive, thrive, and redeem the coldness of heart that is Satan's cruel way. And only by having warm hearts reaching out to others will we fill the vacuum of loneliness so many experience today.

We ask Mother Mary for such neighborly solidarity, to give us her motherly heart, and to pour abundant blessings on community building, so that our area will be a kind place where Eucharistic community spills over into concern for all. For the world's hard, self-centered values and arrogance, of which Satan is lord, pass and are useless in the grave, but

Christ is Lord of grace, peace, and neighborly love forever and ever. Amen.

So as God's own, making hospitality and caring a reality in our hearts and homes, as a Christian people, let's profess our common inherited faith.

## *Prayers of the Faithful*

For our Holy Father and all leaders of God's familial Church, that they may spread Christ's hospitable love, warmth, peace, and grace to the communities they serve.

For civil leaders, that they may not let the hard world of economics rule them to the detriment of care for the people, especially the poor.

For youth, that they may have open, hospitable, warmhearted Christian hearts in their relationships and so be true children of God.

For ourselves, that in home and community we may have that hospitable spirit that is our heritage and so bring God's warmth to all in our houses, especially our children.

For the sick, the old, the lonely, and the depressed in society, that through our reaching out to them in love, they may find hope, peace, comfort, and fullness of life.

For the dead, that, through our caring prayers for them and remembrance, they may be one with us in the communion of saints and come safely to their heavenly rest.

And we ask all these our prayers through Christ, Our Lord and the only Lord of love, peace, grace, and happiness forever and ever. Amen.

### Reflection

In the end we'll be judged by love, according to many of the saints. That is the quality and warmth of our love to those around us will determine our reward in heaven. This is a universal wisdom; the Dalai Lama says that his faith is best summed up by simple warmheartedness. Sometimes, in stressing doctrine or morality or other aspects of the faith, we forget this. Its warm love that matters at last; God won't condemn us for the petty faults that stayed with us. Our charity will cover a multitude of sins. So, conscious of that, let's ask Mary to give us her motherly heart in all our relations with others. Hail Mary.

# Twenty-Fourth Sunday in Ordinary Time A

## *Introduction*

Forgiveness isn't as easy as we think. Many of us carry grudges against others even into the grave. In many families there are estranged members to whom we won't even talk. Let's confess any ways we lack forgiving Christian hearts.

## *Homily*

Some of us hoard hurts like misers hoard gold. I remember a parishioner once berating me for preaching forgiveness; saying she would never forgive a neighbor who had offended her; in fact it was some trivial matter of a dividing fence or some such like, a tree growing in over the fence that the neighbor wouldn't let her cut down. We can let much trivial nonsense come between us in families too, some hurt, real or imagined that we blow up out of all proportion. The human heart is curious and perverse at times. Above all, our anger must be assuaged before it eats us away inside, for it can do more harm to us than to the object of the anger. At some stage we need to lift that burden from our souls.

Today's readings say the same; Ecclesiasticus warns us to stop hating and hoarding resentment in our hearts, to remember God's forbearance and overlook offense. That's not easy, but Christ tells us we'll be judged harshly if we don't forgive others from our hearts. He tells us to be like God, rich in forgiving no matter how deep the hurt. As he forgives us, we should be reconciled with others. That's how to redeem a hate-filled world.

And even from a psychological standpoint it makes sense. Tribunals on abuse have pointed out that, for the offended, the process of healing must involve justice. Yes, but also it must eventually involve forgiveness of the offenders. In this psychologists echo our first reading, which says that harboring resentment and hate can continue the hurt at a deeper, more lasting level. Only forgiving can finally lift even the worst burdens from our shoulders. Eventually letting go, when we're ready to do so, brings healing closure,

Such forgiveness is vital for salvation too. We can't go before God with hating hearts. In life and death we must stand for forgiveness, not hate, or we may have narrow, hating hearts for all eternity. Moreover, as Paul says, the life and death of each of us influences others. If we witness to a life of hatred and resentment, or feuding within or among different families, then we can leave that legacy to our children. Romeo and Juliet is a good example of a poison feud between two families, and the terrible woe it caused.

In that sense, Christ's request for forgiveness is also a recipe for social health. Often I'm shocked by how hard and unforgiving our press and secular society can be. They talk about liberalism, but true liberalism is Christian. Its letting go. It's wrong how totally relentless and ruthless the press and public opinion can be toward politicians, abusing priests, and other public offenders. Of course they must be called to account, but bringing up sins again and again, hounding them even beyond the grave, is not healthy. It's alien to the healthier mentality, which always tends to see and think the best of people and overlook failings after due punishment has been assigned, knowing we're all imperfect. As Christ says of the woman caught in adultery: "he that is without sin among you, let him first cast a stone" (John 8:7, JB). Relentless self-righteous refusal to forgive an offense is a greater evil; it is total hardness of heart.

Curiously, the ones we often find it hardest to forgive are ourselves. Here too we must imitate God, who as the psalm says, "is merciful, tender hearted, slow to anger, very loving, and universally kind" (Psalm 145:8-9, JB). Christ, the living embodiment of God, forgave even those who crucified him. That's our model, and we'd do well to follow it for our health here and hereafter and to redeem a hating world. For its ways pass and leave us empty at last, but Christ is Lord of justice, love, goodness, forgiveness, and peace for our deep happiness in this world and forever and ever. Amen.

So, as God's people called to have a loving and forgiving heart and so redeem our divided world in the merciful image of Christ, let's make our profession of faith.

## *Prayers of the Faithful*

For our Holy Father the Pope, that he may spread forgiveness and reconciliation and help heal the divisions and harboring of wrongs among nations that cause war.

For civic leaders, that, throughout the world, they may help reconcile age-old opposing communities on this planet.

For our young people, that they may abandon the road of hatred and bring about a climate of forgiveness and healing in society.

For ourselves, that at home we may readily forgive and be reconciled with spouses, children, or other family members who annoy us.

For the sick, the aged, the lonely, and the alienated, that they may be brought into the warmth of our love, forgiveness, and care.

For our beloved dead, that, all the trials of this world over, they may enjoy the fullness of eternal life through our prayers, continuing remembrance, and love.

And we ask all these prayers through the same Christ Our Lord, who rose above and redeemed all the petty hatred and divisions of the world, and who constantly intercedes for us before the Father. Amen.

### Reflection

John Paul II, a great man and saint of our time, is a wonderful example of Christian forgiveness. He was shot in the stomach, and this contributed to his health problems in later life. Yet he went to the prison to embrace and forgive the Turkish man who shot him. All of us have people like that to whom we can reach out. Let's ask Mother Mary to help us have forgiving hearts no matter how difficult we may find it to forgive. Hail Mary.

# Twenty-Fifth Sunday in Ordinary Time A

## Introduction

"'My thoughts are not your thoughts, my ways not your ways, (Is. 55:8-9, JB). A huge threat to faith is our twisting of it, for our own sad purposes. Various forms of fundamentalism are examples. Let's confess ways we misuse the faith in this way.

## Homily

There's a story from the apartheid era in South Africa. The black people were not allowed into the churches, but had to receive Holy Communion out the windows. What a travesty of God's Church. It was man's church, man's God. But that's a temptation all of us succumb to, we shape God according to our own thinking. Even the usual physical depiction of Jesus as a fair-haired blue-eyed European type is a distortion, to suit our white-man prejudices. That's why Isaiah's reading for today warns us, "For my thoughts are not your thoughts, my ways not your ways."

Too often we play God. We judge and condemn people according to our own prejudices, and do it in his name. Unfortunately, religious people—and I say this with shame—are often the worst in this regard. Jesus had to confront the Pharisees, supposed people of God, who would stone to death the woman caught in adultery. He said, "if there is one of you who has not sinned, let him be the first to throw a stone at her" (Jn 8:7, JB). We must be careful not to create a harsh God in our image: "My thoughts are not your thoughts." God is infinitely broad minded; most of the time we are not.

And sadly, its often so-called religious people who most claim God for bigoted positions. It's what gives religion a bad name—from Bin Laden to fundamentalist Christians. I think of the north of Ireland, where people like Ian Paisley would claim that all Catholics, including the Pope, are enemies of God. Only his small church, he says, worships the true God. In the same way, Catholics unjustly condemn "black Protestants."

In fact, if we want to even remotely come close to God, we must continually widen, not narrow, our thinking. We must have ever-bigger hearts and ever-more generous souls.

That's what scripture tells us today. The ones who arrive last into the vineyard received the same wages as the ones who toiled all day. They couldn't understand, yet they got what they had agreed on; the master was not being unjust. Their narrow jealously and envy is what fueled their anger. They hated the master's generosity, just as so many strict religious people condemn those who don't think as they do. In fact, with God, all are equal, even sinners. If anyone repents, he or she is welcomed freely, even at the last hour of the day. For God's ways are not our ways; his thoughts not our thoughts.

But narrow mindedness isn't confined to religion; it's universal. Secularists and liberals can be as narrow in their agenda, closed to God or religion, for example, harsh in tribunals and media witch hunts, spiritually blinkered. God's ways are not such either; they are broad as the heavens. All his children are loved equally to the last hour of the day.

Why be envious because he's generous? Let's open our hearts and minds, be as generous and all embracing as Christ. If we come remotely close to that, we will be saints. As Christians, that's what we're called to be. My thoughts are not your thoughts. Let's stop casting God in our harsh image. Let's obey the first commandment and worship the true God in spirit and truth. For only his ways can make us full, open, loving, generous, and spiritually alive. For the cruel ways of the world fade to dust at last, but Christ is Lord of truth, grace, beauty, and generosity, both for our wholeness in this life and happiness forever and ever. Amen.

So as God's people making his all-embracing love our spirit, let's profess our faith.

## Prayers of the Faithful

For the Pope and all leaders of the Churches, may they reach out to all, especially other religions and beliefs, with the generous all-embracing mind and heart of Christ.

For our civil leaders, that they may not impose narrow personal secular ideology in the name of pluralism, but allow the faith and beliefs of all to be furthered to the full.

For our wonderful young people, that they may not become pawns of the prejudice and narrow secular thinking of the times, but be open to God, and the wider aspects of the spirit and the truth he puts before us unto untold happiness in this life and the next.

For ourselves, that in our homes, workplaces, and communities we may not judge anyone, but open our hearts and minds to all with the generous spirit of God and his Christ.

For immigrants to our country of whatever race, creed, or color, that they may find among us an open, accepting Christian spirit.

For the dead, that, shaking off the narrow restrictions of this world, by the help of our prayers, they may come to the limitless and glorious mansions of heaven.

And we ask all these prayers through Christ, the Lord of all people and all the glories of creation, forever and ever. Amen.

## Reflection

There's a popular anecdote told of Mohammed Ali, the great boxer. When he came home from the Olympics with a gold medal he stopped at a restaurant to get a burger. But the man behind the counter is supposed to have said that they didn't serve blacks at that restaurant.

He apparently replied, with typical wit, that he didn't want a black, he only wanted a burger. But he was deeply hurt by these attitudes, after all the glory he had won for his country. Let's oppose any such prejudices among us today. Hail Mary

# Twenty-Sixth Sunday in Ordinary Time A

## Introduction

Keeping one's promises seems a simple thing. Yet we all fail in this duty to our children or whoever depends on us. Let's confess ways we hurt others by not keeping our word.

## Homily

The woods are lovely dark and deep,
But I have promises to keep,
And miles to go before I sleep,
And miles to go before I sleep.

Robert Frost's poem, *Stopping by Woods on a Snowy Evening*, gives us something to think about. Promises to keep. Once, a man's or woman's word was his or her bond, and keeping promises was taken for granted. How seriously do we take promises now? How often do children say, "Mummy, you promised … Daddy, you promised to take me to the seaside today. It's not fair." Children have a great sense of the importance of keeping one's word. Like honor or telling the truth, or fairness, it's a measure of our integrity, and true love.

We Christians make promises to God and others, and should keep them. At Baptism we promise—or parents do so for us—to be faithful, to believe, to practice and pass on the faith to our children. At Confirmation, we promise to be witnesses for Christ and his Church. At marriage, we promise to be faithful to our spouses, to share, to take the good with the bad, to bring up children in the love and security of a good home.

Keeping such promises is the gospel theme. There's the father with grapes ready for harvest. The older son vows to go to the vineyard and pick them, but doesn't go. How hurt that father was. He had relied on the son and was let down badly.

The message for us is that if we make a promise, keep it, or like the younger son, repent, if we disregard our duty at first. Our heart tells us that others as well as God rely on us to keep our promises. We dare not let them down, especially children and relatives dear to us. They look up to us to keep our promises. Do we?

And when we make promises to God, do we easily set them aside? How hurt our Father in heaven must be when we do that: "I will pay what I vowed to the Lord," the psalm says (Psalm 116:18, JB). At ordination, I made promises—to be a good pastor, to preach the Word, to obey my bishop. I pray that I'll keep those vows, and not tarnish the office, like some did recently.

People's word should be their bond at any time. Sure, it may be more difficult to be a person of integrity now. The media, and everything else, seem to advise us to take the easy way out; for example, if things get difficult in marriage, get an easy divorce. In Frost's poem, the poet would like to sleep and forget his promises, but he knows that would be the easy way out. Sleep here suggests death, but "promises to keep"— duties and obligations entered into—make going on imperative.

That's a lesson also for those tempted to give up on life. There are always promises to keep, miles to go before we sleep. We all have things to do in the world that no one else can do. God and others depend on us. The poet is tempted to lie down and sleep, forget such obligations, but deep within he knows that's not the answer to his problems.

Let's keep our promises, our vows—the ordinary and sacred agreements we enter into - however difficult that may be. Let's do so for the sake of loved ones and God. We Christians, the elder sons, should be careful lest prostitutes and sinners enter heaven before us. Let's hold to our pledged faith unto death. For the fickle world fades to ashes at last, but Christ is Lord of truth for our happiness in this world and forever and ever. Amen.

So as the people of God keeping our promises in life and in faith, and as people of fairness, honesty, and integrity, let's profess our faith.

## Prayers of the Faithful

For our Holy Father the Pope and all Church leaders, that, living their sacred vows to pastor the flock well, they may be a light to all those in their care.

For civic leaders, that they may serve the public with fairness, integrity, and justice for all, especially the poor.

For our great youth, that they may keep the promises they made at Baptism and Confirmation to practice the faith and be part of, and workers for, Christ's Church of love and goodness, regardless of the real demands this makes on them.

For ourselves at home, in the workplace, and in community, that we may keep our promises, especially to our children, and all who look to us for integrity of word and action.

For the sick, especially ill relatives, that, through our care, they may know the love of Christ.

For the dead whose faith is known to God alone, that they may come to their eternal home with the help of our prayers.

And we ask all these our prayers through Christ Our Lord, who is our faithful savior forever and ever. Amen

## Reflection

The code of many cultures involves honor and verbal integrity. The old code of chivalry involved a very high regard for honor, and being true to one's word. In Roman culture, one fell on one's sword if one's honor was compromised. Even in the American West of the nineteenth century, being called a liar meant an immediate gunfight. So this Christian code is universal. Through the prayers of Mary, let's hope we can live with real Christian integrity of word and deed and honor today too. Hail Mary.

# Twenty-Seventh Sunday
# in Ordinary Time A

## Introduction

God gave us a beautiful world, food, clothes, families, and more. Our gospel asks us to pay him back what is his due: "Give back to Caesar what belongs to Caesar - and to God what belongs to God" (Mark 12:17, JB). Let's confess ways we fail to give God his due.

## Homily

Christ, in his day met many closed to God, yet open to evil. In our day too, many give all to Caesar, zilch to God?. Nietzsche said we must kill God and follow a will to power beyond his law. This, as the Nazi creed, spawned hell. Yet is it our creed now too? No God, please! We're European, American; we don't have to account to God for anything we do. Satan said the same before his fall. There is no such thing as neutrality here. Christ said that if we're not with him we're against him. He cried when his own shut him out. Is he crying now as he seeks fruits of faith and gets indifference or open hostility?.

Yet as Creator, he's king of our vineyard world and has but leased to us in trust. And as such he has a right to expect due fruits. Yet are we too abusing his gentle trust in handing over the vineyard world to us?. Christ addressed the vineyard parable to his own errant people; but it's a parable for all time. He asks us to give God his due in every age, not to frighten us, but to persuade us into seeing that that is not just our duty in justice to give God his due, but also our freedom and happiness.

Are we giving him due worship and obedience now, and respecting his servants. Or in greedy self-centeredness, like the parable tenants, ignoring his servants and killing his son's voice in our hearts and societies? I fear the latter is the case. If Christ came today to demand the fruits of the vineyard, he'd probably be either ignored, or aborted long before that in the womb, as the embarrassing child of a single mother.

Which brings me to the other theme this Sunday—pro-life. St. John Paul II viewed the modern West as a culture of death, an aging society abandoning faith, even as it killed the vulnerable in the womb, and sought to legalize killing of the old. "He expected justice, but found bloodshed; integrity, but only a cry of distress (Isaiah 5:7, JB). How true of our world where keeping global fat cats happy, is largely put before feeding the world's poor.

It was greed that motivated the godless tenants of the parable. They would keep for themselves what was their lord's. Killing innocent babies in the womb and justifying this evil for narrow, selfish interests, are not the fruits God asks now. True endless children is not the way to free the poor, but is abortion the answer? There is always another way. And we need another way. For the abortion industry just produces an aging society.

But, like the evil tenants in the parable who kill the Lords servants and even his son when they ask for the fruits due, we shut out higher demands. Yet we, like the unjust parable tenants are storing up judgment to come in this. In some ways, the judgment is already come. The average age in the Western world is forty-five now; no wonder our vitality is fading. In God's world the preponderance of youth, and the vitality that brings, is built into the ecosystem. That's why the Church just asks for a generous fertility. It does so, not to oppress women, but to promote population balance and a healthy society.

But I'm sure if God sent Christ now to preach such things, he'd be killed, like the son in the parable. But lets remember that the tenants who failed to produce the fruits required by the lord of the vineyard and killed the son, faced the wrath of the Lord. Are we tempting God's judgment? Abusing his forbearance like the tenants. Are things like the recession his way of shocking us into heeding the gospel lesson, that fruitless greed brings death. But giving God his due, leads to goodness, truth, happiness, peace and salvation for our happiness in this world and forever and ever. Amen.

So, as God's people, charged with producing fruits of faith, goodness, and respect for life as sacred at every stage of its existence, lets profess our faith.

## *Prayers of the Faithful*

As God's people, cultivating his vineyard today in honesty and integrity, and giving him the fruits that are his due, let's pray also to him for what we need.

For our Holy Father and all Church leaders, that they may lead the earth in proper care for it and all its peoples, reminding all of their duties to their gentle loving Creator.

For civil leaders, that they may promote respect for life, for justice and equality for all, and put the earth's fragile environment before endless greed.

For youth, that they may be conscious of their responsibilities to God and all that's good and true. May they be his true and dutiful tenants, building up our world in faith and love and giving him the faithful service that is his due as their loving Lord and Savior.

For ourselves, that in our homes, and communities, we may pay our due respects to our loving Creator and Savior, and give him due worship and free loving service.

For the very young, the old, the sick, and the vulnerable, that, through our loving nurture and care, they may know the love and comfort and healing of God in their lives.

For the dead, that, having been good tenants of God's vineyard the world, they may, helped by our prayers, rise above their sins and come to the joy of a final heavenly banquet.

And we ask all these prayers through Christ, Lord of life, forever and ever. Amen.

## Reflection

We all have roles in God's vineyard. We're on earth to help others as we pass along, and give glory to God by our good works. When we die, lets have fruits to show of giving both God and Caesar what is their their due. So that when the Lord comes on the last day in judgment and asks us to render up the due fruits of our stewardship while on earth, we will be able, and glad, to do so. We ask Mary to help our weakness in this great task. Hail Mary.

# Twenty-Eight Sunday in Ordinary Time A

## Introduction

There's a warning in scripture today. Though we're God's called through Baptism, yet we may not be chosen. We must keep the white garment we received at Baptism on —the garment of faith, holiness, and good works—if we hope to enter the final banquet of heaven. Let's confess ways we fail in living out our Baptismal calling.

## Homily

"Many are called, but few are chosen" (Matthew 22:14, JB). The phrase sticks in the mind; when young we said, "many are cold but few are frozen." Whether our souls are warm or cold when we meet God at death is key. Clothed at Baptism in the white garment of faith and virtue, we promised to keep it unstained unto eternal life. But we must not presume on salvation. The man in the gospel who presumed to enter the master's feast without a white garment on, received a rude awakening. Let's not make that mistake.

For the feast we're invited to is the eternal one of heaven. At one time only the people of Israel were called to that glory. But Christ invited all, without prejudice, to the feast prepared by his Father in heaven. Indeed he says that the blind, the lame, the poor, and the sinful are special invitees. And he warns us, as he did the Pharisees, that "tax collectors and prostitutes are making their way into the Kingdom of God before you" (Matthew 21:31, JB). That warning is apt today. Though specially called, even Church people, as abuse scandals show, failed to keep the wedding garment on. Like the Pharisees, we can all be corrupted.

Even we, the chosen baptized of today, can lose our garment of faith and virtue, succumb to the corrupt temptations of our world. We're his privileged people with untold sacramental aids to salvation, and we are given the very body of Christ as our spiritual nourishment. Every blessing is showered on us as his grace-filled people. But, nevertheless, we mustn't become complacent; others may go into the heavenly banquet before us. For all people in the world are God's children. All receive the means to salvation, especially those who, through no fault of their own, do not know or acknowledge Christ. We have the immense privilege of being part of his holy Church. But we must live up to that gift and try to bring its untold blessings to others. Like the Jews, we mustn't think that, because we're a chosen people, we're automatically saved. Given much; much is asked of us. We must keep the white garment of faith, virtue, and truth on if we're to flower into eternity. As the Baptismal prayer puts it: "May you keep the flame of faith alive in your heart so that when the Lord comes you'll go out to meet him with all the saints." Will he say to us then: "Come, you whom my father has blessed, take for your heritage the kingdom prepared for you since the foundation of the world"? (Mt.25:34-35. JB).

There is always the possibility that we will fail to keep that white garment on, and be cast out into the darkness where there is weeping and gnashing of teeth. We cannot abuse the goodness of God by living lives unworthy of our Christian calling and still expect due reward. Above all we mustn't put worldly greed, power, and pleasure before service of God and others as many do today. That's what the wealthy, hard-hearted Pharisees did. Unlike them, we are asked to be true, kind, faithful people of God. We may not be saints, though that's what we're called to be. But we must bear some fruits of goodness. We may never be perfect, but we must keep striving to be so, so that we'll come before him at death with our Baptismal garment as intact as possible, so that Christ will lead us into the eternal banquet. For the values of which Satan is lord fade to dust at last, but Christ is Lord of life, peace, goodness, truth, and happiness for life here below and forever and ever. Amen.

So as God's faithful, keeping the white garment we received at Baptism as unstained as possible, and so ready to enter the eternal feast, we make our profession of faith.

## *Prayers of the Faithful*

For the Pope and all leaders of the Church, that the white garments they wear may be a sign of their inner grace, integrity, and love, and that they may be lights to our world.

For civil leaders, that they may lead the citizens of our country in integrity, fairness, and dedication, and be especially concerned to help the poor and vulnerable in society.

For our wonderful youth, that they may not become so caught up in the corruption of the world so as to neglect to save their immortal souls as good practicing Christians within the bosom of the holy Church.

For ourselves in our homes, workplaces, and communities, that we may keep the fire of faith alive in our hearts, so that, still wearing the white garment, we may come at last to the banquet of life.

For the sick, the old, the lonely, and the poor, that, through our generosity, love, and care they may know the love of Christ.

For the dead, that, after wearing the garment of faith at death, they may come to their heavenly home with the help of our prayers and masses.

And we ask all these prayers through Christ Our Lord, who is the only Lord of life, happiness, and goodness forever and ever. Amen

## *Reflection*

You may know the story in the Bible of Joseph and the amazing-colored coat (Gn. 37-48). He was the youngest son of twelve, and the coat was given to him by his father because he loved him best. But his brothers, in envy, took it from him and sold him into slavery, telling the father than a wild beast had eaten him. Joseph, however, was taken to

Egypt and became a great man there and later saved his brothers during a famine. All of us are given the many-colored coat of faith at Baptism by God. Let's wear it until we return with many fruits of goodness into the home of our heavenly Father and Mother. And let's ask Holy Mother to keep us faithful to our Baptismal calling to be holy. Hail Mary.

# Twenty-Ninth Sunday in Ordinary Time A

## *Introduction*

As we near the end of the Church's year, she features the end things: death, Christ's Second Coming and the final judgment. She does so, not to frighten, but to keep us on the right path. Let's confess ways we stray, and risk our soul's eternal salvation.

## *Homily*

Remember the old missionaries and their hellfire talks on death and judgment? Now we avoid that, and stress God's love. But its good to reflect not only on our salvation, but also our responsibility for the salvation of others. On Mission Sunday, Saint Paul reminds us that this duty involves more than supporting missions abroad; we're to evangelize at home too. Theresa of Liseux, who never left her convent, is patron of the missions.

Christ's saving work is urgent. At Baptism we were anointed to be its heralds, and at Confirmation we promised, in the words of the old catechism, to "be strong and perfect Christians and soldiers for Jesus Christ." The war of good and evil is endless; Christians must be unequivocally on the side of the angels. Vatican II says, in its various documents on the missions, that Christians can't be passive before the Church's saving work.

And that work is not just for priests or religious. Lay people are asked to take up that role too: as Eucharistic ministers, readers, altar servers, mass goers, preachers, Christian exemplars, and financial contributors. For such active Christianity was never more needed. In recent elections, I was shocked to see some candidates reluctant to admit their Catholic faith, almost apologizing for their belief. How sad, when our ancestors defended the faith unto death. But persecution now is more subtle; to profess faith is not politically correct, but then again God is not so politically correct now either. Let's not be pawns of such ideology, but stand up and be counted for Christ, lest our children have no spiritual birthright, and the pearl of their immortal souls be cast before the swine of the evil one.

Last Sunday Christ said, "give back to Caesar what belongs to Caesar – and to God what belongs to God (Mark 12:17, JB). How many now give all, even their souls, to Caesar and naught to God? What use will Caesar be when our souls will be required of us? But even for this world we need the inner happiness, strength, and grace of faith. Only God can nourish our inner souls unto salvation, and fulfilling our Baptismal and Confirmational duty means bringing others with us to eternal life. Let's do that courageously. And to give us the inner grace to do so, let's often turn to prayer.

For mission begins in the Eucharist and personal prayer. We can render to God what is his, and bring others to him, only if we know him through worship. Then we've the light to inspire others. And to support with prayer and money, foreign missionaries, who, as John Paul II says, not only bring faith to millions, but also help them out of a desert of poverty and injustice. For changing people's lives for the better is a mission too. By helping to transform lives materially and spiritually, we further salvation in every way.

Let me end with the story of a man picking apples. His friend said, "You must have done a lot of work to produce this crop." "No," said the man, "last spring my secret bees did the work." Let's all be bees in God's orchard enabling the world to produce an ever greater harvest of salvation in Christ for this world and the next. For the immersion in this world's corrupt values leaves us empty on the shore of eternity, but Christ is Lord of truth, happiness, love, beauty, and salvation both for this world and forever and ever. Amen.

So as God's own, serving Christian mission in a world of his people crying out for the riches of God, the salvation of their immortal souls and bodies, we profess our faith.

## Prayers of the Faithful

For our Holy Father and all the leaders of the Church, that their missionary zeal may lead to a new spring of faith, equality, and social justice for all in our broken world.

For our civil leaders that, they may further the total good of their people by helping or putting no obstacles in the way of the nurturing and spreading the faith.

For our youth, that they may have the idealism and enthusiasm to go out to the whole world and proclaim the Good News of our salvation in Christ and his holy church.

For ourselves in our homes, that we may bequeath to our children the greatest gift of all, the faith that is their pearl of great price for this world and the next.

For the sick, the aged, and the housebound, that they may offer their prayers and sufferings for the salvation of the world.

For the dead, that through our prayer, a great mission in itself, they may come to their eternal rest and happiness with God and all the saints who have gone before them to everlasting life.

We ask all these things through Christ Our Lord, who is forever the light of the world. Amen.

## Reflection

You may know the story of Saint Francis Xavier, perhaps the greatest of all missionaries. A Jesuit priest, he sailed from his native Spain to bring the Good News to the vast countries of the East. There, in India and other countries, he wore himself out working day and night, preaching and baptizing and building up Christian communities. Tragically, he died on the eve of a great mission to China. Like him, we pray that we'll all have the same zeal for the faith, and we ask Mother Mary to help all missionaries furthering the material and spiritual welfare of the world's peoples today. Hail Mary.

# Thirtieth Sunday in Ordinary Time A

## Introduction

A saint we often ignore is John the Baptist, yet Christ called him the greatest of the prophets. Certainly, he is a model for all of us who are also called to prepare the way for the Lord in our world. Let's confess any ways we fail in this.

## Homily

The word *John* means "the Lord has shown favor." God certainly showed favor to John the Baptist, and he returned that love with interest. That's why, as we gather this Sunday as God's people, we take him as a faith model. For as all of us should, he responded to God's love and favor generously. A cousin of Jesus, born late to Zechariah and Elizabeth, the cousin of Mary, at birth he was chosen as the prophet who would, as scripture says, "Make a straight highway for Our God across the desert" (Isaiah 40:3, JB). He did that with all his heart and was a staunch, unswerving witness for Christ unto death.

As such he's a supreme model of Christian life. For, like us, favored of God, he practiced what we're all called to, to love the Lord our God with our whole heart and with all our soul and with all your strength and with all your mind, and to love others as Christ loves us (Luke 10:27, JB). Like no other, John loved and served God wholeheartedly, eventually giving his life for the truth. He did this because he'd grown steadily in faith from his youth when he went into the wilderness to devote himself to God. Having found God, he didn't stop there; he began a mission of Baptism to prepare for Christ's public ministry.

That's why Jesus called John the greatest of the sons of men and the last and greatest of the prophets. For once Christ came, the law and the prophets were complete. John, the last of the prophets sent by God to foretell the coming of the Christ, lived up to Jesus's expectations in a way that each of us should. We too were anointed to be different present-day prophets at Baptism, not foretelling and preparing for his coming, but helping to spread everywhere the foretold kingdom that he established by his cross and resurrection. Our Baptism is in the Spirit and to everyone. We too promised at Confirmation to serve the Lord wholeheartedly and lead others to God in that new sense. And we too were called like John to wholesome integrity of life and purpose in that great work.

For, no straw in the wind of contrary worldly values, he was an uncompromising prophetic voice, telling the truth and calling people back to God and what's right in the violent, immoral age into which Jesus was born. Yet it was no different from our own or any age. Each age needs a voice to call it from evil to good, from cynical skepticism and materialism to faith, worship, and goodness. John died because he wouldn't compromise with Herod and the powers that be; he called a spade a spade. It is no wonder then that Christ said there's no greater prophet. His greatness was doubly proved when he finally gave way to Christ, saying, "he must grow greater, but I must grow smaller" (John 3:30, JB). He wasn't concerned with his own glory, but with serving God and people's souls.

In our age—the end time of God and his Christ—we're called to be similar witnesses, to stand up for what's true, good, and holy even when it means standing out and suffering. And we're asked to have the humility of John at last. We're to know our limitations and to place ourselves into the Lord's merciful hands with confident trust. Not all of us can be prophets like John, but each of us can do much good, if we live out our Baptismal calling as best we can, and witness in an increasingly godless environment to the timeless saving values of Christ. People need this like never before; for as Paul says, "Now is the favorable time; behold, this is the day of salvation" (2 Corinthians 6:2, JB).

So gathered here in faith, let's vow to bring that salvation to all in the spirit of John so that, like him, we'll be raised up in the Spirit with Christ, Our Lord and Savior. For all else passes, but he is Lord of Glory, truth, beauty, life, and goodness for our happiness in this world and forever and ever. Amen.

So as God's people, baptized to be present day prophets for Christ in these end times, let's make our profession of faith with new enthusiasm.

## Prayers of the Faithful

For Church leaders, especially the Pope, that they may be as faithful witnesses for Christ in our world, as John was for his day.

For our civil leader, that they too may make straight in the wilderness of the modern world a highway for God.

For our great youth, that they may see that it's in giving for God and others that we gain the greatness, peace, love, and grace that flowers in us at last unto everlasting glory.

For ourselves in our homes, that we may be examples to our children, relatives, and neighbors of faith and love.

For the aged, the sick, and all those who suffer in body or soul, that they may find in their faith and our care for them the consolation, healing and peace of God.

For the dead, whose faith is known to God alone, that, through our prayers, any lingering remission for sin may be achieved, and they may come to their final rest with God and all the saints.

And we ask all these prayers through Christ, who is Lord of life and intercedes with the Father for us forever and ever. Amen

## Reflection

A John the Baptist for today, was St. John Paul II. He too was the voice for God for much of our age. He suffered grievously first under fascism's godless creed in Poland. He helped overcome it through an underground church. Later he did the same under communism and helped destroy the iron curtain. As pope he working tirelessly, traveling all over despite being shot. I always remember him on the Vatican balcony struggling to speak to his people, though dead on his feet. No wonder when you go to Rome you find streams of people at his tomb. We pray to be as generous in the Lord's service. Hail Mary.

# Thirty-First Sunday in Ordinary Time A

## Introduction

Scripture today reminds us that our happiness in this world is in serving, not in being served. Like Christ, it is in faith, love, and giving that we achieve true greatness. Let's confess any ways we fail in generous service of God and others.

## Homily

Really good people don't draw attention to themselves; for the most part, they'd be surprised to be seen as holy. For example, I've a friend whose child needed an operation. The doctor was in the theater for nine hours. Before going in, he took time to explain to the parents what he was going to do. After it was over, he took all the time in the world to explain what he'd done. I was amazed at the quality service. It was a living of Christ's teaching, that the great among us are those who serve. This challenges us all. Most of us are in service jobs, or have families who require everyday heroic humble Christian giving.

That's what God commends, simple, authentic, giving people who do good without fuss from innocent hearts. When the apostles were fighting about who'd be top dog, Christ took a little child and placed him in their midst. That was their model, childlike innocence, gentleness, and humility. That's why Saint Paul, such a great man, is concerned in our second reading not to burden anyone. He's the model for our pastoral roles.

Sadly, Church leaders in our day often failed in this respect. Instead of being servants of God's servants, as Christ demands, they lorded it over people. In our first reading, Malachi scarifies the priests of his day for similar pride and partiality And Our Lord attacks the Pharisees in the same way in our gospel. We priests are suffering because we lorded it over people. Christ is teaching us the lesson he taught the Pharisees, that he who exalts himself will be humbled; we're humbled now for our sins, and it's a good thing.

For the main temptation we all face is self-serving pride and power. Satan's fall began with a refusal to serve. Similar pride in us is the root of evil. As Saint James says: "You want something and you haven't got it; so you are prepared to kill."(Jm. 4:2, JB) Even our prayers can be tainted by self-seeking. What we should pray for is to be good servants of God and others; the way to happiness here and hereafter. It was the way Christ chose in the desert when Satan tempted him to be a self-serving Messiah. Christ chose instead to be a suffering servant of God and others, giving all on a cross of love.

Like that tired doctor who spent nine hours in surgery saving a child's life and then sacrificed additional time to inform, console, and heal the parents, our Christian role is to work for others in that way. We're called to dedicated, selfless love and care in the ordinary occupations of life. For only by giving that bit extra for God and our fellow human beings will we redeem a dog-eat-dog world, and make our lives beacons of hope. Alma Bazel Androzzo's song says, "If I can help somebody as I pass along, then my living shall not be in vain." And St. Francis says in his famous prayer, it's in giving that we receive.

Indeed our Baptismal vocation is summed up in generous service of God and others, to build God's kingdom on earth. And its after such service of God and others that we'll be raised at last to the right hand of the Father. For the self-serving ways of the world fade to dust and ashes at last, and leave us empty on the shore of eternity, but Christ is Lord faith, hope, love, goodness, truth, beauty, and salvation both for our happiness in this world and forever and ever, amen.

So as God's people committed to lives of Christ-like love, prayer, and humble self-giving, we profess our faith.

*Fr. Con Buckley*

## *Prayers of the Faithful*

For Our Holy Father, and all the leaders of the Churches, that they may be humble servants of the servants of God, nurturing their flock, and living examples of charity.

For all leaders and authorities in our society, that they may carry out their roles with integrity and responsibility toward all the people they serve, especially the poor.

For our youth, that keeping the faith in love they may gain the deep happiness that service of Christ and others brings.

For ourselves, that our vocations in life may be ones of service of God and those around us, so that the Kingdom of God that Christ came to establish may be truly furthered by our lives.

We now pray in silence, for prayer is a great service of humanity, for our own special intentions.

For the young, the weak, the vulnerable and the sick in our society, that through our humble care they may experience the love of God and his Christ, their crucified Lord.

For the dead, especially those of our parish family who have died recently. May their souls and the souls of all the faithful departed rest in peace. Amen.

Heavenly Father, as true carers for each other, we offer these, our humble prayers, for our real spiritual and temporal needs, through Christ Our Lord who lives and reigns with you and the Holy Spirit, one God forever and ever. Amen.

## Reflection

For a long time I was a De La Salle brother, for the story of the founder of that order inspired me. He was a rich man and a canon of Notre-Dame Cathedral of Reims. But he spent all his riches, and used his very house to start a school for poor children who were running wild in the streets. He set up a religious order so he could teach and live among the deprived. And De La Salle himself was always the first to take on the most difficult tasks of this great work. Let's learn from him the joy of serving others, especially the poor, and ask Mother Mary to lead us in this. Hail Mary.

# Thirty-Second Sunday in Ordinary Time A

## Introduction

As we approach the end of the year and the end of the Church year and winter, let's reflect on the end of all things. Let that sense that all is passing make us wise, so that we'll invest our lives in values that last. Let's confess ways we fail in this.

## Homily

This time of year, as light deserts a winter world, the Church warns us that only active faith saves us from an eternal winter. Christ says the same in today's gospel. He asks us to keep our inner light burning, to store up the extra oil of faith and good works for the final judgment. For failure to do so may mean being shut out from the eternal banquet forever, cast out when the master comes to judge the living and the dead.

This warning is apt for today when an increasingly secular world neglects to fill its inner lamps with the stored oil of faith. So lacking sustenance, the immense light of God's spirit flickers and goes out in many hearts. The sleep of worldliness takes over so that when death comes they will not even want to enter the eternal heavenly banquet. God forbid that he should say to us when we knock at that door: "I don't know where you come from. Away from me, you wicked men" (Luke 13:27, JB). To avoid that fate let's stay awake spiritually. For now is the acceptable time, now is the day of salvation.

Let's fill our inner jugs with the oil of faith and goodness now so that when Christ comes at death or the world's end, our replenished lamps will be burning brightly. For we, like Christ, should be the light of the world. At Baptism our candle was lit from his Paschal candle, and we made a sacred promise to keep the flame of faith alive in our hearts, so that when the Master came we'd be able go out to meet him with all the saints.

Keeping that promise is more difficult today. So much in the modern world would lull us asleep spiritually. Amid the hustle and bustle of getting and spending it's easy to neglect our soul's welfare. We can become lazy about prayer and Sunday mass, or too busy to make time for our family, so our light of salvation can flicker and go out.

In this, faith is like a tender baby. It needs to be fed and cared for regularly in order to thrive. Without regular spiritual nourishment, the inner baby of our faith and relationship with God may pine and die. We'll lapse back into the darkness from which Christ delivered us, the darkness of totally secular lives. If you think this isn't the threat today, look around you at the numbers who no longer practice their faith. In big houses they seem impervious to the gospel warning that God may come at any time to require our souls of us. It's vital in that context for us Christians not to let the great light we received at Baptism fade away. For, like a machine, we can rust and decay within and be cast on the scrap heap of the world's lost souls, unable to rise and shine when Christ comes.

Sure, some say, "I've a vague belief in God still and don't do anything very bad." Reduced to such vague commitment, the little bit of light may inevitably be quenched by life's storms. Without the mass, the Word, and the Eucharist we'll grow weak within and may leave nothing to our children but faith indifference. Like the unwise virgins when the master comes, our lamps will be out, and we'll have no stored oil of grace to relight them.

Will Christ know us when we come to his house on high at death if we've never graced its door on earth? Will those who've lived the faith go into the eternal banquet while we're outside in the dark where there's weeping and gnashing of teeth? Let's get our lives in order now. For worldly values are useless on the shore of eternity, but Christ is Lord of peace, happiness, and salvation both for this world and forever and ever. Amen.

So as God's people keeping faith alive in our hearts by the mass, the sacraments, personal prayer, and active Christian living and so always ready to meet him should he come at our death or on the last day, let's profess our faith.

## Prayers of the Faithful

For the Pope and all leaders of the Churches, that keeping the light of Christ alive in their hearts, they may spread that light to their flock, and all the spiritually needy world.

For civil leaders, that they may promote enlightened policies that serve all the people equally, and render unto God his due too.

For our youth, that they may cling to and spread the faith as they promised solemnly at Baptism, Holy Communion, and Confirmation.

For ourselves in our homes and communities, that nourishing the lamp of our faith and storing the oil of grace in our souls we may be God's light to our children especially.

For our relatives, friends, and neighbors who are sick or in need, that we bring to them the healing oil of faith, love, and genuine, caring hearts.

For the dead who have passed from life to Life, that through our prayers they may reach the highest mansions of heaven.

And we ask these our prayers through Christ Our Lord of light and peace and love forever and ever. Amen.

## Reflection

The story of the death of Saint Bernadette, the seer of Lourdes, is inspiring. For many years before she passed away, she suffered from a painful and incurable leg cancer. Yet she never failed in charity and cheerful love to all around, despite this grievous cross. And as she died, with the sisters around her, she reached out as to someone at the foot of her bed, and her face lit up with intense happiness. Mary had come to reward her for her great faith and love, and the suffering she had offered for the salvation of the world. May we all share that same glory after a life of similar faith and loving service. Hail Mary.

# Thirty-Third Sunday in Ordinary Time A

## Introduction

This is the last Sunday of our year, and the Church continues to put before us the end things—death, judgment, and Christ's Second Coming. As we get old, time flies. So it's wise while active to store up riches in heaven. Let's confess any ways we fail in this.

## Homily

When young, I loved my parents and thought they'd never die. Yet both are gone, and I miss them. The death of those we love is hard. Yet there's only one certainty in life—our death—and no one knows the day or the hour. So it's wise to be prepared. As the psalm says: "Teach us to count how few days we have, and so gain a heart of wisdom" (Psalm 90:12, JB). That wisdom is to live by faith while here on earth and to trust in Christ through all life's trials. For life, though short, is, as Keats wrote, "A vale of soul-making." We should use the time we have to build up faith so that we won't be taken by surprise when Christ comes. As Paul says, "But it is not like as if you live in the dark, my brothers, for that Day to overtake you like a thief" (1 Thess. 5:4, JB).

Christ says that his faithful will never walk in darkness. We'll have the light of his life here and happiness with loved ones when our work is done and he calls us home. So my youthful belief that my parents would live forever was right, for they had faith and goodness of heart. That enriched them to the core of their being and gave them a glory the world cannot give, and that flowered at their death into life with God forever.

Now as days shorten, winter comes, and harsh winds of recession blow, we should be wise and have similar faith. For darkness suggests eternal death and evil, and no one wants to live in darkness forever. That won't be our fate, if, through faith and prayer and active Christian goodness, we keep Christ alive in our hearts. For he promised that those who believe and trust in him will have the light of life. If we are faithful to him and his Church, we need not fear. Unlike the good-for-nothing servant of the gospel, we won't be cast out into the dark, where there is weeping and grinding of teeth.

A headline in some paper I read recently said, in effect, that ten years ago we thought we'd killed God, but now he seems to be alive again. Why is the world so anxious to kill God? Didn't we do enough by crucifying him originally?. Must we do so over and over again in our vain pride and arrogance, or because he challenges our morals.

Perhaps some of you saw the film, *The Omen*, about the anti-Christ. The film is a misrepresentation of the book of Revelation, whose message is essentially positive: if we trust in Christ his coming will be a great joy. But the film is interesting in that the anti-Christ is from a rich, powerful family with global financial interests. Some say the anti-Christ is already present in liberal capitalist excess, allied with materialism and media-driven secularism, the horns of the beast. Be that as it may, our task is to hold firm to Christ's light no matter what worldly philosophy reigns, so that when he comes he'll say to us: "Well done, good and faithful servant!" (Matthew 25:23, JB). For the things of the world of which Satan is lord fade to dust and ashes at last, and we take no ill-gotten riches into the grave, but Christ is Lord of love, goodness, peace, happiness, and salvation both for this world and forever and ever. Amen.

So as God's people persevering in faith, love, and goodness through all the trials of life and worldly attacks and so carrying those riches with us beyond death to join the saints in glory when Christ comes at last, let's profess our undying faith.

## Prayers of the Faithful

For our Holy Father and all Church leaders, that they radiate the steady light of Christ amid the turbulence of our world.

For our civil leaders, that they may not promote any philosophy that is alien to our heritage of glory in Christ.

For our youth, that they may enjoy life's good things given by God fully, and for their happiness here and hereafter keep their white Baptismal garment of faith on so that they may enter the heavenly banquet proudly at last and live forever in the joyful light of Christ.

For ourselves in our homes and workplaces, that, clinging to Christ the light of the world, we may illumine the darkness of our world with his saving faith and presence, and go out to meet him with all the saints when he comes again in glory.

For all those suffering in the present recession and troubles of our world and all the sick, that, trusting in Christ who is the same yesterday, today, and forever, they may have the strength to rise above all trials and sufferings.

For the dead, that, in this time of winter and darkness, they may experience an eternal summer with the heavenly Father through our liberating prayers and petitions for them.

And we ask all these prayers through Christ Our Lord, the light of the world and our unfailing hope forever and ever. Amen.

## Reflection

Some of your may have remembered the old missioners, notably the Redemptorists. They pulled no punches in their lurid depictions of hell's fire and such like gory apocalyptic details. Yet strangely, they were the sermons we most relished and looked forward to; no wishy washy sentiment there. Of course they went too far, but maybe we've gone too far now in the opposite direction. Nowadays no one wants to think of death, and is it because in doing so they will also have to think on the after life and their duty to prepare for it now by faith and good works.

Once upon a time, holy men used to keep a skull alongside their bed, to remind them of the end things. We shouldn't got to that extreme but its good at times to reflect on the reality of death, so that we'll keep on the narrow road that leads to Life. Lets ask Mary to make us wise and faithful on our frail earthly journey. Hail Mary

# Christ the King A

## Introduction

We come to the finale of the Church year—the feast of Christ the King. When God raised Christ from the dead, he made him Lord or king of the universe. At the end of all, he will come in kingly glory to judge the living and the dead. Let's prepare for that day now by cleansing our hearts of whatever separates us from our king of love on Calvary.

## Homily

In the end, we will be judged by love, the saints say. This is also the theme of Christ's Second Coming to separate the sheep from the goats. We will be separated according to our practical charity toward our fellow human beings, or lack of it. This parable shows how important charity is in Christian life. As Peter says, "love covers over many a sin" (1 Peter 4:8, JB). But apart from the fact that charity is the key to salvation, we Christians should make a special effort to help the needy for another reason—because as children of God, they're our brothers and sisters. If your brother or sister were starving, would you walk by? But all people are our brothers and sisters in Christ.

He asks us to love all around us who need our help, in a practical way. Yet many of us walk by brothers and sisters in the gutter. I include myself in this. Every day on TV there are images of starving children in Africa, and I turn away. Are we responsible for righting this wrong? Yes, because we are our brother's keeper, and we're partly to blame for world suffering. When I was abroad in a third-world country, I saw how 60 percent of its GNP went to repay interest on its massive debt to

Western banks. That's the global financial system that even now takes from pensioners to give to rich bondholders.

Charity should start with the needy brothers and sisters around us. As Christmas approaches, giving to Vincent De Paul is one way of helping. Directly or indirectly, we might give of our surplus to the less well off. Indeed that's our Christian duty so as to make the world the kingdom of Christ, the King of Love. Even people living with us can be needy, and we're too busy to notice. In our homes a simple hug costs nothing.

But at home or abroad, we Christians can't ignore others' needs, lest our King says to us when he comes at last, "Go away from me, with your curse upon you, to the eternal fire prepared for the devil and his angels: For I was an hungry, and you never gave me food: I was thirsty, and you never gave me anything to drink etc." (Matthew 25:41–42, JB). If Christ came on earth now and asked us for money for the poor, we'd surely give; but needy Christs beg from us every day. "Give to everyone who asks you," Christ says (Luke 6:30, JB). I myself find that hard, but if someone asks, I always give something. People take advantage, but we can't deny the gospel; it's better to err on the side of generosity than meanness. For only as giving people are we children of a God who gives everything freely: "you received without charge; give without charge" (Matthew 10:8, JB).

Christ was king of love on Calvary, because he gave the last drop of his blood for us. We should also give until it hurts, and even our smallest acts of charity will be rewarded by God. For the hard, self-centered world of which Satan is lord will be cast down at last, but Christ will be eternal king of loving giving people forever and ever. Amen.

So at this end of the Church year, remembering that we'll be rewarded for every ounce of practical charity and love we show, let's make our profession of faith in our King of Love on Calvary, and imitate his selfless giving until it hurts.

## *Prayers of the Faithful*

And as God's people let's pray for our needs and the world's practical needs.

For Church leaders throughout the world, especially our Holy Father and the bishops, that they may be the voice and heart of Christ the King to all those in need in our world.

For civil leaders, that they may make it their special care to reach out to the poor and underprivileged in society.

For our youth, that they may look to the interests to all those in need around them and so make a difference by their lives.

For ourselves in our homes, that we may never be too caught up in work and making money to give the gift of care and affection to our children and aged or sick relatives and neighbors.

For the sick, the aged, the lonely, and the oppressed, that, through our care, they may know that they are loved and cherished as all precious children of Christ the King of Love on Calvary.

For the dead, that our vital charitable prayers on their behalf may lead them out of darkness into the glorious Kingdom of God that Christ the king has prepared for them.

And we ask all these our prayers through Christ our King of love and peace and glory forever and ever. Amen.

## *Reflection*

There's a story told of Saint Martin. One cold, wet winter day, he was riding home and saw a poor man on the road. The man was dressed in scant clothes, and was shivering with the cold. Martin got down from his horse, took off the fine, thick cloak he was wearing, and wrapped it around the man. That night he had a dream. He saw Christ, wrapped in that cloak, saying to him, "Thank you, Martin, for clothing me in my need." This echoes Christ's words today: "in so far as you did this (act of charity) to one of the least of these brothers of mine, you did to me" (Matthew 25:40, JB). Let's all reach out to the needy Christs around us as our greatest service to our King of love. Hail Mary.

# PART II

# Cycle B

# First Sunday Of Advent B

## Introduction

Advent is a preparation for the most amazing event in history, the birth of the Christ. For thousands of years the prophets had been foretelling that coming in the end times, to bring God's salvation to the whole earth. Lets thank God that we live in those end times of the Christ of God, and confess any ways we fail to live up to his promise.

## Homily

The birth of any child is a wonder. Each mother or father feels that as they cradle a new unique wonderful being in their arms. But the birth of God's son is even more special, in the miracle of the virgin birth. Its no wonder then that the church, after ending its year with remembrance of the dead, calls us at the beginning of the new year to prepare for that birth, and mark it with our own spiritual rebirth, as his holy people.

Parent's prepare excitedly for their first born, and the anticipation in the extended family is great too. In the same way the church asks us, the extended family of God, to prepare for our Christ child by being reborn in the Spirit. The candle we light in the wreath asks us to cast off the night of evil and shine for him. That's what Advent's about, renewal, rebirth, for us, the church, the world; recalling us to Baptismal joy and commitment, to revitalized prayer, living of Christian values, rejection of sin, and witness for God.

Christ in today's Gospel describes this as being spiritually awake. Every so often we need to rise from the sleep of sin and death that the old man of the world lulls us into. So that when the lord comes we'll be ready. A common hymn puts it well: "Awake from your slumbers, arise from your sleep/A new day is dawning/For all those who weep".

We need something to cheer us up in this depressing time of dark cold winter weather. Christmas does that; it helps us get over the short days and long nights, with their frosts, snow and chills. But a winter can set in to our soul too; baby Jesus should inspire us to leave our inner Winter and bloom like red Spring roses. For the soul also needs a fillip, lest the evil one grab us and drags us deep into the mire, and keep us there. Advent's inner renewal, prayer, and confession is the perfect pick-me-up, in that context. It enables us to shine up our inner shoes as it were, so that the Spirit can flower in our hearts anew. "Cast out our sin and enter in, be born in us today", the carol says. Christ reborn in us at Advent means spring blooms for us, the church, and the world.

Each child's cry brings hope. Christ birth is infinite hope. Advent calls us to "shine up our buttons with Brasso", as the old jingle says. For now is the acceptable time, now is always the day of salvation. For we prepare not only for his coming at Christmas but at the end of time; now is the time to ready ourselves also for the great judgment day. For, though the evil one would leave us in a winter world forever, the Christ child is lord of ever new life for our deepest happiness in this world, and forever and ever amen.

So as God's people, called to renew our inner life this Advent to prepare for Christ's coming now and at the end of time, we make our profession of faith with fresh enthusiasm.

## Prayers of the faithful

For our Holy Father, the Pope, and all the leaders of the church that they may preach the infinite value of human renewal unto glory in Christ this Advent and always.

For civil leaders that they may promote the spiritual as well as material renewal of those in their care this Christmas and new year.

For our youth that they may make this Advent a times of deep renewal in the spirit of the Lord, and so come to a Christmas of great inner glory, peace and joy.

For ourselves in our homes this Advent that we may blend the spiritual and material joys of Christmas with happy abandon, family gatherings and glorious feasts, for the Word became flesh and dwelt among us in the flesh as well as in the spirit,

For the sick, the aged, the lonely and the poor this Advent, that through our contributions and loving outreach they may know the joy of Christmas as never before.

For the dead that born to new life at Christmas, they may, through our prayers, come to the dazzling glory of their heavenly home, a glory prefigured by the lights and glitter of heavenly Christmas glamor.

And we ask this through Christ, born for us in a humble stable and interceding for us forever before the Father in heaven, amen.

## *Reflection*

I'm sure if the Christ child was born in our modern world, to a single mother, as he was then, that he would probably be aborted in the womb. I read recently how in China, a child born out of the state's one child policy is automatically aborted. Its a terrible prospect, but that's the reality of our modern world. Lets not be totally brain-washed by such values, but appreciate the infinite value of each child in the womb. Each is a sacred being from God, with a potential to be a new Christ to the world. Lets pray for, and help if we can, all the vulnerable children in the world today, caught up in war, famine and neglect; for in helping them we are helping the Christ child. Hail Mary

# Second Sunday of Advent B

Make straight in the wilderness a highway for our God. That's the great cry of Advent. And we have a model in this preparation for the coming of the Christ child in John the Baptist. Lets confess any ways we lack his integrity, love and prophetic commitment.

## Homily

Our gospel for this second Sunday in Advent centers on St. John the Baptist and rightly so. For among the saints we don't always appreciate or praise him enough. Christ revered him so much; he said that of the sons of men there was in no greater than John. Praise indeed. And its justified, for he stands out as a model of godliness and integrity even today. He was as close to Jesus as any of us would like to be. Even before birth he leaped in the womb at Christ's presence. The son of Zechariah and Elizabeth, Mary's cousins, he chose from the beginning to be Christ's prophet. He was, as Isaiah foretold, a voice that "cries, prepare in the wilderness a way to the Lord" (Is. 40:3, JB).

We're called to do the same in our wilderness world; to courageously make a way for Christ in a world of recession, moral collapse, and growing disillusion. And do so humbly like John. For he laid everything at Christ's feet, saying he was not fit to undo the strap of his sandal. He saw himself as a ordained to promote Christ, and then step aside.

There as no Satanic pride there, though he'd a right to be proud. Like all good people he'd have laughed to be called a saint. Yet he was favored of God, and practiced, as we all should, the great law of scripture, that we should love the Lord our God with our whole heart, soul, and mind, and our neighbor as ourself. He left everything, as monks and nuns do today, to witness to Christ, and bring the lost world of his day back to God.

Indeed, when I think of John I'm reminded of Anthony, the great hermit and early model of religious life. He too fled from a corrupt world to serve Christ in the desert with every fiber of his being. Yet though he tried to escape from the world, it flocked to him. Similarly, every aspect of society came to John to learn from him wholesome integrity of life and purpose. And to them he gave real spiritual food, they heard an uncompromising prophetic voice that told the truth, however unpalatable it was.

Advent calls us back to God and right today, as John called his age. Indeed he died trying to save Herod, who'd unlawfully taken his brother's wife. He called a spade a spade, and that world took revenge. Salome demanded his head on a plate. No wonder Christ said there was no greater prophet; for he is also a martyr. But his supreme virtue was humility; he gave way to Christ when his work was done.

In Advent, we're called to be similar prophets for Christ, unworthy servants, even as we do everything right. To exercise our Baptismal prophetic role, to stand up for God and what's right, no matter what. We may not all be capable of John's forthrightness, but each of us in some way can influence our family and community. We can bear witness in our particular environment to God's values rather than those of the cold world of which Satan is lord. So that like John we will also be raised to glory. For all else fades to dust and ashes but Christ is lord of love, goodness, peace, and salvation both for our deepest happiness in this world, and forever and ever, amen.

So as God's people, called in today's spiritual wilderness to make straight a highway for our God, lets profess our faith.

## Prayers of the faithful

And as prophets for today lets ask for all our spiritual needs.

For our Holy Father and the bishops of the church, that they may have courage like John to stand up for, and promote gentle faith and goodness before the world, no matter how much they may be criticized and persecuted as a result.

For civil leaders that they may not persecute the church leaders and prophets of today, as the corrupt powerful of John's day did.

For our youth that receiving a greater Baptism than John, that of water and the Spirit, they may live it out in humble service of Christ, within his Holy Catholic Church.

For ourselves in our homes, that our children and all around us may be inspired by our devotion to Christ, our joyful loving kindness, and our faithfulness to his holy church.

For the sick, that through our care for them as though they were Christ himself, they may know the love and care of God.

For the dead whose faith is known to God alone, that having completed their work in this world, they may come with the help of our communal prayers to their final rest.

We address these prayers, through Christ to God our loving heavenly Father, who always listens to those who call upon him, amen.


## Reflection

We in these islands have had our own John the Baptists. I think, for example, of St. Kevin, the great apostle of Glendalough. He fled to a cave in the wild heart of the Wicklow mountains. But later, it became a monastic city. Seven churches were established there. Like John or Anthony; the whole world came to learn integrity and holiness at his feet. He even persuaded the Vikings to turn from plundering the area. And as archbishop of Dublin, he became a light for his day. Lets ask Mother Mary, that all the Kevins of today may imitate such faith, love and humble service of God and humanity. Hail Mary.

# *Third Sunday* of Advent B

## *Introduction*

"Look, there is the lamb of God", John says of Jesus (Jn. 1:29-30, JB). He pointed to Christ as the way to God. Lets follow the Lamb, and confess if we fail in this.

## *Homily*

We live in throw-away society. Everything reminds us of this. We're told to change our car every few years. Most of us have closets full of clothes that we'll never use again, or many pairs of quite good shoes that are discarded. A consumer society taps into this, producing goods with a limited life; like a *Mission Impossible* tape, they self-destruct.

Similarly, people are disposable now. The part time worker is cheap, so they're used. Workers are made redundant to make a profitable company more so. Over-qualified professors are dumped for cheaper lecturers. Over-forties find it very difficult to get new jobs. Early retirement relieves companies of dead weight. Old people are sent to homes, where we hope they will soon self destruct, lest they be a burden to us.

The Gospel, however, reminds us of another way, of our enduring personal value in Christ. St. James points this out in the first reading, and John the Baptist shows us the Lamb of God, sent to save us. As one church year ends and another begins, we're reminded that Christ came to discard no one, but to raise all to divine heights, especially those scorned by the world. He has a more than satisfying permanent job ready for us in eternity. To him young or old, rich or poor, employed or on welfare, we're valued forever. No one's at the end of their sell-by date, there are no "losers" in his kingdom come.

That's why November, All Souls month, the month of death, leads on to Advent and Christmas, the time of hope. As Christ says to John the Baptist's messengers: "the blind see again, and the lame walk, lepers are cleansed, and the deaf hear, and the dead are raised to life and the good news is proclaimed to the poor; and happy is the man who does not lose faith in me" (Mt. 11:4-6, JB). Advent reminds us of the greatness and eternal newness of not losing faith in Christ; on life's journey, we're cherished at every stage. We don't end up in trash cans, like some in a throwaway society, but in paradise. Because Christ, the Lamb of God, gives us meaning, value and dignity, we should cling to him.

And we should try to live as God's children, well. Advent is a good time to see how were doing in that respect. To take stock of our position, consult our spiritual map and ready ourselves for the great day of the lord's final coming at death, or at the end of the world. For Advent is about preparing for that too, for the great day when the saints go marching in and we are with them; in the meantime lets cherish all as more than disposables, especially the old, the young, the poor, the unemployed and the vulnerable.

Lets also cherish God's holy church anew. For the catechism warns us that "the present time is the time of spirit and witness, but its also a time marked by distress and the trial of evil which doesn't spare anyone, and especially doesn't spare the church. We're ushering in the struggles of the last days" (Cat, 672). In the turmoil of these end times, as James says, we must be patient until the lord comes (JM. 5:7, JB). For the world of which Satan is lord will pass away at last, leaving its devotees on the dust heap, but Christ is lord of human dignity, love, peace, happiness and salvation both for our fullest life in this world, and forever and ever, amen.

So as God's people cherishing all in Christ and raising them up to a dignity, love and happiness the world alone cannot fully give, lets profess our faith anew.

## *Prayers of the Faithful*

And as the people of God lets ask him for all that we need.

For our Holy Father the Pope and the bishops of the church, that they may uphold the infinite dignity of all people as children of God and lead all to the untold riches of Christ this Advent.

For civil leaders that they may not become so caught up in economics as to forget that their main role, is to serve the people, and raise the poor to their full human dignity.

For our youth that serving Christ, his church and all that's good with their whole hearts, they may make a difference by their lives and earn the everlasting reward of the blessed.

For ourselves in homes, workplaces and communities that Advent may be a time to lavish special loving care on those around us.

For the sick and the needy in mind or soul that through our faith and care they may know their infinite value as God's children.

For the dead that their work in this world done they may reap the rewards of their faith and love, and through our prayers come to the home prepared for them from the foundation of the world.

And we ask all these our prayers through Christ Our Savior who came to us in a stable to raise us to God forever and ever, amen.


## *Reflection:*

In hospitals I'm always shocked by the strange logic of our world. In one ward a child of 22 weeks is saved at all cost as a human being, while in another a baby of exactly the same age is dismembered and thrown in a trash can. One is a child, the other a non-being. Mother

Theresa's answer to all this was, give the children to me, I'll love them as the children of God that they are. Lets not see human life as disposable, like our hard commercial modern world does. Lets not sell our souls for its passing consumerism, but have the wisdom to know where enduring values are, in God and the Christ he sent to give human life timeless value, from conception to the grave. Hail Mary

# Fourth Sunday of Advent B

## Introduction

This week's readings remind us of our great inheritance of faith from David, to Mary, to Christ; as the fulfillment of God's saving plan; and his overturning of the hard proud values of the world in choosing Mary. Lets confess any ways we doubt his love.

## Homily

"I am the handmaid of the Lord", Mary says as she accepts her role to be mother of the Savior (Lk. 1:38, JB). As a result of her humble acceptance, the handmaid had a lowly role in the household of the time, she was raised to untold glory; that of the lady standing on the globe with the twelve stars at her feet, and her foot crushing the serpent of evil; the image of popular iconography.

This is a timely reminder to the powerful and the rich, that real glory is in serving God and others without stint. It should bring to their senses people in fine houses who don't have time for God. Getting and spending isn't everything; love of God and others is. Mary as social prophet reminds us of this. She completely overturns worldly values, saying the really important people are handmaids of the Lord, and servants of people.

People like her who spend themselves doing God's will should take heart: selfless priests, monks and nuns; kind carers, selfless fathers and mothers, pious parishioners, caring nurses and doctors; social workers, volunteers in famine-stricken lands.

At Jesus's conception, as always, rich, powerful self-serving people - Herod's wife for example – ruled the world in their interests. But God shunned them and asked a poor obscure single village woman to be his mother. Her yes brought a new order of love, justice, equality and truth into being.

That's the order we should serve. Mary asks us to cop ourselves on, get priorities right. Not to go mad with self, riches and pleasure to the extent of shutting out God and the cry of the needy. Her message is so apt at Christmas, which has become so commercialized. Christmas is a success if sales were up. On Boxing Day, decorations came down and the sales began, as if people weren't fleeced enough. Lets still keep 12 days of Christmas; extended holidays, family gatherings, midnight mass, the crib. Lets not sell this out too.

For our deep happiness is in upholding God's values against those of the hard world. He casts down the rich and raises up the poor, Mary says in her revolutionary speech before Elizabeth – we don't usually think of her as a social seer; but she may have been lowly but she certainly wasn't stupid. Lets also stress the love aspect of Christmas as the key one. Lets raise up someone this Christmas, be extra kind to the weak. For Christmas should reshape the world unto peace, justice and equality. Lets make the church aspect central also this Christmas, for that's what carried us to real joy and glory.

And that's what each Advent and Christmas is really about, the birth of God to raise a fallen world to heaven. Mary's yes to God made all that possible, ensured the eventual victory of God and of his all holy Christ. But he needs us to be his hands in completing the work begun in Bethlehem. Lets be generous in his service as Mary was. For his kingdom can only come through good, holy people like ourselves who serve people and God humbly: through prayer, social work, Vincent de Paul service, caring for the sick, furthering people's spiritual welfare, promoting vocations to the priesthood and religious life. Such selfless spirit-filled people are the Marys of today, birthing Jesus in a world as troubled, violent and sinful as it was in Herod's day. Like Mary they are the wise ones. For the hard world passes and leaves us empty at last, but Christ is lord of love, peace and grace for our deepest happiness in this world and forever and ever, amen.

So as God's people serving people this Christmas, lets live and profess our faith.

## *Prayers the faithful*

Lets ask God the Father to send Jesus into our hearts and homes this Christmas as we pray for the things that we really need.

For the Pope and bishops of the church; this Advent and Christmas may they inspire people everywhere to make straight in the wilderness of our world a highway for God's justice and peace.

For civil leaders that the events of Christmas may inspire them to serve those they lead with humility, integrity and dedication, and to raise up the poor and needy from the dung heap.

For our youth, that they may see beyond the pursuit of power and wealth to where greatness is, in faithful service of God, the church and those who need their gentle care.

For ourselves that this Advent and Christmas we may pause from frantic getting and spending to find time for God and others, for midnight mass, for giving those around us a much-needed hug, especially our aged, lonely or sick relatives.

For the sick that through our care this Christmas they may know the love of Christ.

For the dead brought to life by the child Jesus, that through our prayers they may come to the glittering lights of the heavenly Christmas forever.

And we ask all these our prayers through the same Christ child who stretches out his arms to the world forever and ever, amen.

## *Reflection*

There's a story of a shepherd boy who came to the Christ child. He had no rich gifts to give him, so he thought, "Jesus is cold. I'll collect sticks and make a fire to warm him". But the moss and sticks were wet and wouldn't catch fire. The boy began to cry, but the baby Jesus, seeing his great kindness, stretched out his hand to help, and the fire blazed up. He rewarded the goodness of heart of that simple child, uncorrupted by the world. Lets all have such gentle caring hearts this Christmas. Hail Mary.

# The Nativity B

## Introduction

We come to the joyful goal of our Advent renewal, this glorious night of the Lord. Angels sing to us peace on earth, good will to men. That peace and love is what we should practice at Christmas and throughout the year. Lets confess ways we fail in this.

## Homily

"Feed the world, let them know its Christmas" the *Band Aid* song says. It was only a pop song but it got the message of Christmas. As did the popular hymn we sing all the time at Christmas, until maybe we fail to see its message: "Joy to the world the Lord is nigh, let earth proclaim its king". Certainly the event we celebrate tonight in a blaze of light is a great proclamation, the greatest the world ever knew. For we proclaim our gentle God among us as a frail baby, bringing us from darkness and evil to freedom and light.

Hymns like the 12 days of Christmas also echo that message. It lists the gifts given by the true love God to us the beloved. All other gifts we receive at Christmas pale in comparison to his gift. As the Tony Mathis song says: "all across the land dawns a brand new morn, this comes to pass when a child is born". Boney M's smash hit *Mary's Boy Child* puts it even more powerfully: "Man will live forever more because of Christmas day".

These great hymns and songs celebrate an amazing fact. That the bundle cradled in Mary's arms in a stable far away is God with us. Despite *Jingle Bells*, a booze-up, or shopping until we drop, that's the why of it all. That message of peace and love should soften the hardest hearts, stop war, and feed all our brothers and sisters in Christ.

That is, as we gather in a blaze of Christmas light in a decorated church with angelic choirs singing, we remember the goal of his coming; a better, freer, kinder and more equal world. Glittering lights are vain if they don't lead to brotherly or sisterly love. John Lennon's great song rightly asked the question of a violent world: "do they know its Christmas time at all". For amid the tinsel we can miss the point: no more war, feeding the world, raising all people to salvation, people walking hand in hand: black, white, yellow, red in a world where all equally share earth's riches. That's the Christmas dream.

Sadly the fallen world's Satanic forces still leads us down other paths. Ruthless forces of global power and finance dictate an unequal world. And forces of international power lust, fuel endless conflicts. We saw recently the death of Kim in Marxist North Korea, a state locked in a godless totalitarian nightmare. It reminds us of other secular dictators of our age, from Hitler to Stalin to Assad killing his own with chemical weapons. Christ came as the Prince of Peace, but his work is a long way from finished.

Our task is to finish his work, and its what he trusts us to do. Its God's bright innocent world in Christ that we should dream of this night. Its the gentle one born in a stable and crucified by the world that we should follow. Its his needy children everywhere we should serve. For all else fades to dust and ashes at last, but the Christ child held in Mary's arms, is lord of love, peace, happiness, goodness and grace for the happiness of all in this world and forever and ever, amen.

So as God's own, gathered to adore the baby Jesus, let vow to build his just kingdom of grace, peace, and beauty, as we profess our faith.

## Prayers of the Faithful

And as we gather in this holy night with angels singing for us, lets pray with confidence to the loving God who sent us Jesus.

For the church in the world, in the light of this glorious birth may it inspire the whole world to come to the Lord's cradle and forge liberty, equality, peace and salvation as he desires.

For civil leaders that this holy time may inspire them to lead the people with justice, integrity and wisdom.

For our youth that they may bring to Christ this Christmas and throughout the year their total love and devotion; that those who have wandered from the faith may come back to the arms of the Savior and his holy church to find true peace.

For ourselves that we may bring a harmony, faith and love to our homes this Christmas and that the spiritual riches of the season may continue into a grace-filled, happy and just new year.

For the sick, the aged, the lonely and the needy this Christmas, that through our love, care and practical help they may enjoy the good will of the season to the full.

For peace in our own country and throughout the world, that the spirit of the season may heal all our sad divisions.

For the dead that they may come to the peace of their heavenly home with the help of our prayers.

And we ask all these prayers through the Christ child, who came in answer to all our deepest needs, amen.

### Reflection:

Some say why the Christmas fuss, but that's puritan begrudgery. We should get all worked up at Christmas. For all is calm and bright as "God is with us". The Word became flesh and material aspects of the feast - eating. drinking, parties are a must too. Separation of bodily and spiritual joy isn't Christian. Mary gave Jesus his first kiss on behalf of us, and we can't thank her enough for bringing him to us in the flesh. Lets make him flesh in our real love for all, and feasting, and gift giving this Christmas. Hail Mary

# The Holy Family of Jesus, Mary and Joseph B

## Introduction

The readings echo the fact that Christmas is about family. The first features the third commandment: "honor your Father and your Mother".(Ex. 20:12, JB). Then Paul tells parents and children to practice mutual love, gentleness and respect; and the Gospel shows us the Holy Family. Lets confess ways we fail at Christmas to nurture family unity.

## Homily

Last Christmas abused children and battered wives flooded helplines. Violence, loneliness and alcohol-abuse were major factors in these calls. Not a good ad for our family life, or our sense of what matters at Christmas, peace and good will. Given the scale of family breakdown in society, the picture seem even more depressing. In this context is there any point in the today's feast, that of the holy family?

Certainly not if our image of Jesus Mary and Joseph is of a no-problem home. But nothing could be further from the truth. They were poor. After traveling the long road to Bethlehem, they were shut out of the inn. Jesus was born in a stable. They fled for there lives from Herod, across the desert with scant food and danger everywhere. They were refugees in a far land, maybe excluded and lonely. Nor is Luke's account of the teenage Jesus free from the usual rebellion; when his parents found him in the temple, he said they should know he'd be about his father's business. Yet Jesus submitted to them and grew in grace before God and men.

In effect this holy family survived all that the world threw at them and grew in love and togetherness. Jesus lived for 33 years and spent

90% of this eking out a meager living with Joseph and Mary in an obscure village in the middle of nowhere. Could God have affirmed the value of close family life more? For if that family had plenty of trials it drew them closer together rather than pushed them apart. That's the message of the Holy Family feast. It is about the family who hangs in there, prays together, loves each other tenderly, stays together bonded by trials, who work at family life in the deep love of God and each other. For real love is a deep decision to go on loving no matter what.

Sure this is more difficult today, but it is still very doable. A huge number of families are still getting it right by the grace of God, remaining true to Christian principles of love, unity, faithfulness and non-violence. Sacrificing the pub and personal ambition to be together. Working for each other and children in an atmosphere of affection, trust and peace. Its not easy building such a family, but the alternative is unthinkable. The traditional family isn't perfect but its better than any alternative that's been tried. Without it we risk social disintegration, reversion to irresponsible selfish individualism.

The ones who usually suffer most in this are the most precious people in society, the children. They need the love and security of a good father and mother who are together and there for them. They need a nurturing caring home so as to grow up in age and grace before God and man. The holy family were real. They stayed together, united by love, through all adversity. No less is expected of Christian parents today. They are to create loving caring homes so that children may grow in age and grace like Christ. For all else is dust but he is lord of faithful enduring love and care, forever and ever, amen.

So as God's people promoting in our homes the unity, mutual respect, love and gentle care that is our amazing Christian calling, let us make our profession of faith.

### Prayers of the faithful

For the church, which is the family of God, the true home of all people, that its Holy Father the Pope and all its motherly and fatherly leaders may nurture their large family with the gentle care, respect and infinite love of Christ.

For our civil leaders that promoting the welfare of families may be one of their main concerns, for the greater good of society.

For our young people that they may respect, love and obey their parents in all that's good, and be faithful to their mother the church, so that they may come to the fullness of age and grace both in this world and the next.

For parents who are doing such a wonderful job in nurturing the children of the future, that God may bless, inspire and keep them faithful in this great work.

For all the sick members of our parish family, that God may bring them comfort and healing. Through our care for them may they know the care of God their Father and Mary their mother.

For the dead, especially those of our own families who are still with us in spirit in the communion of saints, and in our hearts, that through our continuing love, remembrance and prayers for them they may come to the fullness of eternal life.

We ask all these prayers through Christ who spent most of his life in a poor village family, amen.

## Reflection

1 read recently a book by Scott Hahn called *Rome Sweet Home.* He was a Presbyterian who became a Catholic. I cite this not to hold any sectarian torch for the Catholic church, but for a reason related to our feast. He used to spent 8 hours a day studying the Bible. From these studies he concluded that the Catholic Church was the true one, for it alone had the image of the church as a *family*, the image of the people

of God throughout the Bible. The Catholic church with its Holy Father, priestly fathers and reverent mothers, and its view of the church as a mother, most fully reflects the homely relationship between God and his people in the Bible. Lets pray to our heavenly Mother that we'll appreciate being part of the great church family of God, and being her children. Hail Mary.

# Solemnity of Mary, Mother of God B

## Introduction

After the feast of the Holy Family as we celebrate the motherhood of Mary. Its the feast of all mothers. The first reading shows the graciousness of God reflected in Mary. Paul talks of God as daddy, Abba, the title we give to our own beloved fathers. In the Gospel we see Mary and Joseph with baby Jesus, and Mary reflecting on his importance. Lets confess if we neglect to reflect the importance of each child in our homes.

## Homily

The hand that rocks the cradle rules the world, they say; mothers are the backbone of society. A good mother or father is priceless. And Mary, God's mother and our's is a model for parents. For God chose as mother for Jesus a real genuine lady: "he has looked upon his lowly handmaid", Mary says (Lk. 1:48, JB). She drew a wide lesson from God's choice: "he has pulled down princes from their thrones and exalted the lowly" (Lk. 1:52, JB). That is, God's choice of Mary is the opposite of worldly values. It says the key people in his world aren't the wealthy or powerful, but those who serve God and others with integral humble love. They seldom receive worldly praise; saintly nuns, caring parents, faithful parishioners, keen nurses and doctors; the sick who offer up their sufferings.

At Jesus's conception there were many rich, powerful, self-serving lords and ladies - Herod's wife for example. Yet God didn't ask her to be his mother; he asked a poor obscure village woman, who had listened to God in her heart and did his holy will all her life. That's the message for us. To serve God and fellow human beings with real fatherly and motherly love, shunning the world's hard greed and lust for power.

For the motherhood of Mary highlights the fatherhood of God, and Jesus become a son to the whole world. This makes all motherhood and fatherhood sacred; for all parents give birth to Christ, if they make their homes into havens of love and peace. Our twelve days of Christmas should focus on such family bonding, and its enhancement by our worship of God as a family. So in this holiday season let's put our energies into faith, family togetherness and good relationships. And in this, let Mary be our model; her kindly spirit inspiring our home life.

So that our houses can become modern-day Bethlehems, lighting up our fallen world with motherly and fatherly care like that of God our Father, and Mary our mother. People with humble, generous hearts who answer God's call to be nurturers of our precious children. We need such good mothers and fathers as never before, to bring human warmth into our world. Look at the difference Mary made by becoming Jesus's gentle mother. She ensured the long-term victory of God. Faithful and faith-filled fathers and mothers make a similar difference. By creating happy united faith-filled families, they become a light to society.

And we don't have to run off for fulfillment elsewhere. There is enduring joy in family faithfulness. And as humble faith-filled parents we birth Christ in a world every bit as troubled, violent and sinful now as it was in Mary's time. "I am the handmaid of the Lord", let all of us parents be just that. For in doing our parental task well, even myself as spiritual "father", we'll draw ever closer to Mary's Son. And all else passes away at last, but he is lord of love, goodness and homely care for our happiness in this world and forever and ever, amen.

So as God people, imitating the motherhood of Mary and the fatherhood of God in our love for and nurture of those in our care, let's profess our faith.

## *Prayers of the Faithful*

As the people of God, with Mary as our mother too, lets pray for what we need.

For our Holy Father; may he guide Mother Church and her children in faith, generosity and all-embracing tenderness, like Mary does.

For civil leaders that their care of those they lead may be marked by integrity, dedication and concern especially for their weaker and more underprivileged citizens.

For our wonderful youth; may they remain faithful to Mother church and their heavenly Father and Mother, and so be safe from the evil one's wiles, and come to happiness here and hereafter.

For ourselves in our homes, that we may be true fathers and mothers to those in our care and bring them up with tender love, faith and goodness so that they may fulfill their great destiny as God's precious children.

For the sick of our families and larger parish family, that as we pray for and reach out to them in love, they may know the healing care of their heavenly Father and Mother.

For the dead that through our love, prayers and remembrance they may reach at last the arms of their Father and Mother in the home that is the destiny of each one of us as the family of God.

We ask all these our prayers through Christ born of Mary and nurtured in her loving arms forever and ever, amen.

## Reflection

I often reflect on that play *Riders To The Sea,* about a mother on the western seaboard who loses her sons one after the other to the sea. "They're all gone now", she says, her grief overflowing, as her last son's drowned body is brought into the house. Its almost a relief to her, for now she won't have to be suffering and worrying for them as they go out on the cruel sea. Mothers endure much, especially when they lose a child. Mary felt the joy of baby Jesus in her arms at Christmas. But later she had to cradle his dead body in the same way. Mothers, as the play says, endure much in their coming in, and their going out of this world. Lets pray for all mothers and their great role. Hail Mary

# Second Sunday after Christmas B

## Introduction

Christmas is about God with us in the flesh. Our first reading puts it beautifully, he pitched his tent among us. Paul says Jesus brings us all the blessings of God. For he is the "only Son of God full of grace and truth". Lets confess ways we fail that loving Lord.

## Homily

"A savior is born to you, he is Christ the Lord" (Lk. 2:11-12, JB). We celebrate to excess this dream come true. For through long ages people in darkness longed for his peace, justice, love and truth to light up their lives. How privileged we are to live in the end time of the Christ of God. For as Isaiah says, because this child is born for us, the yolk across our shoulders is broken forever. Our drab everyday life is raised to heaven.

Yet the amazing thing about the coming of the long-awaited Messiah is its ordinariness. Angelic portrayals of Joseph and Mary in the stable are overdone. There's no prettiness about that journey to Bethlehem for the census. I was in the Holy Land for seven years and it took me four hours to travel that route by car. Imagine a seventeen year old, heavy with child, walking that distance in winter. Winters in Palestine can be severe; during my last winter there we had ten snowfalls. This trek of Joseph, Mary and Jesus was tough. At the end, they had the added worry of a place to stay for a pregnant and sick girl. That's God's humility; born in a stable with animals keeping him warm. Joseph exhausted and Mary without a warm hospital bed in which to bear her child.

Yet the gospel bursts with joy. Born among the poor, the angels announce the Word made flesh first to the poor. Its to humble shepherds that a message of peace and goodwill for the world, is given. God is with us to end sin, suffering and death. Cynics may say "so what", there's pain and violence in our world still. But they miss the point, that God came down to share in and change all that. But it will take time, Rome wasn't built in a day. The good news is that because of his birth, a new world is taking shape with our help, the just Kingdom of God's Christ child.

But as his birth was hard, so his kingdom's coming will be like a mother's difficult birth, slow and painful. Even after the birth of Jesus everything wasn't hokey dory. Joseph and Mary had to rise in the middle of the night and flee across the desert into Egypt. Mary, sick after birth, feeding the baby every few hours, hurried across a wasteland of bandits and searing heat. Here God shared our suffering. So lets be joyful no matter what.

I'm sure many of us will have hard times during the coming year. Sickness, or death of a loved one, or unemployment, or mounting debts. But none of us can say God doesn't care. He's with us in sorrow and joy, affirming our value and his love, healing and leading us to final victory. We can't love enough that baby come to restore our innocence?

But let's not just marvel at, but live this mystery. Lets be his saving and healing hands to the world. T.S. Eliot's great poem, *The Journey Of The Magi*, sees the wise men, after meeting the baby, going back with a completely new attitude to their pagan lands. Inspired by his love, lets also work to make our homes, localities and world better, kinder and more peaceful. For all else fades away but the Christ child's message is enduring happiness for this world and forever and ever, amen.

So as God's people called to continue spreading his holy kingdom which has gradually, inexorably and amazingly expanded in power worldwide from his first coming, let make our profession of faith.


### Prayers of the faithful

And as members of the Christ child's kingdom of love lets pray for what we need.

For our Holy Father and all church leaders that they make God's holy Word "flesh" in the world of today.

For civil leaders that they may work for justice, peace and prosperity for all, the objectives of Christ's coming.

For our youth that reborn as children of God at Baptism they may dedicate themselves to spreading and making "flesh" in our times the healing and saving reign of God and his all holy Christ.

For ourselves that in our homes we may be the faithful loving hands and face of Christ to our children and all in our care.

For the sick that our real practical care for them may incarnate the love and healing presence of God in their lives.

For the dead that freed from sin and death in Christ, they may, aided by our charitable prayers, come to peace and glory.

We ask all these prayers through the Word made Flesh, our great and glorious lord and Savior, Jesus Christ.

## Reflection

I often think that we're so lucky to born into a Church that makes the Word flesh. It retains the fleshly aspect of faith and worship, without which they are but an abstract show. I mean the candles, statues, Holy water, blessing ourselves, incense, bells etc. For these sensuous aspects of faith and worship unite the body and soul in one concrete reality. For since the Word became "flesh" material reality is also holy. There should be no divide between the body and spirit, as some Puritan Christians imposed. Let's have the wisdom to see this, as we pray to our heavenly Mother who brought us the child Jesus in the flesh, in a humble smelly stable of fleshly animals and their cries. Hail Mary.

# The Epiphany of the Lord B

## Introduction

This feast foresees all people eventually coming to Christ as imaged by the wise men. Isaiah says: "the nations come to your light, and kings to you dawning brightness" (Is. 60:3, JB). The Lord was unknown to many nations in the past but, as Paul says, now the pagans share the same inheritance. We were all once far from God but have now come close in Christ. Lets confess any ways we fail to appreciate our great liberation.

## Homily

This is the feast of the wise of the world. Those like you who come every Sunday to worship God, as the Magi did. Like them your reward is deep joy and wisdom, a grace and peace in Christ that will flower into glory here and hereafter. The psalms say that we should realize the shortness of life so as to gain wisdom of heart. That's our main calling, to be wise in Christ, the Way, the Truth, and the Life.

When I was in the Holy Land I was surprised to see Orthodox Christians celebrating Christmas on the sixth of January. I asked them why. They explained that the deepest message of Christmas is that represented by the kings kneeling at Christ's feet. They prefigure all humanity accepting Christ. As the first reading says: "the nations come to your light, and kings to your dawning brightness" (Is. 60:3, JB). That's God's plan, all people sharing Christ's riches. Its only partially happened as yet. This Christmas billions of every color and nation come to the crib. But many still linger outside his cradle.

That's why there's an urgency about the message of today's feast: the first reading envisages God's house as a house of prayer for all people;

Paul talks of the urgent mission to the pagans; and the responsorial psalm prays that all peoples will praise the Lord (Ps, 147). That is, the Christ came so that all God's children of whatever race, color or nation should come his dawning brightness. Our task to help bring that about, and its a mission that starts at home. For western nations are experiencing a drift in faith matters.

Yet we dare not forget that we were once lost to that light like the Magi before Bethlehem. We were far-flung peoples lost in murky pagan practices that brought fear rather than liberation. Then we were brought the faith, and this fulfilled for us the universal salvation heralded by the Magi. What gifts we have brought to Christ since by our faith and missionary endeavor, but we must beware lest all that fades, and the wisdom of all our saints be in vain. God forbid that we should throw that pearl of great price before swine.

So as we face a new year and go back to school or work, amid lengthening days, let faith spring afresh in our hearts. We, like the wise men, have found Jesus. Lets live joyfully in the new year, that priceless gift we've received. Amid the joys, suffering and challenges of the year - bereavement, sickness, financial problems, whatever - let our wise commitment to God's love and peace flower anew with the spring blossoms.

Lets be faithful to the precious faith we received at Baptism and be truly wise, holding that pearl of great price above even life itself. For faithfulness is the gold frankincense and myrrh we bring to Jesus who embraced the world back to life in the manger. By living his love, peace and good will we can bring our dark world back to life too, and it needs that renewal. For all else passes away and leaves us empty in soul at last on the edge of eternity, but Christ is lord of life, love, truth and peace for a fuller life in this world and forever and ever, amen.

So as God's kingly worshipers in the world of today, bringing him the gifts of our hearts, and spreading his light to those still lost in darkness, let's profess our faith.

## Prayers of the Faithful

And as his wise followers let pray for what we need.

For our Holy Father and all the bishops and leaders of the churches, that steeped in the holiness of Christ, and shunning the corrupt power of the world, they may lead all to the infinite wisdom of the Savior.

For civil leaders that they may know where their secular sway ends and where the spiritual freedom and rights of the people begin, may they respect those rights at all times.

For young people; wise in the ways of God as well as the world, may they bring themselves and others from darkness into the Christ's light, for their happiness in this world and forever.

For ourselves that in our homes we may be wise directors of those in our care, nurturing them in the faith as well as giving them the care, respect and love that befits them as precious children of God in Christ.

For the sick, the aged, the lonely and all those suffering in mind or body, that their faith may raise them up, and through our love and care they may know the healing love of God.

For the dead whose faith is known to God alone that through our continuing love, remembrance and prayers they may be raised up to the eternal glory of the Blessed.

And we ask all these prayers of God, through Christ in the wisdom of the Spirit, who lives and reigns forever and ever, amen.

## Reflection:

There's a true story about a man going to scientific congress by train. A small man was in the carriage saying his rosary. The scientist began giving out to him, saying we believe in science now. At journey's end the scientist said to the little man: "by the way I didn't get your name". "My name", the little man said, "is Louis Pasteur". He, of course, was one of the great scientist of modern times. Even greater, he knew where human knowledge ends, and wisdom begins. The wise men were also scientists, yet ones who used their study of the stars to find Christ. We pray all men will be wise enough to come to that eternal font of grace, truth, and all-embracing wisdom. Hail Mary

# The Baptism of the Lord B

## Introduction

As this Sunday we see Christ's Baptism, lets reflect on our own, when God said to us, "I … have called you to serve the cause of right" (Is. 42:6, JB). This call is for all, the second reading says, "anybody of any nationality who fears God and does what is right is acceptable to him" (10:35, JB). "You are my Son, the beloved" (Mk. 1:11, JB), God says to us at Baptism what he said to Jesus. Lets confess if we fail to live our Baptismal vows.

## Homily

What a gift Baptism is. A tiny person becomes God's child, sheltered forever from evil and death. Our Gospel shows this in Jesus's own Baptism. When I was in the Holy Land a group of us relived that experience. In the desert, off with our shoes and into cool Jordan water; knobbly knees, varicose veins and all. As water poured over me I imagined the gospel scene; the rough figure of John, crowds waiting to have cleansing water poured over them. Then a magnetic person comes, ordinary yet full of God's glory. A dove swoops. The Father can't contain himself; he shouts: "This is my Son, the beloved". At our Baptism God says to us also; you are my beloved son, my beloved daughter, for he loves us as he loved Jesus. We in turn should live as his children, and cherish all our brothers and sisters in him, regardless of color or nation, for that's our Baptismal calling.

But in Baptism we receive two other great vocations. Firstly, to be holy as our heavenly Father is, and secondly, to spread the faith to others. Whether we're farmers, shopkeeper, nurses, street cleaners, or the unemployed, as Vatican 11 says, we all receive the same Spirit at Baptism and we're all given two great tasks: to be holy, and to help build God's kingdom as part of his holy church.

For at Baptism we were anointed as priests and prophets to transform the face of the earth. We may say that's impossible. No! We've God's great power to do it in the Spirit that is given to us. Young or old, sick or well, working or pensioners we never retire from that calling, to be Christ's life-long prophets to the world, faithful worshiping members of his church, and everyday saints. For its within that community of faith and worship that our Baptismal promise comes to full flower; the me and God alone view is foolish. So is the view that we just have to avoid sin to live our Baptism; Baptism gives us a much more positive role, to be active workers for the church and good in the world

That's why I say to people at confession, don't list pecadillos. Confess rather the ways you failed to live up to your Baptismal calling to work actively for Christ and his church. Someone said to me once, "I don't practice the faith but I harm to no one". Our morality is not just about avoiding harm, its about doing as much good as we can. Indeed, in the power of the Spirit we're to change the very face of the earth for Christ.

What we should confess then are the problems and issues holding back our progress in active faith and love. For its only through us that the world can become the Kingdom of God in Christ. That's the why of the sacraments; to give us the grace we need to grow in God. For the really important thing is not our external wealth, but our inner riches. And the hard values of the world of which Satan is lord fade to ashes at last and leave us empty before eternity, but Christ is lord of love, goodness, peace, happiness, beauty and salvation both for this world's happiness and forever and ever, amen.

So as God's infinitely valuable children, made so at Baptism, serving all that's good and holy in the world as part of a timeless vocation, we profess our faith.

## Prayers of the Faithful

As glorious children of a loving Father lets ask him with confidence for our deepest needs.

For our Holy Father, may he lead the people of God with fatherly care and be blessed by good health and fruitful ministry.

For civil leaders that they may govern the people with wisdom integrity and justice for all, especially the poor.

For our young people born again by water and the Holy Spirit, that they may live up to their Baptismal and Confirmation vows, to make a huge difference by their lives.

For ourselves in our homes, workplaces and community; may we serve Christ, his church and all that's good as we promised when we became his children, and were anointed as priests and prophets at Baptism.

For the sick, may they be comforted and healed by the presence of God in their lives and through our care know his special love.

For the dead who wore the white garment of Christ at Baptism and at other times in their life's journey, that they may come to the resurrection it symbolizes, aided by our prayers.

We ask all these prayers of the Father as his beloved sons through Christ Our Lord, amen.

## Reflection

Water is a wonderful thing; it cleanses, sustains and nourishes us. I myself often visit Torc waterfall in Killarney. As I listen to the water there, it roars of foams in wet weather, it soothes my soul, and evokes the presence of God, as all beautiful things in nature do. But, as the poet says, we don't always pay attention to beauty around us. Getting and spending, we don't have time to see and grasp beauty. Lets ask God to give us the grace to pause and come into contact with the good earth every so often, for he is in the glorious creation all around us. We ask his holy mother to help us in this. Hail Mary

# Ash Wednesday B

## Introduction

Lent has come again, and our readings echo the themes of prayer, fasting and almsgiving to prepare for Christ's resurrection. Lets confess our sins as we begin Lent's renewal.

## Homily

Welcome to our Special Ash Wednesday mass. You know the story of Lourdes. There was a small girl Bernadette in France. Her family was poor and they lived in one small dark room. They had to gather sticks for a fire to heat the room in winter and Bernadette was often sick because they were living in such conditions, with scanty food to eat. One day her mother sent her up the mountain to get some sticks for the fire to cook the bit of soup they had for lunch. While gathering the sticks she suddenly saw a great white light, and in it a beautiful lady, who later told her that she was The Immaculate Conception, a term Bernadette couldn't have known. Mary told Bernadette to get people to build a church there where people would come to pray and be healed. And she told Bernadette that people should do penance and pray for the conversion of sinners. Such penance, giving up something to show our love for God and to help him bring all to faith, is also part of Lent. With prayer and charity its how we purify ourselves and prepare for Easter. During 40 days of Lent we fast, pray, and give something to help poor people.

In effect, Lent features the main things Our Lady asked of Bernadette. But why forty days? Because Jesus spent 40 days in the desert praying and fasting before he began his public life. And why do we begin with Ash Wednesday, why the ashes. Because ashes are a sign in the Bible of turning from sin to God. A story from the Bible Illustrates this, the story of Jonah.

In Jonah's time there was a great city called Nineveh, and it was a den of iniquity. God told Jonah to go to it, and tell the people to change. At first Jonah refused to do what God asked; he was afraid that if he went to Nineveh the people would kill him, so he ran away. But when he was in the boat fleeing from God a great storm came, and the sailors asked why God send the storm. Jonah said it was his fault, and asked them to throw him into the water so that the storm would stop. They did so, and a big fish swallowed him up. The big fish took Jonah, who was still alive in its belly, to a place near Nineveh, and cast him up on the shore. Jonah realized he'd have no peace until he did what God asked.

He went to Nineveh and said the lord was angry with them, and told them to repent so that God wouldn't destroy the city. Touched, the king of Nineveh repented, left his palace, put ashes on his head, and told the people to do the same. We image a similar conversion when we wear ashes at the beginning of Lent. We say we're going to change ungodly disordered things in our life to prepare for Jesus's coming at Easter, when he called us out of darkness into God's light. So today we put the ashes on our forehead to show that we want to begin Lent in a spirit of penance, prayer and concern for the poor.

So in that spirit of repentant renewal, lets come forward now for the ashes.

And now with the sign of the ashes on our heads we pray that this Lent and Easter may be a special time of prayer, penance and giving to the poor, to show that we want to be faithful followers of Jesus and his church; and we profess our faith anew.


## *Prayers of the Faithful*

As God's people, who depend on his care, lets pray for what we need this Lent.

For all people around the world, that they may be converted to God and to peace and to all that's good at this time of grace.

For the leaders of the churches at this time, that they may never tire of calling the people of the world to peace and holiness.

For our civil leaders that like the ruler of Nineveh, they may keep God in their lives, and rule with moral integrity.

For youth, that this Lent may be a special time of re-commitment for them to what they promised at Baptism and Confirmation.

For ourselves that God may bless us this Lent and Easter with his special grace, and that we may draw closer to him and to each other within our families.

For the sick and the poor that through our little efforts to help, they may, like Bernadette's family, come to better conditions.

For the dead that they may come to the fullness of life in heaven with the help our continuing charitable prayers.

And we ask all these our prayers through Christ Our Lord, amen

## Reflection

I suppose the story of Christ in the desert is each person's story. For the key choice we all face, is to serve God or mammon, to serve others or ourselves alone. Christ went into the wilderness to fast and pray to resist these temptations. Because he was human as well as divine, the temptations were real. So he can identify with us in our weakness. Lets pray to Mother Mary that she will give us the same strength as Christ had, as we're helped by this sacred time of Lent and its desert disciplines. Hail Mary

# First Sunday of Lent B

## Introduction

Today we begin our Lenten trinity of fasting, prayer and almsgiving. The first reading recalls the flood, when people's godless evil brought destruction. Jesus tells us to repent and believe lest we die too. Lent's prayer, fasting and almsgiving puts us on that path; it strengthens us to ward off Satan's wiles. In a repentant spirit lets confess our sins.

## Homily

Perhaps you know St. Augustine's story. A great figure in the Roman empire, in early life he was a pagan. His mother Monica, a Christian, prayed with tears for his conversion. One day in his garden, feeling empty inside, he heard a child's voice say: "take up and read". He picked up a bible from the table, and it opened at Paul's advice to cast off the old man of sin and put on the Lord Jesus. Tears poured down his cheeks and joy entered his heart. He left worldly ways, and became one of the greatest bishops, theologians and saints the church has produced.

Here's a personal response to today's gospel call to repent and believe. Augustine, after years of seeking happiness in worldly pursuits, came alive in the Spirit. Like Christ in the wilderness, he finally saw through the devil's temptation, and turned away from unrestrained worldly pleasure and self-seeking. Lent challenges us to do the same. But it can be difficult today when a new western pagan empire lures us from faith and its values. Lent provides us with an opportunity to answer Christ's call to repent in this context.

For that's a struggle we must keep up, if we're to attain real happiness in this world and the next. Rather than give in to the world, the flesh, and the Devil, our constant challenge is to deepen our life as members of a holy people. To help us achieve this the church puts before us each Lent Christ's death, Resurrection and Second Coming. It tells us to keep us the good fight, so that we'll go our to meet Christ with all the saints at last.

But that struggle to be faithful isn't easy today. The evil one also has his prophets, in the media and elsewhere, that would lead us and our youth to the flood. So we need to keep Christ's invitation to life before us, to purify our hearts with prayer, fasting and almsgiving as a preparation for our own Easter resurrection. As the Baptism prayer says, the challenge is to keep our white garment of faith and goodness on, so that we'll go out to meet Jesus with all saints. Now is the is the day of salvation, Paul reminds us, and Lent is such a day, when the dawn light of Christ comes into our hearts once more.

The air stirs with spring now. Lent asks us to leave behind a soul winter. To revive the spring innocence we had as the baby baptized, when we put on the white garment of Christ. I myself say often say the beautiful words of the Miserere: "God create a clean heart in me, put into me a new and constant spirit" (Ps. 51:10, JB). Lets pray for a spring of faith, new fresh green shoots of the Spirit in our lives, for that's where lasting joy is.

That's what Augustine celebrates in his classic work, *The Confessions*. He confesses not sin, but his joy in the faith. We're called to similar joyful Christian conversion this Lent and Easter through fasting, almsgiving and prayer. What saved Augustine? The prayers of his mother. In the same way we should pray for those we love. To bring them to happiness in this world and the next. For the things of this world fade to dust at last, but Christ is lord of love, goodness, happiness, beauty, and salvation for this world and forever and ever, amen. So as God's people called to renew our souls and rise at Easter with Christ by prayer, fasting and good works now, we profess our faith anew.

### Prayers of the Faithful

As the people of God lets pray for what we need this Lent.

For our Holy Father and all the leaders of the church, that they may continue to call all to repent and believe.

For civil leaders that they govern all with integrity and impartiality, and foster people's spiritual welfare above all, for that is real life for this world and the next.

For our youth, that turning to prayer, fasting and almsgiving this Lent, they may know the deep joy of self-giving in Christ.

For ourselves that in our homes this Lent we may encourage some extra prayers, giving up of some luxury, and setting aside of some of our surplus money to help the poor at home and abroad.

For the sick; through our sacrifice of some of our time to help aged or sick relatives may we gain a great reward in heaven.

For the dead that their sufferings over, they may come to their heavenly home with the help of our communal and personal prayer.

We ask all these prayers through Christ who lives and reigns forever, amen.

## Reflection

The gospel says that man does not live on bread alone. The key temptation in every age is to put our whole trust in passing earthly things. I often think that the debt crisis was partly due to that. As someone said recently, its like the flood that swept away corruption, or the Tower of Babel that came tumbling down around the ears of arrogant men. Certainly the tower of godless human pride, greed and arrogance always topples to dust in the long run. Lets pray to Mother Mary that we'll avoid all that. Hail Mary

# Second Sunday of Lent B

## Introduction

This Sunday features Christ's transfiguration. Usually his divinity was hidden, but on Tabor it shone out for all to see. The Father even appeared and said: "this is my Son, the beloved, listen to him" (Mk. 9:8, JB). Lets confess any failure to listen to God's voice.

## Homily

Rose Kennedy, the matriarch of the great Kennedy clan, states (her words are on a plaque in the rose garden in Tralee): "it is interesting to reflect on what has made my life even with its moments of pain, an essentially happy one; I have come to the conclusion that the most important element in human life is faith". Tolstoy, the author of *War And Peace*, came to the same conclusion; for great minds think alike.

At this time of the year, struggling towards Spring, with a lot of sad things happening in the world, we too should be wise enough to listen to God's voice, and so find the radiant light that will carry us through life's ups and downs. On Tabor the spirit came on Jesus and the Father said: "This is my Son, the beloved, listen to him". If we do listen, light will flood our lives, and we'll find the timeless happiness our hearts seek.

We already opened our hearts to his light at Baptism, when we became his children and received the Spirit. May his Word live in our hearts, through mass, personal prayer, the sacraments; spreading the faith, and being that wonderful word, the faithful. At Baptism and Confirmation we promised to be that, in word and deed; let's renew that vow this Lent.

"This is my Son, the beloved, listen to him". The sad causalities of our age are those who stopped listening to Christ. Deceived by secular propaganda, they let worldliness and Satanic arrogance turn their light into darkness. But scripture warns that it profits nothing for a man to gain the whole world, and lose his soul. Wise people know that godless world's values leave us dead inside, but faith is our everlasting riches.

Which reminds me of the testimony of a Russian believer who spent 15 years in a Siberian labor camps during the communist era. She says that it wasn't so much that she kept the faith, but that the faith kept her alive in every way. So faith is more than believing. Its clinging to God amid life's sufferings; its listening to Christ, the Way and the Truth; Its opening our hearts to infinite grace; its living in the light of the great Holy Spirit.

I often wonder why so many commit suicide nowadays. Perhaps one reason is that increasingly deprived of all that by a hard secular society, in crises they've no solid ground of God to stand on. So I say to parents, appreciate the gift your children receive at Baptism, Holy Communion and Confirmation. For it alone can light them through life's darknesses unto eternal life. Tolstoy, Rose Kennedy and billions of Saints since knew this. As baptized faithful lets renew that light within us this Lent so as to rise with Christ at Easter. For all else turns to dust and ashes at last and leaves us empty, but he is lord of love, peace, happiness and salvation, both for this world, and forever and ever, amen.

So as Gods gathered family, resolving anew this Lent to listen to Christ, to live in the light of his ageless love, and be his church's glorious faithful, lets profess our faith.

## Prayers of the faithful

The just man lives by faith, scripture says: as God's people, listening to and trusting in him, we ask for what we need.

For the Holy Father and bishops of the churches, that they may listen to Christ, and radiating trust in him, bring the church and the world to his glorious light.

For those struggling in the darkness of unbelief, especially our youth, may their doubts be dispelled; like the apostles on Tabor; may they listen to Christ and experience his beauty, truth and timeless radiance, to light up their lives forever.

For parents and teachers, that they may hand on faith in Jesus, the risen light of the world, to the young people of our time.

For those who are sick, lonely or oppressed; may the light of Christ that shone out so powerfully on Tabor light up their lives and may they experience his love through our care for them.

For the dead, especially those who have died recently. or those whose anniversaries occur at this time. May they come into the light, peace and happiness of their heavenly home.

Heavenly Father, as we journey through this vale of joys and tears, help us to listen to Christ and experience his presence in the people around us, and in the events of daily life. We ask this through Christ Our Lord, in the power of his Holy Spirit, amen.

## *Reflection:*

Once speaking in school about faith, I saw a child was miles away. He had a phone and was texting away the whole time. "This my Son, the beloved, listen to him", God says. It can be difficult to do so amid a host of modern distractions - TV, Radio, Video Games, mobile phones, computer tablets. We can be so immersed in these that all other voices fade, especially that of God. So its wise to set aside a quiet time every day to commune with our family, nature and the Lord. Each year I climb a famous holy mountain, and there the Lord speaks to me like he did to the apostles on Tabor. Lets all have a mountain, a room, a sacred place at home and in the church each Sunday, where we can pray and feel Christ's presence raising us up to glorious light and peace. Hail Mary

# Third Sunday of Lent B

## Introduction:

In our gospel Christ drives out traders who were ripping off poor Temple devotees. Yet, because this interfered with the Pharisees' lucrative Temple profits, they had him killed. Greed is as ruthless in our world. Lets repent of any greed excesses in our own lives.

## Homily

What's the most important part of the mass? Of course the communion. But after that some would say the dismissal: "Let us go forth ... to love and serve the Lord". In effect, our mass attendance is a sham if we don't live out its values in daily lives. Our religious commitment must be more than the hypocritical show of the Pharisees, who pretended to serve God, but in fact used their religious positions for sordid gain. They manipulated the difference in money exchange so that the devout poor paid exorbitant prices for offerings. No wonder Christ was filled with righteous anger, shouting: "take all this out of here and stop turning my Father's house into a market" (Jn. 2:16-17, JB).

We too can profess faith, and yet use greedy or cruel methods in business; so our faith becomes a mockery, rather than a real service of God. Of course much of this may come from human weakness: we want to follow God's way, but pressure from worldly norms can be stronger. That's why God gives us Christ, scripture, and the church as guides. With their help and God's grace we can resist temptations to exploit people.

And we must do so, for as Christians, ultimately we're more than citizens of the world. In Christ's power we must at least try to live the values inherent in our belief and worship. Of course where we fail to to do so, we have access to his forgiveness. But that too is hypocritical, if we do not continue to struggle for a wholesome integrity of life.

But why persist in this effort to obey God rather than the corrupt world. Basically because its for our soul's health and happiness here, and its eternal salvation. God doesn't give us laws because he's a policeman; he gives sound guidance because he wants our happiness. The 10 commandments were given to the Jews as their final liberation from slavery. That's also true of Christ's commands; they free us to be light not darkness to the world. Drug dealers with pads in Spain, killing off opposition, may have money but how are they inside? True peace and light is not in soul-destroying riches, but in doing what's right. License leads to enslaving habits, harming us and society, but Christ sets us free.

It was to so free the corrupted Temple sellers, as well as zeal for his Father's house, that he cleansed the dirty money-grubbing Temple. Lets cleanse ourselves of any such corruption in our lives, and return to God's love; lets save the world's soul in saving our own. Lets build his kingdom of love, peace, justice and truth in our age too.

For our so-called liberal and hard capitalist age can be like the buyers in the Temple. It too would serve false enslaving gods of money and greed, and trample on the weak in the process; like taking today from old-age pensioners to give to rich bondholders. And that world would also keep our eyes focused on the earth, never allowing them to look up to the stars. Christ came to cleanse our temple, so that we might live a fine, free, just life. At this mass dismissal lets go out to do so, the temple of our hearts cleansed of greed, violence and immoral living to serve the living God of timeless light. For the corrupt world's ways lead but to ashes and dust at last, but he is the Way, the Truth, and the Life for our freedom and happiness in this world, and forever and ever, amen.

So as God's own, cleansing our inner temple from all enslavements to money, power and exploitation of others, so as to rise with Christ at Easter, lets profess our faith.

## Prayers of the Faithful

We pray for our Holy Father and all the leaders of the churches that they may cleanse the world today, and make it a real Temple that serves God in the poor.

For the civil leaders that they may not worship the gods of corrupt politics, gain, and global money interests, but serve the people, especially the poor, in justice and integrity.

For ourselves, at work or at home, may we deal with those under us with fiscal and other forms of integrity, justice and love.

For the sick, the old, the lonely and the needy that they may know the love of Christ through our love and care for them.

For the dead that cleansed of all evil they may attain to their heavenly home with the help of our prayers and pure offerings.

And we ask all these prayers through Christ who showed us in the cleansing of the temple to the way to true worship of God and true honest service of the world and fellow human beings, amen.

## Reflection:

I sometime think that tackling abuse scandals in the church is a kind of cleansing of the temple. Its forcing us to live up to the real essence of our Christian calling, the care of the young, the weak and the vulnerable. A hierarchical church of power and arrogance, living in palaces, and protecting those who prey on the innocent, is a worldly hypocritical church like that of the Pharisees. We must sweep all that away, and replace it with a humble serving Christian church for our challenging times. For Christ says those who lead in his church shouldn't lord it over others, but be humble servants of all in truth. Lets wash each other's feet, as Christ did, in a simple, integral and humble church. Hail Mary

# Fourth Sunday in Lent B

## Introduction

Our scripture this Sunday sees faith as ongoing conversion. Jeremiah describes the covenant with God as renewed heart commitment, and Christ talks of drawing all to himself in newness of life and faith. Lets confess any refusal of continual conversion, as at Lent.

## Homily

I'm sure you know the story of the conversion of St. Paul. He persecuted the early church, and even had some of its members, like St. Stephen, stoned to death. Yet on his way to Damascus, he tells us, a light of Christ shone around him, and a voice said, why are you persecuting me. After this Paul was a different man, wearing himself out in the service of Christ, in a great mission to the pagans of the day. His conversion led to a great conversion of innumerable communities for Christ. The same is true of the conversion of St. Augustine, or St. Ignatius, or St. Francis. They heard the voice of God and it changed their lives, and the world around them, for good. In the case of Francis, the Franciscan Order and that of St. Clare were born, which still guide us today. Here we have the mystery of conversion and its ongoing fruits such as Christ describes in today's gospel.

As Christ says to Nicodemus, all who want to live the faith must do the same, come out into the light so that what they do is done in God. Paul and Francis saw after years of seeking fulfillment in vain self-glorification, where happiness really lay. Lets do the same this Lent. Flawed human beings, lets recommit ourselves to serving God and others in love. Every Christian needs conversion and frequent renewal, since following Christ is a constant struggle to be freed from the powerful world of darkness, present since the fall.

Such freedom from evil in Christ is our lasting fullness of life and joy. To convince us of this, the church puts before us at this time of year not only Christ's resurrection but also his Second Coming at the end of time. For then he will lead all those who have kept up the struggle of faith, to a final great reward. In that sense its good to keep that final coming before our eyes. So that, as the Baptism prayer says, we'll be always ready to go out to meet Christ with all the saints, wearing the stainless white robe of the blessed.

That's why this lenten season calls us out of the dark of an inner winter to a new spring in our hearts and souls. It calls us to conversion and renewal so that whenever the Lord comes he'll find us free from fallen burdens. I myself say often the words of psalm 51: "create a clean heart in me ... do not deprive me of your Holy Spirit" (10-11, JB). Each of us needs to cling for dear life to that Spirit of holiness we received at Baptism.

Ignatius of Loyola is a another who did just that; early in life, as a soldier he pursued fulfillment in military glory. But when injured, he discovered not only repentance but the deeper love of serving God. From this he forged his book of *Spiritual Exercises* to guide his Jesuits, and all searching souls, to find God in their deep authentic feelings.

I read recently of Liam Neeson, the actor. During a crisis in his Catholic faith, he found his way back through the *Exercises*. Even doubts in our faith, can be a call to new deeper conversion and commitment. Each Lent invites us to so deepen our faith. For now is the acceptable time, now is the day of salvation. As Paul, Francis and Ignatius realized, vain worldly pursuits cannot fully satisfy the heart. They fade to dust and ashes at last, but Christ is peace, happiness, truth and salvation for this world and forever and ever, amen.

So as God's own called to come anew into Christ's light this Lent, and walk with ever renewed hearts in his light, lets profess our faith.

## Prayers of the Faithful

As the people of God lets pray for all the things we need to keep us secure in the light of God and in the arms of holy church.

For the church that having received the glory of Christ itself, it may spread its message of hope and love to the whole world.

For our civil leaders that they may be lights of justice integrity and truth to those they govern.

For youth, that, like St.Francis, they may discover the real joy of following Christ and serving others and the church selflessly.

For parents that they may inspire their children in the faith by their words but above all by example, this Lent and always.

For the sick and the needy in body, mind or soul, that we may be the healing hands of Christ to them through our caring love.

For the dead that freed from their bonds they may come safely to their heavenly home with the help of our prayers.

And we ask all these our prayers through Christ who, glorified by the Father, intercedes for us forever in heaven, amen.

## Reflection:

Christians owe much to the early church in Ireland after Patrick. It brought learning and Christian civilization back to Europe in the dark ages. It was in Ireland that a bell was first used to call people to prayer, and it was in early monastic churches there that individual confession came into being. Before that penance was communal; people were excluded from the Christian community until they had expiated their sins. But in the monasteries the confessor was anam cara, a soul friend. This Lent lets use the gift of confession to cleanse our souls and make fresh progress in our spiritual life. Hail Mary.

# Fifth Sunday of Lent B

## Introduction:

"When I am lifted up from the earth I'll draw all men to myself". Our Gospel sees Christ anticipating the cross and its result, the universal new covenant Jeremiah foretells in the first reading. We're called to dedicated service of our crucified Lord so that we'll be part of his redeemed humanity. Conscious of failures in that, lets confess our sins.

## Homily

Recently on TV, a presenter interviewed youngsters who had camped for days in the cold to get tickets to a pop concert. They suffered for the one they loved. Our reading asks us to do the same for Christ. His great pop show on the cross should win our total worship, so that in the final great light-filled concert of heaven we will share in his glory.

For the cross is both a tragedy and a triumph. Christ says that its only when lifted up on the cross that he will draw all humankind to himself. All human cruelty, Satanic power and worldly corruption were conquered when Christ offered his back to those to those who would strike him, his cheeks to those who would tear out his beard. That's the mystery of faith, our triumph through the Savior's torments.

That is, Christ is the ultimate world pop star on the cross. As supreme lover and Lord he mounts the tree, as in the old Anglo-Saxon poem, *The Dream Of The Rood*, where he is presented as a great warrior, mounting the cross, and stretching his arms to to encompass the four corners of the earth. Not understanding this triumph, the apostles found Christ's talk of the cross shocking. They wanted him to be a worldly political Messiah and themselves top dogs at his side. They were baffled when he chose instead the scriptural role of suffering servant of God and humanity. They didn't understand that true leadership is loving suffering service.

If leaders in society understood this, we wouldn't be in the mess we're in now. That's what Christ talks about when he says that he who hates his life in this world will keep it for eternal life. Only after Pentecost did the apostles make that choice, to offer their very lives in furthering Christ's saving mission.

Our gospel says to do likewise; to choose service of God and others even if it hurts: getting up on Sunday when its easier to lie in bed; visiting sick relative when we want to go to the pub; being faithful to spouse and children in total self-giving; dedicating ourselves to the celibate priesthood or religious life without stint. There's always some dying to self involved in the heroic service of God and others to which we're called.

But in the long run this brings greater glory. Like the grain that dies to bear fruit, there's no lasting Christian joy without the cross. Christ says that those who love him must be prepared to go down the same road of suffering love as he trod. For he knows that in doing so all gain fuller life. That's true of the Christian calling in every age. Standing up for his church in the present climate of increasingly militant secularism requires courage. So does standing against the institutional church itself when its witness is anti-Christian.

For in every age the chief temptation church and people face is to reject the cross of life for the worldly way of death. Look at the many who now abandon faith and become slaves of materialism, drugs, immoral living and worldly greed. There's more life in the celibate priest, the humble religious, the dedicated lay person, the faithful partner in marriage. Suffering self-giving love saves; all else is dust and ashes. Ruthless pursuit of self at all costs may brings temporary pleasure but ultimately it destroys the soul. By the cross Christ overthrew that and its lord Satan. For he wanted us to realize that worldly self-serving values fade to ashes at last, but on the cross of love, we're lords of beauty, truth, grace, peace and salvation for happiness in this world and forever and ever, amen.

So as God's own called to the cross, to self-giving service of God and others for the world's redemption and to enrich our souls, lets profess our faith.

## *Prayers of the faithful*

For church leaders, especially the Pope, that they may abandon pomp and power to fulfill their Gospel role of humble service of God and others, and so redeem the world.

For civil leaders that they may show courage, integrity and total dedication in building up the earthly city in their care.

For ourselves that we may be dedicated to Christ and his church despite the sacrifices this entails, for it is the way of life and salvation for us and the world around us.

For our young people that they may follow Christ in bearing the crosses of faith and loving service of others so as to come like him to the glorious resurrection of the just.

For the sick of our community that they may find comfort in their faith and through our care experience the love of Christ who suffering to free and raise up the oppressed.

For the dead, that the world's trials over and having kept the faith, they may reap the rewards of faithfulness in the happiness of the life to come with their loving Savior.

We ask these prayers through the same Christ who raised up on the cross brought all people to salvation, and who is lord of life, peace, faith, and hope for humankind forever and ever, amen.

## *Reflection:*

You may know the story of Padre Pio the modern mystic. He wore blood-soaked bandages on his hands which were supposed to bear the marks of the nails that pierced Christ. Whether or not that is true is not important. What is, is that he suffered ill-health all his life and offered his suffering every day in union with the suffering Christ. Through this dedication he became a great light to his day and still inspires many people. All of us have crosses, notably illnesses of various kinds, but like Padre Pio if we offer them up they can become a great light for the world. We pray to Mary for that grace. Hail Mary.

# Palm Sunday

## Introduction

As in the liturgy, blessing of the palms.

## Homily

Do you remember the old stations of the cross; they were full of sweat and blood, and a sorrowful Savior rebuking us for our sins. They were both right, and yet at another level mistaken. The cross was hard, yes, but it was also a site of joyful triumph, the triumph of self-giving love. It tells us amazingly what God is like, a being of infinite suffering love for us. That is why we began this mass with the celebration of Christ as king, riding in triumph into Jerusalem, but immediately went on to read *The Passion*.

It seems a contradiction but in fact it is not. For Christ, in the words of the old hymn, is "king of love on Calvary". He made that choice right at the beginning of his ministry, in the desert, when the devil tempted him to be a king who serves his own desires, power and glory. He chose instead to be the suffering servant, despite the urgings of the apostles also that he should be a glory-seeking political Messiah. Christ had to rebuke Peter and tell him to get behind him, Satan; he'd lure Christ from the cross also.

And that's the lesson for us. If we want to be Christ's followers, we too must be suffering servants of God and others, self-giving rather than ruthlessly self-centered. Christ gave all in saving love, to the last drop of his blood, and the challenge is passed on to us to do likewise, for Christ tells us to to love one another as he loved you. He loved us until he'd nothing left except his very soul, which he also gave up at last.

But the main temptation the church and each Christians faces is the temptation to dodge the cross; to serve our own power, wealth and glory ruthlessly, to forget our duty to God and others. So we would avoid the cross of doing what is right; of priestly celibacy, of religious life lived in humility, of poverty and obedience; of being humble lay servants of God in the community; of marriage faithfulness; of generous giving charity. We avoid them because our world tells us to live it up at all costs, to cheat as much as we can, to be assertive and wholly selfish.

That film *Witness*, about an Amish boy who witnesses a brutal murder for gain, and who is protected by an incorruptible cop, is an indictment of modern society's worst aspects of greed and violence. As Christians, of course, we shouldn't go back to a dated world, but we can live apart from today's worst amoral and aspiritual elements. Indeed we must do so, for any society that neglects the soul, or man's thirst for what is right and true, is bound to be a failure to that extent. Doubtless, that is why we have all this reactive fundamentalism and religious extremism, due to people's spiritual and moral frustration, their sense of the exclusion of their deeper needs in a harsh secularist environment where money is god, and unrestrained pleasure and self-satisfaction idols served at all costs. Christian should have the best of both worlds; live in the contemporary world and enjoy its progress, and liberal freedoms, but also witness against its evils.

For there are so many wonderful things in modern society – from the latest technologies, to ease of travel and communication, to the joys of the global village, to grand progressive freedoms. But there are also elements that jar, and are contrary to the way to happiness here and hereafter that we crave, the way of love, beauty, truth and graceful living in God. All that's summed up in Christ's entry into Jerusalem; and in the palms laid before him, the ageless glory of recognizing, and welcoming God into our city.

God raised Jesus up to be Lord and Savior after he became king of love on Calvary. His example of humble self-giving love and sacrifice is what saves, so its what he calls us to. For the cruel, arrogant, utterly selfish ways of the world, of which Satan is lord, are false lures. They leave us empty here, fade to dust and ashes at last, and leave us with empty souls on eternity's shore. But Christ is lord of love, truth, beauty, happiness, grace and salvation on the cross, both for this life's deeper happiness, and forever and ever. Suffering with him in keeping faith, unto untold spiritual riches, and doing what's right to redeem the times, we'll also be glorified at God's right hand, forever and ever, amen.

***Prayers and the rest as in the liturgy***

# Holy Thursday B

## Introduction

A family meal is holy, it binds parents and children together. Christ's supper is similar, it binds us to him and each other. Preparing to eat that supper, we remember our first holy communicants, who like the apostles will share bread with the lord in May, and we welcome Eucharistic ministers to be commissioned. And as we eat together, lets confess any ways we fail to live in loving communion with God and those around us.

## Homily

"This is my body which will be given for you" (Lk. 22:19, JB). Christ's cross and Eucharist are linked. The mass is the cross constantly re-enacted to take away our sins. Like the apostles at the Last Supper we too pray, read scripture, and sing. This is our life, for Christ himself says that unless we eat his flesh and drink his blood we won't have life in us. But he or she who eats his flesh and drinks his blood has eternal life and will be raised up on the last day. No wonder our fathers in hard times walked barefoot to mass.

They were doing what Christians did from the church's origins. The Acts Of The Apostles tell how the early church members met for the prayers, hymns, and the breaking of bread, the old name for the Eucharist. This communion gave them their Christian identity; it also gives us our identity. We can pray at home, but, except for old age or sickness, it can't replace Sunday worship as part of Christ's body. And it must be on Sunday, because that's when Christ rose from the dead; when receiving his body we're raised us too. Coming together each Sunday we become his holy people. For going to the altar and saying amen to "the body of Christ", we affirm both his Real Presence for us and that *we are his body* gathered in church. For faith is never just me and God; its me as a member of Christ's body; this is what empowers us to go live the faith, in charity.

And that's why the washing of the feet is also a vital part of our ceremony tonight. Each communion should inspire us to bring Christ to the world through humble service. By washing the disciples' feet Christ said that communion with him should lead to humble service of God and others. Helping famine victims abroad and spreading charity around us.

But this lesson is especially meant for an institutional church, that too often serves its own wealth and glory rather than washing the feet of God's needy children in the world. Its good that I'm washing the feet of God's children tonight, for the church should do humble penance for its sins against children in recent times. That was a horrible counter witness to the Eucharist. For Christ washed the feet of his apostles to teach church leaders that their role is to be slaves of all God's children, especially the poor and weak. If our mass doesn't lead to such active humble love its an empty ritual; an elaborate lie.

So let our enactment of the Last Supper, in which Jesus instituted the Eucharist, commit us both to life-long Sunday mass and communion, and to a life of humble charity. So that communion may enrich and make us part of eternal life, and enable us to be his healing hands to the world. Asking us to do this in memory of him, Christ asks us to receive him every Sunday, and then go out and wash his needy children's feet. For this world's hard values of which Satan is lord crucifies the weak, vulnerable and frail in our midst. But empowered by this mass, we're asked to be Christ's healing hands of love, happiness and salvation to a needy world forever and ever, amen.

So as God's people gathered on this holy night lets wash feet as a sign of our commitment to the mass, and to humble service of God and others; lets commit ourselves in our small way to turning the cruel sinful world into a humble kingdom of love in Christ.

And having washed the feet, lets affirm our faith with humbler hearts.

## *Prayers of the Faithful*

And as a Eucharistic people lets pray confidently for our needs.

For the church throughout the world that in its great Eucharistic mission it may humbly serve all the children of God, and so build up God's healing kingdom in our needy world.

For civil leaders that they too may humbly serve all the people, especially the poor and most vulnerable in society.

For ourselves that we may constantly give thanks to God for the great gifts of the mass and communion, and spread the dazzling light we receive there to all we meet.

For youth, may they be faithful to Christ who gave all for them, offering himself in the Eucharist as their food of life; may they share in this banquet every Sunday, for their deeper soul happiness here, and forever in the eternal banquet of the Blessed.

For our Eucharistic Ministers who so unselfishly give of themselves to serve God's people that they may be blessed in their ministry and lives in every way.

This holy night we ask God to inspire more young people to become priests, religious and lay ministers in the church.

For the sick, the aged, and the housebound, may they find healing and comfort in the prayers and care of those who help them.

For our dead who enjoy the banquet of eternal life prefigured by their sharing in the communion banquet already in this life.

We ask these prayers on this Holy night of the Last Supper with joyful trust in his enduring love for us here in the mass, amen.

## Reflection

They asked Napoleon when he was dying, what was his happiest moment, "My first Holy Communion", he replied. At last he realized what the greatest thing in the world is, to be one with the Lord. Lets always cherish this gift of his loving presence. Hail Mary.

# Good Friday B

## Introduction:

As in the liturgy.

## Homily

All human life is here, the *News of the World* used to say. That's so true of the crucifixion story. All human life, mainly at its worst, is there: vicarious cruelty; unjust and barbaric torture of the innocent; corrupt law; the envy and vindictiveness of the Jewish authorities; the heartless betrayal of a close friend for money by Judas; the cowardice of Peter and the apostles in abandoning and denying their lord; the violence of the mob; the greed of the soldiers who dice for Jesus's clothes as he dies. Maybe that why some objected to Gibson's film, *The Passion Of The Christ*, it shows us in the raw.

Much of this human cruelty and vice still goes on, in our so-called enlightened world: from Hiroshima, to agent orange in Vietnam, to the torture of soldiers in Iraq? It all happens over and over again, as that song about the first world war, *The Green Fields Of France*, by the Furies, says. If one listens to the news, with its daily accounts of atrocities all over the world, one soon realizes that human nature hasn't changed, despite scientific and technological progress. We just have more sophisticated ways of killing now. A technological savage, some one said, might sum up the man of the wars and genocides of our day. Yet people still say we don't need redemption. Why do many still try to kill Christ's voice in society? So that they can give full reign to their dark desires now too?.

Yet all is not darkness. Though sin pervades the world still, so does the healing witness and hope of the dying Christ. He's the answer to all that darkness, if only we freely accept his redemptive love. And in the Passion story there are also signs that humanity has the capacity to do so: the women staying with and weeping for Jesus; Mary at the foot of the cross, loving to the end; Veronica wiping the face of Jesus and comforting him; the women of Jerusalem weeping for Christ; Saul carrying his cross, though admittedly forced to do so; the centurion suddenly shouting: "in truth this was a son of God" (Mt. 27:44, JB). But above all we've the dazzling example of Christ himself, the God man. Despite sin, greed and brutality, his message is simple; God loves us, believes in us, reaches out to us in loving forgiveness; we can change by his grace.

That's the jewel at the heart of the whole sordid story; we are redeemed and redeemable in Christ. He defeated Satan, evil, death, cruelty and darkness for us. In his holy church now, we've instant access to his other way of light and grace. We can turn the world into heaven, if we but take the hand of the Lord and follow his gentle way. But here's the rub, though light has come into the world, as Paul says, many have shown that they still prefer darkness. Many still reject the hand of God reaching to take their hand.

Thank God we aren't part of that rejection. By gathering here we show that we accept Christ's salvation, and want to be members of his holy kingdom, to light the world, and especially our children, back to original innocent living. For that's the only way evil, cruelty, violence and death can be defeated, by the Kingdom of God come in Christ.

In Gibson film we see the devil cast down to hell as Christ breathes his last. We see those who've crucified him slink away in fear as earth and heaven opens. Yet this is **Good Friday**, when the cross made possible man's salvation, Christ's complete triumph on our behalf. So we already anticipate the Alleluias of Easter as we honor and kiss the cross of a God who gave every drop of his blood to save us. We do so in faith that his great love will eventually redeem the whole world with our help, amen.

**Kissing of the Cross and the prayers etc follow.**

# Easter Saturday (Sunday) B

## Introduction:

Last night (tonight) we lit the holy fire symbolizing the Risen Christ as light of the world. That light shines still. As the Pascal Candle inscription says, "Christ yesterday, today and forever; the Alpha and the Omega, the beginning and the end of all". In the light of that Risen Lord with us, lets confess any ways we shut out his glory in our lives.

## Homily

"Praise the Lord I saw the Light", the Hank Williams song says. Close your eyes, imagine living in darkness. Now open them to a church ablaze with Easter. Before the coming of electricity, when we were young, we lived in the faint light of oil lamps. Doing homework or mother doing her sewing was a strain. Then we were lit up at the touch of a switch. Today's like that. The Risen Christ dazzles a dark fallen world with God's glorious light. Electricity fails sometimes. But the light that illuminated the world that first Easter will never go out, but continue to shine ever brighter until the whole world's lit up. Sadly, as Paul says, some are too caught up in the world to see that, even the church at times.

Watching a priest at midnight mass I was shocked by his matter-of-fact manner. Come on, I said, show some joy. For Easter **is** rejoicing. Our's is the end time of the Risen Lord, the 2000 year dream by the prophets come true. How can we be indifferent; we too should race from the tomb shouting with the angel who announced the resurrection: "he has risen from the dead and now he is going before you" (Mt. 28:7, JB). From the cross of shame came God's stunning victory. The dark that oppressed us since Adam - sin, suffering, evil, violence, death - is gone forever.

For when God raised Jesus and made him Lord and Savior, he banished hopelessness forever. As our common hymn says: "he is Lord, he is lord, he is risen from the dead and he is lord, every knee shall bow every tongue confess that Jesus Christ is Lord". That was the simple creed statement of the early church. It must be our creed statement as we accept this Risen Lord as our personal Lord. For this is special good news in today's world of materialism, violence, cynicism, drugs and youth despair. Once we accept the Risen Christ as Our Lord, a happiness the world cannot give flowers in us.

And that's the resting place of every restless heart. Even for this world, that news contains untold riches. We've vital work to do here and we should enjoy the good things of the world given us by God. But they're only fully enjoyed and meaningful in that dazzling light, that glorious and timeless intervention of God on our behalf, that destroyed sin and death's power over us forever. And not only does this light up our lives in this world and make them infinitely rich in every way, but when the world eventually passes away we've infinite riches in the Risen Christ forever. **Our** final victory here below and forever was guaranteed by **his** resurrection, we're on a winning side for all time. For all else passes but he's now lord of light, love, goodness, happiness and salvation both for our deepest fullest life in this world and with him, our Risen Lord, forever and ever, amen.

So as God's own, reborn in this night of his risen glory, let us live and rejoice in the great faith we profess.

### Prayers of the faithful

Gathered on this holiest of days, the high point of our Christian life and worship, let's pray to the Father through the glorious Risen Christ for the things that we need.

For the Pope, the bishops of the church, and all its leaders throughout the world that they may bring to all the joyful liberating message of the Risen Christ at this time and always.

For ourselves that this Easter mass of light and joy may lighten our own hearts into a grand Spring and Summer to come.

For our youth that the Easter message may be more than cliched holiday cheer, may it penetrate their hearts and bring them to a deep personal commitment to the Risen Lord and his church, as the pillars of their life and faith.

For the old people in our midst that their lives of faith and goodness and service may bring them the Lord's rewards of happiness and peace, and may they know God's love through us.

For the sick, may they know that the lord is with them in their suffering and may they experience the care of the Risen Christ.

For the dead that they come to their own resurrection prefigured this night in the resurrection of their Lord and Savior who when he rose raised all humankind to glory.

And we ask all these our prayers through Christ, our Risen Lord and Savior, who is close to his people and brings them the salvation and light of God forever and ever, amen.

### Reflection:

I talked to African people I had baptized once, and they explained how great a light the Christian faith was to them, burdened by pagan fears and witchdoctors. They had lived in a twilight world, oppressed by superstition and strange dark gods. Suddenly, they were liberated from all that. It was amazingly good news to them that Christ died and rose, that God loved them and was there for them forever in Christ. They found their eternal dignity, value and freedom in him. Yet today many in the west who enjoyed that light for centuries would take us back into a darkness, without the Lord. On TV Tarot cards are OK, but faith is banned. Maybe even us Christians take the glorious faith too much for granted. Lets appreciate it better from now on, and lets pray to Mary to help us in that. Hail Mary

# Second Sunday of Easter B

## Introduction:

We now enter the Easter period, and scripture is full of accounts of the early church's growth in the Risen Christ's Spirit. Today's scripture shows us that at the heart of that authentic early church was charity; they shared everything, no one was in need. That's the model for us; as we begin the mass lets confess ways we fail in generous sharing.

## Homily

There is a story told of a man coming before St. Peter for judgment. "I see you've many sins piled up against you", said Peter, "have you done any good at all in life?". "Well", said the man, "I did give a loaf of bread to a poor person some time ago". On one side of the scales Peter put the man's sins, and on the other the loaf of bread he'd given. Lo and behold, the loaf outweighed all the rest and he was saved! Of course this is just a story but it shows how important charity is in the lives of Christians. As scripture says, it cancels a multitude of our sins. In our reading we see the early church sharing all they had with those in need. And Christ in our Gospel says that if we love God we should show it by making a special effort to help others. If our brother or sister was starving we'd surely help, but all people are our brothers and sisters in Christ.

Indeed, he commands us to love them not just in a notional sense but in a practical way. Yet, and I include myself in this, every day on TV we see images of starving children in Africa or elsewhere, and turn away. Are we responsible for them; yes! Because we are partly to blame for their misery, and we are our brother's keeper. When I was in the Philippines I saw that 60% of its GDP went to repaying its debt to western banks. For each euro we give to poor nations we take out 9 in this way. The rich get richer and the poor poorer. Our Trocaire boxes help to right that wrong in some small way.

But our charity should apply at home too. Needy brothers and sisters in Christ are all around us. Giving to Vincent De Paul is one way of helping. But in whatever way we can we should give some of our surplus to the less well off. Indeed, that's our duty, if the earth is to become God's just world. Even the people living with us can be needy but we're too caught up in the world to see. At home lets give more love and time to family.

But whether at home or in the wider field, we Christians cannot ignore the needs of others. Otherwise Christ may say at the end of time: "Go away from me, with your curse upon you, to the eternal fire prepared for the devil and his angels, for I was hungry and you never gave me food ... etc" (Mt. 25:41-42, JB). If Christ came to us for help we'd give freely; but in the voices of the needy he begs us for help every day. "Give to anyone who asks", he says (Mt. 5:42, JB). I myself find that hard, but if someone asks I always give something. Sure, some take advantage but I can't deny the Gospel. Its better to err on the side of generosity than be mean. For we're sons and daughters of a God who is so good to us; "freely, freely you have received, freely give", the hymn says. Christ gave his last drop of blood for me; I should give to others until it hurts.

And like the man who gave the loaf of bread, the smallest charity will be rewarded. For the world of which Satan is Lord puts the interests of the rich first, but all that turns to dust and ashes at last and leaves us empty, but Christ is lord of all-caring love, goodness and grace forever and ever, amen. So as God's people, reaching out generously to others in love, especially the needy, lets make our profession of faith.

## Prayers of the faithful

And as God's people, we pray with confidence in this glorious time of the Risen Lord for all people's needs in the Spirit.

For the church throughout the world, especially Our Holy Father the Pope and its leaders, that its sharing charity and concern for the world's poor may be a light to all nations.

For ourselves that in our homes, communities and country we may have generous, loving and giving hearts to all, especially those around us who most need our care.

For the lonely and the impoverished in mind, body or soul, that through our love and care they may know the care of God, and of his all-healing and all-loving Christ.

We pray for the sick in our parish, that they may be healed by the dedicated work of those in the medical profession, and our prayers for, and outreach to, them.

For the dead that through our prayers they may be released from suffering due to sin and come quickly to their heavenly home.

And we ask all these prayer through Christ, the only lord of love, goodness and charity forever and ever, amen.


## Reflection

Sometimes we forget that prayer is a great work of charity. I'm always impressed when people organize prayers sessions for sick people; they show great faith that God will help those people in some way, even if he doesn't heal them. Christ says that if we ask of God, we will receive, and our Lady of Medjugorje says that prayer can bring peace to the world; its mysterious power is beyond all imagining. Prayers for the dead is also a great work of charity, especially when we pray for some one who has no one to pray for them. Scripture says, that in view of the resurrection, it is a good and holy thing to pray and make offerings for the dead, "so that they might be released from their sin" (Mc.12:43-45, JB). Lost in that other world our prayers can, in a mysterious way, bring them to light. The doctrine underlying this belief is the "communion of saints". The church consists of the living and the dead, who can help each other. Our greatest advocate there is Mary; lets ask her for prayerful charitable hearts in this, and in every way. Hail Mary

# Third Sunday of Easter B

## Introduction

Repentance is our scripture theme. Peter asks people to repent and believe. John talks of sin and finding forgiveness in Christ. The Risen Lord talks about preaching repentance for the forgiveness of sins to all. Lets confess if we neglect to repent of evil in our lives.

## Homily

You know the Bible story of two sons. The father says to one, "go into my vineyard". He says "OK", but doesn't go. The father tells the other, "go into my vineyard". He says "I wont". But later he repents and goes. He loves his father and knows that the grapes are ripe; it will hurt his Dad if they rot. Love caused his change of heart. Let it be the same with us. I know a young girl whose family didn't practice the faith. Realizing God's love for her, she returned to the church and brought her family with her. That's what we're asked to do at Easter, to leave anything in our hearts or lives opposed to God. To live our faith and inspire those around us to practice it too. Loving God, we should want his wisdom, happiness and peace for all. Did the first son eventually repent of his disobedience. Did he say sorry, and make up with his father later, I hope so. Its cold out there without God.

In our gospel we see the Risen Christ appearing to his apostles and proving he's real by eating food. He asks the apostles to witness to his risen presence and tell people to repent and return to doing God's will. Our faith must be like the son who showed his love by action according to our Father's will, our practical goodness and living faith in his service must not only redeem us but help to redeem our times, where the will of man seems to consistently override the will of God as expressed in his commandments.

Even Christians can be part of this secret apostasy. So many people go through Baptism, Holy Communion and Confirmation today, and promise solemnly before God and the community to follow Christ and his church, and spread the faith. But when it makes practical demands on them, like the first son, they follow their or the world's way instead. Much of this of course comes from human weakness: we want to obey God but are weak.

Today's Gospel shows that God knows and understands that. Christ sent the Spirit to help us and the church in our weakness. And, as John says in the second reading, when we fall we've a forgiving Father, and an unfailing advocate, Christ. He rose that, as the Gospel says: "in his name, repentance for the forgiveness of sins should be preached to all the nations" (Lk. 24:47, JB). We all break some commandments at times, but God still loves us. But we shouldn't make that a license for sin. We must struggle on, pick ourselves up, keep trying. Holiness is in that struggle, none of us will ever be perfect.

And if we cannot persist in the effort to obey God as a response to his love, lets do so at least because its good for us; because freedom from sin leads to inner peace, and happy whole hearts for this life and the next. Selfish license leads to slavery to sin, destructive habits and social chaos. But in obeying God we love ourselves and the world. We build an earth of love, peace, justice and truth. We live our Confirmation promises to help the Risen Christ deliver the earth from evil. We become free children of God and citizens of heaven, and help others around us to be the same.

I knew a man once who had drifted from the faith, but came back at the end of his life. I pointed out that because of him 1000s no longer had faith or higher hope, his children, grandchildren, their children etc. Football signs often say "keep the faith", meaning faith is a struggling club. We should keep the faith for our struggling soul's sake and that of our loved ones. For all else fades to dust and ashes at last, leaving us high and dry, but the Risen Christ is Lord is timeless love, truth, happiness, beauty and salvation, both for our deepest happiness in this world and forever and ever, amen.

So as the Risen Lord's own, living the faith and helping others to salvation within his church, we profess our faith.

### *Prayers of the Faithful*

And as God's living practicing faithful, proud of our Risen Lord, we pray to that lord for what we need.

For our Holy Father the Pope and all the pastors of the churches, that they may not only preach the Word but be examples of Christian life and so light up the world for Christ.

For ourselves that in our homes, communities and country we may proudly profess our faith in the Risen Lord, and live it out in service of God and his holy church, so as to bring ourselves and those around us to happiness, peace and eternal life.

For young people, may they remain true to the sacred promises they made at Baptism, Holy Communion and Confirmation to serve God faithfully and practically within his Holy Catholic Church.

For the sick, the aged, the lonely and the needy in body or soul, that through our faith, love and care they may know the comforting presence of the Risen Christ in their lives.

For the dead, that faithful to Christ in life, through our prayers they may rise with him to everlasting glory. We pray in a particular for those of our community who died recently.

And we ask all these our prayers through the Risen Christ, the unfailing advocate for us before the Father in heaven, amen.

### Reflection:

The great human story is of our salvation and the setting up of the church. In a reading last week about the early church, an opponent said that if the faith is from man it will fade, if from God nothing can defeat it. During its long history the church has seen off persecutions from 1000s of man-made systems, its survival and continuing growth despite fierce opposition, is incontestable proof that its from God. Lets give thanks. Hail Mary

# Fourth Sunday of Easter B

## Introduction

In our gospel today we see Christ the Good Shepherd watching over, caring, and laying down his life for the flock. Now as Risen Lord he continues leading his faithful to green pastures of the Spirit. Lets confess any ways we hurt or ignore that loving Lord.

## Homily

When in the Holy land I'd see shepherds chatting on hillsides their sheep milling together. They'll never sort out that lot I'd say. But a shepherd would call and each lot of sheep would disentangle themselves and trot after their master. Christian life is like that; Jesus calls and we follow freely to green pastures. Each of us does that in specific callings, nurses, teachers, shopkeepers etc. But of course our greatest shepherding role is within our families. Marriage is a sacrament because great grace is needed for loving faithful care of spouse and children. And those who don't marry are free for other caring roles in the church and world. True witness in this, or married and family love, is as important as consecrated ways of life and as vital to the church's holiness.

That said, we pray specially for priestly and religious vocations this Good Shepherd Sunday, for the scarcity of these is worrying. Lay people should take key roles in the church, but we still need priests to preside at the Eucharist and shepherd the flock. And we need monks, sisters and brothers to serve, pray for, and enrich the church beyond measure. But they wont come unless from among us, out of our faith and prayer. There is a crisis in such vocations now, but also ways we can address it: prayer and Eucharistic adoration: suggesting priestly or religious vocations to our children; sharing our vocation story; serving in parish ministry and letting our children do so; supporting those interested in priestly or religious life; and above all nurturing the existing vocations that we have.

For many are shell-shocked in the present secular climate. But that's not our tradition. Its not right that our persecutors are now our own, as if our great spiritual heritage meant nothing. Look where the world is leading us! Recession, despair, austerity and irreligion. A holy person said to me recently I fear we face an increasingly evil irreligious age. Concerted attacks on the church by those who should represent us all fairly, have left many demoralized. Four young young priests left our diocese recently. Sure some disgraced the cloth, but lets not tar all consecrated people with that brush; we don't condemn Christ because Judas was bad. Lets show good clerics and religious they're appreciated or soon we may have none, and the flock left without shepherds.

That's a terrible prospect, for even secular authorities agree that for our inner happiness and very survival we need faith; recently on a radio program, a noted psychiatrist said we should believe for our inner good. Scientific studies show evolution favors those of faith. So we need it to survive, as our history proves, it sustained our ancestors through every persecution. And false shepherds fill the void when good shepherds are lost. So we dare not ignore this crisis. Maybe its God's will that they are fewer so that the laity can shine; and maybe the crisis is God's way of changing a harsh hierarchical church. But we still need priests for the Eucharist and religious to permeate the church and the world with holiness, to foster our moral and spiritual health unto eternity. So lets pray fervently to Christ the good shepherd for more good pastors and religious to renew the faith. For the hard desert world of which Satan is lord fades to ashes, leaving the flock lost in an eternal wilderness. But Christ leads the faithful to green pastures for this life and forever, amen.

So as God's people, by prayer and practical means inspiring a new flowering of consecrated life, lets profess our faith.

## *Prayers of the faithful*

And as the people of God gathered here, we pray to our heavenly Father for the things that we need now, especially good pastors.

For the Pope and pastors of local and universal churches; may they inspire new priestly and religious shepherds who, like Christ, will love and serve God and others humbly.

For our civic leaders that they may not put obstacles in the way of the church, but enable it to live in faith, as it has done since the lifting of past persecutions.

For young people that while enjoying life fully here, they may also see that the world is not enough, and so seek the deeper happiness and inner riches of Christ unto eternal glory.

For ourselves that in our home and vocational work we may shepherd others with Christ gentle care, and live our lives in the uplifting light of his timeless faith, grace and love.

For the sick, the aged, the lonely, the oppressed, and the impoverished that through our deep Christian care and sharing they may know the love of God and his Christ.

For the dead, that through their faith and charity in this world and our prayers they may come to the fullness of light and peace.

And we ask all these prayers through Christ the only lord of life, peace, grace and happiness forever and ever, amen.

## *Reflection*

When my brother was sick and lost in London, mother asked us to pray fervently for him. We stormed heaven, and he was found.

Such a good outcome doesn't always happen, but staunch faith helps whenever trouble comes. For we're led by the Good Shepherd, who always hears our pleas. So lets pray to Mary, mother of the church, for good shepherds for its welfare, that through it, God's holy Kingdom may come. Hail Mary

# Fifth Sun of Easter B

## Introduction

Our gospel reminds us that when we're part of Christ, like a branch on a vine, we stay green and fruitful. That's why we come to mass, so that his life will grow in us, until we flower into eternal life. Lets confess ways we fail in prayerful unity with the Lord.

## Homily

Christ tells us today that union with him makes our lives fruitful. Reading scripture, regular mass, the sacraments and personal prayer strengthens that union; we're gradually grafted onto the true vine. But without that union we wither, like branches fit only for the fire. The old people knew this in their faithfulness to mass and devotion. My mother's prayer is possibly the reason why I'm a priest. I remember when young if I wanted money to go to a film, I'd creep into her room and find her praying. "Look in my purse she'd whisper". When our brother was lost in London for 3 days due to a stroke, she prayed day and night for his safety. He recovered: "Sure we stormed heaven" my mother said.

Prayer is the main way to maintain union with God, tell him our needs and gain strength within. As Christ says, once we're united to him by prayer, scripture and the Eucharist our lives light up and we illumine those around us too. In effect, the key to sound faith is a close relationship with Christ through prayer and the sacraments.

For too long we put the cart before the horse, we stressed morality rather than spirituality, doctrine rather than this relationship. But faith's not an ideology like the "isms" of our day. Its not about ideas but union with the living God whereby we become like spring buds, blossoming into green life here and for eternity. So even Christ himself frequently went apart to pray and commune with his Father; and he gave us the great way to union with God, the mass. Its readings, shared prayer and communion brings us so close to our heavenly Lord, we walk hand in hand like a child and its parent. As Paul says, we become like gods ourselves. Union with God raises us up to more than we can be.

That's why Christians from the beginning gathered for Sunday Eucharist. Acts say they met together for the prayers and breaking of bread on the Sabbath, the day set aside for prayer. The second commandment tells us to keep holy the sabbath day. That's Sunday for us, the Lord's day, when he rose from the dead. Weekday mass can't replace Sunday mass. The church obliges us to attend on Sunday, not to burden but enrich us.

For Sunday mass is our communal faith celebration. We gather as God's family to become one with Christ, and then to live that union in the week ahead. For grafted onto Christ, the vine, at mass, the sap of his grace flows on in our veins, giving us courage and power for life, and to light up the world around us by this engrafted goodness within.

In effect, mass and daily personal prayer not only light us up within but enable us to carry out Christ's saving work. Mary in Medjugorje says in message after message; pray my children, read the Bible, attend holy mass, pray the rosary, in that way you'll save a violent unbelieving world. That world passes away and leaves us empty at last, but united with Christ through personal and Eucharistic prayer we gain fullness of peace, happiness, truth, beauty, love and salvation for this world and forever and ever, amen.

So as God's people, one with Christ the vine and keeping his life green in us by mass, communion and personal prayer, lets profess our faith.


## Prayers of the Faithful

For our Holy Father and all pastors of the churches that, deeply rooted in Christ the true vine, the source of all life and holiness, they may radiate that life to the world.

For civic leaders that they may have the wisdom to facilitate people's spiritual life and development, the thing that matters in the long run and keeps society healthy.

For our youth that grafting themselves onto Christ the vine, through faithful Eucharistic and personal prayer, they may be green shoots of hope and grace to the world.

For ourselves in our homes, workplaces and communities, that we may stay closely united to Christ and the church through prayer and practice of the faith, so that we may be his light, peace and life to our children and all around us.

For the sick, aged, lonely and lost, that heeding Christ's call to bring to him all who labor and are overburdened and he'll give them rest; through our care they may know his love.

For the dead that having been with Christ in life, like branches on the tree of life, they may be united with him forever in heaven helped by our prayers for them here.

And we ask all these our prayers through Christ, our only lord of faith, life, love, truth and glory forever and ever, amen.


## Reflection

There's a story hold of St. Padre Pio, the modern mystic. A person entering his room, found him holding the baby Jesus in his arms. Whatever the truth of that, his union with Christ in prayer was legendary. Millions would come to be at his mass. It lasted two hours, and he often spent eight hours afterward in the confessional. There, they say, he could see in people's souls, what was holding them back spiritually. We may not all be like that, but we can imitate his prayerful union with Christ. Lets ask Mary to deepen that union through devout masses and deep daily personal prayer. Hail Mary

# Sixth Sunday in Easter B (Mission Sunday)

## Introduction

This Sunday's scripture focuses on mission. Christ tells us to go out into the world and witness to him by word and example. Lets confess ways we fail in this.

## Homily

Today, the gospel asks all of us to go into the world and bear fruit from union with him. I say all of us, for all too often we see mission as priests or religious going abroad. But, as Theresa of Liseux reminds us, we should all be missionaries where we are. She never left her convent, yet she is patron of the missions.

Indeed, she tells us that Christ **depends** on each of us to be his light to the world now. We were anointed at Baptism to do that, and at Confirmation received the Spirit to go out and proclaim the Good News as his courageous witnesses. Moreover, at his Ascension Christ sent the apostles, and all of us their successors, to spread his gospel and build his church. That such evangelization is a duty of all God's people was re-emphasized by Vatican 11. It said all the faithful must get down into the trenches with the Lord; as Eucharistic ministers, readers, altar servers, financial contributors, and above all as everyday examples of Christian living.

Such witness was never more needed today when many are abandoning their Christian birthright, going back to the darkness from which Jesus delivered humankind. There they fall easy prey to the world's shallow values, to Satan, drink, drugs, violence and soul-destruction.

To bring as many as possible of these back to Christ and the church's loving arms, is the urgent task of each Christian today.

Christ ascended to the Father, and is with us as Risen Lord until the end of time, but he needs our hands to do his work on earth. Besides active work, we can do this is by prayer. Again look at St. Theresa. She spent a short life in prayer, and is patron of the missions. Giving her that role the church is saying that mission is furthered especially by fervent prayer. That's why I ask daily mass-goers and communicants to pray for young people today. For deluded by empty passing values, many are endangering their souls, abandoning their Savior and his church, going unprotected against evil into the darkness of a world where Satan often reigns. To them we must restore Christ's saving love - by personal and communal prayer, mass and the sacraments, and by active evangelization.

Mission starts at home, and then radiates outwards to bring Christ to those who never knew him. So while doing our bit at home, we might also support with prayer and money those who travel to the ends of the earth with the good news. Thank God we're doing that. A bishop said in a letter for Mission Sunday, in the past years one diocese contributed 183,000 euro to the church abroad. As John Paul 11 said, such contributions also bring people out of a desert of poverty and injustice, as well as spiritual darkness.

Indeed, today we pray also for the aid workers who died in recent times doing God's work, fighting world poverty. Their energy is also rooted in our generosity, prayer and sacrifice. Our missionaries in the past came from the faith of a generous spiritual people. Its the same today. Let me end with the story of a man picking an orchard of apples. His friend said: you must have done a lot of work to produce this crop. No, the man said; last spring while I was asleep my bees, my secret workers did the work, pollinating these plants. Each Christian is one of those bees in God's fruitful orchard. That's how both the home and world orchard will produce a great harvest for Christ, the only Lord of love, goodness and salvation forever and ever, amen.

So as generous witnesses for Christ before the whole world, lets profess our faith.

## Prayers of the faithful

For our Holy Father and all the leaders of the church that their missionary zeal may lead to a new spring of faith and justice in the world.

For our civil leaders that they may put no obstacles in the way of the church's nurturing and spreading of the faith.

For our youth that they may have the idealism and enthusiasm to go out to the whole world and spread the Good News to the poor in body or spirit.

For ourselves in our homes that we may bequeath to our children the greatest gift of all, the faith that is a pearl of great price for this world's fullness and eternal happiness.

For the sick, the aged and the housebound, may they offer their invaluable prayers and suffering for the salvation of the world.

For the dead that through our prayer, a great mission in itself, they may come to their eternal rest with God and all the saints who have gone before them to everlasting life.

We ask all these things through Christ Our Lord who is forever the light of the world, amen.

## Reflection:

You may know the story of St. Paul's missionary endeavors. He traveled all over the world of his day, usually on foot, and beset by every kind of suffering. He tells us that he was often beaten, imprisoned, shipwrecked, and on one occasion he was stoned and left for dead. Yet he kept on in his mission, for the love of Christ, and zeal to bring his salvation to all humanity, burned like an unquenchable fire in his great heart. We may not all be capable of such heroism in promoting the faith, but we can all do some little bit to fulfill the vows we made to do so, at Baptism and Confirmation. Let's pray that we will do so, and let's ask Mary to help all missionaries today. Hail Mary.

# Pentecost Sunday B

## Introduction

This Sunday celebrates the Spirit's coming to the apostles, their Confirmation, when their faith was strengthened and they were enabled to go and establish the church. We received the same spirit at Confirmation. Lets confess any ways we fail to live it in action.

## Homily

Today is the feast of Pentecost when the church was launched. Its right we celebrate it on the eve of summer, for the coming of God's Holy Spirit was summer for the world. For the third person of the Trinity is the key to all goodness in life, the church and the world. But what do we mean by the Holy Spirit? Perhaps, he's best seen in the good aspects of a person, a home, or a country. I once had an audience with with John Paul 11. As he entered his charisma enveloped us. That's true of people we meet every day, they radiate warmth and goodness. That's the Holy Spirit. He resides in all that's individual and best in the world.

But a contrary negative spirit can also possess people. For example, and I hope I'm wrong, I sense a colder spirit abroad today. Is the spirit of the world, and Satan its lord, taking over in hard, secular, atheistic values. Lets beware, for when the Holy Spirit goes out the window, so does our humanity. Certainly the church is feeling a cold wind blowing at present; mass attendance falling, attacks multiplying from secular media and governments. In this climate we who love Christ could easily lose heart.

The feast we celebrate today should snap us out of any such tendency. Its a sign of eternal hope. Christ, ascending to the Father, became universal Lord. From his throne he sent the Spirit so that through his power we'd go out and teach all nations. He guarantees the church's triumph, for as Advocate, he defends it before the world's court, all that fight against God and his Christ. So lets have no fear, in the Spirit all is well.

He constantly gains the victory for God's true people. Just as he sustained the early church in the midst of bitter opposition. The apostles were all killed. Yet, despite this, the power and joy of the spirit enabled them to found the church as a universal mission. So, though the apostles were brokenhearted when Christ ascended, they knew he'd to go. So that the Spirit could come, the church be born and its mission succeed in his power.

For always as scripture says, though sin abounds grace abounds even more. This Easter adults were baptized in churches from China to Ireland. So the Spirit still thrives despite all efforts to silence him. He's why the church has seen off 1000's of opposing worldly ideologies. They all faded, but it thrived in the timeless grace of Christ's Spirit.

But the greater mystery is that he needs our human help for the final triumph of God. At Baptism and Confirmation we vowed to be such lights to a spiritually floundering world. Lets do so. Aided by personal prayer, the mass, the sacraments and living love lets bring his golden light and saving grace to all. For all else fades to dust and ashes at last, and only fools put their trust in the godless spirit of the world and its empty passing values. But in Christ's Spirit can we grow within in the wisdom, love, goodness, peace and salvation that brings overflowing happiness here and peace forever and ever, amen.

So as God's people, spreading faith and goodness throughout our world in the power of the Holy Spirit given to us, lets proclaim our glorious faith anew this Pentecost.


## *Prayers of the faithful*

For our Holy Father the Pope, and the bishops of the church; like the apostles at Pentecost may they fearlessly preach the Good news and bring all to the saving arms of the Risen Lord.

For civil leaders that they may not be so carried way by the hard spirit of the world, so as to hinder the spiritual welfare of the people they serve.

For our youth that having been filled with the Holy Spirit at their Confirmation, when they vowed to practice and spread the faith, they may do so with all their hearts.

For ourselves in our homes, workplaces and communities that we may be apostles for Christ, radiating the Holy Spirit's light of faith to all we care for or come into contact with.

For the sick, the aged, the lonely and the needy in spirit, body or mind that through our care they may know the love of God.

For the dead that they may be raised up in the Spirit to heavenly bliss through their goodness and faithfulness here, and our continuing prayers for them as the powerful assembled faithful.

We ask these prayers of the father through Christ in the Spirit who is with us as the people of God, forever and ever, amen.

## Reflection

Its amazing how the Spirit of certain saints comes down to us and inspires us after thousands of years. People like Paul or Francis or Patrick. The reason, I think, is because they radiated the Spirit who is timeless and whose effects go on and on. We all leave a spiritual legacy of good or ill when we die. Lets pray to Mother Mary, the greatest of the saints who totally lived in the Spirit, that she will help us, despite natural failings that keep us humble, to leave an overall Christian Spirit of faith, kindness and goodness to those who come after us. Hail Mary

# Second Sunday in Ordinary Time B

## Introduction

Its back to ordinary time and Christ's public ministry. The first reading invites us to say with Samuel: "Speak Lord you servant is listening". Paul says to use our bodies for God's glory as modern apostles. Lets confess any failures in faithfulness today.

## Homily

Once in school an older child said to me that the devil doesn't exist. I suppose he was echoing something his parents said, but this view is not Christian. Christ constantly refers to the Evil One and asked us to be on our guard against him. I felt like replying to the child: "that's what he wants us to think. But look at the world we live in, and see that the evil one is still very much alive: daily stabbings, murders, kidnapping, violence, drugs, war, family breakdown, bombings. Look at our age's evils, Hitler's holocaust and Stalin's Gulags; look at the millions killed in the first world war and the use of poison gas on people. Look at the daily slaughter of innocents in our world. Look at shots of soldiers urinating on bodies of fallen enemies. Look at our age's incessant attacks on the faith.

Evil exists, and the evil one, but at the same time we Christians shouldn't be frightened by the fact. God's Christ and good also exist and are infinitely more powerful. Look at all the good people in the world still following God's Spirit, from whatever culture. Look at the volunteers serving to alleviate famine in poor countries. Look at the present Pope, leaving his palace to live simply with the people; look at the United Nations and its peacekeepers; and so on.

The good Spirit is universal. If we give him half a chance he'll conquer all evil for us. But we are most effective against evil if we ask for his help in prayer, and remain practicing members of the church as we promised at Baptism. Its only when we leave such havens, provided by God, that we're open to the world's forces of evil. Christ said the gates of hell wouldn't prevail against his church, but we must freely choose to be part of it.

In effect, we must be like the apostles. They came to and stayed with the lamb of God. We must be like Peter, that Christ called the rock. Sure that faithfulness is more difficult now. Our world still harbors the illusion it doesn't need God, we can be our own God, make our own laws to suit ourselves, we don't need to be saved. That world persuades us that Satan doesn't exist; that sin is OK. So Satan smiles, as in arrogance like his, we rush headlong to doom in body and soul. Do what you like, he says, justify every evil with every argument you can think of. So the blind lead the blind into the ditch.

Yet we still feel guilty when we do wrong. We cant kill the conscience God put in us. And without seeking his forgiveness, that inner bother goes on and on; there's no rest for the wicked, scripture says. Maybe its why Psychiatrists are doing a roaring trade today. But they are no help against the ills of the soul, the emptiness of the Spirit without God, the slavery to evil. There is evil, sin hurts, and our inner devils can only be cast out by Christ's redeeming power, the presence of his Holy Spirit in us.

So lets be wise and follow him like the apostles; for our souls, like the body needs protection, nourishment and regular food from God. So lets say like Samuel; speak Lord your servant is listening. For, as Paul says, only by his power can we rise above sin and soul death. Only the lamb of God who delivered us from inner death by his death, is our everlasting hope. Let's be wise enough to see this and like the apostles follow him to where he lives in truth, glory, and happiness forever. Sadly, as a wise man said, instead following Christ along the way we're often by the way or in the way. Lets not be so. For the ways of the world of which Satan is lord turn to dust at last, leaving the soul empty and desolate, but Christ is lord of love, goodness, peace, happiness, beauty, truth and salvation both for this world and forever and ever, amen.

So as God's people secure in the Lord's arms from evil, and following him along the way of life, we profess our faith.

## *Prayers of the faithful*

And as God's people let's pray for what we need, especially protection against evil.

For the Pope and all church leaders, that following Christ faithfully themselves, they may be a light of faith, goodness, and truth to the whole world, delivering it from evil.

For civil leaders that they may put no obstacles in the way of the faithful following of Christ in freedom.

For our wonderful youth that they may not walk away from the faith and leave themselves wide open to the machinations of the world and the devil, but stay safe in the arms of Christ and his holy church for their lasting happiness here and hereafter.

For ourselves that we may trust in the lord of Life to deliver us from evil, and like the apostles follow him faithfully along the Way.

For the sick, the aged, the lonely and the oppressed in body, mind or soul that through our faith and love they may know the love of God and his Christ in their lives.

For the dead that through our prayers they may attain to full happiness of the Lord with all those who have gone before them in faith to eternal life.

We ask all these our prayers through Christ the only Lord of life, peace, happiness and salvation forever and ever, amen.

### Reflection:

The classic book, *The Lord Of The Rings* was made into an award-winning film. Its by J.R.R Tolkien, an orphan who was brought up by his uncle, a Catholic priest. A strong sense of life as a struggle of good and evil comes out in the book. Curiously, its a little Hobbit who saves the world from the Satanic Mordor. All of us are like that Hobbit, small beings, yet with a key part in our world's salvation. We pray to Mother Mary that we will not shun the task of leading the struggle against evil. Hail Mary.

# Third Sunday in Ordinary Time B

## Introduction

Readings this Sunday anticipate Lent. The story of Jonah in the first reading sees him asking a corrupt city to repent. Paul in the second reading reminds us that our time is short, the world as we know it is passing away. This sets the scene for the gospel where Christ's call as he begins his ministry, is to repent and believe (Mk. 1:15, JB). Lets do so.

## Homily

I'm sure you know Ignatius of Loyola's story. Early on in life he sought glory as a soldier. But badly wounded and lying on a hospital bed, he had a conversion experience. Christ called him to a different warfare, a battle for souls. He went on to found the Jesuits, become a great missionary, and guide many souls to God.

Yet in all this he just answered Christ's gospel call to repent, believe and follow him devotedly. Reading the lives of the saints and finding Christ in a vision, Ignatius came to see the uselessness of vainer pursuits. He realized that true glory and happiness was in serving God. Like Christ in the desert he rejected Satan's service and gave all to God.

We should do the same. For lasting joy, happiness and glory is in loving others and God with all our heart. We're to do so through all trials. The world throws many temptations in our way to lure us from faith's enduring values. So we must constantly renew our Christian commitment. Our soul's journey needs constant repentance and faith renewal. And that struggle ends only in the grave and the freedom of the Blessed.

Christ says only he who perseveres to the end will be saved. So the challenge is to keep firmly to the path begun in Baptism. Then we were delivered from evil and made members of God's holy people. Our life's great task is to remain an integral part of that family, to journey with it to eternal life, like the apostles who followed Christ even unto final martyrdom. We may not be required to die for Christ, but we're asked to live for him. This means rejecting the world's contrary ways despite its lures, for it has many false prophets.

One way to rise above all that and remain steadfast in faith, is to keep the vision of Christ's final coming in glory to judge the living and the dead before us. We want to be among the faithful to whom he'll say then: "take for your heritage, the kingdom prepared for you since the foundation of the world" (Mt. 25:34, JB). For to be wise is to follow Christ with joyful hearts like the apostles or Ignatius, through the trials, sufferings and temptations of life so as to gain the crown of life at last when we'll go out to meet him with the saints in the heavenly kingdom, wearing the white robes that we have kept intact since Baptism.

One way to keep that white garment bright is to live in the world with pure hearts. I myself say often repeat the words of psalm 51 which is a prayer that we will stay free from sin and faithful to the pure spirit of God within us. That's what Ignatius prayed also in his *Spiritual Exercises*, which are a way to remain true to God's Spirit. By prayer, good example and practice of the faith we're to be a light of Christ for our families and the church? So that we'll have treasures in heaven when the wheel of life runs down and when the angels beckon us into the home of the Blessed. For the godless values of this world pass and are empty at last, but Christ is lord of love, goodness, happiness, beauty, truth and salvation both for this world and forever and ever, amen.

So as God's people called to constant repentance, renewal of belief and faithful practice of the faith, so as to be lights to the world, let's profess that faith anew.

### Prayers of the Faithful

For our Holy Father, the Pope, and the bishops of the church that they like the apostles may follow Christ faithfully and lead the whole church and the world to justice and equality.

For civil leaders that they may not put any obstacles in the way of the church's mission and the free work of God's Holy Spirit.

For our youth that like the young apostles they may seek out and follow Christ the Way, the Truth and the Life, to find rest for their souls both in this world and the next.

For ourselves that in our homes, workplaces and communities we may be a light of Christ and his church to our families and all we associate with.

For the sick that carrying their unavoidable crosses after Christ in faithful discipleship despite all trials, they may turn those sufferings into gold and enjoy untold rest and reward hereafter.

For the dead that having followed Christ faithfully along the road of life, they may come to the reward of the blessed, with the help of our continuing love and prayers.

We ask all these our prayers through the same Christ Our Lord whose wounds constantly intercede for us before the Father, amen.

## Reflection:

There's a story told of St. Ignatius, that after founding the Jesuits, they made a pilgrimage to the Holy Land to seek God's will. But they were prevented by circumstances from completing their journey. So instead they went to Rome and placed themselves at the service of the Holy Father. Sometimes in following Christ, the will of God is revealed to us in strange ways. Lets do our bit for God, however the Spirit calls us to serve. Hail Mary.

# Fourth Sunday in Ordinary Time B

## Introduction

Readings today feature prophecy. The first reading affirms true prophecy against those who invoke God for worldly ways. Paul in the second reading affirms the prophetic aspect of celibacy for the Lord. Christ in the gospel teaches with authority and casts out unclean spirits when others fail. Lets confess ways we put worldly thinking before God's.

## Homily

I read recently of a Chinese priest who spent many years in a concentration camp there for his faith. Despite ill-treatment by ruthless atheistic authorities there, he harbored no ill-will after his eventual release on health grounds. His faith, strengthened by his horrific ordeal, remained untouched. He even learned from his experience, because his life was ruled by a higher authority than that of the communists prophets of a worldly system, who oppressed and tried to indoctrinate him; they bowed his body but not his spirit.

We too should trust in faith rather than its worldly opponents. For the church embodies an apostolic tradition that comes from Christ. We should put that before the passing trends and ideologies of a godless world of which Satan is Lord. For when we experience suffering or a crisis the uncaring self-seeking and commercially ruthless world has little to offer. Its like the scribes in our gospel who could do nothing for the man with the unclean spirit. Like the false prophets of our first reading they claimed to speak for God but in fact spoke with the voice of worldly self-interest, cruelty and corruption. By contrast Jesus's message had as its source God's love. As St. Paul says, like priest and religious now, he gave his undivided attention to God and the needy. That saving presence is still with us. In the storms of life we've a safe harbor in his holy church.

Indeed the great legacy of the lord is the authority invested in his church. At Baptism we became part of that apostolic faith community. And despite its human faults we can trust it's teaching in matters of faith and morals. For Christ promised to be with it for all time and that the gates of hell wouldn't prevail against it. So even modern flabby devils of materialism are fighting a losing battle. The church goes on forever like a river.

For Peter, the first Pope, was given the keys of the kingdom. God gave Christ all authority in heaven at the resurrection. He in turn passed that on to his church and Peter its head at his Ascension. So our house of faith is built on that solid rock, not on sand. Lets remember that when the world makes a football of the church, attacking its moral authority and trying, like the false prophets of old, to water down the faith to suit its ways. A host of self-appointed Popes on TV or Radio would replace the rock as our masters.

They'd impose a way of thinking often contrary to God, who reminds us in scripture, that his thoughts are not our thoughts, his ways are not our ways, that the heavens are as high above the earth as his ways are above our ways (Is. 55:8-9, JB). Lets not give in to the spiritual chaos of our often blinkered, often self-serving, and certainly always less wise ways. Rather than building on the world's shifting sands of every new trend, straws in every wind, lets stand by the one true church founded on the rock of Peter, maintaining the full truth in season and out. For its not the disordered babble of arbitrary men twisting the truth to suit their whim, its a rock built on on the gospel and maintained by elected legitimate authority. Like a river it flows forever past every human folly. While all else fades to dust leaving us empty within, the church built on Christ the Risen Lord, is truth, beauty, happiness and salvation, for our happiness in this world and forever and ever, amen.

So God's people safe under the authority of his Christ present with the church and in scripture forever, lets proudly profess our faith, founded on those unshakeable rocks.

## Prayers of the faithful

Lets pray for the authorities in our church - Our Holy Father and the bishops especially - that they may be rocks of faith and truth, raising all up to God's wisdom.

For our civil leaders that they may protect and not infringe on the spiritual rights of the church to teach the truth freely.

For our youth that they may not be ruled by the false prophets of the sinful world opposed to God, but be wise and build their house on the rock that is Christ and his eternal church.

For ourselves in our homes that we may be true prophets to our families and all those who depend on us, bringing them up in true faith, and with real caring and nurturing love.

For the sick, the needy aged, the lonely and the deprived in body, mind or soul; through our care may they know God's love.

For the dead whose faith is known to God alone, that remaining true to God and his church here below, they may, with the help of our prayers, come to the highest happiness in heaven.

We ask all these our prayers through the same Christ who is lord of truth, love and salvation forever and ever, amen.

## Reflection

Once when in the USA, I was on a bus, and a wonderful old African American woman came up to me and said: "there is another way". It struck me as a good slogan for our troubled world. Every day we read of people beating up the old and weak for a few euros, high on drugs or drink. Stabbing each other or giving up on life because they've no sure spiritual ground under their feet. The challenge for us is to show them that there is another better way in Christ and his Church. Each of us must, like that woman, help all to find faith and peace in these progressive yet troubled times. Lets pray to Mother Mary, that all the lost souls of our world may come to the healing grace and peace which is Christ and his holy church's way of true life-giving prophecy and timeless wisdom. Hail Mary.

# Fifth Sunday in Ordinary Time B

## Introduction

Today's readings feature healing. Job is anguished at life's suffering but Paul gives us the remedy, heart rest in Christ, whom we see in the gospel healing all who come to him. Lets confess if we doubt his healing love, or fail to be his healing hands to others.

## Homily

There's a story told of Mother Theresa that I never tire repeating. One day in a Calcutta street she saw a poor man in the gutter, thin, sick and covered with flies and sores. She lifted him up, took him to her house, washed him, put ointment on his wounds and gave him fresh clothes and food. Soon after he died. Her helpers said: "what was the point, he died anyway". "The point", she said, "was the smile on his face as he died".

Once, I was chaplain in a Catholic general hospital. Reading its history I was struck by how its aims resembled Mother Theresa's: to care with human warmth for the sick and dying, especially the poor, aged and underprivileged. They aimed to serve not only physical needs but the whole person, each one's dignity as a child of God.

Suffering is a mystery, part of the human condition since the fall, but its not God's will. If it were God's will why did Christ, his son, spend his life combating it? A mystery differs from a problem, which can be solved. Suffering, part of our fallen human condition, is a mystery. But the ministry of healing is not. It is best seen in medical science aided by Christian virtues - charity, compassion, social conscience, concern, caring, sympathy, brotherhood, kindness, love. For healing must include the whole person, body and soul.

This wholistic approach continues Christ's extensive healing ministry while on earth. We see him in our gospel curing the outcast leper. But a huge part of his public life was spent in such work. For if suffering and sickness is part of human existence, a source of redemption when offered up, its not God's will. Its part of a fallen world we redeem, like Christ did, by active charity. That includes healing mental and spiritual ills too. Christ didn't just heal physically, he healed minds and souls even more so. Indeed, faith has a huge part even in his physical healing. As Mother Theresa was fond of pointing out if our ministry of care to others is done from deep love of God then it has a timeless dimension.

Again the hospital manifesto come to mind. The sisters' ministry was all embracing. A Cork Protestant wrote in the local paper in 1879, when the sisters were collecting for a hospital: "if everyone had been able to see the intelligent and devoted care given by the sisters in time of suffering as I have, then the sum which they need would not be difficult to collect". Later, when they were celebrating 100 years of service to Tralee, a *Kerryman* editorial noted: "The sisters of good help came to a poverty stricken town in 1878 to move among the sick, nurse them in their homes. They have served the community well with their nursing skills and with a sympathy engendered by the holy life they lead".

But the ministry of healing is not just for religious, its the duty of all Christians. St Theresa of Avila observed that Christ has no hands on earth now but ours. All Christians are called by Baptism to be healers. Indeed as religious decline you lay people must take up that work as never before, especially at home with sick relatives We should do that work with Christ's love and compassion. For the sake of our eternal reward and to imitate Our Lord. For the hard values of the world of which Satan is lord turn ashes at last but Christ is lord of living compassion, for healing in this world and forever and ever, amen.

As God's own, called to be his healing hands to the needy around us, let's profess our faith.

## Prayers of the Faithful

For the leaders of the church, especially our Holy Father, that they may promote the key work of charity and care for others in body and soul, to continue the healing work of Christ today.

For our civil leaders that their main focus may be the healing of the sufferings of people who elected them, especially the disabled in body or mind, the house-bound, the sick, the aged and the underprivileged in society.

For our youth that their whole focus may not just be on their own wealth, big houses, well-paid jobs, pleasure but also have compassionate hearts to reach out to the needy and give of their time to helping and healing the sick.

For ourselves in our homes, workplaces and communities that we may have time to listen to the worries and needs of those around us and respond with the love and care of Christ.

For our sick that through our care, and that of medical professionals and pastoral priests they may know the love of God.

For the dead that their joys and suffering in this world over they may know eternal peace, rest and happiness with the Lord, helped on their way by our personal and communal prayers.

We ask these prayers through Christ, the healer of the world forever and ever, amen.

## Reflection

The story of Lourdes is a good example not only of the desire of God to heal us in body and soul, but also of the heavenly care of Mary, our Mother. She appeared to the poor asthmatic Bernadette and made her an instrument of universal healing, both physical and spiritual. The same is true of Marian shrines all over the world. She came to Knock after the famine, because her heart was broken by the sufferings of her children during that catastrophe. Lets pray to her that she will help all of us and all people to reach out with healing help to those suffering in body or soul, in our world. Hail Mary

# Sixth Sunday in Ordinary Time B

## Introduction

Our readings this week continue the healing theme. Moses says to shun the leper for the sake of the community, but Christ by healing a leper, changes the law of exclusion to one of inclusion. Lets pray that we may reach out to the sick and excluded in our midst.

## Homily

I am a leper, deformed, shunned by everyone. Children run into houses when they see me coming. I've to shout "unclean" everywhere. Life is pain, suffering, loneliness, dirt, poverty. I wish I were dead. Someone please help. Wait the teacher and healer I've heard about is coming. Jesus, the holy one of God, have pity on me, I shout. Shut up, Peter says, get away from him you foul thing. I shout louder. Jesus comes. I say please heal me. Jesus touches me, the first time anyone has done so in 20 years. And I can't believe it, the sores are gone, I'm well. Thank God, now I can go home to my family.

That's the Gospel as told by the leper. Who now has a similar story; a person infected by aids, an old person in a home, the poor excluded in cosy middle-class mores? But in that world there are lepers too, spiritual lepers insulated in big houses from their neighbors, and from God on Sunday, choosing to shop rather than keep the Sabbath. To these Christ brings a healing message too, repent and believe lest you perish forever.

Like in Jesus's day, many would retire into an escapist world, from all those who would remind them of their deeper human duty: the aged, the mentally ill, the intellectually impaired; travelers, migrants, beggars. Similarly, we'd turn our face from God and deep spiritual demands. All we need is the pub, TV escapism, the culture of the lager lout and the premiership game. No room for the challenging message of Christ or our humanity. Like Dives in the gospel, we shun the beggar at our gate. Yet when Dives in hell wanted that man's help, it was too late. Lets be wise enough not to share that fate; for if we exclude people in need, we risk being excluded on the great judgment day which will come when we least expect it, the gospel tells us.

As Christians, unlike Cain, we must be our brother's keeper; we must at least try in some small way to be Christ's healing presence to spiritual and physical lepers around us. As St. Theresa says: Christ has no hands on earth but ours, he depends on us to be his healing to a world full of broken and discarded people, children of God. We mustn't fail them. For so many of God's children out there need a healing touch, from the tramp to the abandoned street child. All are equal children of God, our brothers and sisters in Christ. We can't pursue ruthless self-interest like Satan regardless of needy neighbors, faith or salvation. Our Christian family includes the homeless, the refugee, the addict, the agnostic. The latter especially must know that worldly power is no use at last, only faith and charity carry us beyond the grave to glory.

For the key temptation we all face is that of Christ in the desert. To pursue our own power and pleasure regardless of God or the crying needs of humanity. Jesus resisted Satan's worldly wiles to opt for suffering service of God and humanity. So must we. Defying the world, Jesus reached out to the leper, his friend in low places, as the song says. We must have similar open hearts. For hard worldly values fade to dust and ashes at last leaving us empty before eternity, but to the Christ of all-healing love and faith, belongs the kingdom, the power and the glory forever and ever, amen.

So as God's people called to steadfast, real and caring charity towards the needy, we profess our faith.


## Prayers of the faithful

And as the people of God lets pray for all our needs, and the needs of the most needy.

For our Holy Father and all church leaders, that they may live a message of inclusiveness and healing, and so bring the world to equal nourishment and care of all God's children.

For civil leaders; may they promote ever more and better hospitals and caring institutions, so that all may feel equally valued in our country, especially the sick in mind or body.

For our youth, that they may choose to be the caring hands of Christ to all those suffering or in need in any way.

For ourselves in our homes, workplaces and society that we may not exclude anyone from our care, and treat all those in our household with great respect and nurturing healing love.

For migrants, especially those fleeing from persecution or exclusion in their countries, may they feel included and welcome in our country, so famed for its openness and hospitality.

For the dead, that healed of all the lingering effects of their sins, they may come with gladness to the open arms of the Lord, with the help of our charitable prayers.

And we ask ask all these prayers through Christ who spent his life on earth healing the sick and reaching out to the downtrodden and marginalized, amen.

## Reflection

Once I knew a young person with MS; she followed a trendy set with no time for God or others. Their philosophy was enjoy yourself, have sex, if others hurt you pay them back. When she became disabled they deserted her; and their philosophy left her spiritually dead. But Christian friends rallied round to visit, wash and take her out; from them she experienced new love and faith. She asked me to bring her communion and pray with her. Our faith must be like that; persevering with the alcoholic relative or troubled teenage child; not counting the cost of faith or charity. Lets ask Mother Mary to help us in this. Hail Mary

# Seventh Sunday in Ordinary Time B

## Introduction

"You have burdened me with your sin, troubled me with you iniquities" (Is. 43:24, JB), God says in our reading. In the gospel Christ forgives the sins of the paralytic as a deeper healing. Do we ignore the seriousness of sin, if so lets confess our's now.

## Homily

Nowadays we tend to ignore how serious sin is for God, the individual and society. Yet its effects are obvious in the news every day; stabbings, murders, kidnappings, rape, violence, drugs. At one time murder was a wonder, now its a daily occurrence. Sinful human greed on a huge scale brought the recession, a reminder of the wages of sin. So is the result of our era's spiritual and moral regression into senseless killing. During the revolution in China up to 10 million from churches, temples and the middle class went to the killing camps, where ideologues ate the bodies of the victims. How could this happen in an enlightened age, how did it produce a savagery unprecedented in human history.

One answer is failure to acknowledge the reality of evil, and arrogant refusal to avail of the solution, God. So, spurning his light, we plumb the depths of depravity. Perhaps you saw the film, *The Killing Fields*. In it an escapee walks from a communist extermination camp over a roadway of human bones. Still secularists say there's no such thing as sin; we don't need to be saved, or can save ourselves. The devil laughs and rubs his hands.

But God says "You have burdened me with you sins", for, seeing us destroying ourselves in body and soul by cruel sinful acts, breaks his heart. Are we to conclude then that humankind in general is bad news?

No! the fall and Satan is also to blame. Two years ago in school a child said to me, Satan doesn't exist. I smiled for the more we doubt him the more power we give him. I felt like saying: listen to radio's daily news son, and tales of crimes so gruesome they can only come from some extra force of evil.

Of course we may blame Adam and Eve. But modern theologians see their story as an ongoing parable. Adam and Eve is each of us. We all face the choice of good or evil every day, and only God's grace can save us from the wrong choice. Lets wake up to that fact and pray like Christ's does in his key Our Father prayer: "lead us not into temptation but deliver us from evil". Christ came precisely to free us from evil.

Because we fail to see the need for redemption from sin, our age's genocides echo the biblical Tower of Babel story. Man invents false gods, or tries to be God, and produces hell after hell. A holy person said to me recently that he saw the recent collapse of the banks as a modern Tower of Babel built by two deadly sins, arrogance and greed. All this images a deeper malaise whereby we reject God, see sin as outdated, and feel no guilt.

Yet anyone with even half a brain can see the terrible world this creates: crime, drugs, violence, sexual promiscuity, breakup of the family, greed, license, suicide. Sin is real and when unchecked destroys us in body and soul.

But there's the hope amid this gloom, the other message of our gospel: the Son of Man has power to forgive sin. He delivered humankind from the evil by his coming, and delivers us in a special way within his church, through the sacraments notably confession. There he redeems our inner corruption and brings us freeing forgiveness. If we just trust in him, all will be well. He will guarantee our bright future and that of our children.

Satan still exists, sin still exists, but the good news is that we can gain the victory through Our Lord Jesus Christ. For all else fades to ashes but he is lord of love, peace, freedom, happiness and salvation, both for this world and forever and ever, amen.

So as God's people given eternal hope to overcome sin in the saving and loving presence of our triumphant Lord, we profess our faith.

## Prayers of the Faithful

And as the people of God lets pray for what we need to be free of spiritual slavery.

For church leaders that they may preach the reality of sin as a burden on God, each person and society, but also preach Christ as the way to freedom from sin, forgiveness, and a return to innocence.

For civil leaders that they may allow the church to bring its saving liberating message to all for the true enlightenment and freedom of society and the individual.

For our youth that realizing that the wages of sin are death they may reject the evils that destroy them, and come to grace, glory and freedom in God and his church.

For ourselves; in homes, workplaces and areas; may we be beacons of faith, forgiveness and trust in Christ who dying destroyed our death and rising restored our life.

For the sick and all oppressed in body or soul by the evil one, that by faith and love in Christ they may be healed and freed.

For the dead that freed from the sins still weighing them down in the other world, through our prayers they may come to the fullness of light and peace in the Lord.

We ask all these prayers through Christ Our Lord whose body and blood was given up for us so that sins might be forgiven, amen.

## *Reflection*

Graham Green's novel, *The Power And The Glory*, depicts Mexico during the communist era when priests were hung from lamp-posts.

Eventually only a whiskey priest remains. They lure him back, saying a dying man needs confession. As the commandant shoots the priest he says, "ah now we'll have a perfect state". "Ah", the priest says, "you forget about sin". After the commandant shoots the priest, a boy who has been watching spits on the smoking revolver. Lets all see that only in Christ, are we really released from sin. Hail Mary

# Eight Sunday in Ordinary Time B

## Introduction

Our scripture today sees our relationship with God as precious. In the first reading its compared to a husband treating his bride with tender love. Paul sees our relations with God in Christ as endless riches. And Christ compares the new kingdom he brings to fine wine that gladdens the heart. Lets confess any ways we fail to trust in his love.

## Homily

"To live is to change and to be perfect is to change often", says Cardinal Newman. Our era has seen amazing changes. From the horse and trap to traffic jams in one generation; from oil lamps to electric light, from planes to rockets to the moon; from typewriters to word processors; from basic computers to do-all tablets. Our faith should adapt to such changes. Jesus in the gospel reminds us that new wine doesn't go into old wine skins. Certainly the temptation to hold to a fixed way of celebrating faith is perennial.

But we need only look around us to see the stupidity of that view. Moslem, Hindu and Christian fundamentalists alike would imprison us in static culture, rigid law, lifeless beliefs, mad violent impositions. This is what Jesus warns against. God is bigger than our narrow thinking; any faith that stifles change stifles the human spirit. God's love and our response to that love is the only constant. But new ways ways of living that love always open up. Unless we embrace them, we can become irrelevant. Lent challenges us to leave lifeless ways and move forward with the world, while remaining in Christ.

As we approach Spring renewal that's the challenge Jesus also puts before us, new wine, new wine skins. Our church is changing now, being dragged out of old sinful ways. Its slowly and painfully shaking off a legacy of child abuse, harsh authority and misrepresentation of a loving God. In that sense the crisis the church is going through is the Spirit's doing. He's making us more accountable, more pure in heart to live the love, justice and truth we profess. Old self-serving structures are bursting and decayed wine leaking away. A new church is emerging where lay people take over. Convents are closing to make way for religious in ordinary houses. Priests are serving people's spiritual needs rather than running the whole show. Pope Francis is leaving his palace for a humble flat.

Thank God for all that, and for Vatican 11 that made it possible. But let's be careful also. The faith's essentials must not be sacrificed to fashion, structures may change but key truths remain. 2000 years of faithfulness to key doctrines and beliefs can find new expression. But this does not mean that the church must now conform to the ways of a corrupt world. Nor must it jump on the bandwagon of every crazy new ideology, or dump its beliefs willy-nilly for secular or liberal way of thinking that lead us away from essential Christian truths and our eternal salvation.

That is, good change involves wisdom and insight, to be "with it" but also to continue to challenge our troubled world with irrevocable values - respect for life, faithfulness in love, authentic family life, peace in a violent world. For our world has changed for the worst in some ways; with more crime, violence, suicide, abortion, selfishness, unbridled greed, disregard for God. We must both move with our times and challenge its regressions. Each Lent we must try to change our and the world's heart from sin; so that Jesus can become alive anew in the world. For all else passes away but to him, in a changing world, belongs the kingdom, the power and the glory forever, amen.

So as God's people, changing what needs to be changed, leaving corrupt ways and renewing our souls in Christ and the church's timeless truths, lets profess our faith.

## Prayers of the faithful

For church leaders throughout the world, that they may have the wisdom to bring out from the infinite store of Christ things that are both old and ever new.

For our civil leaders that in advocating change they may discern what's expendable from what is essential and precious in our unique spiritual identity as a nation.

For ourselves in homes, workplaces and communities, that we may move forward always and find fresh ways of keeping and expressing the faith.

For our youth that they may keep the faith, the timeless pearl of great price, amid the ups and downs of an ever-changing world.

For the sick in body, mind or soul that through our faith and love they may find the riches, peace and healing of Christ.

For the dead that through our prayers they may enter quickly the perfect way of life Christ has prepared for each of his children.

We ask all these our prayers through the same Christ Our Lord whose Gospel is ever old yet ever new, amen.

## Reflection

I remember when the radio came to our area. People would gather in houses that had one, to hear stirring commentaries on football matches. Then all got transistor radios and moved on to TV in the Fifties. Indeed, the rapid and massive degree of technological change in one generation has been mind-boggling. There were also seismic changes in the church with Vatican 11, and that still goes on today with new parish clustering to maximize a dwindling pool of priests. In all this the faith, and its embodiment in the church, has weathered many changes, and continued to grow. We pray that it will come out stronger as a result of modern changes too. Hail Mary.

# Ninth Sunday in Ordinary Time B

## *Introduction*

"Remember to keep holy the Sabbath Day", God says in our first reading. Do we do so with mass and leisure activities as God intended? I hope so, for we are earthenware jars, as Paul says, that yet hold the treasure of Christ within. A day set aside for our souls is vital. But as Christ shows, let's not make that a rigid law but a joyful commitment.

## *Homily*

When we were young people took the Sabbath seriously. We were even reluctant to save hay on the day. We obeyed what the first reading says: "for six days you shall labor and do all your work but the seventh day is a Sabbath for the lord your God" (Dt. 5:13-14, JB). This gave us time for recreation, a slap-up Sunday dinner and playing or watching games. It all began with dressing up and going to mass. We carefully kept the second commandment: "Observe the Sabbath day and keep it holy" (Dt. 5:12, JB).

But we also kept its spirit; Sunday was a day we looked forward to, never a rigid law. I remember when I was in the Holy Land in the strict areas you could not even drive a car on the Sabbath. That type of imposition is criticized by Christ. But that said, we still need such a day of rest, for recreation and satisfying the deeper needs of the soul. But we must do so from the heart, happily setting aside time for God and play.

For as Christ says, the Sabbath was made for man, not man for the Sabbath. Like all the commandments this is for our liberation not our enslavement; it gives us room for the joyful things of the soul. And in all his teaching Christ is concerned with the life-giving spirit of the law. That's why the Sermon On The Mount, his revision of the ten commandments, has not thou shalt nots. He emphasized not law, but the blessedness that came from doing all he commanded joyfully, for they are our happiness.

But the temptation is that in abandoning rigid law, we may also forget to uphold the spirit of this essential command of God. We should still set aside time for rest on a Sunday, for mass, for going out with the family, for celebrating, for all the essential life-giving things we can't do during the week, because we're too busy getting and spending.

God's laws are wise, for as Wordsworth writes, getting and spending we can lay waste our powers. We need to build them up again on Sunday. The workaholic is the most unfree person in the world. Working on a Sunday, the Sabbath day, is more common; some of it required by industry, some of it not. But even when free on the Sabbath, having spent the whole week frantically making money, the temptation is to spend the whole weekend frantically spending it; so as to again leave no time for God or family matters.

We Christians must avoid such an imbalance; we must find a creative way to keep the second commandment, and make Sunday a special day. To find time during that day for God, for mass, for our family, for rest and recreation together. For during the week, due to work, we may have little time for our spouse and children. If, even on a Sunday we immerse ourselves in frantic pursuit of riches and consumerism, we may neglect such deeper more important things altogether, and eventually destroy our souls.

That point is made well in the film *The Devil Wears Prada*. In it a girl is sucked into the ruthless world of fashion where people are owned body and soul, and where she is expected to be at the beck and call of a ruthless employer, regardless of her family and love commitments. Eventually, she says the price is too high. We can learn from such examples, to get our priorities right on Sunday, and every day.

Christ healed on the sabbath. We must keep Sunday's rest and godliness in some active way. For the devil may wear Prada, but Christ, the lord of the Sabbath, is lord of love, goodness, freedom and peace both for this world and forever and ever, amen.

So as Gods people making space for mass, prayers, rest, recreation and building family togetherness on Sunday, lets profess our faith.

## *Prayers of the Faithful*

For the church throughout the world that it may not neglect to remind people of the crucial making holy of Sunday, the Sabbath Day, so that in the frantic world of today too, people may have a time set side for God and recreational renewal.

For our civil leaders that they may not so encroach upon Sunday for all sorts of economic activities, as to destroy its spiritual and recreational importance altogether.

For ourselves in our homes that pausing on Sunday for Mass and spiritually bonding family activities, we may be ready for the new week renewed in body and soul.

For our youth; may they not lose a sense of the sacredness of Sunday as the Lord's Day, the Sabbath Day, set aside for Mass, and recreational soul-building activities.

For our sick, aged and lonely relatives, that through our caring visits, especially on free days such as Sunday, they may find the healing, comfort and relationship with God that they need.

For the dead that, their work done, they may find happiness and rest in the arms of the lord, helped by the powerful prayers of the assembled people of God here on Sunday.

We ask all these prayers through the Lord of the Sabbath, Jesus Christ Our Lord of not law but life, forever and ever, amen.

## *Reflection*

The Bible tells how God made heaven and earth in six days and on the seventh rested from labor. If God needed a day of rest, surely so do we. We cannot burn the candle at both ends, and remain sane balanced human beings. We pray to Mother Mary that she will help us to see the importance of keeping the Lord's day holy, so that we'll be constantly renewed in soul and body. Hail Mary

# Tenth Sunday in Ordinary Time B

## Introduction

Our readings today deal with doing God's will. Adam and Eve in the first reading refuse to do so and suffer as a result. The same is true of Satan. But from a positive viewpoint doing God will makes us his happy children: "Anyone who does the will of my Father in heaven, is my brother and sister and mother" (Mt. 12:50, JB). Lets confess any way we do our own perverse will, rather than God's good one.

## Homily

What is holiness? the answer is given in our Gospel, to do God's will. Mary was the most holy human being because she did just that. Yet Christ says **all** who do the will of God are his mother and sister and brother. That doesn't mean being perfect, no human being is that, but trying to do his will despite our faults. Holiness is a call continuously answered rather than ever fully attained. Some of the saints were cantankerous odd-balls, like Jerome; or the pious tramp Francis Laboure. Yet loving God heroically, they were holy.

Let me tell you two stories. There was a priest talking about holiness in a hall one day and someone at the back stood up and started ranting and raving against the church's faults. The priest waited until he had finished and said quietly: "OK, so go find the perfect church and don't join it!". For, of course, the perfect church wouldn't be human at all. That's the mystery of the church, holiness in the midst of human mess. Like the whiskey priest in Graham Green's book, *The Power And The Glory*, we can be holy and also a mess. Though a flawed human being he eventually redeemed himself by giving his life to bring confession and peace to a dying man. The truth is that the only true utopia is in the non-worldly heroic effort to answer to God's call, to do his holy will. Our ancestors through every persecution followed Christ; they did his will in hard times, and attained wisdom.

We should also remain true to the church despite its faults. An article in a newspaper recently said people should leave the church because of scandals. I thought of Christ's words to the apostles: "do you want to go away too"; and Peter's reply: "Lord who shall we go to? You have the message of eternal life" (Jn. 6:67-69, JB).

Our faith is not in a few corrupt church members but in Christ. Our role is to try to adhere to his will as expressed in the Gospel, despite our recurrent human weaknesses. For even in establishing his church Christ didn't call perfect people but flawed blusterers like Peter, or greedy tax collectors like Matthew. He showed them the way to do the will of God. They struggled, and abandoned him in Gethsemane when he needed them most. Yet they eventually give him their all. As the church today does despite its failings.

Lets follow its teaching on faith and morals then, not the will of the corrupt world of which Satan is lord. That's our model and I'm amazed how many ordinary people I meet every day who are doing just that. Yet most of these would be shocked to be described as holy. St. Paul says "this is the will of God, your sanctification". And the main aspect of being holy is faith and love. Vatican 11 says again and again, all Christians in any state or walk of life are called to the fullness of the Christian life and to the perfection of love. Lets really mean the Our Father words we pray all the time, "Thy will be done on earth as it is in heaven". For the the will of the world that's contrary to God, fades to dust and ashes at last, but Christ is lord of love, holiness and truth forever and ever, amen.

So as God's own, doing his will as best we can, we profess our faith.


### Prayers of the Faithful

And as his flawed faithful saints lets pray for what we need.

For our Holy Father, and all church leaders that they may serve the will of God not their own power and glory.

For civil leaders that they may serve the people with integrity, justice and special concern for the poor and vulnerable.

For our youth that they may have the wisdom to see that real truth, grace, humanity and freedom is in doing the will of God in Christ, as faithful members of his holy church.

For ourselves in our homes and workplaces and society, that we may bear witness to the will of God in love and faith to redeem the times and make all associated with us free and happy.

For the sick in mind or body, that through our care and love they may know the deep love of God for them, and that sickness is not the will of God - Christ spent his time healing it - but part of our fallen human state that we must do our best to transcend.

For the dead, that having done the will of God on earth as best they could, and endured also human weakness, sin and suffering, they may come to their heavenly home with the help of our prayers.

And we ask all these prayers through Christ who is lord forever and ever, amen.

## Reflection

Fisher, a martyr of the Reformation in England, was a man who believed originally in the divine right of kings. But, realizing that a human being is not God, and we should not do his will if it is contrary to our conscience and God's law, he opposed the king's claim to authority over the church. There is always a tension between obeying the will of the times, its prevalent man-made ideologies, and faithfulness to the more enduring truths and wisdom that comes from God. Lets ask mother Mary to have the wisdom, like the martyrs, to see the difference. Hail Mary

# Eleventh Sunday in Ordinary Time B

## Introduction

Our readings today deal with God's kingdom come in Christ. Ezekiel compares that to a tiny sprout God plants in the earth that becomes a great tree of life. The gospel has the same image of the tiny seed that grows into huge shrub where birds rest. We're birds resting on Christ and his church's branches. Lets confess ways we fail in this loyalty.

## Homily

Recently, I watched the Queen giving her state of the Union address, and thought what a wonderful example she is. But I also thought that human kings, queens and kingdoms in general haven't had a great record. So many of the high kings and queens lorded it over, and failed, their people.

One kingdom that will never fade, however, is Gods deeper perfect kingdom in Christ. For unlike human kingdoms its universal, eternal, peaceful and timeless; its citizens include the living and the dead. As Christ said to Pilate, his kingdom is not of this world. In its mystic aspect its all good people in the world who do what's right. In its bodily aspect, the church, it crosses all borders and includes all races and nations. The varied languages and colors of people at the Eucharistic Congress recently reminded me of that.

Lets rejoice that we belong to that great universal kingdom of grace and peace and truth in Christ. It started from a tiny seed, the resurrection, and has grown into a mighty tree, under which all peoples rest, find light and are saved. For its focus isn't worldly power but God's truth. The apostles went out at Pentecost to set it up in answer to Christ's command: "go, therefore, make disciples of all the nations; baptize them in the name of the Father, and of the Son and of the Holy Spirit. And know that I am with you always; yes, to the end of time" (Mt. 28:19-20, JB). That it is from God is proved by the fact that it has gathered a universal harvest of souls since and encompassed the globe.

We're privileged to be citizens of that Kingdom, and serve its king, Christ. But with privileges goes responsibilities. As vowed at Baptism, the key to the kingdom, we must help build it on earth; bring it to fulfillment, so that God's will may be done on earth as it is in heaven. For that's the Kingdom's aim, a total fallen world totally redeemed.

We celebrate Father's day at this time and parents in the home have a huge role in building that kingdom. In the Our Father we pray, thy kingdom come. But it won't come without our help. Christ needs our hands to build it, and we are the kingdom as practicing members of the local church. For its there that the kingdom is incarnated; in the here and now its made visible in authentic church structures we help to build and maintain.

Nowadays the failings of the church deter some from this great task, but we mustn't throw out the baby with the bathwater. Despite flaws, its human as well as divine, the Risen Lord is at the church's center. So hang in there, active members of the party structure as it were, canvassing for it, not just passive card-holders. For in its deeper aspects the church is the life of the world, embodied in our own local and particular churches.

Seeing beyond the church's human flaws to that glory is wisdom. Seeing it as a human flawed but yet essential instrument of victory over sin, death and evil in Christ. For this world's contrary kingdoms of which Satan is lord pass and leave us empty within at last, but Christ is Lord of grace, and salvation for this world and forever and ever, amen.

So as God's own, building his church kingdom generously, we profess our faith.

## *Prayers of the faithful*

And as God's people of the eternal Kingdom of truth, lets pray for what we need.

For leaders of the churches throughout the world, may they serve the Kingdom of God and bring all to its fullness in Christ.

For civil leaders that in serving their own kingdom of earthly power and glory they may not put any obstacles in the way of the growth of the greater Kingdom of God in the world.

For young people that they may see beyond the passing kingdoms of this world of which Satan is lord, to the deeper and more enduring Kingdom of God in Christ, and remain true and practicing members of his holy church, its frail earthly embodiment.

For ourselves in our homes, workplaces and communities that we may be witnesses to the Kingdom of God, and bring its riches to our children, and all we come into contact with.

For the sick, the ages and the lonely that through our love and care they may know the consolations of God's healing Kingdom.

For the dead that they may come to the final kingdom prepared for them since the foundation of the world helped by our powerful communal prayers as the body of Christ.

We ask these prayers through Christ Our Lord, to whom belongs the Kingdom, the power and the glory forever and ever, amen.


## *Reflection*

Our world is full of nation Kingdoms, where the local and particular culture is embodied. For the nature of the world is variety, in that area as in every other; what Louis McNeice called the drunkenness of things being various. If all countries were the same, or all people the same, it would be a dull world indeed. That's why I think the superstate idea is a mistake, especially if, like the EU or the old Soviet Union, it tries to quash local variety and color in the interests of grey superstate conformity and ideology. That's why the variety of the churches can be a good thing too, as long as it doesn't lead to conflict and disunity and violence, which is a counterwitness. Lets pray for church unity in diversity, under the great unifying banner of Christ, the Alpha and the Omega of all truth. Hail Mary

# Twelfth Sunday in Ordinary Time B

## Introduction

Trust in God bears us up in life's Tempests, our first reading says. And Jesus stills the storm in the Gospel, saying: "Why are you so frightened? How is it that you have no faith?" (Mk. 4:40-41, JB). Lets confess any lack of trust in God amid life's troubles.

## Homily

"I feel just awful, I wish someone would shoot me, I can't go on living", a person said to me once. I was shocked because for me life is precious, I can't imagine anyone giving up hope. But maybe I'm naive. I know that even in times of affluence, and more so in times of recession, many are troubled. Multitudes ring The Samaritans and helpline every day. We all go through rough patches in life; as problems and difficulties pile up we're tempted to despair. Don't, listen to Christ instead: "Why are you so frightened? How is it you have no faith".

The apostles lost faith during the storm but he rebuked them and calmed the waves. In the same way he'll lift us up in dark times, lighten our burdens. Scripture tells us to cast your care on the Lord for he has care of us. And Christ says: "Do not let your hearts be troubled, trust in God still, trust also in me" (Jn. 14:1-2, JB).

"Be not afraid for I am with you" was the motto of the late John Paul 11. He lived this gospel of trust in Christ. It enabled him to survive the storms of fascism in his native Poland and later terrible communist repression. He had to be ordained in secret because the church was banned. He also survived the early death of his parents, and, as Pope, an attack on his life. Trust in Christ carried him past every trial. If we imitate him we'll be wise, trust will sustain us also. For God is not a luxury to take or leave, he's as necessary as the air we breathe. People lose out when that sure ground is taken away.

For without God's healing presence life is ultimately empty and meaningless, there are fewer reasons to go on. This is a proven fact. Psychological studies in hospitals have shown that those with faith are more likely to recover from illness and recover more quickly. And I read recently about Pierce Brosnan, the movie star who seems so self-assured. In fact he suffered many crises of late. He wrote that without his Catholic faith he'd never have got through or made those trials a source of growth in his life.

This is the great consolation of us all as God's people. We're not alone. God is with us in Christ and enables us to grow, even through our troubles. His love endures forever, and as St. Paul says nothing can separate us from the love of God in Christ Jesus Our Lord. If we trust and pray he'll turn our weaknesses into strengths. For Christ cares. He spent his public life caring for those in society who were sick and scorned by the world. He loves us. We must never forget that we're children of an infinity caring God who doesn't judge by worldly standards.

The Sacred Heart feast we had recently illustrates that, his heart burns with love for each of us. He's just waiting for us to ask him to lighten our way in life's dark hours. That's wisdom, to acknowledg our need for him, for it really hurts him when those who need him most turn away. He can heal and bring us eternal life but many won't let him. So when things get ever rough, we've no sure ground to stand on. As God's people lets avoid that trap. For the world and its trials pass, but Christ is lord of hope, love and inner peace for this world and forever and ever, amen.

So as God's people trusting in Christ to calm life's storms and bring us safely home, we profess our faith.

## *Prayers of the faithful*

For our Holy Father the Pope that he may be an example to the whole world of the trust in God which brings peace.

For civil leaders that as the American dollar says "in God we trust", they may not exclude God from their governing spirit.

For our youth that amid the storms of life they may find a safe anchor in Christ their loving Savior.

For ourselves that in our homes when things go wrong we may turn to Christ and his blessed Mother as our one sure harbor.

For the sick that they may trust in the Lord through all their sufferings and through our care know his presence in their lives.

For the dead that the storms of life over they may rest in the Lord forever, helped to their heavenly peace by our prayers.

We ask all these prayers through the same Christ who is lord of consolation, inner strength and peace forever and ever, amen.

## *Reflection*

One of the great scenes in the Old Testament is David's confrontation with Goliath. David says to this giant come to fight him, that he trusts in his shield and armor, but David trust in the lord God. Of course, through that trust, the boy David was able to overcome the mighty arrogant warrior of the Philistines. We pray that we will have the same trust, and through that trust rise to true greatness of life, like the saints. Hail Mary

# Thirteenth Sunday in Ordinary Time B

## Introduction

"The world's created things have health in them", our first reading says. Healing is part of our faith. We see Jesus in our gospel healing the woman with a haemorrhage and curing Jairus's daughter. Let's seek his healing in our lives, as we confess.

## Homily

Maybe you've heard of Brid McKenna, the miracle-worker. As a young sister she suffered from arthritis, and this was hard to bear for one so young. One day she went to the church and begged God to heal her. Suddenly a voice said: "Brid you are healed, go and heal others". She got up from her knees free of pain. Now she goes round the world preaching and holding healing masses. She wrote a best-seller, *Miracles Do Happen*, telling how in that ministry she has witnessed many miracles, physical and spiritual.

She has a special mission to heal priests, for she says, the devil is launching an assault on them today, because they're in the front line of God's work. Brid has seen many spiritual miracles, notably hardened sinners embracing the church. These wonders usually happen at mass when the people are blessed with the monstrance containing the Blessed Sacrament. The healing is not her's but Christ's. She tells a story of a sick baby in its mother's arms who suddenly looked at the Monstrance and cried out; he was healed.

You may say why this extraordinary activity? Faith shouldn't depend on signs and wonders. But there's nothing extraordinary about Brid's ministry. She's doing what Christ did. In our Gospel we see him healing a little girl. When he went in to heal her, the crowd laughed at him. Just as the cynical world laughs at spiritual healing today. But Christ dismissed the crowd and said, "little girl I tell you to get up" (Mk. 5:42, JB).

He raises us up and heals us in some way, even if we're not physically cured. Sr. Brid heals by recourse to God and the power of prayer. So must we Christians, for our life in Christ is healing. Of course in this, we must first use to the full God's ongoing miracle of medical science. Faith healing shouldn't bypass that. Sickness is part of life and hard to explain, but without it we wouldn't have the wonderful work of accomplished doctors, nurses and house carers. In these Christ the healer is most alive. But faith adds a further dimension to this healing. Only in God is healing complete; even doctors agree that we the whole person must be treated, for many illnesses have psychosomatic roots.

That's why modern scientific studies have shown that those in hospital who have faith are more likely to recover from sickness. Moreover the study found they recover more quickly, and are less likely to despair if terminally ill. We should not be surprised. Even non-believers see the need for faith and prayer faced with the mystery of suffering and death. For only God enables us to bear suffering courageously, and offer it up if it can't be healed by the ordinary means he provides.

Finally, Christ healed the scars of sin as well as physical ills. For sin is a sickness related to our fallen human condition. In Christ it can be redeemed and turned into spiritual gold. So like Brid McKenna or the little girl in the gospel, lets turn to God for every healing. For the world's hard values pass and something always comes to bring us to our end, the one sure thing in this world is that we must die, but Christ is lord of healing love and salvation both for this world and forever and ever, amen.

So as God's people consoling the sick in whatever way we can and praying for the dying, we profess our faith.

## Prayers of the Faithful

And as the people of God lets pray for what we need.

For our Father and all the leaders of the church that they may be shining lights leading all to the healing arms of Christ.

For civil leaders, through funding our health system to the full may they be part of the great work of healing in society.

For our youth that realizing the shortness of life and its emptiness and pain as well as its joys, they may come to where deeper life, happiness, healing and wealth is in Christ.

For ourselves that in our homes we may be the healing love and hands of Christ to those around us, especially our children, and sick or aged relatives and neighbors.

For the sick in body, mind or soul that they may, through our prayers and care, come to healing, comfort and peace.

For the dead that the fever of life over and their work done they may come quickly to the heavenly home prepared for them, helped by our prayers.

We ask all these prayers through Christ the only Lord of life, healing and grace for this world and forever, amen.

## Reflection

The death of Michael Jackson shocked many. It reminded me of mortality; that, as scripture says, none of us have here a lasting city. Knowing that should make us wise. Sure, while here lets live life fully, the glory of God is man fully alive. And let's use our talents, as Jackson did, to enrich the world. But for inner depth and greatness lets also have faith, so that our work here will be more complete, our happiness deeper, and at last we'll flower into glory. But even for this world, we need the deeper life and inner wealth faith gives; otherwise we flounder in a short meaningless life ending in darkness. Drugs or alcohol are only false bridges over the void created by the emptiness of existence and the suffering of being; we need deeper inner hope, love and light. Lets thank God for the faith that provides such light and brings us peace in Christ both for here and forever. Hail Mary

# Fourteenth Sunday in Ordinary Time B

## Introduction

Our readings deal with faith and justice. In the first the prophet scarifies the wealthy who in pride harden their hearts against God. And Christ is shocked at the lack of real faith among wealthy, haughty religious authorities. Lets confess ways we shut out God too.

## Homily

There's a story told of an African pastor during apartheid. Asked to preach at a "Christian" service he accepted only on the condition that colored members of the congregation be allowed in. Prejudice was so rife, some ministers gave communion to colored people out the window. We needn't go to Africa for such practice. I remember at home when dues were read out in church. Poor people who gave only 10 shillings were humiliated. The rich owned pews in churches, one dare not sit in their privileged seats.

But that's not new. Christ himself met with snobbery. The fiercest unbelievers were in his own town, for he was just the carpenter's son. He himself treated all as equal. Were he alive during apartheid, I'm sure he'd have pulled many a pastor's head out the window and scarified those who attended to the big shot in church while ignoring the poor. Christ soundly rebuked the apostles for keeping the so-called riff-raff away from him.

So should we. Rather than judge people according the ways of a cold, money-adoring world, we too should judge all people as equal children of God, and pay special attention to the poor or excluded in society. For Christ said they'd enter the Kingdom of God before the rich, who in pride think they don't need God or man; money is enough.

But Christ didn't endure holy snobs easily; people who professed faith but didn't live it. Indeed, he saw the worst form of sin as self-righteousness, thinking ourselves better or holier than others. He, the holiest person ever, washed his disciples feet. He was turned way by the rich, was born in a stable, and was a traveling preacher with nowhere to lay his head. He was poor in spirit, so that he could serve the poor.

The challenge for us is to do the same, to make no distinction between man and man, woman and woman, child and child. To respect the god-given dignity of each person whatever his or her state in life. "Let not a man guard his dignity", the famous philosopher Emerson is suppose to have said, "but let his dignity guard him". We can do much harm to peoples dignity by prejudice; looking down on the poor, or the disabled, or travelers.

Church leaders must take this lesson too. There's more than one way to give communion out of the window, more than one way to humiliate the disadvantaged, more than one way to pander to the rich and turn our faces from the needy. Some say the abuse scandals were about power. But not just church people can fall into that trap. Look at the adoration of pop stars who turn out to have clay feet, and are often destroyed by our adoration. As one theologian noted, the main temptation we all fail over and over again, be we church or lay people, is that Christ faced in the desert, to put pride, wealth and power before God and the poor. Christ chose to be a suffering servant of all.

The church is humiliated now because it failed to follow his example. As an old man said to me recently, we kept priests too fat. Certainly, with palaces, wealth and unfeeling institutions, the church of the past was more like the Pharisees than Christ. In this, however, none of us need be smug. We too connive in injustice at times, and despise the weak. We too fail to imitate the carpenter's son who was raised by God. But the more we imitate his humility the higher we're be raised up. For the world's gods of power, wealth and fame turn to ashes at last, but Christ is lord of all inclusive faith, love and goodness for this world and forever and ever, amen.

So as God's people keeping a true and humble sense of our worth, and cherishing all God's children equally, we profess our faith.

### Prayers of the Faithful

And as God's children we pray for what we need.

For church leaders throughout the world, especially the Pope, that they may come down from their palaces and be one with the poor and suffering Christs of the world.

For civil leaders that they may not indulge in corruption and misuse of public funds but use taxpayers money to serve all the people, especially the poor and underprivileged.

For our youth that they may not put their whole trust in wealth, fame and power but cherish the Christian ideal of humble service of God and others, especially the needy.

For ourselves in our homes; may we treat all our children with equal love and fairness, and reach out to the needy around us with compassion and unprejudiced care.

For the sick, the aged and the lonely that through our finding of time for them they may know the love of God in their lives.

For the dead, especially those holy souls who may have no one to pray for them, that they may come to the all-embracing arms of Christ and the heavenly home where all wrongs are righted.

We ask all these our prayers through Christ to God the only and equally-loving Father of all his children, amen.

## Reflection

The great condemnation of snobbery in the Gospel is the story of Dives and Lazarus. Dives and his brothers feasted every day, and ignored Lazarus, a poor man at their gate covered in sores, who begged only the crumbs from their table. Then both Dives and Lazarus died. The rich man went to hell, but the poor man went to heaven where he finally received the justice denied him on earth. Its a warning to all who trust in riches and grand houses, who ignore God, and despise their poor neighbor. Lets ask Mother Mary to help us to open our hearts to God and others, whatever our circumstances. Hail Mary

# Fifteenth Sunday in Ordinary Time B

## Introduction

Our readings focus on mission. In the first reading the prophet is commissioned to go out and proclaim God's word. Christ tells the apostles to gather all into the saving nets of God. Lets confess ways we fail to be the missionaries for Christ in or world.

## Homily

Reflecting on mission I always think of John Paul 11. He carried the gospel to over 100 countries and ministered to billions by his preaching and writing. His books outsold the best authors of our day. He made the Papacy a powerful moral and spiritual force in an increasingly hard secular world, constantly challenging it with God's deeper values. Family planning, abortion, euthanasia, divorce; the break-up of the family, the death penalty, war, the unequal distribution of wealth; even those who disagreed with him recognized the power of his dialogue with the world on such pressing issues.

And his stress on the sacred nature of each human life still resonates in a world where economics is often made into a god, and human life, from conception to the grave, is disposable. Yet even when criticizing a culture of death in consumerist society his kind Christ-like nature shone through. As did his courage in championing human rights under Fascist and Communist systems. Psychologists say good parents are loving yet consistent and just; with this Holy Father everything was reasoned and explained.

But above all he helped Christians hold their nerve amid present spiritual chaos. We must hold our heads high and keep the faith in the same way today. For we've the message of eternal life, and the world is not enough for our children. That why Christianity has survived 1000s of worldly social and political systems over 2000 years. It'll see off present-day attacks too in the power of the Risen Lord which cannot be defeated in the long run. John Paul defeated tyrannical fascism and communism in Poland. He constantly challenged the emptiness of the world, calling it to follow Christ, the way, the truth and the life. So must we. For all else leaves us empty and lost on a cruel meaningless earth.

This highlights the urgency of Mission, the crucial struggle today is for the salvation of our children's souls. As Christ sent out the apostles, we're sent out at Baptism and Confirmation and never was our Christian witness more needed. Today the harvest is indeed great, and the laborers are few. We must gather that harvest now for people's happiness both in the next world and in this one. I read an interview with Seamus heaney, the great poet, recently deceased. He said we should keep the faith we've received for happiness on this earth even if, like many today, the next world seems too remote. He's right, we must must live our faith heritage of truth and goodness for our welfare at all levels. For our children's earthly happiness, inner mental peace and final eternal life.

As we live so shall we die and many give up on life now because they've no deep hope or truth to enrich their existence. Faith is necessary for us in every way. Here we come to another key point John Paul stressed that that the only real happiness is to be found in the church's deep scriptural wisdom and Eucharistic sharing. Our mission is to bring that to all in its full richness, for happiness here too. Lets bring to our children and those we influence at work or communally fullness of life in Christ and his church. For godless worldly values fade leaving us empty before eternity but Christ is lord of truth, goodness and happiness for this earth and forever, amen.

So as God's people, living faith and mission against all attack and like John Paul proclaiming it to the world for its enrichment in every way, lets profess our faith proudly.

## Prayers of the faithful

For church leaders now, that like John Paul they may work tirelessly to bring all to the arms of Christ and what's right.

For civic leaders that they may leave the church free for its vital mission to bring the saving life of Christ to all.

For our youth that they may not drift away from the church, and back into the darkness from which he delivered us, but stay with the lord of life as active members of, and everyday witnesses for his holy church.

For ourselves in our homes that we may pass on to our children the gift of faith we received, and so help continue the church's saving mission until all achieve final happiness in God.

For the sick that offering up their sufferings for the salvation of the world they may turn their unavoidable sufferings into gold, and know God's love through our care for them.

For the dead that having finished their work in this world and kept the faith, they may enjoy the rest of the Blessed with their Father in heaven.

We ask all this or the Father through Christ who is lord of truth, life and salvation for this world and forever and ever, amen.

## Reflection

Ancient monks were great missionaries. St. Brendan sailed from Ardfert to seek foreign lands for Christ in a boat of canvas and pitch. In the old manuscript, *The Voyages Of St. Brendan,* we see him braving endless icy seas in such a craft. It may even have carried him to America via Iceland, experts say. The voyages mention mountains of crystal, icebergs, and sheep big as cattle, probably polar bears. The explorer

Heyerdahl traced his probable route to Canada using a similar boat. We face dark icy seas of societal and even government irreligion today in living and spreading the faith. Lets do so with hearts as wise and brave and generous as our great saintly ancestors. Hail Mary

# Sixteenth Sunday in Ordinary Time B

## Introduction

In our first reading, Jeremiah attacks bad pastors and God vows to raise up true shepherds to look after all. Christ saw the lost of his day as sheep without a shepherd. Lets pray for good shepherds for today, and confess ways we fail our own little flocks.

## Homily

"Doom for the shepherds who allow the flock to be scattered" (Jr. 23:1-2, JB). These words send a shiver down my spine. So do Christ's words: "he took pity on them because they were like sheep without a shepherd" (Mk. 6:14, JB). There are many like this today. Abandoning the church, they are rudderless, living as I read in a recent survey of young people's attitudes, in the here and now, with no regard for their soul's salvation for this world or the next. Its frightening but not new. Jeremiah's words, from 3000 years ago are still true. But there is also consolation in God's promise to the prophet: "I will raise up shepherds to look after them … no one shall be lost" (Jr. 23:4, JB). We priests, bishops, and lay ministers must be such shepherds, leading all back to the fold.

We find criticism now in newspapers and *Prime Time* of those who failed in this. But Christ was as hard on corrupt shepherds of his day, religious authorities who served their interests rather than the needy flock. He told the people to be guided by them in matters of faith, but not to imitate their lifestyle. He himself not only preached but lived the true shepherd role, washing people's feet and saying that the greatest is the servant of all. The true role of priests, bishops, and even the Pope is as servants of the servants of God.

Are we that? Have we rather palaces to protect? Do we rather cover up for one another, like a self-serving club, not God's church? History doesn't change; the church, human as well divine, always needs reform. The consolation is that Christ constantly does that, creating new prophets and leaders when administrations become partial.

This is true not only of bad shepherds of the church but also of the state. He constantly brings down the mighty and exalts the lowly. So I see Providence's hand in recent revelations of priestly and ministerial corruption. For the abuse of the weak or the people's trust, is a crime God dare not ignore. His prophets today, in highlighting a criticizing all such, are the media, but the corrupt powerful always encounter some scourge of God. For he abhors corruption and injustice, whatever its source. Scripture rings like a bell down the ages: "doom on the shepherds who allow the sheep to be scattered".

Indeed, modern organs of criticism join scripture in this, they are part of a divine process by which, as Christ says, the one who exalts himself will be humbled and the one who humbles himself will be exalted. We priests need a dose of humility. Archbishops in their palaces, indeed all of us, should shiver at God's word, that shepherds must not lord it over the flock, but be humble servants of all. And this applies not just to spiritual and government leaders but to each of us. We're all shepherds in some form, at home, in school, in the workplace. We all face justice for any oppression of innocents in our care.

The Lord hears the cry of the poor scripture says. He demands real humble service of others like Christ gave unto death. The flock are out there, crying for caring mothers and fathers too in a violent, godless, immoral age. We the shepherds, whatever our leadership role, must lead all with humble love. For every day we read of young people beating up the old and the weak for a few euros, high on drugs or drink. Spiritual foundation gone, they've nothing to sustain them in the jungle of a recession world. The challenge for shepherds is to be there for them, lights and true examples. For we need to be saved in every age from the ruthless shepherd that is Satan and his worldly minions. We must be the Savior's hands of love and care for all our children. For all else fades but only our love and goodness in Christ is light forever, amen.

So as God's people praying for good shepherds in church and state to lead us with wisdom and integrity, lets profess our faith.

## Prayers of the faithful

For our Holy Father and bishops of the church that they may feed the people of God by preaching and living the Word humbly, and so pointing all to happiness, wisdom and integrity in Christ.

For our civil leaders that they may serve the people under their care well, especially the poor and most vulnerable in society.

For our young people that they may come every Sunday to the table of the Word and the Eucharist, and so be fed by Christ, the good shepherd, unto greatness of life for this world and the next.

For ourselves, may we go from the table of the Lord to carry his faith, love, peace and grace to our children, our workmates and our community, and so be good shepherds of our small flock.

For the sick that through regular or First Friday reception of the Eucharist they may know the comfort, care and healing of Christ, the Good Shepherd.

For the dead that having received Christ regularly here below they may come to the promised final resurrection and to the highest heaven through our prayers and masses.

We ask all these prayers through Christ who is lord of all the living forever and ever, amen.

## Reflection

You may know the story of the king who went down among his people as a common laborer and learned much as result, even true love; its a common theme of folk tales. It illustrates what Christ says of leadership; it must be in touch with and serve the real needs of the people. This is true of shepherds of church of state; no true leader can afford to live in an ivory tower of privilege or grand isolation. Lets ask Mother Mary to help all leaders to be God's humble tender hands and heart to all those in their care. Hail Mary.

# Seventeenth Sunday in Ordinary Time B

## Introduction

Our gospel sees Christ feeding the crowd in the desert. He still feeds us with himself. Lets confess any lack of appreciation of our communion with him in the mass.

## Homily

Once at Easter I asked an adult about to be baptized what becoming a Christian meant. "Really receiving the body of Christ", she said. After her communion, she lit up. "For first time I've real peace and happiness within", she said. Christ feeds the crowds in our gospel. He still feeds his people at mass and we're satisfied in body and soul. But receiving every Sunday, we can take him for granted. So as we gather here to share the bread of life, lets renew our love for this gift whereby were united with the Lord and raised to heaven. Lets reaffirm his presence for us as real, in communion and in the Tabernacle.

I sometimes think that he gets lonely waiting for people to come and speak to him in the Tabernacle. That's why perpetual adoration is wonderful. It gives us a chance to be with the Lord and make up for general indifference. For faith is a growing relationship with God and communion is the kisses of that relationship. There's a story of a man who'd visit the church each evening on the way home from work. He'd say "heh Jesus, its me Tom". One day he'd a heart attack and his heart stopped. Before doctors brought him back he experienced Jesus coming to him with open arms saying: "heh Tom, its just me Jesus".

Whether the story is true or not it illustrates and important truth; that faith is really about a growing relationship with the Lord. This relationship is built in weekly or daily communion, visiting him in the church, and personal prayer at home. Once we know him in this way, he'll come to meet us at last and know us, and join us to our relatives who have gone before us in faith, and to the saints in glory. For he promises: "anyone who does eat eat my flesh and drink my blood has eternal life, and I shall raise him up on the last day" (Jn. 6:54, JB). Imagine that! We're part of eternal life already when we receive him in communion, and assured of being raised up at last. Moreover, he remains with us for our earthly struggles during the ensuing week; so mass is not a duty but life in Christ.

For the Christ we receive isn't remote. After he died, God raised him and gave him all authority in heaven and earth. By regular communion we grow in intimacy with that glorified lord until we flower into eternity. Communion also enriched us for life, intensifies our joys, and helps us bear life's burdens and sufferings. For in each Eucharist we share God's life, commune with the saints in glory, and unite with the local and universal church. On Sunday he rose, and each Sabbath he feeds his lambs in the desert of the world.

Moreover, communion enables us to live a life worthy of our calling in complete selflessness, gentleness and charity. Fed by Christ, we can feed others, especially the needy around us. He washed the feet of his disciples at the first mass to tell us that communion with him should lead to humble service of God and others in daily life. He asks us to make our world a Eucharistic community of service. Not only to enrich and make us part of eternal life but also to heal the world. For godless values fade to dust and ashes at last, but Christ is lord of life, love, peace, happiness and salvation in the mass, both for our happiness in this life and forever and ever, amen.

So as God's people sharing in his bread of life, and bringing its fruits to others in overflowing love, we profess our faith.

## Prayers of the faithful

And as a Eucharistic community, united with God, let's pray for what we need.

For our Holy Father and all church leaders, that they may feed the people of God by giving them the Word and the Eucharist, for their happiness here and for eternity.

For our civil leaders that they may serve the people under their care well, especially the poor and most vulnerable in society.

For our wonderful youth that, coming each Sunday to the table of the Word and communion, they may be energized for graceful living in this world, and an eternity with the saints when he come again.

For ourselves that we may go out from the Lord's table with faith, love, peace and grace for our children, workmates, community, and all we encounter.

For the sick that through regular or First Friday reception of the Eucharist, as part of our Christian care, they may know the comfort, care and healing of Christ.

For the dead, that having received Christ regularly here they may come to the promised resurrection and the highest heaven through our prayers and masses for them as their ongoing Eucharistic family.

We ask these prayers through Christ, lord of the living forever and ever, amen.


## Reflection

The story of how God fed the Israelites in the desert, during the exodus from Egypt, underlies much of the Eucharistic symbolism in the

New Testament. Wandering in the inhospitable desert, the people of God cried out for food, and water. He made water gush from the rock when Moses struck it, and he sent a white powdery food, that settled on the ground, and the people collected it each morning. It was called manna, and sustained the people until they reached the promised land. Christ feeding us with the Eucharist, in our journey through the desert of the world today, or at any time, is similar. It is the spiritual food that sustains us, the new people of God, until we reach the land flowing with milk and honey, the promised land awaiting us in heaven. Lets partake of this food with grateful hearts and ask our Mother Mary to keep us faithful in receiving it each Sunday. Hail Mary

# Eighteenth Sunday in Ordinary Time B

## Introduction

Our first reading describes the manna by which God fed the Jews during their desert journey. It prefigured the Eucharist by which he feeds us, his new people in Christ, for our spiritual journey; "he who eats this bread will never be hungry" Jesus says. Lets confess any failure to appreciate the importance of this bread of life.

## Homily

Last Sunday showed us Christ feeding people in the desert. Today's gospel continues that story. They sought him again for bread. But he rebuked them saying they shouldn't work for the food that passes away, but for the food that the endures unto eternal life, the Eucharist. This answers questions some ask nowadays. Why the mass? Why's it a matter of life or death to go every Sunday? Why did our ancestors attend mass under threat of death and walk barefoot to mass when times were hard?

The answer to these questions is given in accounts of the early church: "they remained faithful to the teaching of the apostles, to the brotherhood, to the breaking of bread, and to the prayers" (Acts. 2:42, JB). What united and gave believers their identity then was an early form of the mass. Its our Christian anchor in life's storms now too.

Sure, we should pray at home too, but not as a replacement for our worship as the body of Christ every Sunday. And it has to be on Sunday; daily mass is not the same. For Sunday is the Sabbath day, the day we're to set aside for rest and worship of God. Its also the Lord's Day, when Christ rose from the dead. Coming together on Sunday, we share his risen life, and become his risen body. For when we go up to communion and say amen to "the body of Christ", we not only affirm our faith in real Christ's presence in the bread and wine, we also say that we **are** the body of Christ gathered in church.

Christianity's not an individualistic religion. We're saved as part of a community of faith and worship and Christian action and witness. Baptized into that family, if we stay aloof from it, we're Christian in name only. We may still keep the commandments and pray, but something vital is missing for our Christian journey; that's why the church once said missing mass was a mortal sin. Christ himself says that unless we eat his flesh and drink his blood we won't have life in us; without that food our spiritual life shrivels.

That may even be true at the social level. As it increasingly abandons mass our predominantly Catholic society increasingly disintegrates into violence, family breakdown, drink, drugs. Without Christ's sustaining presence we can lose touch with God and whats right. He says those who aren't with me are against me, so we can soon end up serving the prince of this world instead.

But people say, "but oh, all these people going to mass are so hypocritical, they're sinners too". Sure, we don't automatically become saints thereby; the struggle to be holy is life-long. But the presence of Christ in communion and the Word broken open every Sunday, accelerates the growing life of our souls. Don't t take my word for it, take Christ's: "if you do not eat the flesh of the Son of Man and drink his blood, you will not have life in you" (Jn. 6:53, JB). No wonder our mass-going ancestors were saints.

Today some say, "mass is boring". But its not entertainment, or a quick fix, but something deeper; it needs active participation. But even at the modern cynical level of whats-in-it-for-me it makes sense. Its fruits in our lives can't always be seen but deep down it brings peace and spiritual riches. Again Christ affirms this: "Anyone who does eat my flesh and drink my blood has eternal life, and I shall raise him up on the last day". That is, through each Eucharist we grow in God's life, until we blossom into heavenly glory. For all else fade to ashes at last, but regular Sunday communion with Christ brings untold happiness for this world, and forever and ever, amen.

So as God's people, eating the bread of life each Sunday, and becoming the body of Christ in our gathering, we profess our family faith.

## *Prayers of the faithful*

And as the gathered Eucharistic Family of God we pray for what we need.

For church leaders, that they may bring all to a deep appreciation of the centrality of the Eucharist for the lives of the faithful, and for the salvation of the world.

For our civil leaders that they may not put obstacles in the way of our children's sacramental faith and life in our schools.

For our great youth; may they be wise and see the importance of Sunday mass; that receiving the bread of life is as important for their souls as food is for their bodies.

For our homes and families that Sunday mass and communion may still be the key way of keeping holy the Sabbath Day, a way to unity, peace and grace.

For the sick that they may find in the communion brought to their homes, a way of participating in the church body, and sharing in Christ's comfort, healing and strength.

For the dead; having received Christ's Body, may they be raised up to the glory it promises, as we pray for them here in a communion that includes the living and the dead.

We ask all these prayers through the same Christ, the bread of life, from whom all good things come, amen.

## *Reflection*

Let me tell you a story of St. Maximilian Kolbe, who died in the Auschwitz concentration camp. Bread was scarce there, and wine even scarcer. But they always saved a morsel of bread and a sip of wine for mass. They passed it around among them in their cells every Sunday. It gave them grace and strength to endure their unimaginable sufferings. Kolbe eventually gave his life for one of the other prisoners, a family man, enriched by his union with Christ. We have plenty of bread and wine, but do we cherish mass and communion as much; lets pray to Mary that we'll always do so. Hail Mary

# Nineteenth Sunday in Ordinary Time B

## Introduction

This is the third Sunday that features the Eucharist. Elijah journeyed for forty days and forty nights to God's mountain, fortified by bread from heaven. This prefigures the Eucharist. Jesus is the bread sent from heaven to nourish us for life's long journey. Lets confess failures to appreciate the importance of Communion for our Christian life.

## Homily

"I am the living bread which has come down from heaven", Christ reminds us today, "Anyone who eats this bread will live forever" (Jn. 6:51, JB). What a wonderful summing up of the importance of Holy Communion. Indeed Christ makes no bones about it, unless we eat his flesh and drink his blood we will not have life in us. What a strong statement. We avoid that fate by coming every Sunday for the bread of life. At this sacred meal he feeds his people not just for Sunday, but the week that follows and life's journey.

In the first reading we see Elijah spiritually and physically exhausted. Then an angel brings him bread from heaven, a sign of the Eucharist. We're told: "strengthened by that food he walked for forty days and forty nights, until he reached Horeb, the mountain of God" (1K. 19:8, JB). People say, "why the mass?". There's the answer. With its help, we walk through life's journey confidently, protected like Elijah, until we reach the mountain of God, our eternal home. Indeed Christ reminds us that in Holy Communion we're already part of eternal life and sure to be raised up on the last day.

But, as Paul reminds us, Holy Communion is not just for our benefit. Its given so that we can bear the fruits of good and holy lives for others. It showers us with grace so that we can witness to Christ and all that good before the world. The Holy Spirit we receive in communion enables us, above all, to live charitable lives. Never bear grudges, Paul says, never lose your temper or raise your voice to anyone or call others names (Ep. 4:31, JB). That is, communion with Christ should make us kind, loving, and forgiving, gentle in speech and act. For we grow in the life of the lord we receive; our lives become a fragrant offering to God in goodness, justice, holiness and peace.

What great food from heaven! In its power, frail human being though we are, nothing is beyond us. Whereas without it we can die within, go the primrose way to the everlasting bonfire. But with it we'll never die, for the lord and his Holy Spirit is present in our hearts, making us infinitely greater than we can ever be.

You raise me up to more than I can be, a popular song says. By regular Sunday communion we become ever more like the glorious Christ who conquered sin, suffering, death, and every earthly trial. In communion he makes us part of his divine glory, bears our burdens, and enriches us until, as Paul says we become little less than Gods. For we share God's life, commune with the saints in glory and become one with the local and universal church. That's why Sunday mass is life and death for us. We gather as the people of God and he feeds us with the bread of life. That's the only enduring food, for all the things of this world pass away to dust and ashes ar last but in that glorious communion Christ bring us life, love, goodness, happiness, beauty and salvation both for this world and forever and ever, amen.

So as God's own, communion in Christ filling us with glorious life for here and hereafter, lets profess our faith with overflowing joy.

## Prayers of the faithful

And as the living body of Christ lets pray for what we need.

For church leaders that after the International Eucharistic Congress they may inspire a new flowering of Eucharistic devotion.

For civic leaders that they may promote the spiritual as well as social and political good of the community they serve, for without that no society can thrive.

For our youth that coming weekly to the table of the lord they may walk in its power, in grace and beauty of life here and so eventually reach the mountain of God, and their heavenly home.

For First Holy Communion and Confirmation children, continuing to eat the bread of heaven every Sunday as their food for life, may they grow in wisdom, age and grace before God and men.

For the sick in our parish that by our regular bringing of communion to them they may know the love, grace and strength of God in their suffering, and our deep care for them.

For the dead that they may share the eternal banquet of Christ in heaven, helped by our prayers and prayerful remembrance.

We ask all these prayers through the only Lord of Love, present to us forever in the bread of life, amen.

## Reflection

I see ripe corn in the fields around me here now, and its an amazing thing. As Christ says, it grows from the tiny seed to first the shoot, then the ear, and then the full grain. Like the fruitfulness of the earth, all the crops that God provides nourish and cheer our hearts and bodies. But the miracles of nature are ones we can take for granted. Instead of always complaining about the rain or whatever, projecting our discontents onto nature, lets praise the green wonders of the world around us. And above all lets rest in the infinite joy and wonder of natural wheat, become the Bread of Life. Hail Mary

# Twentieth Sunday in Ordinary Time B

## Introduction

For a fourth week readings deal with the Eucharist. This in itself tells us of its paramount importance. In the first reading its associated with wisdom. Christ tells us communion with him is the way to happiness, a share in the life of God even in this world. Lets confess ways any failure to appreciate the mass as our spiritual treasure.

## Homily

When my family is on holidays the first thing they always ask is where to find mass. Its part of their life and that's as it should be. For the mass is a heritage since penal times, when people huddled in fields, or in makeshift houses, with a priest on the run. I remember my mother telling me how, before horse and traps or cars, they'd walk miles to mass, barefoot, over rough puddle-filled roads or on the back of the ditches. Their shoes were tossed over their shoulders; they'd put them on when they reached the church. They wouldn't dream of not going to mass, it was as natural as the seasons and very scriptural. For Christ says that unless we eat his flesh we wont have life in us. The intense life of the mass, like a diamond, enriches us with infinite facets of God's beauty.

The word itself comes from the old dismissal phrase "ita missa est". We're asked us to go and live in daily life the holiness we celebrate. As a Eucharistic People we should live in the everyday the union with God and others what the mass signifies, a life of thankful charity. Indeed Eucharist is an old Greek word which means to give thanks. In it we give thanks to God for Christ, for life, for nature, for salvation, and above all for the gift of himself to sustain us for life's journey to eternal happiness.

Yet another insight into the mass comes from its title "the breaking of bread". After the resurrection, the disciples recognized Christ in the breaking of bread. At the Last Supper he broke the bread and gave it to them. Acts describes the early Christians as meeting every Sunday for prayers and the breaking of bread. This is what gave the early followers of Christ their communal identity as Christ's people; its the same today.

Then again, another word for the mass, Aifreann, comes from the Latin word for offering. This reminds us that the mass is a reliving of Christ's sacrifice on the cross and a participation in its merits. There Christ offered himself to the father for us, in the mass we unite our joys, trials and sufferings with his perfect offering for our and the world's salvation. We're not silent spectators but join our lives, joys and sorrows, our own and community needs with Christ's offering of perfect praise.

The names for the mass then contain many aspects of its mystery They signify what wise and holy people know instinctively, that its the essence of Christian life. That's why we wisely offer the holy mass continually for deceased loved ones. We know its power and efficacy for liberating the dead, often lost in darkness, for it is the supreme sacrifice of redemption.

So all in all, lets continue to give thanks and glory to God in the breaking of bread, scripture reading and communal prayers that is the mass; remembering and making real for us the life, death and resurrection of Christ. For his continual presence with us in communion guarantees our triumph and that of the church over the world, the devil and all that drags us down since the fall. For all else fades to ashes at last, but to Christ in the Eucharist belongs the Kingdom, the power and the glory forever and ever, amen.

So as a glorious Eucharistic People, lets profess our faith with joy.

## Prayers of the faithful

And as Christ's body gathered in the Spirit to share in the bread of life, we pray confidently to the Father for our needs.

For the church throughout the world that it may live out its universal mission, and in the power of the Eucharist transform the whole world into the glorious Kingdom of God.

For ourselves in our homes, communities and country that witnessing to Christ and all that's good, we may practice and pass on to our children the gift of Eucharistic faith.

For missionaries at home and abroad that through the mass they may bring Christ's living saving presence to all people.

For the old, the lonely, the sick and the neglected in our society that through our love and care they may know the saving love of God in Christ, and bear their sufferings like he did on the cross for the salvation of the whole world.

For the dead, especially those who have died recently. Having shared in the Eucharistic banquet here, may they enjoy it with loved ones forever.

And we ask all these our prayers through Christ Our Lord from whom all good things come to us in the holy mass, amen

## Reflection

Sometimes we're all doom and gloom about weather. Psychologists say this is a way of venting discontent. For even if the weathers "good", we say "ah but in two weeks time its going to rain". We see only "bad" weather. I put the word "bad" in parenthesis, for as a wise southern woman once said: "sun, rain, frost, snow, they're all my friends". She's right, all nature is positive when seen aright. People in arid areas of the world, dream of rain. We'd have no growth, green fields, fresh lakes or rivers without it. But for some the glass is always half empty. Its similar with faith, God gives this great gift, but some see only abusing priests, and use that as an excuse for apostasy. Lets not let anything separate us from the glory of God in Christ Jesus our Eucharistic Lord. Hail Mary

# Twenty-First Sunday in Ordinary Time B

## Introduction

"We have no intention of deserting the Lord our God" our first reading says. Yet many do today. As some did when Christ taught the physical reality of his Eucharistic presence. "Do you want to go away too", he said to disciples (Jn. 6:67, JB). Lets confess ways we desert the gospel, when it doesn't agree with the views of the worldly.

## Homily

Many news items today are so shocking, we wonder what the world is coming to at all. Such as the case of a man in Austria who kept his daughter locked up and fathered children by her; or mass killings in many parts of the world. Is this decadence a warning? If we continue to follow our desires blindly, abandoning God and the sacredness of life, will worse happen? Christ says, "will you also go away". Let Peter's answer be ours: "Lord, who shall we go to? You have the message of eternal life" (Jn. 6:68, JB).

Yet though vowing at Baptism to be faithful, some do defect to a dog-eat-dog world, saying, in effect, who cares about God's laws? We will pursue our own desires. Advances in technology today give the illusion of general progress, but spiritually, morally and humanely are we going backwards? A young person said recently on radio that his new year resolutions were three: "put myself first, put myself first, put myself first".

But such self-centredness leads to community collapse. Whenever I go on visiting to communities and estates I'm always shocked to find how many do not know their neighbor; the usual response is to say, "well they come and go, but we don't have much to do with them, we don't disturb them, and they don't disturb us". Neighbors are seen not as a plus, as an opportunity for broadening our social world, but as a potential threat to our seclusion. People make excuses, it was worse in the old days. It wasn't. We were poor, so we'd no room for heads in the air. We cherished neighbors and kept basic laws of God, notably the law to love our neighbor. Now, with the rise in crime, our neighbor seems more as someone to avoid or to use for our own benefit. Every day we see mass killing on TV. Have we gone mad with self, sold out to godless heartless worldly values of which Satan is lord, under an illusion of progress? Maybe! But we Christians can never be pessimists. God is still in charge and the wheel always turns back to good.

Which brings me to happier news on the media. A report on sky news said that there's an increase in England, America and the continent in people joining the priesthood. They interviewed one such, an engineer who'd left all for the seminary. Why? "I went through it all", he said, "money, sex, the blind pursuit of all I wanted without restraint. But my heart was empty. Then I copped myself on and said there must be more than this, am I an animal? Surely human Life has a deeper purpose. Suddenly I realized it in serving God and others, in building Christ's better world of love, goodness and truth. OK, my priestly celibacy is foolishness to a sex-mad world but that's precisely its witness value".

Our readings echo that young man. The first says we'll not desert the lord our God. The second begs us to gain infinite riches in obeying Christ. And Peter says to Jesus in the gospel: "You alone has the message of eternal life". We might add that he alone is the source of happiness and fulfillment for this world too. For he is the lamb who takes away the sins of the world. We should follow him in faith and trust like the apostles, spurning the hard cold world that leads us away from eternity and its values.

In the light of eternity, we're to be rocks of faith like Peter, beacons of charity like Paul, cherishing and loving all as our neighbors in Christ. For worldly pride and Satanic self-centredness fade to ashes at last leaving us empty within, but Christ is lord of life, love, happiness, grace, beauty, and salvation for this world and forever and ever, amen.

So as God's people saying "we have no intention of deserting the Lord", and cherishing our neighbor in his light, lets profess our faith.

## Prayers of the faithful

And as God's children lets pray to our heavenly Father for the things that we need and are for our lasting good.

For our Holy Father and all church leaders that they may draw the flock, and all the world's people, back to the saving arms of God and his Christ, where true faith and neighborly love resides.

For civil leaders, may they see that man does not live by bread alone, and further the spiritual welfare of all by wise laws.

For our great youth, may they be safe from the self-destruction of excessive drinking, drugs and suicide. In the Lord's arms, may they find the happiness, grace and love they crave.

For ourselves in our homes and workplaces, that we may draw all to the fountain of life, love and salvation that is Christ.

For the sick and all suffering during the recession, especially those unemployed and on social welfare, that the lord may make us all strong, united, and mutually supportive in these hard times.

For the dead that they may come to the fullness of life hereafter with the help of our powerful communal prayers.

We ask all these prayers through Christ, in the Spirit, to the Father of all, amen.

## Reflection

A person came to me once with a story of how he'd lost his faith, and wandered into every excess of drink, drugs, and womanizing. One day, he found himself out in the street, not knowing even how he got there. Shocked at how low he had sunk, he decided to go home and try and rebuild his faith, for he knew that leaving it was the source of his downfall. Lets all appreciate how important the faith is for our deeper welfare. Hail Mary.

# Twenty-Second Sunday
# in Ordinary Time B

## Introduction

"Pure, unspoilt religion, in the eyes of God our Father is this; coming to the help of orphans and widows when they need it, and keeping oneself uncontaminated by the world" (Jm. 1:27, JB). Like James, Christ criticizes those who honor God with their lips, but whose hearts and lives are far from him. Lets confess any hypocrisy in our faith.

## Homily

Today's scripture is about religious hypocrisy. One can profess the faith, attend mass each Sunday, and yet be a living terror. Christ attacks the Pharisees as such. They kept the letter of God's law, and yet were corrupt in action. As Christ says, quoting Isaiah: "this people honor me only with lip-service" (Mk. 7:6, JB). Jesus despised outward law, his concern was purity of heart, and faith issuing in just charitable living. He wanted us to harness the horse of spirituality to the cart of ethics. For him the soul is true to God within, and proves this by good living. So his approach to morality was wholly positive. No "thou shall nots", his commandments, the Beatitudes say **act** from a merciful, charitable, peaceful, pure heart and you'll be God's own. St. James says the same; pure religion is coming to the help of orphans and widows, and being uncontaminated by the world.

A film I saw recently shows such an uncontaminated soul in action, Fr. O'Flaherty, the famous World War 11 priest. From the Vatican, during the Nazi occupation of Rome, he helped thousands of Jews and prisoners-of-war escape. At one stage the Pope called him aside and said:

"Be careful, the Germans can destroy the church in occupied lands, invade the Vatican". "Ah", O'Flaherty said, "I'm a simple man, I know nothing of politics. When I see people in need my heart just tells me to help them". Here was a man whose heart was truly uncontaminated by the world. Later, after Rome's liberation, the Pope admits: "its because of people like you that the church has credibility in every age".

The Pope was right. What makes us Christian is good works stemming from a faith-filled, compassionate heart. Christ is the model, in God's light, he reached out to heal the blind, the lame, the deaf and the dumb. The world crucified him, but he triumphed in defeat. Christ asks us to live our faith in the same way; but we're imperfect, so its not easy. The key is to keep up charitable efforts despite our weakness, and to fight all life long to free our hearts from the worldly vices that contaminate the soul. Christ lists such: fornication, theft, murder, adultery, avarice, malice, deceit, indecency, envy, slander, pride.

When the Nazi commander confronts O'Flaherty, in the film, he speaks from such a toxic soul, voicing the hard immoral secular thinking that rules the world. He shouts: "there's no God, right or wrong, only service of one's own desire and power". Satan and the world always tempts us to abandon innocence in this way. Believers shouldn't be fooled but pray with scripture, that God may take away our hearts of stone, and give us hearts of flesh instead. For worldly values fade to dust at last leaving us empty inside but Christ is lord of love, goodness, faith, peace, beauty, truth and happiness both for this world and forever and ever, amen.

So as God's people, acting to help the needy and keeping our hearts pure and compassionate, with Christ help, lets profess and resolve to live our faith in love.

## Prayers of the faithful

And as God holy people practicing faith in spirit and truth lets pray to our Father with confidence for the things that we need.

For our Holy Father the Pope and all church leaders, that they may preach and live the Christian Gospel from pure faith-filled uncontaminated hearts and inspire others accordingly.

For civil leaders that they may avoid worldly corruption and self interest and serve the people with integrity and justice, helping especially the poor and underprivileged in our society.

For ourselves; may we live and bear witness to the faith even against the world's contrary values, so as to be lights of faith, goodness and love to our children in particular.

For our wonderful young people, that they may not go the way of the corrupt world to soul death, but bear witness to Christ by faith-filled pure hearts within his holy church.

For the aged, the sick the lonely and the oppressed in our world, that through our heartfelt care and charitable action they may encounter the real loving and healing presence of Christ.

For the dead who passed from this world to the next and await a heavenly reward for their active faithfulness to Christ and all that's good; we pray especially for those who died recently.

We ask all this through Christ Our Lord who in love and concern for our welfare constantly intercedes for us before the Father.

## Reflection

Abuse scandals in the church is a warning that even consecrated religious people can go wrong. Some priests were corrupt like the Pharisees, preaching one thing and doing the opposite. Its hard to imagine that ordained ministers were so hard of heart as to abuse vulnerable children, and that bishops covered that up. Saving the church's skin seemed more important than doing what Christ tells us to do; cherish his little ones. One of my favorite writers in scripture is St. James because, as in our reading today, he pulls no punches about religious hypocrisy. We priests needed the shock of recent revelations, lest we lose the plot altogether. Lets pray to Mary that we will produce a better more accountable truly Christian church, uncontaminated by clericalism. Hail Mary

# Twenty-Third Sunday in Ordinary Time B

## Introduction

"Then the eyes of the blind shall be opened, the ears of the deaf unsealed". Our readings envisage the cleansing of the earth and the coming of justice in Christ. James shows that this was needed even in the early church, where distinctions were made between the poor and rich at the Eucharistic celebrations. Christ in the Gospel heals the deaf man. Lets open our ears to the Lord's words, and confess any failure to heed them.

## Homily

At one time, priests were all powerful. Some were wonderful pastors, some lorded it over people contrary to Christ's command; a few, we now know, abused the people's trust. I love St. James, because he fearlessly attacks abuses even within the church. In our reading he berates those who discriminate against the poor at mass. Like Christ, he called religious leaders to account, for fawning on the big shot, and humiliating the poor.

Christ's healing of the poor deaf man in today's gospel has a similar message. He healed the needy that the apostles tried to keep away. Church people must do likewise; rather than judge people accord to class. Christ said sinners and prostitutes would enter his kingdom before the proud religious leaders of the day. For arrogant pride, thinking oneself better than the poor, is present in all social spheres, even the church. For that reason Christ, though Lord, washed the feet of a common thief, Judas, and chose a humble fisherman as Pope. He himself, born in a stable, lived as a lowly carpenter.

Our challenge is to be like him, making no distinction between man and man, woman and woman, child and child, respecting the god-given dignity of each person whatever their state. "Let not a man guard his dignity", the philosopher Emerson said, "but let his dignity guard him". We can do much harm to that human dignity by social prejudice, against the disabled or travelers for example. And all of us unwittingly at times humiliate the disadvantaged, and pander to the famous. From the beginning, as James shows, even the church did this. Indeed, throughout its history it has constantly put wealth and power before God and others. Its time now to change all that.

To do this, and become credible, it must dump palaces and large cold institutions. An old man said to me recently, our mistake as a people was to feed our priests too well. Be that as it may, St. James would have judged severely the contemporary sin of our church, turning a blind eye to corruption in the ranks. The devil is prince of that world. Our challenge is to constantly reform ourselves in the image of the carpenter's son, the homeless nomad who reached out to serve and heal those despised by the world.

But not only church ministers but all the baptized have this role, to establish Christ's just reign in the midst of an often unjust world, to spurn the world's corruption and social snobbery. For only by imitating Christ's gentle selfless non-discriminatory service will we transform the earth into the Kingdom of God, he came to establish. That's our task and lets do it humbly for the Lord with generous open hearts. For the world's hard values of which Satan is lord fade to ashes at last but Christ is lord of compassionate non-discriminatory faith, love, justice and goodness for this world and forever and ever, amen.

So as God's people cherishing all his children equally as Christ did, and striving to right injustice whether inside or outside the church, lets profess our faith.

## Prayers of the faithful

And as the people of God lets pray for what we need humbly.

For church leaders throughout the world, that they may turn from power, palaces and wealth to the humble service of the physically needy, and the spiritually disadvantaged.

For our civil leaders that they may govern with justice, integrity and special care for the most needy in society.

For youth, that seeing beyond vain wealth, power and fame, they may practice the faith, goodness, truth and just living that the God's grace within the church makes possible.

For ourselves in our homes and among our loved ones, that our love may flow equally to all, and we may rid our hearts of overweening pride, snobbery, and prejudice.

For the sick and those suffering in body, mind or soul in any way that through our care they may know the healing love of Christ.

For the dead that, healed of all the effects of their sins while on earth, they may come with the help of our prayers to final rest, glory and happiness.

We ask these prayers through the all-compassionate Christ who reaches out to us with his saving love forever and ever, amen.

## Reflection

There's a story told of Cassius Clay, the great boxer who became Mohammed Ali when he converted to Islam, because he was fed up of the racialism he found among so-called Christians. After winning the Olympic gold medal for the USA he describes going home to his native southern USA, and stopping at a fast-food restaurant to buy a burger. "We don't serve blacks here!", the waiter said. "I don't want a black, I only want a burger", he supposedly replied, with typical wit. But it hurt him. Indeed, we don't know how much we hurt others by intolerance, discrimination and lack of fairness in our treatment of them, especially children. People can have the scars of being unloved or excluded, for life. Lets ask Mother Mary to help us avoid perpetuating that evil. Hail Mary.

# Twenty-Fourth Sunday in Ordinary Time B

## Introduction

Constant faith through every sufferings is our theme today. In the first reading we have the image of the suffering servant who trusts in God despite fierce torture. Christ in the gospel, points to cross. Lets confess any ways we lack trust in God during trials.

## Homily

One thing that always impresses me when I go to the homes of sick people is their faith and courage. So many, especially of the older people, show an amazing trust in God despite all their suffering. Recently, I had to attend a relatively young man, with young children and young wife, who was dying of kidney cancer. Yet all through the sickness, which was obviously terminal, I found no bitterness, only constant entreaty for prayers; for that man had tremendous faith, so much so that it put me to shame.

But this experience is not an isolated one. I find the same faithful endurance when I go to hospitals and old people's homes; people with kind wise faces, and unbelievable faith who say to me, again and again, without faith and prayer I'd never get through this sickness, or the trials of old age and infirmity. This strength that faith brings, is borne out by scientific studies which say that those with faith, in hospitals, tend to recover quicker. Trust in God, and union with him in prayer gives an inner strength that nothing else can.

At this time, with sad things happening in the world we need that saving strength. Today's gospel tells us where its to be found, not only in the light of Christ's teachings, but also in the everyday reality of bearing our crosses with Christian fortitude. By carrying our crosses with Christ, who suffered for and with us, the unavoidable suffering of life can not only be endured, but turned to gold. Peter, like Satan in the desert, wanted to keep Christ from the cross. But since suffering is an inescapable part of human life, our faith isn't about trial-free witness; its about taking up our crosses and following Christ in a believing that illuminates suffering, and perseveres no matter what pain the world throws at us. Continuing to attend mass and the sacraments and continuing to witness to the faith as his church faithful. For only by facing ills courageously will we grow in God's life and in a faith that makes everything both bearable and deeply meaningful.

For our trust is in the crucified Christ, not a corrupt passing uncaring world. The saddest causalities of our age are those who stop walking the way to happiness in Jesus because of the challenges he poses. They pursue instead the illusory seemingly painless pleasures, values and wealth of this world, of which Satan is Lord, and let their light fade to darkness. So when trials come they've no solid ground to stand on. Like wise people such as the people I mentioned, they should realize that the world, the flesh, and the Devil leave us empty, but clinging to Christ brings untold riches for every challenge of life.

In effect, faith is more than believing, its an eternal optimism, clinging to God through all crises. I often wonder why so many give up on life today. Perhaps one reason is that, deprived of God by a hard secular society, when they enter a crisis they've no solid ground to stand on or reason to go on. I say to parents bringing children for Baptism, what a gift you give your child, the Lord's light to guide them through every trial to glory.

For without faith, when the world fails us, all is darkness. But carrying our crosses with Christ we can turn our pain to light. And as all wise people know, the world's vain godless values fade to ashes at last, but the crucified Christ is lord of love goodness, peace, and grace for this world and forever and ever amen.

So God's own, passing all tests to our faith, persevering through all the sufferings of life, and growing through them by Christ's grace and example lets profess our faith.

## *Prayers of the faithful*

"The just man lives by faith", scripture says; as the just people of God trusting in him always, we ask him now for what we need.

For our Holy Father and all church leaders, that by their luminous faith they may bring the whole world to fuller life and endless inner strength.

For civil leaders, may they see the infinite value of people's faith and in governing never hinder its growth in any way.

For our youth, especially those tempted to give up on life because of trials, that in Christ they may find the grace and strength to light them through every suffering to glory.

For all in these difficult times, struggling families and the unemployed, that faith and trust in God may enable them to stay the course, until we return to better times.

For the sick and all those suffering in body or soul, that having recourse to every medical help first, and comforted by our love and care, they may face unavoidable suffering with courage and faith, and offer it up for the salvation of the world.

For the dead that the sufferings and joys of life at an end and their work done, they may come to the reward of the blessed.

We ask all these our prayers through the same Christ Our Lord who on the cross won the victory for us his followers, amen.


## *Reflection*

St. Paul said that he made up in his bodily suffering for anything lacking in the sufferings of Christ. Its hard to see anything lacking in the cross. But in some mysterious way suffering borne for God and others in love is also redemptive. It can be joined to the sufferings of Christ for the salvation of the world. That our pain is not in vain is a great consolation for the sick, it can help heal others. Lets pray to Mary for such faith. Hail Mary

# Twenty-Fifth Sunday in Ordinary Time B

## Introduction

Today's readings tell us that goodness is attacked by the envious world. The first reading details attacks on the virtuous man by godless opponents. In the gospel Christ tells the apostles that because of his godly preaching he'll be tortured and killed. Lets confess ways we follow the cruel cynical world, rather than the suffering Christian path of virtue.

## Homily

Goodness doesn't advertize itself. Really good people are surprised to be described as such. For example, I've known so many great nuns, priests and religious who do untold good, and give up everything – a spouse, children, property, independence – and do so with a smile on their face, for Christ. People may laugh at enclosed nuns, or monks, speaking from behind grills to visitors, and say they should be out there living it up, and satisfying themselves. But this is the thinking of the cynical world, not the thinking of the deeply happy lover and server of God and his holy people. I am often amazed at how young enclosed nuns always look, with clear complexions; its the good life and the peace it brings. And above all these are serving the whole world, witnesses to deeper more transcendent values, that, in some mysterious way, is the yeast to the world's dough. And this is why they are universally revered as the high point of culture, like Hindu or Buddhist monks and nuns also are, fed and sustained by the people as the deeper life of the world.

Yet this Christian model of self-giving service for the enrichment of the church and the world is the opposite of what the apostles expected

at first. Their original vision of the Christ was worldly. They saw him
is as a step up the ladder for them. They wanted to be self-glorifying
top dogs in a worldly kingdom won by military force. Christ put them
right by setting a small child before them. In his kingdom the great
are innocent little ones; like those religious dedicated to holiness as the
praying heart of the church's success.

In putting this ideal of innocence before us, Christ warns us against
our greatest temptation, self-centered people-trampling ambition. The
devil's fought to rule heaven; we fight to rule the earth. As James says:
"You want something and you haven't got it so you're prepared to
kill, you've an ambition that you cant satisfy so you fight to get your
way". Even prayers can be tainted by this: "you pray and don't get it
because you pray for something to indulge your own desires". This is the
opposite of what I mentioned; those who serve, toil and pray, wanting
nothing for themselves, in selfless holiness and love of God.

That's also our path to greatness. We too should live out our
Christian life in loving service of God and others no matter the cost. For
the laity, living God's holiness and innocence in the world, this means
worshiping God faithfully every Sunday and caring thoughtfully for
others amidst life's struggles; this is what makes life worthwhile. As the
common song says: "If I help somebody as I pass along then my living
will not be in vain". By living our vocation in this way we're happier
and we change the world for good.

And curiously we will achieve all our inner ambitions in a more
satisfying way; we'll win friends and honor in this world and treasure
in heaven that will not tarnish or fade away. For the hard self-centered
world fades to ashes at last, but to Christ the Servant king on the cross,
and us his faithful imitators, and dedicated religious saints, belongs the
kingdom, the power and the glory forever and ever, amen.

So as the people of God called to serve God and others faithfully
with humble caring praying hearts to fulfill our deeper humanity, we
make our profession of faith.

## *Prayers of the faithful*

Conscious of his Son's self-giving love for us we make our prayer to our Father in heaven for the things we need.

For church leaders that they may make the same choice as Christ to be the suffering servants of the faithful and all humanity, and so bring the world to fullness of life and salvation.

For civil leaders that they may take the path of honest service of those they govern not that of corrupt self-service and power.

For our youth that they may choose Christ's way of faithfulness to the church and humanity, and so as to make a difference by their lives and gain an eternal reward.

For our wonderful religious, that their witness may continue to enrich us and the world beyond measure, in the holiness, truth and beauty of the consecrated life.

For all parents in the home and all married couples, that they may dedicate themselves to faithful long-suffering loving service of their partners, spouses and children, rather than giving all to ruthless pursuit of ambitions and worldly riches and pleasure.

For the sick, the aged, the lonely and the poor that through our our loving care for them, they may know the love of God.

For the dead, especially those of our parish family who have died recently.

We offer these our humble prayers for our real spiritual and temporal needs, through Christ Our Lord who lives and reigns forever and ever, amen.

## Reflection

Recently children asked me how the Fatima seers died. I was surprised, but they'd seen the film on TV. I told them that Lucy lived to a ripe old age, visited by bishops and cardinals for advice. But the younger children of the apparition were told by Mary that they wouldn't be happy in this world. They would die young, but by their suffering they'd redeem many. They were happy to do so. They never complained but lived their short lives of illness with great devotion and love. Lets pray to Mary that we'll lead innocent, charitable, faith-filled lives like those children, even in the face of sickness and suffering, for our reward will be great when we come before the throne of God. Hail Mary

# Twenty-Sixth Sunday in Ordinary Time B

## Introduction

"If only all the people of God were prophets and he gave his Spirit to them all", the first reading says. That kind of prophecy is seen in James' condemnation of rich who exploit the poor. Similarly Christ condemns those who give scandal to the young. Lets confess ways we fail in concern for the vulnerable.

## Homily

In modern life have we lost our sense of responsibility towards our neighbor? Rather than caring concern, is indifference or exploitation of them for profit, such as James condemns, the norm today? Certainly, the old values of hospitality seem to be fading in towns and cities. I once served in a large town; and visiting in the estates I was shocked find how many confessed to not knowing who lived next door. Security may exclude open houses now but there's no excuse for shutting ourselves off from all around us. Even in our homes we may fail to spot the child who is being bullied in school or the teenager who is a drug addict; I think of that film *Traffic*, where the man chosen by the president to lead a war on drugs, doesn't know his daughter is addicted. Our human and Christian duty remains, to know and love our neighbor, even if it requires extra effort today.

Do we make that effort? Recently, we'd the shocking case in America of a man who kept women locked up for many years to serve his lusts. Yet neighbors somehow didn't see what was going on next door to them. We don't want to pry into our neighbor's business of course, but when someone is in need next door to us, its our duty to do something. The "I'm all right Jack" view, I'm not my brother's keeper, is the spirit of Cain.

Our readings warn of the spiritual emptiness of this view and pinpoints its cause in affluent isolationism. Our first reading sees the arrogant wealthy swapping open-hearted godliness for the hard spirit of a money-mad world. St. James calls to account those living a life of luxury who ignore or oppress needy neighbors. And Christ in that gospel says that even a cup of water given to a needy person in his name will be rewarded.

Also, a related theme, he calls us to protect the innocent. Those who scandalize his little ones should be thrown into the sea with a millstone around their necks. His words apply to a church of bishops in palaces ignoring child abuse. But we can all scandalize youth by sexual promiscuity, non-practice of the faith and lack of love. When I was chaplain to a hospital, recently, I saw that it was a good center, because each patient was treated as a person. In a strange place they'd someone who cared about them.

This caring attitude should apply in our home too. For in big houses we can become less affectionate towards our children and spouses, or too proud to open our hearts to neighbors. When I was young, our house was always open, not just for a cup of tea but for personal worries and family issues to be aired. We can't roll back the clock, but we can still have homes where all are welcome and cherished.

And we must still have homes where little ones are protected against a world that exploits the weak, even on the internet. And at home, spouses might be more than just two people living together. Some women say to me that their husband spends his time reading the paper. Husbands say, she's great around the house but I feel like a stranger. With neighbor, workmate or children, wealth mustn't replace human warmth. Lets always put people first. For worldly wealth passes and leaves us empty but Christ is lord of faith-filled caring hearts forever and ever, amen.

As God's own, committed to open caring hearts and homes, lets profess our faith.

## *Prayers of the Faithful*

And as God's children lets pray to our heavenly Father for the things that we need to be his faithful people.

For church leaders, especially the Holy Father, that they may be caring pastors of their flock, protecting the innocent and bringing the boundless charity of Christ to all.

For our civil leaders that they may not be ruled wholly by cold economics but rule with integrity, and serve the needs of all the people, especially the poor, sick and vulnerable in society.

For ourselves; at home, in our work place and neighborhood, may we be the caring face of Christ to all, with open, loving and welcoming homes, hearts, and arms.

For our youth that they may realize that loving service of God and people is the road to happiness in this world and the next.

For the sick in our homes, among our close relatives, or in our neighborhood that through our care and prayers they may come to know comfort, healing and the love of God.

For the dead that they may reap the reward of their charity in this life and through our prayers and continuing love and remembrance come safely to their heavenly home.

We ask these our prayers through the all-loving and caring Christ whose wounds intercede for us before the Father in heaven, amen.

## *Reflection*

When I was young, when one needed help the neighbors rallied round; gathering hay before rain pelted down; or at thrashings, drawing sheaves and feeding them into the machine; or bagging the grain for storage. Stout, tea, and cakes were passed around during breaks in the work. We came to see, as the poet says, that no man is an island. Lets rediscover that today too, the loving human solidarity that is Christian life. Hail Mary.

# Twenty-Seventh Sunday in Ordinary Time

## Introduction

Scripture today says of marriage, that those who leave parents for spouses, are united by God, and shouldn't be sundered by man. And Christ rejects divorce, saying also that what God unites, man mustn't divide. Lets confess any marriage unfaithfulness.

## Homily

Marriages are made in heaven. Christ says spouses should leave their parents, become one, and stay faithful. Vows taken, nurture of children, true love, and Christ's command means we should accept no less. Marriage mustn't be like the countryman's ad: "wife needed, donkey dead". It should be a bond of mutual love even death won't destroy.

That fine film, *Sleepless In Seattle*, makes the point well. The heroine is engaged to a man she likes, but doesn't love. Realizing this, he hands her back the ring saying marriage is too serious to be entered into lightly. The film ends with a Jimmy Durante song, "make someone happy, and you will be happy too". That's the challenge for couples, to make and keep each other happy. Christ asks us to love one another as he loves us. He loved to the last drop of his blood; marriage commitment should be as heroic.

Its because a marriage is so sacred, that Christ began his ministry at one. He turned water into wine so that the wedding could go on. He wanted his relatives to be happy, and that's his wish for all couples, to remain united. For a true marriage mirrors his enduring love for his bride the church, and begets life. Each child born of real enduring love; a world of happy united fathers, mothers and children, that's the Christian dream.

But we live in a fallen world and the strains on marriages made in heaven are immense today, with devaluation of the marriage ideal by easy divorce, and a wholly sexual approach to love. All the more reason why Christian couples should cling to God's vision of a better way. Which remind me of another joke: the first year of marriage the husband speaks and the wife listens; the second year the wife speaks and the husband listens; the third year they both shout and the neighbors listen. The joke has a message. Communication is vital: talking to each other; sharing problems; remembering birthdays and anniversaries, making up quarrels; being sensitive to each other's feelings, for they're easily hurt; and continually giving tokens of love, people need to **know** they're loved.

But even in the best of marriages, life is seldom rosy all the time. At times the wine runs low. But such tests should strengthen rather than break the union, so that it produces the good wine at last. And for the long haul, the church dimension is vital. The sacrament gives us extra grace to live what's seems foolishness to a cynical world.

If couples keep God as part of their lives, honor their vows and pray when things get tough, they're more likely to survive. They can be faithful, share, take the good with the bad, bring children up in the security of a good home, and keep alive the precious fire of love celebrated at their wedding, until the lord receives them, and they are united forever with each other in the home of the blessed. For cynical worldly values fade to ashes at last, but Christ is lord of dedicated enduring love and faithfulness, for our happiness in this world and forever and ever, amen.

So as God's people, committed to marriage as a permanent union of love and honor, ordained by God and affirmed by Christ, lets profess our faith.

## *Prayers of the faithful*

And as his faithful people lets for what we need.

For our Pope and all the leaders of the churches, that they may continue to put before the world the sacred ideal of marriage faithfulness until death.

For civil leaders that they may act with integrity in governing us, and uphold marriage and integral family life, for the good of society.

For our young people that in their love relationships may chose the Christian ideal of a permanent sacred union, and invoke the extra help of the sacrament, the vital extra grace of God it confers.

For our own marriages and families; that God may bless us with continuing love, union and graceful living among happy children.

For the aged, the lonely and the sick in body, mind or soul that through our care and prayers they may experience God's love.

For those of our families who have died, especially spouses, that through our continuing love and prayers we may stay united until we're joined forever in the home of the faithful prepared for us.

We ask these prayers through Christ, Lord of faithful love unto death for this world and forever and ever, amen.

## *Reflection*

Surveys show that marriage is less common in Europe now. With this goes ever increasing family break-down. So commitment to Christian marriage was never more needed. For our youth's future, and society's health, hinges on this ideal. So, while, of course, having compassion for those separated due to irretrievably broken or abusive relationships, lets reaffirm life-long Christian marriage. While recognizing that we're all sinners and dare not judge anyone, we pray to Mary for a fresh commitment to Christian marriage, so as to help to redeem the times by loving Christian faithfulness. Hail Mary

# Twenty-Eight Sunday in Ordinary Time B

## Introduction

Today's readings touch our times. They ask us, rather than putting our trust in riches, to trust in God, our real wealth. In the gospel the rich young man rejects Christ's call, because he's rich. Lets confess ways we sometimes put money before God.

## Homily

You know that Abba song "Money, Money, Money, in a rich man's world". Is it a rich man's world? Is getting and spending the meaning of life? Certainly, even the once socialist countries, who made a living by condemning capitalist greed, have jumped on the gravy train, where the rich man reigns as king. Even the corruption of the former Soviet Bloc, seems to show that the ideal of equal sharing is a pipe dream, that the world is made up of winners or losers in a rat race where money is the prize, and the rats are winning. But is there still another way?

That there is, is the point of today's Gospel, where the rich man is asked to follow Christ, to walk from slavery to wealth to freedom within; to follow Christ in detached service of God and humanity, especially the poor. But like many in today's west of liberal capitalism, the young man cannot break free. Christ looked at him as a person, loved him, and offered him a more fulfilling role; "Go and sell everything you own and give the money to the poor, and you will have treasure in heaven; then come follow me" (Mk. 10:21-22, JB). It was a noble call; he saw the young man's potential for greatness, but he reckoned without the enslaving power of greed. The young man couldn't break free from his chains; though deep down he knew Christ was right, for we're told that he went away "sad".

Is this the state of many in a money-mad west? Is it why the vocations there are drying up; there's no room for the true God's call in a world that worships mammon, and has little room for Christ's perfect world of detachment and selfless sharing. But the recent recession did make people think again about this philosophy. Maybe it will bring people back to the more enduring humane values of the Lord, though, that said, the cult of economics seems to reign now. I thought economics served people; now the opposite seems to hold. Schools and hospital beds are closed to rescue rich foreign bondholders and toxic banks; the poor bail out the rich, who always rule the world in their interests.

That's the kind of vain worldly "wisdom" our scripture attacks. Christ doesn't say that working hard for a good standard of living is wrong. What he warns against is allowing riches to enslave us, and make us indifferent to the suffering of the less well off. What does it profit a man if he gain the whole world and suffer the loss of his soul, he says. The right Christian attitude towards earthly goods is to use them well and wisely in a sharing culture. His detachment philosophy, further developed in the Beatitudes, is recipe for a perfect world, for if all shared unselfishly, free from possessiveness, no one would want. There's more than enough in the world to feed many times its population; the problem is that some gobble up so much, the others inevitably suffer want.

But Christ not only gives a recipe for world justice and equality, he also gives us a motive for implementing that recipe, to build treasure for ourselves in heaven that will never decay. In this, Christ also offers a special way of perfection to some, monks and nuns who reject property for prayer and holiness. But even Christians in the world should be free from excessive greed, sharing surplus goods with the poor. Thereby they gain inner freedom and treasure in heaven. The most enslaved man is the one constantly worrying about his wealth, and because of this worry, never having enough. So God and things of the soul tend to be banished to limbo. But any day his soul may be required of him.

So lets re-evaluate our priorities and follow the perfect way of Christ, the poor nomad who gave up everything to serve God and humanity on the cross, and yet to whom belongs the kingdom, the power and the Glory forever and ever, amen.

So as God's people called from total soul-destroying greed to detachment and a related generous charity, and so build treasure in heaven, we make our profession of faith.

## Prayers of the Faithful

And as God's people we pray for the things that we really need, not just want.

For church leaders, may they continue to remind people that man does not live on bread alone.

For the world's political leaders, that in serving economics they may not neglect to serve the spiritual as well as material needs of those they govern, especially the poor.

For the sick, the lonely, the aged and those among us who need our care, that we may find the time from getting and spending to be there for them, and be Christ to them.

For ourselves, that we may give our children the riches of love and care, as well as the material benefits that they deserve.

For the dead, especially those who have died recently in our parish and for all those whose anniversaries occur at this time.

We ask all these things through Christ Our Lord, from whom all good and holy things come, amen.

### Reflection

There's a story told of early Christians. They could save themselves from the lions if they abandoned Christ and worshiped the Emperor. For this they received much money. One Christian took the cash. As he watched fellow Christian going to death, a soldier said, "aren't you lucky, you're alive and wealthy while they're dead meat". "No", he said, "they're the ones who are alive, I'm the one who's dead". He'd sold his soul, and knew it was a bad bargain. Like that man we too can sacrifice everything, even our souls, for filthy lucre, which Paul calls the root of evil. Lets ask Mary to help us avoid that trap. Hail Mary.

# Twenty-Ninth Sunday in Ordinary Time B

## Introduction

Redemptive suffering features in today's reading. The first, a prophecy about Christ, says: "by his suffering shall my servant justify many" (Is. 53:11, JB). And in the gospel Jesus tells the power-hungry apostles they must also embrace the cross. Lets face our crosses and humbly serve God and others, so as to help him redeem a fallen world.

## Homily

Recently we celebrated the Triumph of the Cross. Our readings today show how that triumph came about. "Can you drink the cup I must drink", he says to apostles who craved worldly power and glory (Mk. 10:38, JB). That cup was the scriptural one depicted by Isaiah: "by his suffering shall my servant justify many" (Is. 53:11, JB). And that's the central paradox of our faith, Christ became King through the cross's counterwitness to a corrupt world of power politics. He became the perfect image of God's gentle being when he mounted a blood-soaked tree, rejecting a false throne of power won by violence and oppression. The apostles, all for such power, found this shocking. Like Satan, they wanted Christ to be a Hitler Messiah, and they basking in ill-gotten power and riches at his side. Christ showed them that this was the world's way, not his. He came not to be served but to serve and to give his life as a ransom for many. Later they saw the wisdom of this.

So must we. Like Christ we must choose to be suffering servants of God and others in love. For Christ shed his last drop of blood in love, on the throne of the cross, and passed the crown to us: "What I command you is to love one another" (Jn. 15:17 JB). And he shows us what real love is, by giving everything, even his soul. Yet the church and Christians through the ages have more often followed Satan's way of ruthless self-serving power and riches, trampling on the weak. Present Church scandals show how the church needed in this age to be toppled from such a throne of self-service.

For in every age this is the chief temptation the church and all of us face. Look at the many who walk away from faith today to serve money and pleasure; who avoid the crosses of moral living, of priestly celibacy, of religious poverty and obedience, of humble lay service in the Church community, of suffering marriage faithfulness, of self-giving charity. Instead they tell us, live it up, get as much as we can at whatever cost.

But these are soul-destroying illusions. For ruthless pursuit of possessions, sex, and self-satisfaction, though it bring temporary pleasure, turns to dust and ashes in the long run. As one one holy person put it, if we choose the worldly way in the long run we may be left with just hardened hearts, and an empty grasping soul for all eternity.

Christ on the cross tells us to follow a more satisfying long-term way of selfless love; a way of suffering faithfulness; a way of healing sacrifice. Sadly even such a simple sacrifice as getting up on Sunday to go to mass seems too much for many. Yet that's where enduring happiness is. Serving Christ and what's just, we'll make a difference by our lives and be raised to glory. For the ruthless values of this world of which Satan is lord turn to ashes at last and leave us empty before eternity, but Christ on the cross is lord of life, love, truth, and beauty for happiness this life and forever and ever, amen.

So as suffering servants of God, others, and the church in real giving love, to redeem a ruthless self-serving world, lets profess our faith proudly.

## *Prayers of the faithful*

As God's own called to love Christ and others faithfully despite and through the crosses this entails, we pray for what we need.

For our Holy Father the Pope, the bishops and all leaders of the church, that they may lead the flock with humility and be examples of charity and faithful loving service.

For all leaders and authorities in our society that they may carry out their roles with a true sense of love, integrity and responsibility for the welfare of all the people they serve.

For youth, may they humbly serve God, others and the church in love, and so transform the world into Christ's gentle kingdom.

For ourselves that we may grow in that deep love of God through every suffering and trial, and truly love and humbly serve those around us and in our homes, especially our children.

We now pray in silence for our own special intentions.

For the young, the weak, the vulnerable and the sick in our society, that through our care they may experience the love of God, and Christ the healer.

For the dead, especially those of our parish family who have died recently.

We pray for these spiritual and temporal needs through Christ whose wounds pleads for us forever before the Father, amen.

## Reflection

Our call to redeem the world through imitating Christ's suffering love, is reflected in the life of Edel Quinn. She suffered all her life from severe ill-health, but she did not let that prevent her from traveling to Africa to spread the Legion of Mary. Indeed, she died young, worn out by her work and foreign travel for Christ. But in that suffering service she gained so much. As she said herself, her greatest joy in life was to be able to suffer for Christ. Lets pray that we'll be as noble and generous in his service. Hail Mary.

# Thirtieth Sunday in Ordinary Time B

## Introduction

Scripture today features blindness and seeing. The first reading sees the Israelites returning to the Lord, "all of them, the blind and the lame" (Is. 31:8, JB). Similarly Christ heals the blind man in body and soul. Lets confess if we're blind to the truth in our lives.

## Homily

Before I begin the homily, close our eyes. Imagine living in darkness. That was the blind man before Christ cured him. Now open your eyes. See everything. That was the joy of the blind man when his eyes were opened, and who did he see when he opened his eyes? the Lord. Jesus opened his eyes in that way too. What did the blind man do then? Did he walk away? Did he go back into the darkness? Did he abandon Jesus? No! "he followed him along the road" (Mk. 10:52, JB). We're called to do the same. We began on that road of faithfully serving the Lord, at Baptism, where we vowed to leave behind unbelief, sin and death. Have we followed him faithfully on that road of life since?.

For its not enough to have our eyes opened, they must stay so. We must walk with Christ as faithful members of his church. We must come each Sunday to hear his word and receive him in communion. We must go out and bear the fruits of that faithful discipleship in everyday life, witnessing to his values and lighting up the world by our witness. For only by such living worship and faithful witness do we keep our eyes open, and keep safely on the right road that makes us wise and happy. For following him is happiness for this world too, besides leading to a final vision of God in heaven for all eternity. That's the goal, the end of the road in an unending paradise.

But its one thing to say we'll do this, and another thing to actually do it, for its not easy. We're constantly tempted to go back into the darkness by the powerful anti-Christian forces of the world, the flesh and the Devil. Hence, as Paul says, though many have seen the light, some show they prefer darkness. So the call for us today is keep our eyes open, to be wary of any distraction that leads us away from the faithful following of Christ, any watering down of the faith, any abandoning of the Word and the Sacraments.

Eyes wide open, we must be on our guard lest the evil one lure us down another road, the road where the blind lead the blind into the ditch. For as one wise unknown said, though all are called to follow Christ faithfully along the way, many are more often "by the way" or "in the way". And that's the other lesson of the gospel today. Like the blind man we mustn't just open our eyes to Christ and follow him **on** the way, we must help others, especially loved ones, to follow the path as well; like the blind man preaching even to haughty Pharisees, we must be his light to all around us, leading them from darkness too.

Its to keep us on the way that, as the year ends and days get cold, the church puts before us the end things, death, judgment and Christ's Second Coming. Not to frighten us but keep us focused on the path, so that when the end comes, Christ will meet us with all the saints and say, well done good and faithful servant. For the cold values of a godless world of which Satan is lord, pass and leave us lost by life's roadside, but Christ is the way, the truth and the life for happiness in this world and forever and ever, amen.

So as God's own, cured of blindness by Christ's death and resurrection, following him faithfully and leading others along the road to every happiness, lets profess our faith.

## Prayers of the faithful

Lets pray now for the things that need to that glorious lord.

For church leaders, especially our Pope, may they follow the way themselves and lead their flock and the whole world out of darkness and into God's saving light of truth.

For our civil leaders that they may follow the right way of public life, one of integrity and service of all the people, especially the poor, needy and oppressed of our society.

For youth, may they not wander from the way they began at Baptism and continued in Holy Communion and Confirmation, but follow Christ faithfully along life's road, practicing their faith so as to come safely to their heavenly home, and show others the way.

For ourselves in our homes, may we lead our children wisely on the right way, sharing our faith with them and bringing them to the light of life in God, for happiness here and hereafter.

For the sick, the aged, the lonely and the troubled in mind, body or soul that through healing love and care they may be comforted and healed and know the love of God.

For the dead who still need our remembrance and prayers to light them home, that they come safely to their heavenly rest.

And we ask all these our prayers through Christ, the way, the truth and the life forever and ever, amen.

## Reflection

We all get lost at times, bewildered by a maze of roads before us; driving round and round, not knowing where we are. In Christ and his church we're never lost like that. Even death is not a dead end, but journey's end. Like someone who comes to his home, turns off the engine and the car lights, and walks up the driveway to a house where his relatives, friends and loved ones wait in light. Lets keep on the right road with Christ in this world, so as to reach that happy journey's end, and lover's meeting. Hail Mary

# Thirty-First Sunday in Ordinary Time B

## Introduction

Today's readings sum up our faith. We're to love the Lord with all our heart and soul and love our neighbor as Christ loved us. Lets confess any way we fail in love.

## Homily

Love is our vocation. But what is love? Its a much abused word today, meaning anything from vague affection to sexual intercourse. So as Christians we must look to Christ to teach us what love is. That's easy, his whole life was one of total love of God and others unto death. And that love was not exclusive. He opened his arms to embrace all on the cross and gave to the last drop of his blood, even for those who crucified him. Our love must be like that, non discriminatory, self-giving, given even to those we dislike.

In a film of John Paul 11's life, a wonderful scene shows such love in action. A Polish friend says that they should attack Nazi persecutors mercilessly and kill all collaborators. "No", John Paul replies, "we'll defeat them by love". We know how effective his way was in defeating fascism and communism in Poland. He won out against overwhelming odds because one can't defeat love in the long run. No wonder two miracles have been found for his canonization. For today's readings echo his words as gospel truth. Loving God and each other is the way to redeem a hating, divided, violent world.

Sadly some "love" God in a different way, hating and killing in his name, and so-called religious can be worst in this. Christ had to confront the Pharisees who'd stone the woman caught in adultery.

Many still do Satan's work by religious fanaticism, remaking a loving God in their distorted image, people like Ben Laden who blow up innocent people. Or Paisley who claims Catholics and the Pope are God's enemies. Or Catholics who can see no good in so-called "black Protestants".

All this is an abomination to the true God, as our readings make clear. To be like God, we must constantly widen our thinking, have ever bigger hearts, ever more generous souls, ever more forgiving minds. That can only come from knowing the true God. John Paul also said that if we accept the true and living God, he'll walk with us in love. Scripture says the same. God's love should lead to unconditional love even of enemies. This is redemption. Someone said to me once: "I'm a sinner so God is sure to hear my prayers", how wise. God's love is wider and deeper than anything we can imagine.

As such his ways are not those of fanatical secular liberals either. They too hate and condemn those who don't agree with their agenda. They close their hearts to God, or religion, or the other world, and they can be so self-righteously harsh in their tribunals, and so spiritually dead in their philosophy. God's ways aren't so narrow. They're deep, broad, generous and warm as the heavens. If we open our hearts and minds to this living God our hearts will also open to all our fellow brothers and sisters; we'll imitate Christ and be saints. We'll stop casting God in our image, or excluding him altogether in self-centered secularism. We'll love God and others as Christ loved you, unconditionally. We'll be open, loving, generous, spiritually alive human beings. For all else fades and leaves us empty at last, but Christ is lord of real love for our happiness in this world and forever and ever, amen.

So as people called to love God and each other in Christ with our whole hearts, souls and minds lets profess our faith.

## Prayers of the Faithful

And as the people of God lets pray to our loving Father for the things that we need, especially open loving hearts.

For the church throughout the world that, eschewing power and self-service, it may witness to love in everything it does.

For civil leaders that their love for the people they govern may be shown in the integrity of their dealings and the wise laws they make for the people's good, especially the most vulnerable.

For our youth that their love of God and others may be the cornerstone of their lives so that they may achieve happiness in this world, and with all they have loved forever in heaven.

For parents that their constant, affectionate and indiscriminate love for their children may bring them to fullness of life.

For the sick, the aged, the lonely and the disturbed in mind or soul that through our care they may know the love of God.

For the dead that having lived in love of God here below they may come to fullness of life with him forever helped by our loving prayers for them, a love which continues after death.

And we ask all these prayers through Christ the living lord of love forever and ever, amen.

## Reflection

When we were young everyone went to mass to honor God. And when anyone was in trouble or needed help the neighbors rallied round. As they did cutting the turf and drawing it home in the autumn, or stacking it in the outhouse for the winter. The tea, sandwiches and cakes brought by womenfolk, that we ate on the banks of turf on fine summer days, tasted like the glorious heavens over us. We came to see, as the poet says, that no man is an island, that we are greatest when one in the human and divine solidarity of work and loving comradeship. Lets pray to discover that in our way now. Hail Mary.

# Thirty-Second Sunday in Ordinary Time B

## Introduction

Readings today focus on widows. In the first we have the widow who succors Elijah. In the second we've the widow who gives all she has to the temple. Both deal with generous giving to God. Lets confess ways we fail in such love and generosity.

## Homily

There is an extraordinary contrast in today's gospel, between authentic religion and false religion. The so-called religious scribes pretended long prayers, but oppressed the poor for money; their faith was a soulless sham. By contrast we've the widow; out of her livelihood she gave all she had to the Temple treasury. No wonder Christ was awestruck. She lived perfectly his command to love the lord with our whole heart, our whole soul and our whole mind. Also she lived his new commandment in the Beatitudes: "happy are the poor in spirit" (Mt. 5:3, JB). Detached, she didn't hoard even the little money she had.

Christ asks us to have the same freedom in serving God, and the same freedom from possessiveness, as the way to solve world poverty also. To give generously from a faith-filled loving heart, to bring justice to the earth by sharing our surplus with the needy everywhere, for the love of God. And that's good for us too, for we free ourselves from enslaving greed and possessiveness and build up treasure in heaven that will last forever.

That lesson came home to me when I was buying a site for a house. When fencing it, I made sure I got every inch of ground. "Ah", the fencer said, "a few feet of ground is all we have in the end". A slap in the face for a so-called man of God.

Christ warns us in the same way today. He says the way to end injustice is not "me me", but "give, give", like the widow. This blessed way isn't easy in a money-hoarding and money-accumulating culture. That's why this gospel's so relevant, it warns that the pride of wealth can close our hearts to the poor and to God. In the pride of riches we may need neither God nor man. So as wealth increases, our practice of faith declines. But those in Grand houses with 4-by-4 cars abandoning the faith of our fathers are fools, when our souls are required of us riches will be no use to us, only heavenly treasures last.

Its interesting that the pious widow not only showed her overwhelming love for God by her total giving, but also gave that to the Temple so that God could be loved and honored, and his house properly cared for. Giving out of our surplus to the church today is as important, for it needs material sustenance for its missionary outreach and charitable activities. As scripture says, we should use money, that tainted thing, to win treasure in heaven. We're not asked to give all we have in this; but once we have more than enough for ourselves and our families, then we should share some of our surplus. We should have plenty, but it will be of lasting value only if we share it generously with those in need and the church. Then we'll raise up our world, and make a difference by our lives. And finally we'll share in the glory of a Lord who gave all to the last drop of his blood for God and us. For the world's hard greedy values pass and leave us empty before eternity, but he leads generous souls to happiness in this world and forever and ever, amen.

So as God's people called to the generous sharing with the needy around us, and with the church of God, from a faith-filled heart like the widow, we profess our faith.

### Prayers of the Faithful,

Giving thanks for any prosperity we have and praying that in this time of recession all may return to it, we ask also that we may learn the uselessness of excessive greed and worldliness, and give generously to God and others from rich non-hoarding hearts.

We pray that the church and its leaders may continue to remind people that man does not live on bread alone.

For our political leaders, that they may not neglect to serve the spiritual as well as material needs of those they govern, and work for a more equal distribution of wealth.

For our youth that they may not be so caught up in the pursuit of worldly things that they have no time for God and the deeper more lasting goods that enable them to serve the needs of others and grow into everlasting life.

For ourselves that in our homes we will have generous and loving hearts towards our children, the church, and all who need our material and spiritual support.

For the sick the lonely, the aged and those who need special care, that we may find the time to be there for them, and so bear witness to active Christian love.

For the dead, especially those who have died recently, those whose anniversaries occur at this time, and all those on the November list of the dead.

And we ask this through Christ Our Lord in whom all good, holy, and generous souls find happiness forever and ever, amen.


## Reflection

Recently our neighbor died in a ruin of a house with the cold wind blowing in broken windows. Yet, when they consulted his affairs, they found he'd hundreds of thousands in the bank. It was no good to him on earth, and relatives have fought over it ever since. Life's short, we're foolish to put it all into money making, and money hoarding. For we carry nothing into the grave but faith and good deeds. Others will spend the earthly wealth we've accumulated, but the wealth we accumulate in heaven is our's forever. Let be wise then, and share from the heart, like the widow in the gospel. Hail Mary

# Thirty-Third Sunday in Ordinary Time B

## Introduction

Our scripture at this dark end of the year naturally deals with the end things, death and judgment. The first reading deals with the end of the world, and so does the gospel. Lets confess any ways we fail to prepare by good deeds and faith for the end of all.

## Homily

Recently, I said to someone: "We've only thirty years left". A article said a meteor heading for the earth, could strike in the year two thousand and thirty, with the force of a hundred atom bombs. Thirty years hence many of us won't be around. But even the youngest of us needn't worry. The odds on the meteor hitting earth are five hundred to one. Such reports are grist to the mill of a press, who play on apocalyptic fears. During the Millennium there were daily predictions of disaster. We should treat all such doom and gloom with a grain of salt. For they usually misrepresent apocalyptic writings, which say that Christ's Second Coming will be a cause for joy, not fear.

Yet we do need to be reminded that the earth will end; even scientists agree on this; that it will wind down, and could be destroyed at any time by some cosmic cataclysm. And despite all those films where heroes stave off world destruction at the last moment, we're really powerless before the vast forces of the universe. If the world shifted on its axis, we'd all be wiped out, and there's nothing we could do about it. Local national disasters, such as tsunamis or severe earthquakes remind us of our limitations before the forces of nature. Such disasters happen because the world since the fall is imperfect; and corrupt human agency adds to that; global warming caused by human greed, is a case in point. Forces of greedy industry need to be tempered lest the apocalypse come sooner that expected. We can all help the environment and stave off disasters.

But ultimately all is passing. If God took his hand away it would all be over. Our consolation is that he loves us despite our failings, and won't take his hand away until Christ's Second Coming. That won't be a so much a taking way of his hand as a triumph of his love. The world, theologians argue, wont be so much destroyed as transformed. When will that be? No one knows. Even Christ in the Gospel says he doesn't know.

What we do know is that though the Book of Revelation says fearful things will happen, we shouldn't worry, Christ will be there to save us. The more immediate truth is the end of each of us, death. We could face that, and judgment, any day. But the gospel message is optimistic here too: Christ says at his rising not to be afraid, he is with us. Yet it makes sense to be prepared, within, to meet the Lord should he come at any time.

That's why today's Gospel, at the end of the church year, and in the dead of winter, jolts us into sober reflection on the end things. The threat of eternal darkness shouldn't so much frighten, as wake us up spiritually. Christ says that if we thus remain faithful, the Second Coming will be our triumph. That's why in the mass, and at Christmas, we say, "Christ had died, Christ has risen, Christ will come again". We joyfully proclaim his resurrection and look to his coming again to fulfill God's plan, the final triumph over sin, suffering and death. This is the message of the Book of Revelation. Christ has won the victory for us. We needn't fear though the very sky fall down.

Moreover, when the world ends so will all immoral godless values of which Satan is lord. Only good will remain and Christ will gather his faithful into an eternal kingdom of love, peace and joy. In that light to be faithful is the goal of life on earth. To enjoy life fully as his people here, until he fulfills our dreams in heaven. For worldly values fade and leave us empty before eternity, but Christ is lord of enduring goodness, happiness and salvation both for this world and when it ends, forever and ever in heaven, amen.

So as God's people, keeping our souls ready for death and judgment and looking to his final coming with joy, but also preparatory spiritual activity, we profess our faith.

## Prayers of the faithful

As God's church people, as the year ends and we're reminded of the end things, lets pray for our ongoing safety and salvation.

For church leaders, especially our Holy Father, that they may lead all in faith, truth and goodness, so that they whole world may be prepared for the final coming of Christ.

For civil leaders; may they further people's spiritual as well as material welfare and govern with integrity and justice, knowing they always face the judgment of the people.

For youth, may they see through passing worldly values to those of their timeless Lord, for their lasting happiness here and hereafter.

For ourselves in our homes, workplaces and areas, may we prepare ourselves and loved ones for the Lord's coming, by faith and the charitable works that give it credibility.

For the sick, the aged and the housebound that through our care they may know the love and care of God.

For the dead that through our prayers, love and remembrance they may come to final judgment cleansed of sin and ready for heaven.

And we ask all these things through Christ Our Lord whose Second Coming we look forward to with great joy as his faithful people, amen.

## Reflection

Some people are natural pessimists. A friend of mine when he has any ache or pain says, "I'm finished, its all over". Some are full of glee when a storm or other disaster nears, maybe because we need a bit of drama to add spice to our lives. I know a person who says the recession marks the collapse of the Tower of Babel that's western culture now. This doom-and-gloom brigade will have a field day at the apocalypse. We shouldn't share that gloom, for Christ is merciful, but at the same time lets pray to Mary that our souls will always be prepared for his coming at death, or at the world's end. Hail Mary

# PART III

# The Cycle for Year C

# The First Sunday of Advent C

## *Introduction*

It seems curious that today's Gospel, on a Sunday which begins our preparation for Christmas, should talk about the world's end. But, in fact, the new heaven and the new earth that will begin at his Second Coming is already prefigured at his birth. Conscious of the scripture call to stay awake and be ready whenever he comes, we confess our sins.

## *Homily*

I remember when we were young how we stayed awake the night before Christmas, too excited to sleep. Anticipation of the feasting on the morrow, the opening of presents, and the family gathering from all over, kept us on tenterhooks. Christ sees the same exuberant excitement associated with his Second Coming on the clouds with power and glory. It won't be a sad time but the fulfillment of all our hopes. We're to stand erect then, our heads held high, for it will be a time of liberation for us. All our chains will fall away,

Our scripture, however, also contains a warning, a warning to be prepared for that great event. For it could happen at any time, and come suddenly, like a thief in the night, or like the great flood of Genesis, when they were eating and drinking and practicing every kind of debauchery up to the time when the waters swept them away. Spiritual awakening and staying awake, is the theme of preparation for Christ's birthday surprise and the surprise he will spring on the world at the end of time.

It will be a pleasant and joyful surprise for us the faithful who have remained so, but a trap sprung on the evil doers who have affronted the justice of God, and taken advantage of his forbearance, and think they can mock him with impunity, and desecrate the earth with iniquity. They'll be confounded, but the just will stand confident before God at his coming, having through prayer and good works kept their souls pure and ready for the coming of the Lord in judgment.

Christ talks of not letting our hearts and souls become coarsened by debauchery and drunkenness and the cares of life, lest we too be all at sea on the day of his coming. And that's a salutary warning for us today. In an often libertine and agnostic world, where every law of God is flouted, we can tag along, afraid to stand up for higher standards of living and believing. We can become a straw in the wind of every worldly trend and forget out Christian calling to holiness of life and witness, to be the salt of the earth and the light of the world. Prayer is the key to authentic witness and being ready when he comes, as the gospel says: "Stay awake, praying all the time for the strength to survive all that is going to happen, and to stand with confidence before the Son of Man" (Lk.21:36 JB),.

And that is the message of Advent also; we are given this time of prayer, fasting and alms-giving to strengthen us, and purify us both for his coming at Christmas and at the end of time, or at our own death, which could be at any time also. That's why we have this season, to prepare for any of these comings. That's why we light the first candle in the wreath. It signified the casting off of the night of evil in our hearts, and our shining up of our souls for Christ. For that's what Advent means—rebirth in faith, peace, and love for us, the Church, and the world. So that we'll be ready, and his work complete in us, when he comes at last in glory to judge the living and the dead.

In the meantime, we must remain watchful, tuning up our souls so that there will be no false notes there when the Lord comes. Advent's prayer, fasting and almsgiving enables that retuning, so that Christ will find a grand welcome when he comes to our inn at Christmas; a warm bed in our heart's manger; a family of renewed warmth love and peace at home; a Church buoyed by our attendance; a world renewed by our prayer, charity, and witness. For the worldly values of which Satan is lord, fade to dust at last, leaving us empty before eternity, but Christ is Lord of life, love, goodness, peace, and happiness both for this world, the end times, and forever and ever. Amen.

So as God's people renewing our inner light this Advent to prepare for Christ's coming now, at death, and at the world's end, we profess our faith.

## *Prayers of the Faithful*

For the leaders of the Church, that this Advent and Christmas they may bring God's light in Christ to the world as never before.

For civil leaders, that the Christmas gift may soften their hearts and make them reach out to all the needy children in their care.

For our youth, that, like the Christ child, they may be a light to our world by their faithfulness to Christ and all that's good and true.

For parents; may they love, bless, and give to their children with all their hearts this Advent and Christmas, so that this may be a time of good will and peace in each home.

For the sick and all those suffering in mind, body, or soul, that this Advent, through our love, care, and prayers, they may experience the peace, comfort, and healing of the Christ child and this may continue into the New Year.

For the dead to whom Christ opened the gates of heaven by his coming, that, helped by our prayers, they may enjoy the fruits of Christ death and resurrection in heavenly bliss.

We ask all these prayers to Christ, the child born for us and given to us at Christmas as the eternal light of the world. Amen.

## Reflection

"All across the land dawns a brand new morn, this comes to pass when a child is born." These are Fred Jay's lyrics to *When A Child Is Born*. The Christ child has no particular color or social class. He is black, white, yellow, or whatever. All are his children, and they are equally cherished. May it be the same with us. May we treat all God's children with equal dignity, love, and care. We ask Mary, who bore the Christ child for all humanity, that she will give us the open heart of Christ toward all this Advent, Christmas, and throughout the New Year, so that we will stand with joy and confidence before the Lord when he comes at last. Hail Mary.

# Second Sunday of Advent C

**(if the birth of John the Baptist is celebrated
see second Sunday of Advent A)**

## Introduction

The preaching of John the Baptist about Christ features in our scripture this week. Already the fruits of Christ's birth are predicted in the first reading in terms of the blessings showered on the exiles returning to Israel. And John prepares the way for the Lord in our gospel, he makes straight a highway for the Christ in the world and prefigures all people's return to the Promised Land in Christ. Let's return to God at this time, confessing our sins.

## Homily

Modern highways are a wonder, multi-laned and teeming with automobiles of every kind, flashing lights and streamlined junctions, and clear directions at every few miles of the way. They are a long way from the twisting tracks that must have served as roads in John the Baptist's and Christ's day. Only the Romans had large paved roads, and those leading to Rome, such as the Appian Way, were especially wide and straight. For Rome was the center of the world at that time, and people streamed to it from all over.

But when the scriptures talk about making straighter roads, it obviously has a deeper moral and spiritual import than facilitating speedier transport. This is especially true when John talks about highways in the desert, which would make little sense economically. If we see the desert as a spiritual and moral one, however, then opening it up so that God can come more easily, makes sense. Clearly John, aware of Isaiah's text, is talking about preparing a way paved for the Christ's coming, for John was the herald of the Messiah.

That's why the church puts him, and this text, before us on the first Sunday of Advent. For Advent is our preparation for the Lord too; it creates highways in our hearts for his coming at Christmas, with hints also of cleansing our hearts for his coming at the end of time. The highway, path or road in the wilderness of the world, is the high moral and spiritual way of Christ, the straighter way of God we must build within us in this time of grace. And the fruits of that grace we should produce are summed well in today's first reading: "peace through integrity and honor through devotedness." (Bar. 5:4 JB).

Certainly a new peace, integrity and devotedness to God is asked of us at Advent. Like John we're asked to love and serve God with hearts renewed. The spiritual practices of Advent, are calculated to bring about this renewal in holiness, straightening of our crooked muddy tracks as it were: extra prayer, fasting and almsgiving. The gradual lighting of the candles, each Sunday leading up to Christmas symbolize its gradual building up of our renewal through confession, repentance and gradual conversion. Advent is like a great symphony of renewal building up to a Christmas crescendo.

But what are the valleys to be filled in, the mountains to be laid low, the rough ways made smooth? Obviously, again, these are concerned with filling in any lacks, straightening out any twisted ways in our souls. So that our witness can be more powerful, at the end of one year and for the beginning of another. And we can be newly polished and shining lights for Christ at Christmas and into a new year of hope and resolution in Christ. For all else fades away and leaves us empty here and for eternity, but he is Lord of light, truth, goodness, and happiness both for this world and forever and ever. Amen.

So as God's people, called this Advent to shine for Christ anew, humbly rededicating what talents we have to his service, let's profess our faith in anticipation of his birthday.

## Prayers of the Faithful

For our Holy Father and all the consecrated leaders of the Church, that they may be as faithful witnesses for Christ in our world as John was for his day.

For our civil leaders, that they too may make straight in the wilderness of the modern world a highway for God's life, justice and truth.

For our youth, that they may see, through these days of Advent renewal, that it's in giving for God and others that we gain that inner greatness, peace, love, and grace that flowers within us at last into everlasting glory.

For ourselves in our homes that we may be examples to our children, relatives, and neighbors of the faith, love, and renewed goodness that Advent calls us to.

For the aged, the sick, and all those who suffer in body or soul, that this Advent and Christmas they may find in their faith, and in our care for them, the consolation, healing, and peace of God.

For the dead whose faith is known to God alone, that, through our prayers, any lingering remission for sin may be achieved, and they may come to their final rest with all the saints in glory.

And we ask all these prayers through Christ, the Lord of Life, who intercedes for all before the Father forever and ever. Amen.

## Reflection

A person who recalled people to the straight way of God in our times was the great recently canonized Pope St. John the XX111. Like his namesake, John the Baptist, he certainly stirred up the church of his day, and heralded a great renewal by calling the Second Vatican Council. A church mired in traditionalist gridlock was suddenly trust by him into the modern age, launched on a great Adventure of renewal, and a return to simpler and more authentic Christianity where the ordinary people were given their true voice. He was like an Advent for the church in our time, the fruits of which we are still enjoying. But that is not only why he was made a saint; no, that was due to his intense simple holiness that radiated warmth; he was perhaps the most loved Pope of our times, though his reign was short. Let's pray that we'll be as faithful and generous in God and humanity's service, and let this Advent be the beginning of that rededicated love and faithfulness. Hail Mary.

# Third Sunday of Advent C

## Introduction

"I want you to be happy, always happy in the Lord (Phil. 4:4. JB), Paul says and that's our theme. Faith is not about long faces, but joy. That's what we celebrate this Gaudete, or joyful, Sunday. Our pink candle reflects the tiding of great joy the angels proclaimed. Let's confess ways we fail to spread joy and laughter around us.

## Homily

The great joy in life is to be close to someone we love. I saw on TV a few weeks ago teenage girls at an event featuring the boy band Westlife. One of the girls was in tears: "O my God! I can't believe I'm close to him!" she said. "He actually spoke to me!" I laughed that a pop idol could evoke such adoration. It seemed out of proportion. Then I realized that we all need someone larger than life to fill our hearts and lives, to look up to and love. Our readings see the most worthy subject of that love as Christ, the Savior who gave all for us, and who rejoices over us continually as his holy people.

That's why this Gaudete Sunday we light a pink candle. Our scripture says that the the Lord "will exult with joy over you" (Zeph. 3:17, JB). We rejoice that God is close and comes intimately to us in Christ. This should dispel all anxiety as our second reading says, "The Lord is very near. There is no need to worry" (Phil. 4:5-6. JB). He's with us in each Sunday Eucharist, and he's coming in the flesh at Christmas.

I watched that funny film, *The Pope Must Die*, again recently, about a simple, guitar-playing priest who becomes pope and spreads the simple message that we shouldn't be kill-joy about the faith. He's right. God doesn't want long faces, only our happiness.

The American declaration has as one of its aims the pursuit of happiness. Christ in the manger enabled that, for, as Isaiah says, he broke the yoke that has weighed us down since the fall (Is. 10:27, JB). He gave us the real way to happiness through believing, loving hearts following what's right. He restored our inner freedom. It's no wonder then he says: "I have come that they may have life, and have it to the full" (John 10:10, JB). So let's rejoice in the lord, enjoy our faith like a good meal.

We often seek that fuller life in worldly crutches like drink or drugs, but our greatest joy is the Lord. We soon grow tired of pleasures, but never of grace. Only God fully fulfills our deepest thirst for happiness and gives us the deep values by which it is achieved. That's why all Christ's new commands—the Beatitudes—have no "thou shalt nots." he just says that "they are happy" who follow him. For, like that girl at the Westlife event, we dream, idealize, and seek a worthy object to love. Christ satisfies that inner need fully.

Saint Paul says: "No eye has seen, and no ear has heard, things beyond the mind of man, all that God has prepared God for those who love him" (1 Corinthians 2:9, JB). As believers, we enjoy many of those good things while on earth and are storing up unbelievable joys for the next world. As Isaiah says to the people: "Cry out for joy and gladness, you dwellers in Zion, for great in the midst of you is the Holy One of Israel" (Isaiah, 12:6, JB). He is here with us always and comes in glory at Christmas.

And that's the why of the Christmas glitter; it rightly expresses the joy of God's baby among us, setting us free forever. That's why I love the Christmas lights, giving of presents, reunion of families, and so on. For we should exult beyond measure, enjoy ourselves in the body too. Paul says: "I want you to be happy, always happy in the Lord."(Phil.4:4 JB). As his beloved people, like that girl close to her idol, we should not apologize for overdoing it at Christmas in lavish feasting, peace on earth, good cheer. The glory of the Lord is all around us. This should drive out all our worry, for as Paul says, God guards our hearts and minds in Christ Jesus, Our Lord. And he is now our grace, peace, and deepest happiness for this world and forever and ever. Amen.

So as his joyful followers gathered here in his presence this glorious season let's profess of faith with great rejoicing and gladness.

## Prayers of the Faithful

"There is no need to worry; if there is anything you need, pray for it."(Phil. 4:6. JB). As Christians, natural optimists and joyful believers we pray for what we need.

For all Church leaders, that joy in the Lord may light up their leadership.

For civil leaders this Christmas and New Year, that they may bring joy to the people, especially the old, the weak, and the vulnerable.

"I want you to be happy, always happy in the Lord" (Phil. 4:4, JB). In the spirit of St. Paul, let's pray silently, with joyful confidence, for our deep personal intentions.

Committed in this season to giving presents to all around us as part of our joy in the Lord, we pray that our generosity may extend especially to the poor and the needy.

For sick friends and relatives at this time, that, through modern medicine and our loving care they may know the healing presence of the Lord this Christmas and always.

For our dead, especially those who have died recently, that they may now enjoy ultimate joy and happiness in the presence of the Lord and their loved ones forever.

And we ask all these things through Christ the joy and salvation of the world and our near and loving Lord forever and ever. Amen.

## Reflection

The film *Love Story* features love between a rich Harvard boy and a poor Italian emigrant. She develops leukemia and dies, leaving the boy distraught. When his rich father comes to say "I'm sorry", the boy repeats the girl's mantra: "Love means never having to say you're sorry." The God of the boy's father was wealth and social status. He gave his son no love like that he received from the girl. The message is that to love and be loved for ourselves is real riches. Christ should inspire that love in our lives. He told us to love one another unconditionally. Let our Christian hearts reflect his love to all today. Hail Mary.

# Fourth Sunday of Advent C

## Introduction

"He himself will be peace," the prophet says of the Christ (Micah 5:5, JB). In our gospel we see the peace, love, and joy that Mary brings when, heavily pregnant, she visits Elizabeth. Let's confess ways we fail to spread love and peace around us at Christmas.

## Homily

"Christmas is coming, the geese are getting fat," we sang, in a folk rime, when young. Christmas is near now, and Irish writer John B. Keane talks about the unique urgings it brings. He describes a neighbor who normally wouldn't give the crumbs from his table to a starving child, yet full of Christmas spirit one year, phoned his estranged daughter in England and begged her to come home. She came, all was forgiven, and he wasn't half as mean thereafter. Keane adds that we should take Christmas by the horns, because the milk of kindness doesn't come from cows and goats, but from the human heart—softened, we might add, by the grace of God and the humanity of his Christ.

That overflowing Christmas faith and love has survived Stalin, Hitler, and all secular efforts to snuff it out. It has survived human greed, intolerance, and all worldly attacks imaginable; even modern consumerism. As we might point out, there are three dimensions to Christmas now: the commercial Christmas with its carols, reindeer, Santa Claus, and the hard sell; the Charles Dickens Christmas with its images of snowy scenes, roaring fires, turkey, ham, plum pudding, mince pies, universal good will; and the Christian message that is really its heart. For without it, Christmas may bring but a brief uplift, a few jolly songs, a few gifts given and received, then back to the grind. The third dimension, the reason for the whole thing, is the Christmas miracle with its timeless message. Two thousand years ago was born for us God's son. Now humanity's vocation is unity, peace, joy, and love.

But lest I seem to be preaching Puritanism, God forbid, let me hasten to add that the first two dimensions have a role to play too. As in Dickens' story of Scrooge, pious condemnations of Christmas hoopla can create a division between spiritual and material realities. That's deeply unchristian, because what we celebrate is the Word made flesh. Christmas joy must be lived in the flesh. We can and should have the best of both worlds. Parties, gifts, eating, and drinking anchor our Christmas in bodily pleasures (excluding, of course, excessive drinking or driving while intoxicated, which damage rather than build harmony). Don't be afraid to let yourself go in Christmas buying and selling, in gift-giving, in good works, and in every kind of family good cheer.

Indeed, the gospel highlights the key family togetherness theme of Christmas. Mary goes to her cousin Elizabeth to share her joy. They experience mutual happiness in the children about to be born. And Elisabeth loves and supports the young saint in the onerous role trust on her. Mary, doubtless afraid and confused, needed a shoulder to cry on.

Christmas is like that; it's about family visiting and supporting relatives troubled or lonely. We do Christ's work in uniting and comforting each other. And, like that old rhyme, "please put a penny in the old man's hat", let's help the poor too. For example, donations placed in the crib box might go to the Vincent De Paul to help families suffering financially. Mary carried Christ as a gift to all. Our gifts to the poor bring warmth and love to those who most need it. This is a time when we experience the Lord's grace and favor. Let's spread that favor around us. For the Christmas child is the timeless Lord of life, love, and salvation for all people's happiness in this world, as well as forever and ever. Amen.

So as God's people glorying in this feast of Christian light and joy to the world let's profess our faith with renewed charitable hearts.

## Prayers of the Faithful

And as God's family gathered in Christ and called to charity and faith now and throughout the year, we pray for what we need.

For the Church throughout the world, especially its leaders, that, full of Christmas joy, they may radiate that joy to the world.

For our civil leaders, that, as they concentrate on the commercial benefits of Christmas, they may not forget to respect also its spiritual dimension.

For our wonderful youth, that they may appreciate their deliverance by Christ by practicing their faith; and that those who've drifted from the Church may come back to joy.

For ourselves, that in our homes and communities this Advent and Christmas, we may be a light of faith and love for our children and those around us.

For the sick, the lonely, the aged, and the troubled in body or soul, that, through our prayers and caring love, they may find peace, comfort, and healing.

For the dead for whom the Christ opened heaven's gates, that, helped by our prayers and remembrance, they may come to final peace.

We ask these prayers through Christ, who came to us as a frail baby and will come again at last to answer all our prayers. Amen.

## Reflection

Saint Joseph is a much-neglected Christmas saint. He never put himself forward, yet he played a key role in the incarnation. He saved Mary from being stoned to death as a single mother, and he saved the child Jesus from Herod by taking the family across the desert to Egypt. Jesus must have loved him very much, for he spent thirty of his thirty-three years on earth in Joseph's job as a carpenter. Let's pray to Joseph this Advent and Christmas that we will be as faithful and loving in our families:

Jesus, Mary, and Joseph, I give you my heart and my soul.

Jesus, Mary, and Joseph, assist me in my last agony.

Jesus, Mary, and Joseph, may I breathe forth my soul in peace with you. Amen.

# The Nativity C

## Introduction

What we celebrate tonight was the goal of all scripture and the prophets, the coming of the Christ. "Look, your Savior comes!" Isaiah proclaims (Isaiah 62:11, JB). The infinite kindness and love of God is revealed at last in him. Let's pray this holy night for the grace to live in his light, and let's confess ways we fail in to bring his light to others.

## Homily

What was the best event in your life? The one that brought you most joy. Your first kiss? Your wedding day? Your first job and paycheck? The birth of your first child? The event we celebrate tonight with such a blaze of light is all such joys rolled into one. For it is God among us, come to save us in the form of a tiny child. The impact of this for all people is earth shattering: final freedom from darkness and evil; the coming of the dazzling light of God to transform our darkened world; the birth of hope and truth for man; the Advent of the Savior promised from the beginning of the world.

Traditional hymns like *The Twelve Days Of Christmas* but faintly capture that miracle. This song lists all the gifts given by the true love to his beloved. The true love is God, and we're the beloved in the original meaning of the song. We all receive gifts tonight, but they are paltry in comparison to the gifts showered on us by the infant Jesus. That small bundle cradled in a mother's arms in a stable far away conquered despair, darkness, death, and evil for us forever. Choirs sing: "Joy to the World, the Savior reigns." his coming was just that—untold joy to the world.

Lest we reduce Christmas to a cynical booze-up, let's remember that our heavenly Father loved us so much, he sent us his son. People come home this time of the year. We all came home at the Nativity. God opened a home of love for us all in the form of his frail human son, and his outstretched arms should soften the hardest heart. The fact that you're here means you've come to God's home to say thanks, to shout like the angels: "Glory to God in the highest heaven, and peace to men who enjoy his favor" (Luke 2:14 JB). For the call is not only to celebrate, but to live the peace brought by Christ. The Christmas decoration of love in our hearts is the real tinsel God wants, treating all our brothers and sisters on earth with equal respect, peace, and love. They're all our family now, especially the old, the sick, the poor, and the lonely.

The Word became flesh and dwelt amongst us. As the children sing for us, we remember that the joy of Christmas is also in dance, music, and partying. Indulging in fine food and drink remind us that this is a time when we rightly celebrate to excess. Worldly cynics say, "Why all the fuss about Christmas?". But that makes sense only to faithless hearts. Mary cradles Our Lord in her arms, and all *is* calm all *is* bright now. For we're also safe in her arms from cold and darkness.

Though some regress to dark paganism today, rejecting that light of life, we make no apologies for celebrating *The First Noel* in a blaze of light. For tonight Mary gave Jesus his first kiss on behalf of us all. It's our first kiss, our wedding, our first baby too; all our joys rolled into one. It's the restoration of the paradise our first parents threw away. The wise celebrate that to excess at Christmas to give thanks. For the godless values of a hard, materialistic world pass and fail to satisfy us, but the Jesus, born for all in a humble manger, is Lord of life, love, happiness, grace, beauty, and peace, both for this world and forever and ever. Amen.

So as God's people gathered in faith, love, and joy on this night of nights, with angelic choir voices lifting us up to heaven, let's profess our faith with boundless joy.

## Prayers of the Faithful

And as God's people rejoicing at his birth and working to bring peace, love, and enjoyable living to all this Christmas and in the New Year, we pray for what we need.

We pray for the Pope and Church leaders, that they may be ambassadors of peace and world equality, and so bring the Christ child's saving presence to the whole world.

For ourselves, that, where there is darkness in our lives, we may dispel it with God's light, attain peace, love, and happiness in our hearts, souls, and homes.

For the sick, the old, the lonely, and the depressed, that, through our love and care, they may know the love, comfort, and healing of Christ this holy Christmastime.

For lasting peace in our country and in the world, that brotherly togetherness may break out everywhere, all may live the angels' message of peace and good will among men.

For all those who have died in the peace of Christ, especially the relatives and friends who can't be with us this Christmas, that God may lead them safely to the heavenly home where we will be reunited with them in full eternal love and happiness.

And we make all these prayers with confidence on this holiest of nights, through Christ Our Lord, born for us in a stable of love.

## Reflection

Santa Claus is very commercialized today. But the original Santa Claus, Saint Nicholas, echoes the main Christian spirit of Christmas—charity. He was a rich man who lived in a country that was very cold in winter, hence the woolly clothes and sleigh. He gave away all his riches to the poor. But being a humble man who didn't want to trumpet his Christian goodness; he went around at night, in the dead of winter, and especially at Christmas, to leave goodies on people's windowsills, or at their doors. When they got up in the morning they found the presents and rejoiced. Santa Claus was born in this great saint who made giving his life. We pray for the same warm giving Christian hearts at Christmas and always. Hail Mary.

# Feast of the Holy family C

## Introduction

We may think of Christ as beyond things like adolescence, but he was fully human. Today we see his teenage rebellion. Yet we also see him submitting to his parents and growing in age and grace. Lets confess ways we fail our parents.

## Homily

Last Christmas calls from battered wives and children flooded helplines. Violence, abuse, loneliness dominated these calls, and alcohol was a major factor. Not a very good ad for family life, or our sense of what matters at Christmas, peace and good will. Add to this a huge increase in family breakdown in our society and the picture can seem depressing.

In this context is there any point in the today's feast, that of the holy family. Certainly not if our image of Jesus Mary and Joseph is of a no-problem family. But nothing could be further from the truth. They were poor. After traveling the long road to Bethlehem, they were shut out of the inn. Jesus was born in a stable. They fled for there lives from Herod, across the desert with scant food and danger everywhere. Then they were refugees in a strange land, threatened, excluded, lonely. Nor is Luke's account of the teenage Jesus free from the usual rebellion; when Mary and Joseph found him in the temple, he said: "did you not know that I must be busy with my father's affairs" (Lk. 2:49-50, JB) Yet he obeyed them, and grew in age and grace before God and man.

In effect this holy family survived all that the world threw at them and grew in togetherness. Jesus lived for 33 years and spent 90% of this eking out a meager living with Joseph and Mary in a quiet village in

Palestine. Could God have affirmed the value of close family life more. For if that family had plenty of trials it drew them closer together rather than pushed them apart. That's the message of the feast. It is about the family who hangs in there, prays together, stays together, bonded by trial and difficulty, who works at marriage and family life in the deep love of God and each other. For love is a conscious decision to go on loving and nurturing life no matter what.

Sure, this is increasingly difficult today, but its still doable. A huge number of families are still getting it right by the grace of God, remaining true to Christian principles of love, faithfulness and non-violence. Sacrificing the pub and personal ambition to be together. Working for each other and their children in an atmosphere of affection, trust and peace. Its not easy building such a family, but the alternative is unthinkable.

Traditional Family life isn't perfect but its better than any alternative that's been tried. Without it we risk social disintegration, a reversion to irresponsible individualism. The ones who usually suffer most in this scenario are the precious people of our society, the children. They need, deserve, the love and security of parents who are there for them. They need a real home, a nurturing caring environment so that they can grow up "in wisdom, in stature, and in favor with God and men", as Jesus did (Lk. 2:52, JB). The holy family were a real family. They stayed together, united by love, through all adversity.

No less is expected of parents today. They're called to create loving caring homes so that all children may grow in age and grace, like Jesus, Our Lord of all faithful enduring love and nurturing care forever and ever, amen. So as God's own gathered here, praying for loving united families to our heavenly Father and Mother, we profess our faith.

## *Prayers of the Faithful*

For the Pope, the Holy Father of God's people, that he and all the local bishops and fathers who pastor God's family the church may do so with the love, care and diligence of Christ himself.

For our leaders in public life and government that they may promote and support family life by their laws and rule, and so bring about a healthy and nurturing society.

For ourselves in our own families and homes, that we may love and nurture equally all those of our family, feed, clothe, nurse and educate and bring them up in age, grace and truth before God and man.

For husbands and wives especially those in endangered marriages, may they continue to grow in the love that first brought them together and be one forever in love in their final heavenly home.

For our aged sick or lonely relatives, friends and neighbors that we may reach out to them in familial love and care and so bring to them the love of God.

For the dead members of our families that they may, with our prayers, come to their heavenly home where we will be reunited with them one day.

And we ask all these prayers through Christ Our Lord who spent most of his life in a humble family home.

## *Reflection:*

Home is where the heart is, as that great Christmas favorite, *The Wizard Of Oz*, tells us. Certainly, a good home where love flourishes, is never forgotten. Its where we return to again and again when life lets us down. Its where we are laid at last, surrounded and mourned mainly by our family. Others may love us but not in the same way, or as deeply. Lets ask Mother Mary, the perfect mother, and Joseph the caring father, to watch over our homes in peace and love this Christmas and always. Hail Mary.

# Feast of Mary Mother of God C

## Introduction

Our scripture today reminds us that we're God's family gathered here. We've a father and mother in heaven who loves us. Lets confess ways we fail our loving parents.

## Homily

Christmas is about family. And that is very evident in the theme of today's scripture, where we have shepherds coming to honor a mother and a child, a special mother and a special child, but also an ordinary mother and a human as well as a divine child. The overall theme is one of wonder, and reflection. The shepherds wonder at the strange tiding of the angels about this child, and the message of peace and good will to all people, that he brings from God himself, as his Son.

Indeed as the Son of God born of Mary, you'd think there would be more fireworks at his birth than there were. The extraordinary thing about this birth, apart from the angels and the wise men, is its ordinariness. The setting of the humble stable, the village simplicity of Mary and Joseph, and their following of the ordinary custom of having the child circumcised on the eight day after birth, and their naming of the child at the same time. Though it is the feast of Mary, the mother of God, there is actually little about her in the scripture; except that she treasured all these things and pondered them in her heart.

For the amazing things about his birth is that Mary too is finding out about the child, reflecting on who he is and naming him Jesus according to the instructions given to her at the annunciation and the conception of the child. In this, however, one thing is certain, Mary is obeying God, reflecting on and reflecting his will always in her life.

And that is the message of her motherhood of the Savior; Mary is, in all this, a simple handmaid of the lord, always looking to his will not her own. And there's the message for us, to ponder on our faith and to seek, and do, the will of God, as we discern it, or as it has been revealed to us. For the other theme of the feast is that as mother of Jesus, Mary is mother of the church, which is his body, and as each of us as adopted children of God in Christ; and of the whole world as God's creation.

And what a mother God chose for Jesus and for us humans. For the first thing we should see and celebrate in Mary is her humility, her sense of her herself as a lowly servant of God. "He has looked upon his lowly handmaid", Mary says (Lk. 1:48, JB) And she drew a wider lesson from God's choice: "he has pulled down princes from their thrones and exalted the lowly". In effect, though chosen this does not give Mary a swelled head, it makes her even humbler and more appreciative of her dependence on God. There is a lesson there for us. Yet though a simple village maid, Mary is not simple; she is a person who ponders things deeply in her heart. She is a contemplative who doesn't say much, but when she does speak, she really shakes things up. Her Magnificat shows her, curiously, as also an intellectual and a social revolutionary. For that speech, is about casting down the proud and raising up the poor.

That is the motherhood of Mary is about a new just order in the world, her son is to bring about. Her role is to raise up the lowly and watch over all her children as a gentle and caring mother of the whole world as Christ is its lord. "I am the handmaid of the lord", lets each of us say that too. As such praying people, dedicated social workers, Vincent de Paul volunteers, pastoral carers, priests, nuns; active parish laity, volunteers who help the poor at home or abroad, kind dedicated educators of the young - we are the Marys of God's Kingdom today. Humble faithful, under Mary's banner we are to birth Jesus in a world every bit as troubled, violent and sinful as it was in Mary's time. "I am the handmaid of the Lord", Mary said (Lk. 1:38, JB. Let each of us say that each day. For that lord is love, goodness, happiness for this world and forever and ever, and Mary is at his side in that role as our gentle mother and mother of the whole world, of God's just nation, amen

So as the people of God called to serve God and others with humble and joyful hearts in the light of Christ and our wonderful mother, let us make our profession of faith.

### *Prayers of the Faithful:*

And as God's family lets pray confidently to him for what we need.

For the Pope, and all leaders of the churches that they may serve God and all his people with humble care and love like Mary did.

For all those who govern us that they may not lord it over the people but give humble, honest and equal service to all.

For our youth that, like Mary, they may serve God and others with generous and unpretentious hearts.

For ourselves in our trials and difficulties, that we may turn to Mary our mother, and mother of the church, at all times, and ask for her healing help always.

For the sick, the old, the lonely, and the oppressed that through our love and care they may experience the love of Christ, and his gentle caring mother.

For the dead that they may come to their heavenly home with the help of our communal and personal prayers for them, and Mary's advocacy in heaven.

And we ask all these prayers to Christ, who is or lord forever and ever, amen.

## Reflection

The story of Lourdes gives a good image of Mary. There she came to a poor girl and addressed her with gentle love: "would you do me the kindness to come here", as if she was the servant and Bernadette the lady. Bernadette says that she was very beautiful, but also very young, very humble and all radiant with light. That's our gentle mother. Each of us are her beloved children as brothers and sisters of Christ, and how happy we should be to be her children. So proud of her, and confident of her care, we pray, Hail Mary.

# Second Sunday of Christmas C

## Introduction

This Sunday celebrates Christ as the universal Lord. For when he became flesh, as John writes: "we saw his glory, the glory that is his as the only Son of the Father, full of grace and truth" (Jn. 1:14, JB). Remembering ways we fail him, we confess our sins.

## Homily

The words of a song I heard during the week is apt for today. Its about a mother and son. He comes in and puts a paper before his mother asking money for household tasks: mowing the lawn, watching his little brother, putting out the garbage etc. The mother turns over the page and writes a witty response: for the 9 months she carried him growing inside her no charge; for the times she sat up with him, and for buying his clothes and wiping his nose no charge. She finishes by saying that true love is given without charge.

We're sometimes like that son with God. He might reply: for the world and life I gave you no charge; for still loving you when you turned away from me to follow your own sinful way; for sending my son to bring you back to happiness, perfection and innocence; for the agonies he suffered for you; for the church he set up as your guide; for the heaven he prepared where we can be happy forever – no charge.

At Christmas we celebrate that parental love poured out for us in his Son. For this is a wonderful mystery; God, lord of the universe is a loving Father. Our response should be love in return, and ensuring that his children walk in light. For his birth is useless unless he lives in an earth reborn to his glory, peace, love, innocence and truth.

So that he'll come at last in triumph. For Christians also look to his Second Coming, when we'll go out to meet him with all the saints, having lived in his glorious light all our lives. For sinful worldly values fade to ashes at last, but he is lord of love, peace and salvation for this world and forever, amen.

So as God's people serving him in returned love and witness, lets profess our faith.

## Prayers of the Faithful

For our Holy Father and leaders of the churches, that they may be humble servants of the Word made flesh, promoting light, love, peace, faith and justice in the world.

For youth that, enlightened by Christ, they may keep the faith and work for his kingdom.

For ourselves that in our homes and communities, may we be faithful servants of Christ.

For the sick, the aged, the lonely and the oppressed that we may be the hands of Christ reaching out to them with love and care.

For civic leaders, that they may serve all the people under their care, free from corruption, favoritism and self-seeking greed.

For the dead that they may share the glory of the Word made flesh in the heaven that he has prepared for all his faithful.

And we ask all these prayers through Christ, our Prince of love and care forever, amen.

## Reflection:

The late Mother Theresa was a perfect example of someone caring for all, as the hands of Christ healing the world. She tells of going in to conference on world poverty one day and seeing a poor sick man lying just outside the door of the conference center. She picked him up and cared for him. She notes that all the grand people inside were waffling away, solving all the world's problems in theory, while that poor man, like Lazarus in the gospel, was dying at their gates. We pray that our charity in the service of Christ, the light of the world, may be more than words but help for God's needy around us. Hail Mary.

# The Epiphany C

## Introduction

Our Christmas season ends with the Magi feast, little Christmas as we used to call it at one time. Scripture sees it as the feast of all the world coming to Christ in the form of foreign kings. Lets confess ways we fail to be wise servants of God and humanity.

## Homily

We honor the wise men today, but what's wisdom? Obviously, like the wise men, to seek and serve the source of wisdom, truth and goodness, God. We can have all the knowledge in the world but as the psalms repeatedly say, without the wisdom that comes from God, its all in vain. The Magi knew this. Sometimes I think modern man doesn't. All too often we think we know all, can control all, even the universe and the elements; but when a severe hurricane or tsunami comes we are helpless; if the earth shifted fraction on its axis we'd all be wiped out and could do nothing about it. In comparison to the vast forces of the universe we are very small indeed. Do we have savvy enough to see this.

The Magi did and were wise; they were astronomers who studied the movements of the heavenly spheres. But they used their knowledge – they were doctors and scientists - to also seek and find the Christ. This feast says that all humankind should do the same. As the first reading says: "let all the national come to your light, and kings to your dawning brightness" (Is 60:3, JB). Billions have already done so, but many still hold back.

Scripture calls the latter to saving faith. Our first reading envisages all people coming to praise the lord for their happiness. Paul also talks of the urgent mission to bring all earth's people to God. Christ in the

Gospel reaches out to the pagan Canaanite woman, and the responsorial psalm anticipates his kingdom come everywhere: "may every race in the world be blessed in him, and all nations call him blessed" (Ps.72:17, JB). That's God's plan, that humankind should come to wisdom, not languish in darkness.

As a new year dawns and its back to work, back to school, lets make a new year resolution to continue with fresh hearts the joyful Christian journey we started at Baptism. Lets pray that our own country and all nations will, like the wise men, accept and worship the universal Lord born to save all. And as individual believers, having kept the priceless wisdom of the faith, lets help in whatever way we can to bring that about. For as Christ's kings, the gold frankincense and myrrh we bring to him is devout lives and witness. That's the challenge for the new year with the suffering and joys it has in store.

As truly wise men and women, faith, hope and charity are the gifts we're to bring to Our Lord in the coming year. For the light is given us not to be hoarded but to be shared. For only Christ's love can spread peace, and save a sinful broken world from meaninglessness and spiritually empty living. Lets be wise and know, like the great scientists that the Magi were, where true lasting wisdom, truth and salvation is. Lets bring our hearts joyfully to the baby Jesus waiting in that cold manger with Mary and Joseph.

That's the challenge for the new year with the suffering and joys it has in store. We should open our eyes in the new year to fresh wisdom; notably to realize that the things of this world fade to dust and ashes at last, but truly wise people see that Christ alone is lord of love, light, peace, truth, beauty, happiness and salvation both for this world and forever and ever, amen.

So as modern wise people, men and women of grace and truth, spreading God's light to those still trapped in futile darkness and despair, lets profess our faith.

## Prayers of the Faithful

And as the Lord's wise ones, lets pray to him and his mother for what we need.

For Our Holy Father the Pope and all the leaders of the churches that they may reach out to all people with a message of healing both for this world's ills and their eternal salvation.

For our civil leaders that they may help the practical and spiritual welfare of all the citizens and reach out generously with what aid they can to those in need abroad.

For the sick, the aged, the depressed, the lonely and those who lack the saving wisdom of Christ, that through our care they may come to fullness of life both for here and hereafter.

For our young people that they may not just concentrate on self, wealth, power and fame but be conscious of their responsibility to walk in God's wise light, and be his faith-filled and caring hands to those around them.

For ourselves that we may welcome all people as our brothers and sisters in Christ, and deepen our own faith, hope and charity in the light of Christ's true wisdom, so as to be true saving lights to the families and community we love.

For the dead who have passed from the cares of this world that they may come safely to their heavenly home, especially all our loved ones and sisters and brothers in the parish who have passed away recently, or whose anniversaries occur at this time.

And we ask all these our prayers through Christ who is universal Savior and Lord of all wise people forever and ever, amen.

### *Reflection:*

An example of a modern wise holy man who served God and others with Christ's heart is the famous Jesuit scientist and scholar Pierre Teilhard De Chardin. He worked tirelessly through his writings to bring together science and faith. Indeed, his famous theory is that through modern science and especially progress in medical science, man is part of the redemptive work of Christ, to bring about a perfect heaven on earth in the long run, as scripture predicts. Evolution, he thought, is now a redemptive process through the increasing enlightened consciousness of man, which is from God also. Lets affirm and pray for all scientists in their work to further human wisdom and healing. Hail Mary

# The Baptism of the Lord C

## Introduction

As we start a new year we're reminded today that our spiritual journey begins with Baptism. God says of Christ at Baptism, as he says of us, "This is my beloved". Lets confess ways we fail to live our Baptismal and Confirmation promises.

## Homily

The gospel features Christ's Baptism in the Jordan river. When in the Holy land, a group of us relived that experience. In the midst of the desert, off with our shoes and into the cool water; knobby knees, varicose veins and all. As water poured over us, I imagined the gospel scene: the rough figure of John; crowds gathering to be baptized; someone special coming, ordinary yet full of God's glory; the dove descending and the father shouting, "You are my son, the beloved; my favor rests on you" (Lk. 3:22, JB).

Yet God says the same to each of us at Baptism; "you are my son, you are my daughter, the beloved". For when he rose Christ made us all God's children, and the Father loves us hopelessly, as he did Jesus. So we should cherish all as brothers and sisters. For by Baptism we're God's family, our innocence and heavenly destiny restored.

But at Baptism we receive others vocations too, mainly to be holy as God is. Farmers, shopkeeper, nurses, street cleaners, the unemployed, whatever, we're all priceless. As Vatican 11 says, at Baptism we're called to live as children of God and to actively spread his goodness and holiness in the world. We're to do our Father's work, by being holy ourselves and passing the faith on to others, especially our families.

Young or old, sick or well, working or pensioners, we never retire from that dignity and calling.

For it is an urgent work and each of us must carry it out conscientiously all life long. I'm reminded of a story a lapsed Catholic told me. When he went abroad, he stopped practicing his faith. But when he retired, he realized his mistake and came back to the church. But when he went to the local priest to be received the back, the latter gave out to him: "you've a lot to answer for", the priest said, "as result of your apostasy thousands are and will be lost to the faith; your children, grandchildren, great grandchildren". A person can make a huge difference for good or ill by keeping the faith or not. For ill, by abandoning the faith and so gravely endangering one's soul and those of loved ones. For good, by remaining faithful members of the church and spreading it to others, especially our family, furthering Christ's saving work through our church work.

For we're saved not as individuals but as part of a **community** of faith, worship and charity. If we abandon that community and its worship, then its likely our faith will disappear also. That's why I say to people at confession, stop repeating minor faults and ask yourself instead, am I living out my Baptismal promise to deepen and spread my faith as a faithful and active part of the church community. For the real trust of Baptism is that we're anointed to be a living active members of the holy church.

Not that we'll ever be perfect. But despite our very frailty and sinfulness we should remain faithful to God and his church. For what's important is not the quantity of our money, but the steadfast quality of our faith. As Mother Theresa of Calcutta used to say, we don't have to be ultra successful, only to be faithful. For every breath we take from first to last is precious and vital to God's plan. So lets persevere in serving God and the church to the end, so that when Christ comes to judge the living and the dead he'll welcome us as one of his special ones, the saints on earth, and join us to his saints in heaven forever. For this world fades to dust and ashes at last but Christ is lord of life, love, goodness, happiness, truth, and salvation for this world and forever and ever, amen.

So as God's beloved, blessed with his Spirit at Baptism and anointed to do his work as faithful members of his church and his light to the world, we profess our faith.

## *Prayers of the Faithful.*

For our Holy Father, the Pope, and all leaders of the churches, that they may remain true to their Baptismal calling to lead the faithful in humble service of God and each other.

For ourselves, that in our homes, community and local church we may serve Christ faithfully and live out our Baptism in goodness and holiness in our daily lives.

For all our children who were baptized and received First Holy Communion and Confirmation, that they will live out their Christian calling to be worshiping members of his local church and witnesses for Christ and all that's right before the world.

For the sick, aged, lonely and the mentally depressed that conscious of their dignity as precious children of God through Baptism, they may know his love through our care.

For the dead who wore the white robe of Christ's resurrection at Baptism, that they may enter into the fullness of life promised then, by coming safely to their heavenly home.

And we ask these prayers through Christ to the heavenly Father in the Spirit we received at Baptism, amen.

## *Reflection:*

I baptized a mother and her three children of various ages, once. We priests, usually baptize infants, so it was great to be able to baptize people who were aware of what it was all about. Indeed, in the early church most of those baptized were adults, and at one stage in the church's development, many waited until late in life to be baptized, because they said that once they were baptized they should live blameless lives. St.Ambrose, the great bishop of Milan, was elected bishop by the popular acclaim of the people, and was baptized, made priest, and ordained as bishop all in one go. We, who were baptized as infants, did not get the chance to make that adult commitment to Christ and his church. Lets us do so this Easter, and ask Mary to keep us faithful to our Baptism. Hail Mary.

# Ash Wednesday C

## Introduction

Welcome to our Special Ash Wednesday mass. It always reminds me of the story of Lourdes and Mary's call there for a life of penance to atone for sins and bring the world back to God. Lets pray for some such renewal in our own lives this Lent.

## Homily

Lourdes featured a small French girl, Bernadette Souberous. Her family were poor; they lived in one small dark room. They had to gather sticks for a fire to heat the room in winter and Bernadette was often sick, because they were living in dank conditions with scanty food to eat. One day her mother sent her up the mountain to get some sticks for the fire, to cook the pot of soup they had for lunch. While gathering the sticks she suddenly saw a white light and a beautiful lady who later told her that she was the Immaculate Conception. The Lady told Bernadette to get people to build a church there where people would come to pray and be healed. She also told Bernadette that people should do penance and pray that sinful people would be converted, and so be saved.

That's what Ash Wednesday also tells us; to deny ourselves in some way so as to show our love for God, and prepare for Easter, and help convert the world to faith and peace. Hence Lent's 40 days of fasting, praying and helping poor people like Bernadette.

Why forty days? Because Jesus spent that time in the desert praying and fasting before he began his public life. Why ashes?. Because ashes are a sign in the Bible of spiritual renewal and conversion. The story of Jonah illustrates this well. In his time there was a great city called Nineveh which was noted for unbelief and immorality. God asked Jonah to go there and tell the people to turn back to God. At first Jonah refused to go; he was afraid that if he went to Nineveh with a message of repentance, the citizens would kill him. So he ran away. But when he was in a boat trying to escape a great storm came. The sailors asked why God sent the storm. Jonah said it was his fault, because he was running away from God. So they threw him in the water and a big fish swallowed Jonah up. The fish took him, still alive in its belly, to a beach near Nineveh and coughed him up. Jonah realized that he should do God's will. He went to Nineveh and said to the people that the lord was angry with them because of their evil ways. He asked them to repent or they would be destroyed. Heart struck, the king of the city came down from his throne, put ashes on his head, and told the people to do the same. The city was saved.

By wearing ashes this Wednesday, we signify similar conversion. We say we're going to give up what's wrong in our lives to prepare for Jesus's coming at Easter. To better follow his holy church, we also commit ourselves to some extra prayer and charity. We do so for our spiritual welfare and that of the whole world. For we Christians are to be a light to our broken world. So in a true spirit of conversion and renewal in heart and soul, lets come forward now for the ashes.

With ashes on our foreheads, praying that Lent and Easter may be a special time of prayer, penance and giving to the poor and bringing all back to God, we profess our faith.


## Prayers of the Faithful

For our Holy Father and all the leaders of the church, that this Lent they may be renewed in Spirit for their great work in the church and for the world.

For civil leaders that the world of politics may be cleansed of corruption and truly serve all the people, especially the poor and oppressed.

For youth, that this Lent any who have strayed may return to God and his holy church with glad repentant hearts.

For people around the world that they may be converted to God, to peace, and to just and integral living, this Lent and Easter.

For ourselves and our families that Lent and Easter may be a time of great grace, love and happiness in Christ.

For the sick and poor that through our efforts they may come to better conditions.

That Mother Mary may bless us all this Lent and Easter and bring all to the healing font of confession and penance.

For the dead, that their work in this world over, they may come safely to their heavenly home with the help of our prayers.

And we ask all these our prayers through Christ Our Lord who resisted the temptations in the desert on our behalf, and who intercedes for us forever before the Father in heaven, amen.

## Reflection

Every year I climb Croagh Patrick. On the last Sunday in July thousands of pilgrims make their way up the mountain, often in difficult conditions, praying at stations along the way. At the top they attend mass. Many try to climb barefoot, and start early in the morning to be at the top for the first mass at 8.30 am. Once I saw a man of over seventy climbing in his bare feet, to be there for that mass; he started that climb at about 6 am, on a cold wet morning. All this might seem foolishness to a self-centered world, but it reminds us Christians of the great tradition of dedicated prayer and penance we have inherited. Lets pray to Mother Mary that we will continue that tradition, in our own small way, this Lent, for the good of all. For prayer is the most powerful thing on earth and penance makes it a thousand times more powerful. Hail Mary

# First Sunday of Lent C

## Introduction

Our scripture this first Sunday of Lent features Christ's temptations in the desert. There he resisted key temptations we all face, to put self, power, and wealth before humble service of God and others. Lets confess ways we let selfish lust for money rule our hearts and prevent us living in faith and charity.

## Homily

The film, *The Boy In The Striped Pajamas*, got no hype or media attention but its a parable for our time. Bruno, the small son of a concentration camp commander, befriends a Jewish inmate, Shimone. Every day they'd sit, one inside, one outside, the barbed wire to play and eat food Bruno brings. A guard finds Shimone eating the food and says, "you Jewish dog, you stole the food". "No", he said, "I got it from Bruno". But when the guard asks the German boy, he says, "No I didn't give it to him"; he lied our of fear. Later, finding the Jewish child beaten up, he says, "I'm sorry I don't know why I did it, forgive me". Shimone does so, though he's been hurt by his friend's betrayal. Then he begins to cry, his father has disappeared. Bruno says, "I'll come into the camp and help you look for him". The father has been gassed, and while the boys look for him they too are rounded up and taken to the gas chamber. They die together holding hands, the innocent German and Jewish child, victims of a cruel world they can't understand.

The film is very Christian. The little boys practice the indiscriminate loving way of Christ as against the cruel Satanic way of the divisive hating world of power politics. The key temptation Christ faced in the desert was to ape that Satanic way. To be a Hitler-like Messiah winning power and glory through the blood and oppression of fellow human beings. Like the Nazi creed Satan said in effect: forget God, worship me, exercise power without moral restraint, crush the weak, serve your own power and wealth and pleasure, forget the rabble. You may say we're not like that, but the modern libertine philosophy of western Capitalism has elements of that philosophy: do what you like, pursue money and pleasure at all costs; to hell with God, the weak, or higher values if they get in my way. It was the creed of the boom, unrestrained greed, and look where that landed us.

Dictators such as Stalin or Pol Pot who killed millions while demolishing temples and churches and sending opponents to concentration camps, built a similar world. Satan wanted Christ to do the same, but he chose instead to be the humble suffering Servant of God and humanity unto the cross; to serve not dominate, to redeem not crush.

Its a choice we Christians make also. For Satan's way destroys the soul and creates hell on earth, it destroys innocence, as in the film. Lent is the time to rid ourselves of such hard worldliness by prayer, fasting and giving generously to the poor For prayer unites the soul with God; fasting purifies the heart of self-seeking; and giving to the poor rids us of greed, so that everyone will have enough. For the hard worldly values of which Satan is lord leaves us empty here and for eternity, but Christ is lord of goodness, peace, love and happiness for this world and forever and ever, amen.

So as God's people following the way of prayer, fasting and almsgiving to build faith, innocence, love and generosity within, so as to rise with Our Lord, we profess our faith.


### Prayers of the faithful

For our Holy Father the Pope and all the pastors of the churches, that they may lead the people of God and all the world's peoples on the way of innocence and charity.

For civil leaders that rejecting the way of corrupt power, they may serve all the people in generosity and fairness.

For youth, rejecting the cruel ways of the world, may they follow the gentle Lord and his church in innocent faith, love and service.

For ourselves that this time of Lent may be a time of grace, peace and inner growth for us as we devote ourselves to self-denial, prayer and almsgiving in imitation of Our Divine Lord.

For those of our world who reject God, that they may heed the call of Christ to repent and believe, to find rest, happiness and salvation for their souls, and come to the fullness of truth.

For the sick, aged, lonely and oppressed that through our care this Easter they may know the healing presence of God's love.

For the dead, those who need our prayers to come to the fullness of light and life, that this season of grace may be a final liberation for them, and especially those for whom we pray.

And we ask these our prayers in this grace-filled time of Lent, when the ashes on our head symbolize the rekindling of grace and holiness in our hearts, through Christ Our Lord, amen.

## Reflection

An example of the contrast between Satan's and Christ's way is the story of Max Kolbe. Sent to Auscwitcz for condemning Hitler in his newspaper, as a priest he was subjected to extra cruelty there. After a resistance attack, the camp commandant decided to shoot 10 inmates. As they were selected, Kolbe saw that one of them was a family man. He asked to be taken instead. Injected with poison but slow to die, they eventually beat him to death with their rifle butts. A crucifix was found scratched by his nails on his cell wall. What a witness to Christ's way of love, peace and self-giving. Lets give similar witness to a deep faith and love, that alone can redeem the cruel world. Hail Mary

# Second Sunday of Lent C

## Introduction

Today we've the wonderful story of Tabor. On the mountain, Christ's divinity shines for a moment through his humanity. Yet his talk coming down the mountain is not about glory but the cross. Lets confess ways we fail to carry our crosses to redeem the world.

## Homily

"She walks in beauty like the night/Of cloudless climes and starry skies". You know Byron's poem. At a dance one night he was smitten by a lady's beauty and purity of soul; "A mind at peace with all below/A heart whose love is innocent". Our gospel shows Christ bathed in similar beauty. Yet the world hated and killed him. His soul, united with the source of goodness, showed up its corruption. God's glory, veiled in his humanity, was ordinarily seen only by eyes of faith, but on Tabor the veil slipped; his divine beauty was revealed and was so heavenly Peter wanted to stay there forever.

Yet descending the mountain, Christ talks not of glory but of the cross. Moments of joy are often like that, short-lived, yet they make subsequent trials easier. The honeymoon or holding our first child can sustain us in marriage crises. Jesus came down the mountain to face his sufferings with fresh strength. We might go out today in the same spirit to face life's suffering. For the luminous encounter with Christ in communion here should stay with us, and give us untold strength. As should the Lenten prayer, fasting and charity which we undertake to deepen our faith, and strengthen us for life's crosses.

There is a common saying that there are no crown bearers in heaven who were not first cross bearers on earth. Because of our freedom God doesn't take away suffering; if he did so we'd be spoilt puppets. Suffering is part of life since the fall. But faith enables us to turn unavoidable suffering into gold as Christ did. He gives us a joy, even in suffering, that the world can't give.

In my visits to hospitals I am reminded of this. I see sickness, but also God-given strength and faith which enables people to transcend even the trials of extreme old age. Don't heed the ads which says only young slim, shiny haired people who use costly make-up are beautiful. The closer we get to God the more human and beautiful we become, the more immune we become even to age and suffering. Look at Mother Theresa. Even when old and wrinkled, her spiritual radiance was amazing. Someone working with her in Calcutta told me that when she entered patients' rooms everyone lit up. That's why euthanasia's evil, people take the easy way out, instead of letting suffering deepen their souls.

Its no coincidence that as faith declines despair increases. For its through prayer, weekly communion, and the Word that we gain the inner depth to bear even the hardest crosses of life. We gain a loveliness of life, thereby, that's more than skin deep. Christ was beautiful on the cross. And each of us is infinitely beautiful when one with Christ in unavoidable suffering well borne. That's why we can say of his church, "she walks in beauty like the night". Despite her institutional layers of bureaucracy, her sufferings due to the opposition of the world gives her Christ's beauty. For this world's false superficial glitter soon fades, but Christ is Lord of a radiant inner life and a peace that endures and transcends all pain, and brings untold happiness for this world and forever and ever, amen.

So as God's people radiant in the Risen Lord and carrying our crosses with him in love and goodness, lets profess our faith.

## Prayers of the Faithful

And as the people of God gathered in the radiance of Christ our Risen Lord lets pray confidently to the Father for our needs.

For our Holy Father the pope and all church leaders that walking in the light of Christ, they may bring that light to the world by their grace-filled words and deeds.

For civil leaders that they may serve the people they govern with integrity, justice and concern for all, especially the poor and the most vulnerable in society.

For our youth that receiving the radiant light of Christ at Baptism, Holy Communion and Confirmation, they may continue to live an active faith life, and so have God's radiant light within, and be witnesses to that light amid the darknesses of the world.

For ourselves in our homes, that through our faith, love and goodness our children may be bathed in God's living radiance.

For our own personal intentions or those of the community we now pray in silence.

For the sick, the lonely and those suffering in body, mind or soul that through our love they may know God's comfort and care.

For the dead that they may enjoy the eternal radiance of heaven helped, where still weighed down by their sins in this world, by our continuing prayers and loving remembrance.

And we ask all these our prayers through Christ our radiant lord of love, forever, amen.

## Reflection

Perhaps the great failure of our world is its neglect of man's inner life. All is surface glitter and worldly clamor. Yet its what's within that matters. We can have every luxury, yet be empty inside. Faith carried our parents through tough times. We need the same spiritual depth today to carry us through life with grace. For when the materialistic world fails us we've zilch left. But all the while Christ knocks at the door of our hearts with the way, the truth and the life. Lets open our hearts to him this Lent and Easter. Let him light our souls out of all adversity and darkness to joy and inner peace. And lets fervently ask Mary, to open our and our youth's souls to his radiance, for now is the day of salvation. Hail Mary

# Third Sunday of Lent C

## Introduction

Scripture today revisits the theme of sin, which, though it is a bad word today, remains, and so does its grave consequences for our souls. Christ says: "unless you repent you will all perish" (Lk. 13:5, JB). Lets confess ways we fail to repent of sin in our lives.

## Homily

"Unless you repent you'll all perish". Christ's words may shock us, but the fact remains that sin is death, and remorse life. Even the world knows this. Secular papers say about terrorists bombers: "They're monsters, without remorse". They say the same about unrepentant child-abusers; they recognize that sin is evil, and humanity demands remorse.

If even non-believers see unrepentant wrongdoing as inhuman, how much more should we. Saying sorry is life. If Christians, called to high values, are hardened in sin what hope is there for the world. We may share the view that guilt's unhealthy; but surely its a healthy warning sign, like pain alerts us to physical disease. God put a capacity in us to know when we are doing wrong. Only the psychopath is immune to guilt.

Why can't we let children out now? Why do old people hide behind locked doors? Sin is abroad, and repentance is needed lest society disintegrate altogether. So is the need today to re-tune our consciences, dulled by a worldly ignoring of sin. Otherwise individuals and society will continue to suffer. For God doesn't ask us to avoid sin because he's a tyrant; he is perfect, he doesn't need our compliance. As our loving Father, he asks us to avoid sin because its just plain bad for us. Untold social ills come from a libertine blurring of right and wrong – family breakdown, widespread crime, shooting sprees, a drug culture, to name but a few.

But apart from its adverse consequences, deep down we're all adverse to sin. Even high profile figures such as Mel Gibson came to see this. He recovered faith and conscience by reflecting on Christ's Passion; it saved him from a self-destructive drug and alcohol abuse spiral. "Unless you repent you too will perish"; that warning still holds.

So does the church's warning not to abandon confession. When we go wrong, we need to be reconciled with ourselves, others and God. Confession is the perfect way to do that, and the great aid in our journey from sin, to the freedom of God's children. But its not enough to confess privately to God; that's a cop out. James says: "confess your sins to one another, and pray for one another, and this will cure you" (Jm. 5:16, JB). We need to confess to another human being to be made really whole. Even Psychologists agree. They say abusers, for example, won't know peace until they show remorse and admit their wrong openly before their accusers. Its why we're bombarded with pictures of Fr. Smith, a notorious abuser, and with headlines like, "this inhuman monster showed no remorse".

The cure for sin and guilt is remorse and divine forgiveness; for, though our sins be scarlet, as the first reading says, God can make them white as snow. But unconfessed and unrepentant, the pride of sin may harden into the unredemptive obstinacy of evil. The barren fig tree in God's vineyard, a gospel image, symbolizes those who refuse to bear fruits of repentance. As members of Christ's kingdom through Baptism, let's not ignore God's Word: "repent and believe ... the Kingdom of God is close at hand" (Mt. 3:2-3, JB).

The fig tree had useless bitter fruit; sin prevents us from bearing good fruit, but through confession, remorse, and divine forgiveness we're liberated to bear the fruits of goodness and inner peace; the burden of guilt is lifted from our shoulders. Hence in Celtic monasteries, the confessor was "anam cara", a soul help in our journey to God. For sin leaves us empty and heavy with guilt before eternity, but Christ's ready forgiveness restores us to love, peace and happiness both for this world and forever and ever, amen.

So as God's people constantly repenting and confessing for our inner peace, and lest we go the primrose way to the everlasting bonfire, lets profess our faith.

## Prayers of the Faithful

And as God's people called to constant repentance and spurning of sin, lets pray to our Father for our on-going spiritual health.

For our Holy Father and church leaders that they may courageously call the world from sin to all that's right, true and good.

For civil leaders that facilitating their people's spiritual and moral welfare they may exercise a wise stewardship at all levels.

For youth, may they retain a consciousness of sin and the need for repentance when they do wrong, so as to be free children of God and people of wise integrity.

For ourselves, at home may we encourage our children to practice confession, a meeting with Christ that bears fruits even if we do no wrong, for it nourishes us on our spiritual journey in God.

For the sick in body or soul, through our prayers and love may they come that fullness of life and healing which is God's will.

For the dead that freed at last from any residue of sin they may come to the full glory of heaven helped by our prayers.

We ask this through Christ Our Lord of love, life, and forgiveness, forever, amen.

## Reflection

In the Celtic church the confessor was a friend who helped people by encouraging them to talk about moral problems and experience forgiveness. Ideally, confession isn't a mechanical listing of sins, but an aid to spiritual, psychological and moral health. Helped by confessors, we reveal habits that trouble, hold back, or oppress us; confessors are spiritual psychiatrists. But even if we've no serious sins, regular confession's sacramental meeting with Christ, brings great grace. So whether we prefer confession as a chat with a priest, or prefer the old way, lets pray that either way we'll see how healing it is for us. Hail Mary

# Fourth Sunday of Lent C

## Introduction

This Sunday we've the parable of the prodigal son. Its a reminder that we all drift from the Father at times, and need to return with all our hearts from sinful ways. Lent is such a time for conversion. Lets repent now of any sins, small or big, as we confess.

## Homily

I'm sure you know St.Agustine's story. Early in life he was wildly pagan. His mother Monica, a saintly Christian, suffered as a result and constantly prayed for his conversion. One day while sitting at home, feeling empty and dissatisfied, he heard a child's voice say, "take up and read". He picked up a bible from the table and it opened where Paul exhorts the people to cast off the old man of sin and put on the Lord Jesus. Immediately, tears poured down his cheeks; he renounced his former life, and went on to become one of the greatest bishop, theologians, and saints of the church.

His story is similar to that of the prodigal son. Like the prodigal, Augustine turned to God not out of fear but need. After years of seeking happiness in other ways, he found real love, joy and freedom in Christ. That's what we should grasp at Lent, that true happiness is in God's arms. But the path to his arms can be made difficult by this world; assailed by Satan's temptations its easy to drift from Christ, the church and what's right. So we need to come back every so often. Our Christian journey is one of ever renewed faithfulness, a life-long struggle against the false lures of the world, the flesh and the devil.

But its worth the effort, for it leads to Easter joy. Its to encourage us in this path that the church puts before us at this time of year Christ's death, resurrection and Second Coming at the end of time. For his resurrection anticipates our own resurrection body and soul at last when Christ will come to judge the living and the dead. In the meantime we must continue to keep steadily on the path to glory so that we will be part of the saintly throng going to meet Christ at last. We walk in light here so as to do so for eternity.

But darkness always threatens to engulf us while we're in this world. So we have this season to recalls us from any dark winter elements in our lives. Spring in the natural world is matched by a new flowering; a conversion of heart and soul, so that when the Lord comes at death or the end of the world he'll find us awake, free from the hell of unrepentant sin. The words of psalm 32 express this freedom well: "Happy the man whose fault is forgiven, whose sin is blotted out" (Ps. 32:1 JB). At Lent and all life long we need to return to innocence, and the arms of the Father where true love is. That's what the prodigal son discovered. That's what Augustine discovered.

Indeed, his book of *Confessions*, aren't about sin but how God lit up his life and led him to help others. We too are called to return to God, and to help bring others to do the same. By prayer, good works and service of the church we're to help transform the world into God's kingdom. But, like Monica, that involves above all praying for and saving those we love. So that they will be at our side as we go out to meet Christ at last.

Monica reminds us of the key role mothers play in fostering the faith at home. And the other saint we celebrate at this time, Patrick is a perfect example of fostering love and faith far from home; he turned a whole people to Christ. Lent and Easter we're asked to follow the example of these saints, by helping the missions at home, by our witness, and abroad, by our contributions. For all else passes and leaves people empty, but Christ is lord of love, goodness, truth, and salvation for this world and forever and ever, amen.

So as God's people constantly turning to Christ to bring ourselves and others to lasting joy, lets profess our faith.

## *Prayers of the Faithful*

And as we prepare for Easter as Christ's faithful saints lets pray confidently to the Father for the things we need.

We pray for the Holy Father, that he will lead the church wisely and well in these challenging times, so that this Easter will be a special time of renewal for the church and for the world.

For civil rulers that they may not put obstacles in the way of the faith, but serve all with integrity, justice and be specially mindful of the needs of the poor and deprived.

For our youth, like the prodigal son if they have drifted from the Father may they see where true peace, happiness and salvation lies and return to his loving arms and those of mother church.

For our homes that they may be places of faith where every child is cherished and we pray especially at this time for mothers.

For the sick that through our care and love they may know the love and care of God their Father.

For our own special intentions we now pray silently to the Lord.

For all those who died recently, may their souls and the souls of all the faithful departed rest in peace.

And we ask all these things through Christ who is Lord forever, amen.

## *Reflection*

Another conversion story is that of Tolstoy. At thirty feted everywhere as the world's greatest writer, he had everything. Yet he felt empty inside.

Then he discovered Christ and his life was suddenly lit up. He thought the Sermon on the Mount was the great blueprint for earthly utopia, and he corresponded with Gandhi about it, inspiring the latter with the Sermon's message of non-violence. Lets realize also how universal Christ's truth is. And lets ask Mary to keep us faithful to him and his church in on-going conversion. Hail Mary

# Fifth Sunday in Lent C

## Introduction

One great temptation we all face is self-righteousness. We see that in our gospel in the form of the woman caught in adultery. The Pharisees wanted her stoned, but Christ says, "If there is one of you who has not sinned, let him be the first to throw a stone at her" (Jn. 8:7-8, JB). Lets confess any ways we unfairly judge others.

## Homily

Tradition has it that when Christ bent down to write in the sand, after the Pharisees presented the woman caught in adultery before him, he was writing the particular sins of each of those gathered to condemn her, notably their sexual sins. He was condemning not her, but the hypocritical men who wanted her stoned to death for a sin they themselves committed with impunity. Their whiter than white attitude was real sin. Jesus saw through it, and they knew he did, for they went away, starting with the eldest (Jn. 8:9, JB).

That is, Jesus used the incident of the adulterous woman, to highlight a greater sin, that of hypocrisy and hard self-righteousness. He calls all to have humble non-judgmental hearts. The reading from Isaiah for today says the same thing. We must be rich in forgiving, for God's thoughts are not our thoughts, his ways are not our ways.

Yet too often we judge and condemn others in God's name, making him responsible for our narrow views. Unfortunately, religious people, I say this with shame, are often the worst in this. We should not represent our own narrow thinking as God's.

Yet today too many are doing just that in bigoted or violent ways. It's what gives religion a bad name - from Bin Laden to militant fundamentalist Christians. I think of Northern Ireland where people like Paisley would claim that all Catholics, including the Pope, are enemies of God. Only his small church, that perpetrates division, worships the true God. And some Catholics can be just as divisive and exclusionary at times; when we were young some Catholics abhorred and condemned the so-called "black Protestants".

But, in fact, if we want to come even remotely close to the true God, we must widen not narrow our thinking. We must have ever bigger hearts, ever more inclusive souls. That's what the Gospel tells us. The woman caught in adultery was not condemned by Christ, but those who would condemn her was. In this, as in other areas, Christ was leading the people away from bigotry to worship of the true God. Yet they hated his generous forgiveness and love of sinners, like many strict religious people do even today.

God's ways are not our ways, he is generous as the heavens. Even anti-religious liberals fall into the trap of the Pharisees, just as intolerant and narrow-minded in their libertine agenda, souls closed to God and spiritual values. They should learn from the fanatical secularist totalitarian systems of our age. God's ways are far from that way too.

In effect, we must shun every narrow thinking of men, of whatever ilk, and imitate God's generosity and celebration of difference in the glorious variety of nature. We must keep open hearts and minds, judge no one, embrace all as Christ did. He said prostitutes and sinners would enter heaven before the Pharisees, the righteous in their own eyes. If we come remotely close to his generous loving inclusiveness, we'll be saints. And as Christians that's what we're called to be; to follow his broad ways, not man's narrow ones.

Lets stop casting God in our own image. Lets stop making the hateful world and its values our idol. Lets worship the true and all-loving God, the end of our quest. For only that God makes us open, loving, generous and spiritually alive in Christ who embraced all, even enemies, on the cross. For narrow minded ways, be they secularist or religious, liberal or conservative, are a dead end, but Christ is lord of love, faith, forgiveness, beauty, truth, happiness, peace and salvation for this world and forever and ever, amen.

So as God's people following the truly gracious way of Christ's all-embracing love and non-judgmental faith, lets profess our own faith with open hearts.

## Prayers of the Faithful

And as God's people lets pray to be his open heart to the world.

For the church that it may emerge from present crises more open, accountable, humble, contrite, democratic and people orientated.

For civil leaders that a narrow focus on economics may not close their hearts to the real purpose of politics, the service of all people, and especially those most in need.

For the victims of child abuse that they may find healing and redress for the hurt they have received at the hands of some church members, and some of the hierarchy.

For ourselves that we may not be discouraged by failure, but emerge from it with stronger faith in following Christ and the church, despite its flawed human instruments.

For the sick, the aged, aids patients and all we may be tempted to ostracize, that we may make them our special care.

For the dead, that in that great act of charity on their behalf, our prayers, we may bring them to their final rest.

And we ask these prayers through the all-compassionate Christ.

### Reflection:

The church's apologies for clerical child abuse remind us that we all need to repent at times. I hope it will make church authority more open, humble and accountable in the gospel model of leadership. If Christ were among us today I'm sure he'd be saying that abused people should be heard and healed. And that sex predators who target the young must be exposed and punished, and structures put in place in society and the church to protect the vulnerable. Already we've that in our diocese, but we must implement it rigorously, and do everything possible for the victims. If the financial pay-outs makes the church poorer, good! The weaker the church is, the freer it is to serve God. Lets pray for an open and loving church to its Mother Mary. Hail Mary

# Palm Sunday C

## Introduction

The theme today is that Christ is a King of humble suffering love. As we enter Holy Week lets follow him in all the ceremonies through the Last Supper, the cross of love, and the resurrection. and lets confess any ways we fail this great Lord and Savior.

## Homily

"Take up your cross and follow me". Sacrifice for a greater good isn't promoted as it should be today. Many waste their souls, and their latent idealism, in vain pursuits that would avoid any higher challenge. Passion Sunday should wake us up. Seeing Christ's suffering should remind us of the deep wisdom of the cross. And that we must work in its power to bring God's great love to all.

Christ's answer to Pilate is so important: "my kingdom is not of this world". Even the apostles wanted him to be a kind of Hitler, imposing his reign by power, the world's way. But that would negate his greatest gift, our freedom. So Christ took the way prescribed by the prophets, that of the humble suffering servant of God and humanity.

That choice, which speaks louder than words of God's love, should touch the hardest heart. A man in the USA confessed to a murder after seeing Mel Gibson's film *The Passion Of The Christ*. A young person coming from the movie said its hard not to pray seeing that. Our response should be to work to transform a world of greed and violence into his gentle kingdom; bearing the cross of faithfulness to him for the world's salvation.

And God is with us in this. For when Christ died in intense mental and physical pain on the cross, God hadn't abandoned him. Again the Gibson film makes that point well. As Christ dies, a single tear of the Father splashes on the ground, and suddenly all is changed. His triumphant human tormentors slink away on their donkeys, and Satan, who has been in the background, triumphantly gloating over Christ's pain, is plummeted back to hell. Gibson then switches the scene to the Last Supper and Christ's words: "this is my body given up for you". By giving up his body, even his soul, Christ gained everything. God raised him up and made him king of heaven and earth. But he was already that on the cross, a king of love.

Our way to glory is similar, faithfully giving all for the faith, the church, and the good of humanity. For the universe is God's, but he handed authority over it to his Christ at the resurrection. He, in turn, handed that authority to the church at the Ascension: "Go, therefore, make disciples of all the nations, baptize them in the name of the Father and of the Son and of the Holy Spirit, and teach them to observe all the commands I gave you. And know that I am with you always; yes, to the end of time" (Mt. 28:19-20, JB).

How privileged we are to be part of his church then. Lets be faithful to it no matter what the world throws at us; the 2013 papal election reminded us how universal and glorious it is; always throwing up surprises in the Spirit. Through it we should struggle to transform our violent unjust world into the grace-filled kingdom of our crucified king for, because that Risen Lord is with us forever, our victory in that struggle is assured. And the cruel world of which Satan is lord passes away, as do the inevitable failures of the church in its human aspects, but the Risen Christ, present forever with his holy people is Lord of love, peace, happiness and salvation both for this world and forever and ever, amen.

So as the people of the crucified lord in these the end-times of his kingdom come, as foretold by the prophets, lets make our profession of faith.

## Prayers of the Faithful

Lets pray in all the coming Holy Week ceremonies that the kingdom so wonderfully won by Christ's cross may transform our world.

That the church, as our Holy Father prayed, may be the humble suffering servant of God and others like Christ its lord on the cross.

For civic leaders, that their rule may also be one of service of the people who elected them, especially the weak and vulnerable.

For our youth, that they may follow the example of Jesus's disciples on the first Palm Sunday and lay their hearts at his feet.

For all gathered here, that we may be aware of those who suffer, and ensure by their help, that suffering relatives or neighbors do not carry their cross alone.

That we too may bear and offer up our sufferings in a Christ-like way for the salvation of the world.

And we pray for all in the parish, who have died that the lord may raise them up with himself to the eternal glory of the blessed.

God our father we ask you to listen to the many needs of your people as we offer our prayers through Christ your Son, amen.

## Reflection

The *News Of The World* used to boast, "all human life is here". Certainly the events of the Passion contain all that's worst and best of human life. On the one hand we have Roman state cruelty; unjust barbaric torture of the innocent; the terrible corrupt envy and vindictiveness of religious authorities; the heartless betrayal of Christ for money by Judas; the cowardice of Peter and the apostles; the cruelty of the mob; the greed of the soldiers as they dice for Christ's clothes. It shows us ourselves in the raw, and its all happening today too. Sophisticated savagery might sum up the terrible wars and genocides of our era. Yet people still say we don't need redemption.

Yet, on the other hand, the crucifixion is not all dark: we have the weeping women; Veronica wiping his face; the affirmation of faith by the Centurion and so on. Though sin pervades the passion so does grace. And its larger message is joy; despite sin, greed and brutality, God loves us, believes in us, reaches out to us. Lets ask Mother Mary to help us to appreciate that love, and stand by the Lord in this week's ceremonies. Hail Mary

# Holy Thursday C

## Introduction:

Tonight we begin a trilogy of Holy week celebrations with the liturgy of the Lord's Last Supper. About to die, Christ gave his very self to us for all time to nourish and sustain us in grace. Lets thank him for that gift, and confess ways we fail to live its love.

## Homily.

Before the giving of the Eucharist tonight, Judas walked out and sold Christ for 30 pieces of silver. Today many walk out on him too for money and worldly values. We must all avoid that Satanic trap. Like the apostles we must stay at his table, loyal to the mass, the faith and the church. We mustn't sell our souls for any quantity of silver, but follow the Jesus who washed the feet of the apostles to give a lesson of humble serving love.

For those walking dry Palestinian tracks in sandals, without socks, naturally ended up with dusty feet. So these were usually washed when they entered a house for dinner. The person who did this was the lowest servant in the house. While the apostles were arguing who'd be top dog, Jesus, the lord of all, washed their feet like the lowest servant. They were shocked, but took the lesson. The greatest in Christ's kingdom are those who serve.

Authorities in church and state should heed that lesson. Significantly, it was after the washing of the feet that Jesus gave the apostles the first Holy Communion. Because this too was a great act of service. "This is my body which will be given for you" he said (Lk. 22:19, JB). Those words are repeated at every mass, because he told them to do this for all time: wherever his followers gather. That's what we're doing tonight. For in this mystery he's with us for all time, providing the food by which we grow strong in faith, fit to serve God and others. And its the living bread that we need for a journey through life to glory.

But its happiness in this world too. This food given to us, his modern day apostles, is the sustenance we need for an integral life. That's why the church insists we come to mass every Sunday. This food gives us the strength to live as he told us to, in love, goodness, truth and happiness; its by its power that we can grow in God's life.

If you don't believe me, believe Christ; "if you do not eat the flesh of he Son of Man and drink his blood, you will not have life in you" (Jn. 6:53, JB). That how important it is. No wonder the church said at one time that it was a mortal sin to miss mass. Thank God, they no longer stress that; we should not come to this table in love not compulsion. For Christ goes on to say: "Anyone who does eats my flesh and drink my blood has eternal life, and I shall raise him up on the last day" (Jn. 6:54, JB. In the strength of this food, eaten regularly, we grow in God's life here below, until we flower into eternity.

That is, having thus shared God's life, when he comes again at the end of the world we'll go out to meet him with all the saints in the heavenly kingdom, and be raised up in body and soul. For the things of this world pass away and leave us empty at last. But Jesus in communion is lord of life, love, happiness, truth, beauty and salvation both for a fuller life in this world and forever and ever. Each mass and communion anticipates the final great banquet God has prepared for us his faithful. So to signify our duty of humble love for others, the fruit of this sacrament, I'll wash the feet of 12 people.

And as God's people caring for those around us with Christ's humble serving love, lets profess our faith.

### Prayers of the Faithful

And having washed feet in imitation of Christ lets ask our Father who loves us for the things we need.

For the church throughout the world and its leaders that they may not lord it over the people but always witness to the humble service of others that brings Christ to earth.

For our civil leaders that they may not use their office to serve themselves, but the people, especially the poor and most vulnerable.

For our youth that they may not spend their lives in pursuit of wealth, pleasure and fame alone, but also in serving God and others, the path to lasting happiness and peace.

For ourselves in our homes, may we inspire our children and all around us to come each Sunday without fail to the Lord's table.

For the sick, the lonely, the old and the neglected, that through our washing of their feet, our care for them, they may know the love of God.

For our own special needs, we pray silently on this holiest of nights.

For those who have died, that having partaken of his body and blood in this life they may be raised up to glory as he promised.

And we ask all these prayers through the same Christ Our Lord who as the bread of life is with us forever, amen.


## Reflection

It is good that we wash the feet of the God's children tonight for the criminal failure of the church in modern times has been the abuse of vulnerable children. It was like Judas's betrayal of Christ, only more so. To walk away from the table of the lord and sell out Christ present in his most innocent children, is a crime even worse than that of Judas. For its about unaccountable power. So at this feast its right we wash the feet of God's children to make reparation for those wrongs. To remind us that we should all serve others and be innocent like children. So lets pray to Mary that we may turn away from all exploitation and be true loving servants of God and others as Christ asked. Hail Mary

# Good Friday C - The Passion

***Introduction*** (as in the liturgy)

## Homily

Life is a series of deaths. We come crying into life. Dying to childhood follows in adolescence. Later again, we give up multiple partner choice to grow rich in the love of a spouse and children. Growing old we die to vitality; to so many things we can no longer do. Always, there's dying of some sort. We're constantly put to the test, but that's how we grow. Through faith borne in suffering we grow too, until our souls flower into eternity.

That's what the passion is about. Christ's passed the supreme test of faith on the cross; and thereby restored light to a world lost since the Fall. There he canceled out the original sin. By steadfast faith and love we too die to self, to bring the world back to life.

The ways we do this are many: faithfulness in marriage; loving and nurturing our family through ups and downs; faith, kindness, honesty and integrity in the work place; facing trials and carrying our crosses with courage; witnessing courageously for Christ before the world; showing Christian heroism as dedicated religious, celibate priests, lay ministers, Vincent De Paul volunteers and so on. These are the ways to walk through the world with Christ in constant suffering giving; giving up so as to gain everything.

For Christ says that unless a grain of wheat dies it cannot yield a rich harvest. Part of that dying will be forced on us by the world. For the world of which Satan is lord will hate and persecute us because of our devotion. We'll challenge it to deeper life as Christ challenged the corrupt world of his day. But in imitating him we'll gain our souls and those of others. For every Christian is called to live the passion of Christ in his or her own life.

But if, imitating Christ, we face our crosses, we will rise with him also. For the self-centered world of which Satan is lord, leaves us empty on eternity's shore. But Christ on the cross is lord of goodness, happiness, freedom and salvation forever and ever, amen.

**Prayers etc, as in the liturgy.**

# Holy Saturday and Easter Sunday C

## Introduction

This feast of light is the high point of our year, the central feast of the faith; humanity redeemed and raised to glory with Christ. So having lit the Easter fire and pascal candle, lets purify our souls to prepare to celebrate the world's greatest event.

## Homily

Close your eyes and imagine living in darkness. Now open them to dazzling light. When we were young we read by the frail light of oil lamps. Doing homework was a strain on the eyes. Then electricity came to illumine our home. Our feast is like that. Christ's rising bursts like dawn on the world. Our cold lost night blazes with God's warmth in Christ. What joy, yet sadness too, that some still prefer darkness, unable to bear the light, or too caught up in the world to let it enter their hearts. Sometimes even the church doesn't always grasp this glory. Lackluster Alleluias show that. But Easter is about joy; the dream dreamed for 2000 years by prophets has come true.

Like the women we should race from the tomb with the news: "he has risen from the dead risen and now he is going before you" (Mt. 28:7, JB). For out of the cross of shame came a stunning victory. The darkness that oppressed humankind since the fall dissolved into glorious sunshine. Our mission is to shout that to the world. God raised Jesus, made him universal Lord and Savior, we no longer live in a pitch black night of pagan despair. Our response should be boundless joy. We should shout the words we often sing after the mass's consecration; that he is Lord, he is lord, he is risen from the dead and he is lord, every knee shall bow every tongue confess, that Jesus Christ is Lord.

Indeed, our mission is to confess that before an increasingly dark world. Where many reject God's light and love in Christ we must work hard to restore the light, lest ignorance and worldly blindness drag us back to pit where Satan reigns as the lord of darkness.

Instead lets celebrate being God's glorious children in light. Our ancestors suffered in heroically opposing those who'd snuff out that light. In today's world of increasing materialism, secularism, violence, cynicism, drugs, and youth despair, we must do the same. As Christ's glorious faithful we must proclaim the eternally liberating Easter message. This holy Easter lets do that, joyfully accept Christ as our personal Lord and Savior and proclaim him enthusiastically before the world. For only his happiness and spiritual depth can light up souls here below until they flower into eternal life. Lets spread that news, that the Risen Christ is the resting place of every restless heart.

As Easter people lets shout that with resounding alleluias; the risen Jesus is Lord to the glory of God the Father. And in that light lets joyfully do the vital work of faith we pledged at Baptism. In our ordinary job or vocation we shouldn't be afraid to witness to joy in the Lord. For we enjoy fully the pleasures and good things of the world he gave us, and when the world passes we gain the even fuller riches of life with the Risen Christ forever. For a world without God is death and despair, but Christ is lord of light, love, goodness, happiness and salvation both for this world and forever and ever, amen.

So as God's people born to everlasting light on this Easter of his risen glory lets rejoice that we're people of the light and profess our faith with renewed love.

### Prayers of the faithful

And gathered on this holy Easter, the high point of our Christian life and worship, lets pray confidently to the Father through the glorious Risen Christ for all that we need.

For Pope Francis, and all the world's church leaders, that they may bring to all the joyful liberating message of the Risen Christ this day, and always.

For civil leaders that they may help keep that light of our heritage burning among us and not fall prey to militant secularism.

For ourselves that this Easter mass of light and joy may lighten our own hearts into a grand spring and summer of faith to come.

For our youth that the Easter message may be more than cliched holiday cheer, may it penetrate their hearts and bring them to a satisfying personal commitment to the Risen Lord and his church.

For the old people in our midst that their lives of faith, goodness and service may bring them the Lord's rewards of happiness and peace and may God's love come to them through us.

For the sick, may they know that the Lord is with them in their suffering, and may they experience through our care the Risen Lord's love.

For the dead that they come to their own resurrection prefigured this night in the resurrection of their Lord and Savior who when he rose raised all of us to glory.

And we ask all these our prayers through Christ our Risen Lord and Savior who is close to his people and brings them the salvation and light of God forever and ever, amen.

## Reflection:

Once I talked to African converts I'd baptized, and they explained how great a light Christ was for them, oppressed by pagan witch doctors and dark gods. It was great news to them that Christ died and rose to bring them God's love. They found a new dignity, value, freedom and peace in him, and their lives lit up. We've the faith so long do we take it for granted? Have we lost its wonder? Lets appreciate it anew this Easter, and live it anew for the rest of the year. Lets pray to Mary to help us in this. Hail Mary

# Second Sunday of Easter C

## Introduction

We continue to celebrate Christ risen. The first reading and the Book of Revelation show the apostles preaching Christ risen after Pentecost. They begin the universal salvation predicted by the prophets. Lets confess any failure to help in that mission.

## Homily

"Doubt no longer, but believe" (Jn. 20:28, JB). In an age when cynics and skeptics abound, lets heed these words. And refuse to make ourselves God, truth our whim, right whatever we desire. Lets listen to God, the church, and the Pope who show us the more timeless way to life. For the faithless way is inner death in the long run; Satan's sin of I will not serve, that brings hell after hell to earth, ever deepening darkness.

For if we're not obeying one Master we're obeying another. and new secular masters would have us ignore our precious inner life, our dignity and moral conscience, the ground of God we stand on, the salvation of our immortal souls. No wonder when crises come young people, conditioned by this ethos, flounder. With no solid ground to stand on in a faithless, immoral world, they have nothing to satisfy the deeper needs of their souls.

I think that's why Our Lady of Medjugorje says our's is Satan's age. Even as 20th century godless systems that spawned awful inhumanity and destroyed billions of bodies and souls, continues into today, the world it created, from Stalin to Hitler to the killing fields, should teach us that abandoning God only produces hell. Kim in Korea imposing that ideology now threatens to use nuclear weapons. Just as libertine capitalist secularism, a related ideology, secularizes schools, constantly highlights church mistakes, and sidelines faith. Must Christ come now, show his wounds and plead: "Doubt no longer, but believe"; he came that we might have life and have to the full; but many prefer death.

So his words are urgent. Our scripture describes Christ's resurrection, his showing of his risen body to win us to faith and goodness; to bring light back after thousands of years of fallen darkness. Yet a faithless generation won't believe though he be risen from the dead.

Unbelief is always hard-hearted, unreasonable and closed. As they say of charted miracles at Lourdes, for those who do not want to believe, no amount of proof is sufficient. In his own day, hard-hearted unbelief broke Christ's heart; we see him crying over Jerusalem: "How often have I longed to gather your children, as a hen gathers her chicks under her wing, and you refused" (Mt. 3:37-38, JB). Its no different now; I'm sure if he came back and stood among us and showed his wounds many would refuse to believe or, offhand, crucify him again. Or start a 50 year tribunal of inquiry that would end up with a million-page document and no firm conclusion. That's why Christ's words are urgent now: "Doubt no longer, but believe". Our forefathers through war, famine and colonial persecution believed and were saints. But an affluent generation says we don't need God anymore. That affluence is probably behind modern unbelief is shown by the fact that the only place where the church is not growing is in the first world.

Fools! What good will money be when your souls are required of you, and your possessions consist of a six foot box. Our forefathers will have the last laugh at the side of the Risen Christ. Love and faith gave them the victory over every worldly oppression. They knew that only faith makes us human, infinitely dignified and eternally wise. For the things of this world of which Satan is lord fade to dust at last, leaving us empty inside before eternity. But Christ is Lord of goodness, love, faithfulness, freedom, happiness and salvation both for this world and forever. Its to him, and not hard faithless worldly self-servers, that the kingdom, the power, and the glory belongs forever and ever, amen.

So as Gods people, the blessed believing saints of the Risen Lord, destined to share his glory, lets profess our faith anew.

## Prayers of the Faithful

As the people of God, solid in faith and trust in God, lets ask the heavenly Father for the faith that we need most of all.

For our Holy Father and leaders in the church that they may bring all the healing faith and saving presence of the Risen Lord.

For civil leaders that they may not go against our eternal good by ruthlessly promoting irreligious and secular ideology.

For youth, that heeding the words, "Doubt no longer but believe", and following Christ in living faith within his church, they may gain his glory in this world and the next.

For ourselves in our homes, that teaching our children to believe; they may learn the joy of keeping Baptismal and Confirmation promises as Christ's blessed faithful ones.

For the sick, the aged, the lonely and the oppressed that through our care they may know the love and care of God.

For our dead, having the kept the faith and run the race, may they receive the crown of life helped by our communal prayers.

We ask all these prayers through the Risen and glorified Christ who pleads for us constantly at God's right hand.

## Reflection

There's a story of Henry V111 at death, which may or may not be true. A friend said: "aren't you proud, we defied the Pope and even God". "No", henry said, "we **lost** everything". Be that as it may, as a man lives so shall he die. If we have unbelieving souls in life, that's what we'll have for all eternity; I find that frightening, but obviously, hardened in unbelief, some don't. Lets not be so blind, but heed Christ's words, "Doubt no longer, but believe". Lets be like the many saints who brightened the human soul with a great faith, and by the greatness of spirit it enabled, lit up the world. We ask Mary to help us to be one of the faithful saints in light here, and forever more. Hail Mary.

# Third Sunday of Easter C

## Introduction

They gloried in suffering humiliation for Christ's sake, our reading says. Like all creation our role is to serve God. And that's best done as part of his church led by Peter, to whom Christ said. "feed my lambs". Lets confess ways we stray from the true fold.

## Homily

This time of the year is all green leaf, flower and fragrance. Nature blossoms around us in fresh dazzling beauty! Our life in Christ is such an eternal flowering grace amid the darknesses of life. We first produce the buds of faith at Baptism. Then it blossoms in glorious Spring beauty at Holy Communion and Confirmation. And as we move towards summer and autumn of our life it produces fruits of timeless grace.

It's sad to see many abandoning that flower of life, for the flabby devils of secularism and materialism. We too, influenced by this world, can let our flower of faith wither and fall to be trampled underfoot; ourselves and our offspring can be left back in the pagan darkness from which Christ delivered us. But that uncaring commercial world has little to offer when suffering and death comes, and it certainly won't give us eternal life.

Only the apostolic church, born with the Risen Christ, can give us flowering life here shading into fruits of eternal glory. We see it in infancy in our gospel, where Christ gives it a leader for all time, Peter. At Baptism we were initiated into that holy family which will endure forever and against which, Christ promises, the gates of hell can't prevail. So even modern devils of materialism and indifference won't in the long run stifle its flowering grace and beauty and its timeless fruits. Christ's rose in triumph; the church is his eternal hope.

For the keys of the Kingdom were given by the Lord to Peter on the shore of Lake Galilee. For having received all authority in heaven and earth, Christ passed it on to his church and Peter its head, at the Ascension; he built our house on that rock. Lets remember that when worldliness assails it. Apostolic truth and authority was given by Christ to the church, ensuring its faith and unity for all time. That is our belief.

And never was that authority more needed than today, when powerful trends, within and outside the church, would water down the faith to suit passing worldly fashions. Of course the church must adapt to modern ways, otherwise it can become irrelevant. But there is a fine line between adaption in non-essentials and abandoning the basics of the faith. The latter would be disastrous in the long run; it wouldn't be a church of Christ but of men, in which self-appointed popes in the media and elsewhere would replace Christ as our masters. That's where the sane unifying voice of Christ's eternal church comes in, a church founded on the apostles and Peter as their head. Less apostolically grounded churches, though retaining much truth, are more tempted to drop what don't suit the times.

But there is a price to pay for any drift from age-old unity of faith and practice that stems from, and is maintained by, legitimate elected authority from apostolic times. As Cardinal Newman noted, once churches have split from the church of Rome, they've split again and again. So that now, anyone can set up a church, as in Waco, and call it what he will; too often its just the church of his bizarre prejudices. By contrast, the one true Catholic church, founded on the rock of Peter, despite its faults, maintains Christ's truth in season and out. The Risen Lord is at its heart in timeless gospel and apostolic values. Other mainstream churches, of course, also have a high degree of validity and faithfulness.

So lets heed all that, rather than the babble of men twisting truth to suit themselves, constantly changing according to fleeting fashion. Christians as straws in that wind make no sense. What does make sense is the true church, built on a Pope who serves rather than controls the Gospel and tradition. One whose no power to change anything that's part of the living memory of Christ and the church. For even the doctrinal development theory can be an excuse for anything goes; we follow desire and then invent specious reasons.

Rather, we must build our house on the "the rock" amid the world's shifting sands of which Satan is often lord, and which fades to ashes at last, leaving us empty on the shore of eternity. For Christ, present in the Word and apostolic authority, is lord of truth, salvation, and happiness both for this world and forever and ever, amen.

So as God's own safe on the rock of Christ and his elected, we profess our faith.

## Prayers of the Faithful

For the churches throughout the world; led by Peter's successor, may they keep the worldwide lambs of God in the authentic evergreen blossoming pastures of God.

For civil leaders that they may cherish all the people equally according to their dignity as children of God, especially the poor, weak and oppressed in society.

For our youth, that following the church's elected leaders who serve in the spirit of Christ as passed on through scripture and apostolic tradition in unbroken truth and beauty, they may come to a peace, grace and salvation the world's shifting sands cannot give.

For ourselves that in our homes, communities and country we may bring the faith of the Risen Lord to all those we serve.

For the sick that through our love and care they may know the love of God and find strength and consolation in suffering.

For the dead that they may be raised with Christ to glory, helped by our prayers.

We ask all these prayers through Christ, our Risen Lord forever and ever, amen.

## Reflection

Christ links authority in his church with love. For true leadership is tender service of the people. We talk of people or parties being "in power". But surely the role of those in charge should be service of people and society rather than furthering their power. Certainly, by washing the feet of his disciples Christ gave that service model of leadership to the church. We pray to mother Mary that all leaders will follow that model. Hail Mary

# Fourth Sunday of Easter - Good Shepherd and Vocation Sunday.

## Introduction

"The sheep that belong to me ... will never be lost" (Jn. 10:27-28, JB). This Good Shepherd and vocation Sunday we pray for shepherds for the flock, priests, lay people and religious, to be Christ's pastoral presence now. Lets confess a failure to nourish vocations.

## Homily

While in the Holy land I'd see shepherds chatting on the hills, their sheep mixed together. They'll never sort out that lot, I'd say. But each shepherd would call, and each lot of sheep would disentangle themselves and trot after their master. Christian life is like that. Christ calls and we follow freely to ever greener pastures.

In thus following Christ within the church, though our main call is to be holy, each of us also has a general vocation. For most its marriage and great grace is needed for a life of love, faithfulness and family care. Some are called to Christian single life and this is also valuable. Then again we all have special life vocations; nurses, teachers, shopkeepers etc. Each of us has a special role in God's plan for a balanced society. Most Christian witness is shown in family and worldly work. Christ spent 30 of his 33 years in the family carpentry business. Ordinary Christian family and business witness is as important as consecrated religious life. What keeps the world from chaos is loving Christian homes. And celibacy in religious and priestly life, though vital to the church's holiness, is no less demanding an ideal than marriage faithfulness.

That said, on this Good Shepherd and vocation Sunday we're asked to pray especially for priestly and religious vocations. For an increasing scarcity there is worrying. The laity's new prominence in the church is a must, but priests are still needed to preside over the Eucharist and shepherd the flock. Similarly monks, sisters and brothers provide such service and prayer the church would be immensely impoverished without them.

"A crisis in ministry", a media headline said recently, "Only 10 sisters joined up this year". No wonder the church calls for prayer and Eucharistic adoration for vocations, and lists practical steps we can take: suggesting a priestly or religious vocation to children; sharing our vocation story; serving in parish ministry and encouraging them to do so; supporting those interesting in priestly or religious life; and nourishing existing vocations.

The reason for the vocational fall may be affluence (for vocations are growing everywhere except in the affluent countries of the west). This and scandals in the church, have left many priests and religious demoralized; in the last few years four priests left in our diocese. Sure, some priests disgraced the cloth, as did some religious. But to tar all consecrated people with the same brush is like ignoring Christ because Judas was bad.

No! We must affirm good clerics and religious anew lest we end up with none. Maybe its God's will that we've fewer priests and religious so that the laity can be more prominent. Maybe this crisis is providential, bringing down harsh hierarchical church structures. But even in this scenario we must support vocational events and pray constantly for new vocations, as well as a new more open and humane church to fit the times.

Good shepherds are more needed in a new evolving church where priests and bishops return to the gospel role of love and humble service; where the church's message of eternal life comes to the fore, not power politics. So lets support and pray for good consecrated priests and religious to lead a new flowering of the church. So today too Christ can lead the world from darkness into light. For this world's values fade to ashes at last, but Christ is lord of happiness, truth and salvation now, and forever and ever, amen.

As God's own, living our vocations in Christian love and by prayer and practical means aiding a new flowering of consecrated and priestly life, lets profess our faith.

## Prayers of the Faithful

And as God's people, trusting in him always, lets pray for our needs.

For our Holy Father and all church leaders, that they may promote good vocations for a fruitful new apostolate to our age.

For ourselves that we may promote, support and encourage vocations to the priestly and religious life, so that our church may grow and thrive to enrich the times.

For young people, that they may find in Christ and in priestly and religious service of God's people, rich fulfillment and never turn away when the Lord calls them to such fulfilling devoted service.

For the sick that through medical and other caring vocational people they may experience the healing hand of God.

For the dead who have fulfilled their work in this world that they may reap the rewards of their endeavors in the life to come.

And we ask all these prayers through Christ, the Good Shepherd, who never neglects the flock in their need, amen.

## Reflection:

The story of St. Padre Pio's vocational struggle is inspiring. Initially, he was rejected from the Franciscan order because of illness; he was sent home for a while until his health should improve. He persevered, though it was a struggle to get ordained, and the person who ordained him is supposed to have said that much couldn't be expected of this poor friar. Little did he realize the influence Padre Pio would have in later years, due to his holiness. A vocation is a mysterious thing, and its fruits can be extraordinary. Lets pray for good vocations today for the enrichment of the church and all people. Hail Mary

# Fifth Sunday of Easter C

## Introduction

Our readings this week feature God's kingdom on earth in Christ. The first reading sees that Kingdom come with joy to the pagans, and the second sees it come to completion in a final perfect heavenly Jerusalem. Christ says in the Gospel that the way to bring that about is our active unfailing love and faith. Lets confess ways we fail in this.

## Homily

Once I ministered to a person with advanced MS. She'd been part of a trendy set with no time for God. They said, enjoy yourself, have sex, if anyone hurts you pay them back. When she got sick they ignored her, she now hindered their pleasure. They left her spiritually dead. They had just used her. But Christian neighbors rallied round, gave of their time to come and feed and take her out; from them she relearned faith, and real love.

Am I being unfair in saying that such a giving caring society is rarer now? "Me" seems most people's priority. Listening on the radio to a young person's new year resolutions I was shocked to hear his list: "put myself first, put myself first, put myself first". And is the relation between men and women increasingly, "I love you but."; always conditions; what about the ideal, when I give my heart it will be completely. And is loving one's needy neighbor reduced to sending a small amount to Africa. Love at a distance.

Be that as it may, I may be misjudging people, lets look at what Jesus asks. He not only says, "love one another", but "as I have loved you, you also must love one another" (Jn. 13:34-35, JB), which is a much more radical demand. He loved to the last drop of his blood, so he is asking a very serious love indeed. Yet such love is central to our faith; it shows us how to transform the world around us. Even if it means suffering we give for God and others without precondition.

This means not treating God as a cheap Sugar Daddy we love as long he gives us what we want, cures our ills, solves our problems; its loving him through all our trials and difficulties of life, when the easy way out isn't given. For God doesn't normally interfere with life's processes. That would destroy our freedom. But he gives us the grace we need in sufferings, so that we can carry our crosses and those of others; putting up with people's faults and failings, making sacrifices for them in love, without seeking a return.

That is, we're not to love at a distance, but close to the bone. For example priests are asked to persevere in the celibate priesthood, or religious are asked to give all in consecrated life. They love God and give undivided service to his people, though it means much sacrifice, such as giving up family joys. Often, baptizing children I feel it would be nice if I'd one of my own. Then I reflect that I've 1000s of children in the faith. I know it would be easier to satisfy myself; avoid sacrifice. Yet I know there is more life in total giving, like volunteers risking disease in famine areas, healing the world's injustice.

But we don't have to be priests or religious, or go abroad to love. There are many opportunities at home: persevering in love of an alcoholic relation; helping a troubled drug-addicted teenage son or daughter; supporting a neighbor in need when its easier to keep to oneself; giving time to a bed-ridden relation. There's nothing impossible about such charity. Its what billions of secret saints have done since Christ, setting aside personal interests to serve. We're called to be like that; and if we change the world into a caring place, it will bring great reward eventually, for in the grave it turns to glory. Whereas worldly arrogant self-centered values, of which Satan is lord, fade to ashes at last. With Christ on the cross of love we're lords of peace, faith, and lasting goodness, for our deeper happiness in this world, and our glory forever and ever, amen.

So as Christ's body, loving God and others with real caring hearts to make a difference by our lives, and make the earth God's Kingdom in Christ, we profess our faith.

## *Prayers of the Faithful*

And as the people of God sorely in need of his care and help, we pray for the things that we need.

For the church throughout the world, especially the Pope and the bishops, that their charity may help all in need, inspire selfless giving and sharing, and so help bring real love and justice to our much ravaged and unequal world.

For our civil leaders that their leadership may be in the interests of all, especially the poor and underprivileged, and not just serve their own power.

For our young people that they may not just work for their own welfare, but we reach out to others in the love of God and make a difference by lives of real charity, faith and grace.

For ourselves that we may make our homes places of real love and care for our children, neighbors and all those who need us.

For the sick, the aged, the poor and the oppressed that through our love, care and generous hearts they may know God's love.

Knowing its a good and holy thing to pray for the dead that they may be released from their sins, lets pray for the dead as a great act of charity towards our dear departed.

And we ask all these prayers through Christ the lord of real and giving love forever and ever, amen.

## Reflection

Charity covers a multitude of sins, St Peter says in his epistle. The Lord at last will not look at our riches or petty faults but our generous hearts. As St. Theresa says at last we will be rewarded according to the quality of our love while on earth. Lets pray to Mother Mary that we'll make a difference by lives of real charitable living. Hail Mary

# Sixth Sunday of Easter

## Introduction

In the first reading the apostles resolve disputes in the church, and John has a vision of its mystical holiness based on its apostolic foundations. Christ in the gospel sends the spirit to be with the church always. Lets confess if we fail the holy apostolic church.

## Homily

"Peace be with you", Christ says, showing his wounds after the resurrection. This reminds us that he suffered for us, and is most close to us in our suffering. One suffering many face today is addiction; finding peace there is difficult. At this time Confirmation children are taking the pledge and we might all reflect with them on the dangers of drink and drugs. There's a joke about the man who went to the doctor. "What's the matter", the doctor said. "Its my throat", he replied. The doctor looked: "I see nothing wrong", he said. "Ah, you should see something", the man said, "two farms went down that throat".

Joking apart, many a person's life has been ruined by alcohol, giving them no peace until the grave. Many a business or farm or house has been lost, many a marriage broken, many a bright young future destroyed by the "demon drink". Yet there are no warnings on whiskey or gin bottles like we have on tobacco packets. Indeed drink and even heavy boozing is often seen as part of our culture. I asked a young person once what they did on nights out. He said, "the fashion now is binge drinking". A survey done recently said that many teenagers, especially in towns and cities, begin drinking at the age of 14. At least a fifth of those will be alcoholics before 25, the survey concluded.

Its a sad prospect. I myself have often gone to squalid flats and seen young people dead on the floor, victims of continuous heavy drinking or drug-taking. George Best, the great footballer, is a good example. He had a liver transplant, yet died at the age of 56. And how many marriages made in heaven have been ruined by drink?

But addiction is not only bad for relationships and businesses but also a major threat to health and life. So its good that our children at Confirmation promise to abstain from drink at least until 18; and we hope it will be for life. And parents if you love your children, you'll watch over them and not let them fall into this trap. If they do drink stress that it should be in moderation. For of course drink isn't evil in itself. Its a good if used for recreational purposes; Christ drank and was accused by the Pharisees of being a wine drinker. It was the common drink in his land; he turned water into wine at Cana to help people celebrate. Moderation is key, being able to take or leave it, not letting it enslave us.

An even greater menace today is drugs. Confirmation children also promise to abstain from drugs for life. For once people start taking drugs at all, they can quickly become enslaved. The middle road is almost impossible. I remember, when I was in a large town parish, going to a squalid flat one night and seeing a young girl, barely in her 20s, dead on the bed from drugs. The sight haunted me for months.

When visiting Mountjoy prison as part of my training for the priesthood I visited a young man about 27 who described how his life was ruined by drugs. He abandoned his wife and child and resorted to robbing tourists' wallets in the streets. When arrested he was only seven stone weight. He begged me to ask the warden to get him on the drugs program. So as Confirmation children make their promises, we might all examine our lives and see if drink or drugs are too prominent.

"My peace I bequeath to you", Christ says. He loves us and weeps for any of his children enslaved. AA says that one of the first steps for recovering addicts is invocation of God. Lets invoke his help for all addicts. And as the people of God practicing moderation in drink and other things that can destroy us in body and soul, lets profess our faith.

## Prayers of the Faithful

As the people of God lets pray now for the things that we need.

For our Holy Father the Pope and all the leaders of the church that they may bring the peace and freedom of God and his Christ to addicts, or any enslaved in any way.

For civil leaders that they may provide proper facilities to help rehabilitate those suffering from addictions.

For our youth, may they be safe from excessive drinking, drug-taking and whatever ruins their future; through our care may they may grow in age and grace before God and men as Christ did.

For the sick, the aged and those who need special care, that through our care they may know the love of God and his Christ.

For the dead whose faith is known to God alone, the all merciful judge, that through our prayers they may come safely to the fullness of light, happiness and peace in heaven.

We ask all these prayers through Christ from whom all good things come. Amen.


## Reflection

There's a joke about a man who entered a pub and ordered an array of drinks. The bartender set them and the man drank them fast. "Why are you drinking so quick", the barman said. "You'd drink fast too", the man said, "if you'd no money". The barman was angry but then laughed saying, "we can take a joke here, if you pulled that trick in the bar across the road they'd break your back". "Well", said the drinker, "why do you think I'm bent over like this". The joke has a lesson. Many a person's back and very soul has been broken by addiction. Lets pray for and reach out to heal as best we can all those around us who suffer from addictive diseases, and ask Mary's help in this. Hail Mary

# The Ascension C

## Introduction:

We end our Easter celebrations with the ascension of the Lord. He had to go so as to send the Spirit and begin the church. But he is with us in Spirit until the end of the world. Lets confess any ways we may have failed to live in his spirit.

## Homily

Nowadays the church is in turmoil; scandals, mass attendance down, atheism growing. We who love Christ and his church could easily lose heart. But we shouldn't. Christ's ascension is the perfect antidote to pessimism. It guarantees the faith and the church's bright future. For Christ ascended to the father not to abandon us but to be with us forever. From God's right hand he orchestrates the world's and his church's inevitable triumph. He sent us his followers out at the Ascension to "teach all nations" and bring his salvation to the ends of the earth (Mt. 28:19-20, JB). In effect, he trusted us to finish the work he began. But knowing we'd need special help he sent his Holy Spirit to be with us. And he himself remained with us as Risen Lord: "know I am with you always; yes to the end of time" (Jn. 28:20, JB). What consoling words. Lets have no fear, however bleak things seem. God ensures that Christ will rule forever, in the Spirit.

And in him all are saved whether they realize it or not. Of course there's evil still - wars, famines, injustices. But as scripture says, where sin abounds grace abounds even more now. Even in recent revelations of the institutional church's failings the Spirit is present, renewing and reforming it. I see his work myself in the holy people I encounter everyday, their work is not mine but his. Though church leaders can be a stumbling block, Christ is Lord. The apostles tried to stop his Ascension. But he went to let the Spirit come, the church be born, and its mission succeed in his divine power.

Everywhere this Easter untold numbers were baptized around the world. This reminds us of the universal expanding church we're privileged to be part of. It will survive today's troubles as it survived 1000s of political and ideological systems that attacked it since its foundation. For at its heart is not human ideas or systems but the Risen Lord. That's why, despite constant onslaught its not only survived but grown. You know the *Star Wars* slogan "the force be with you". The force of the Risen Christ with it can never be defeated.

But does that mean we can sit back and let it happen. No! Christ needs our help, we must be his saving hands now. He ascended so that we could finish his redemptive work. The church was born at his Ascension and Pentecost, when the apostles went to teach all nations. That glorious work of Christ will continue until the end of time through us.

And when he comes again, he'll gather the vast universal number of the saved into the eternal Kingdom of God. Lets play our part in that victory by actively spreading and defending the faith, fulfilling sacred Baptismal and Confirmation vows. Having done that we'll ascend also to the Father. For the corrupt world of which Satan is lord turns to dust and ashes at last, but the ascendant Christ is lord of life, goodness, peace and salvation both for happiness in this world and forever and ever, amen.

So as God's people empowered for mission by his ascension and presence with us forever as Lord, lets reaffirm our faith.

## *Prayers of the Faithful*

And as his equally glorious people lets pray for what we need.

For the church throughout the world that it may never lose heart but grow and thrive in the power of its Risen and ascended Lord.

For ourselves, that we may never be just passive Christians but active builders of his kingdom of saving love at home, in the work place, and wherever we are.

For our young people that they may be inspired to become priests, religious and lay workers for Christ and his church, new apostles of our age.

For those suffering due to sickness, old age, or poverty, that they may be helped by our generous and caring love.

For the dead that the ascension of the Lord may bring them all to the heavenly mansion prepared for them from the foundation of the world.

And we ask these prayers through the Risen Lord of life, amen.

## *Reflection:*

There's a story told of St. Theresa of Avila. One sister stole into church to watch her at prayer. Suddenly her body actually left the floor and was lifted up into the air. Certainly, prayer raises us all up to God; its our Ascension while on earth. We pray that through deep personal and communal prayer such as the mass, we'll be raised up to great grace, glory and fervor in the lord service and in the service of humanity. Hail Mary

# Seventh Sunday of Easter C

## Introduction

Christ in our Gospel prays that we all may be one as he is with the Father and the Spirit. Such unity is urgent in a world filled with hatred and division as never before. Lets repent of ways we ferment division in our relationships, churches, community or country.

## Homily

There's a joke about the Unionist-Nationalist divisions in the north of Ireland. A member of Ian Paisley's church at death's door converted to Catholicism. There was uproar among his friends. They went and pleaded: "please don't do it. We wouldn't mind any other church, but Papism, how could you?". "Well lads", he said " I'll tell you the truth. I knew I was dying of cancer so I figured it was better for one of them to die rather than one of us". Joking aside, church divisions are a great scandal. In the early church pagans admired Christians for how they loved each other. Is that how they see us now.

Of course a "them and us" mentality is part of human nature. They say if you put a group of people in a room, in less than a day they'll divide into opposing camps. One need only look at gang wars between rival soccer groups to see that tribalism is still very much alive everywhere.

Recently I read the biography of Roy Keane. He talks about the famous world cup match in Belfast. The Republic went there needing a draw. Keane describes the absolute hatred the team encountered when they went out onto the pitch, a complete shock to most of the Irish team, who'd been born in England. Keane didn't even try to explain;

he knew it would take more than a few minutes to explain the history behind this virulent hatred.

There's no doubt if we did try to explain the cause of the vicious divisions in Northern Ireland the roots would be found more in political history than religion. But to the extent that the churches contributed to this we must beat our breasts. In a modern EU and post-Vatican 11 world these divisions are medieval at best. Until we're a loving united people, we can't call ourselves Christian. For Christ's central message was unity, and he gives the antidote to all division in his injunction to love our enemies. He prays fervently in our Gospel: "may they all be one, Father, may they be one in us" (Jn. 17:21 JB).

That's our Christian calling, to promote unity among races, churches, creeds and nations. And to foster justice as a prerequisite for such unity. That's the Kingdom of God on earth Christ came to establish as Prince of Peace. Its not better than one of them should die rather than one of us; it is our duty to help each other on the way to the larger world cup, peace on earth, goodwill to men. For that's the true destiny of our little planet, to bear witness to our common Creator by the unqualified and unifying nature of our love.

And this is not a matter of feeling, but a conscious decision to love others, even our enemies, as Christ did on the cross. Its to be a sign that the world is not made up of them and us, but that all of us as are one family. For this world's divisions of which Satan is lord fade to dust and ashes at last but to Our Lord, the Prince of Peace, belongs the kingdom, the power and the glory both for this world and forever and ever, amen.

So as God's people, called to promote loving unity at home, in our country, among our churches and creeds, and in our warring world at large, lets profess our faith.

### Prayers of the Faithful

And as the one people of God lets pray for our needs, especially for peace.

For our Pope and the leaders of all the churches that they may be signs of unity and peace in a war-torn world, and so be real representatives of Christ.

For civil leaders that they promote unity in their country and throughout the world.

For our youth that the they may work as the future generation for peace in our country and promote loving unity wherever they go.

For ourselves in our homes, community and country that we may keep our families united and spread peace all around us.

For the sick, the aged, the lonely, the poor and the oppressed that through our love and help they may find peace and justice.

For the dead that they may come quickly, with the help of our prayers, to the unity and eternal peace of their heavenly home

And we ask these prayers through Christ the prince of love, unity and peace forever and ever, amen.

## *Reflection*

One of the great promoters of unity and peace in a racially divided America was Martin Luther King. His rightly famous, "I have a dream" speech is deeply Christian, for he was essentially a man of faith in the perfectibility of man. He envisaged an America where there were no racial divisions, and everyone worked happily together according to their shared dignity and equality as children of God. Sadly, like Christ, he was killed by those who could not bear such a pure vision. But this is a universal aspiration. Gandhi that great non-Christian saint used to the same approach to free India. So lets pray to Mother Mary, that we will abandon violent division in every aspect of our lives and bring the unity and peace of Christ to all. Hail Mary

# Pentecost C

## Introduction

Today, Pentecost Sunday, celebrates the coming of the Spirit on the apostles, their Confirmation, when their faith was strengthened and they were empowered to go out to establish the church. All of us received that Spirit at Baptism and Confirmation. We too are sent out to spread the faith and build the church. Lets confess if we don't keep our vows.

## Homily

Today's the feast of Pentecost when the church was launched. And its right we celebrate it in summer, for the coming of God's Holy Spirit was a summer for the world. And the third person of the Trinity is the key to all warmth in Christian life, the church and the world. That's what we mean by the Holy Spirit? He's best seen in the finest kindest aspects of a person, a home, or a country. I once met Mother Theresa, and her warmth enveloped me. But that's true of people we meet every day, they radiate kindness and goodness. That's the Holy Spirit, what's individual and best in humankind.

But a contrary negative spirit can also possess people. For example, and I hope I'm wrong, I sense a colder spirit evolving in our world today. Is the spirit of the world and Satan its lord taking over, in colder, harder, secular atheistic values. Be that as it may, when the Holy Spirit goes out the window, so does humanity. The church is feeling such a cold wind blowing at present; mass attendance down, attacks from a more secularist media and government. In this climate we who love the Spirit could easily lose heart.

The feast we celebrate today should snap us out of any such tendency. Its a sign of eternal hope. Christ, ascending to the Father, became Lord. From his throne he sent the Spirit to us so that in his power we could bring his salvation to the ends of the earth. He guarantees that triumph. So lets have no fear, in the Spirit all is well.

He constantly gains the victory for us over the destructive spirit in the world. Just as he sustained the early church in the midst of bitter opposition and martyrdom of the apostles. Despite persecution the power and joy of the spirit carried them eventually to glory. They were brokenhearted when Christ ascended but they knew he had to go. So that the Spirit could come, the church be born, its mission succeed.

Paul says where sin abounds grace always abounds even more. This Easter adults of many countries were baptized in churches from China to Africa. The Spirit thrives despite efforts to snuff him out. The church has seen off 1000's of opposing worldly ideologies through time. They all faded like grass, but it continued to grow in the Spirit.

Lets be wise then and serve him with all our heart, as we promised at Baptism and Confirmation, when the Spirit was poured out upon us. Aided by personal prayer, the mass, the sacraments and living love lets bring his golden presence to all. For all else fades to dust and ashes, only fools trust in the spirit of the world and its empty passing values. But in Christ's Holy Spirit we grow within in untold wisdom, love, goodness, and salvation unto great happiness here below and forever and ever, amen.

So as God's people, spreading faith and goodness throughout our world in the power of the Holy Spirit given to us, lets proclaim our faith with new enthusiasm.

## Prayers of the faithful

As servants of God praying in the power of his Spirit, we ask for what we need.

For our Holy Father and leaders of the church, that, like the apostles at Pentecost, they may fearlessly preach the Good News and bring all to the arms of the Risen Lord.

For civil leaders that they may not be so carried way by the spirit of the world so as to hinder the spiritual welfare of the people they serve.

For our youth that having been filled with the Holy Spirit at their Confirmation when they vowed to practice and spread the faith, they may do so, and be the light of God to the world.

For ourselves in our homes, work places and communities that we may be apostles for Christ and his Holy Spirit to our children, and all with whom we come in contact.

For the sick, the aged, the lonely and the needy in spirit, body or mind that through our care they may know the love of God, and the comforting presence of his Holy Spirit.

For the dead that they may be raised up in the Spirit to heavenly bliss through their goodness and faithfulness here, and our continuing prayers for them as the powerful assembled faithful.

And we ask all these our prayers of the father through Christ in the power of the Spirit who is with us as the people of God forever and ever, amen.

## Reflection

Its amazing how the Spirit in certain saints still come down to us and inspire us even after thousands of years. People like Patrick or Francis or Brendan or Peter and Paul. They still inspire because they were filled themselves with the Spirit of God which is timeless, and whose effects go on and on. But that's true also of good people in general, for the Spirit is present in the world at large too; in people like

Nelson Mandela, or Martin Luther King. Indeed, we all leave a legacy of good or ill when we die. Lets pray to Mother Mary, the greatest of the saints, who totally lived the Spirit of holiness, that she will help us, despite our natural failings that keep us humble, to leave an overall Spirit of faith, kindness and goodness to those who come after us. Hail Mary

# Trinity Sunday C

## Introduction

In today's celebration of the Trinity, our readings deal with each person in turn. The first describes the majestic Father, the second the power of the Spirit, and third the Risen Christ as Lord of all. Lets confess ways we fail to glorify the infinite triune God.

## Homily

"The world is charged with the grandeur of God", the poet Gerard Manley Hopkins writes. That grandeur comes from the Trinity, which is not a remote mystery but the root of all goodness, beauty and truth in the world. The earth teems with threesomes that reflect that Triune God - sun, moon and stars; earth, sky and the sea; and notably father mother and child. God's threefold nature underlies all the great dynamics of life.

Is it even why we're male and female? Genesis says; "in the image of God he created him, male and female he created them" (Gn. 1:27, JB). Though some scholars argue that "him" here refers to man specifically, and not a generic term for humanity, one can, nevertheless, argue that gender difference, like so many aspects of the beauty of creation, echoes the triune nature of the Creator. For the loving union of man and woman begets a third, a child. As God is three in the heavenly home, so it is in the earthly home.

Certainly, God's great plan ensures that each person born is generated from a loving union like that of the Trinity. That's why rape's such a sin, it turns that plan to violence and cruelty. For everything is male and female and produces offspring. So all is sacred, our human rights come from being sacred creative children of the triune God.

Sadly today we often ignore that centrality of the Trinity in our faith. Our forefathers can teach us a lot in this. Look at a typical early Christian Celtic prayer: "I invoke the three in one and one in three; depth of earth, height of heaven, deep of ocean". For our ancestors the triune God wasn't an abstract idea but all around them in the grandeur of the created world. St.Patrick supposedly used the humble three-leaved shamrock to explain that mystery; it has three leaves but is one plant. Whether Patrick actually did this is irrelevant. He Christianized the natural sense of God in Celtic culture. Just as the Celtic cross unites the cross and the sun, the twin sources of natural and spiritual life.

Then again the Trinity dominates the sacraments. We baptize in the name of the Father, the Son and the Holy Spirit; we absolve from sins in the name of the Father, the Son and the Holy Spirit, we confirm in the name of the Father, the Son and the Holy Spirit; and all our mass prayers are trinitarian. We pray them all through Christ to the father in the Spirit. But our greatest trinitarian prayer is the simple blessing of ourselves. We impose the cross of redemption on our bodies, even as we invoke the Trinity; the two central mysteries of the faith are embodied in one simple act of prayer.

Why then is the Trinity sometimes played down. Maybe the culprit was the reformation which overstressed Christ, as some sects still do today; Christolatry. As today's gospel makes clear this fails to see that everything Christ did came from his union with the Father and the Spirit. Also Reform fundamentalists tended to overstress the Bible, Bibliolatry. Our faith is not a matter of a book. Its center is the living person of the Risen Christ in the midst of his church, and Christ always in intimate relation with the Father in the Spirit. For everything he did on earth came from that union. So also God's presence among us as a community is trinitarian. Its in the power of the Trinity that we live and move and have our being. Its our endless strength, grace, and guarantee of eternal life. For at last we'll be swept up by Christ in the Spirit into the eternal kingdom of the Father. With our loved ones we'll be part of the life of God in a heaven of love, peace and happiness. For the values of the divisive world of which Satan is lord fades to ashes at last, but Christ, one with the Father and Spirit, is lord of life forever and ever, amen.

So as people of a trinitarian faith let us say the creed now in a new way, noting its trinitarian format: the first part deals with the Father, the second with Christ, and the third with the Spirit which is linked to the church as his outpouring to the world.

## *Prayers of the faithful*

As God's people, rooted in the mystery of God as Father, Son and Spirit lets pray for what we need to our infinite triune God.

For the church in the world, especially our Pope and the bishops, that they may reach out to all in power of God as Father, Son and Spirit, and so bring the world to similar unity in diversity, for the essence of the world is infinite variety.

For civil leaders that they may promote unity in the country, north and south, and among all the people in the Republic; unity in recognition and acceptance of difference.

For our youth that the mystery of the Trinity may surround them with love and bring them to the love of Christ and the church.

For ourselves and our children that as we bless ourselves with holy water for protection and grace, we may become ever more aware of the Trinity's presence in us, above us, and around us.

For the sick and all those suffering in mind or body that the three persons in one God may raise them up to new life.

For the dead, may they enter through Christ, the door, in the Spirit, the key, to the eternal House of God the Father.

And we ask all these prayers through the same Christ, in the Spirit to the eternal Father of us all forever and ever amen

## Reflection

Christ be beside me, Christ be before me, Christ be behind me king of my heart. Again in this ancient ancestral prayer the triple nature of God's presence is invoked. We pray that Mother Mary, part of the Trinity that was the home at Nazareth may bring us all to a living relationship with the triune God. Hail Mary.

# Corpus Christi C

## Introduction

Today we celebrate the Risen Lord's bodily presence with us. In the first reading Melchizedek offers a similar thanksgiving offering of bread and wine. The epistle retells the Last Supper's giving of the Eucharist, and tells us to celebrate it for all time. The gospel has Jesus feeding crowds in the wilderness; he still feeds us in the same way with his real presence. Lets confess ways we fail to appreciate this great gift of Christ.

## Homily

Since Renaissance Platonism and the Reformation we've played up the soul and played down the body. Hence stresses on the spiritual and condemnations of materialism, but that's not Christian. Ours is an incarnational faith, the word became flesh. It must always be incarnated in worldly fleshly terms. Hence the church thankfully kept all the sense aspects of the faith, candles, incense etc. I shiver when I enter some other churches, they are so cerebral and bare, and in that sense inhuman. We are body and soul, and both are equally sacred; we go to God through the senses.

That's why we have the feast of Corpus Christi, the body of Christ. To remind us that his presence to us in communion as real as someone walking into our house. You know when some people enter a room, there's a buzz. It was like that with Christ. His powerful gentle presence made all flock to him and hang on his words. We may say I wish I were there. Actually we are "there" at mass. He's with us in a real way; in each mass the substance of bread and wine becomes his body and blood, soul and divinity.

A person can be talking to you and miles away. Jesus's presence in communion is not like that. Its an active intimate presence that makes faith hope and charity bloom, it makes us Christian to the core. It keeps us healthy within, like good eating does our bodies. It sustains us for life's trials, enables us to grow in God's life, binds us to his body the church, gives us strength to witness to Christ, and enables us to defeat sin, suffering and death. They say we become what we eat, and what we eat here is Christ.

But priceless blessings come to us also from visits to his sacramental presence in the church. He is present for us at all times in the tabernacle. Now if you knew Jesus was visiting your area in the flesh you'd rush to meet him. But he is in the church all the time. Benediction and exposition are great reminders of that fact as is prayer in his sacramental presence. Visiting him brings strength for life's struggles and deepens our prayer life.

All in all then we cant overemphasize how precious a gift the Eucharist is. Our wise forefathers knew this as they made going to mass as essential and natural as the seasons. Jesus was there for them, they wanted to be there for him. Those who say I believe but don't go to mass are deluded; they throw away the essence of the Faith in an amazing show of religious ignorance; for the Eucharist is the absolutely essential food of Christians. Don't take my word for this. Christ himself says: "if you do not eat the flesh of the Son of Man and drink his blood, you will not have life in you" (Jn. 6:53, JB).

In effect, regular communion is as vital to our faith as eating is to our bodies; without it we grow thin within, easy prey to evil. But with it we flower into eternal life even here below. No wonder the church once said missing mass was a mortal sin. It alone can transform our lives into graceful living. So that when we see Christ face to face at last we won't be strangers. Christ also said emphatically: "Anyone who does eat my flesh and drink my blood has eternal life, and I shall raise him up on the last day" (Jn. 6:54, JB). Imagine that we are already part of eternal life through regular communion, sure to be raised up when he comes. To know that is wisdom. For the world fades to ashes at last, but Christ in communion is life for us both here and forever and ever, amen.

**So conscious that we Christians are in essence a Eucharistic Sunday people, lets profess our faith** with new enthusiasm.

## *Prayers of the faithful*

And as God's people, one in the lord, present to us here in body and soul, lets pray confidently for what we need.

For the leaders of the church throughout the world, especially our Holy Father the Pope, that they may always enthusiastically encourage the people of the world to receive and be the living Body of Christ in grace, beauty and timeless truth.

For our civil leaders that they may facilitate every aspect of the practice of faith, for the deeper good of all their people.

For our young people that they may realize how vital Sunday mass and communion is, as their very life in God as his people.

For ourselves that we may never fail to come every Sunday to be nourished at the table of the lord, bring our children, and spread his loving healing presence to the world.

For the sick, the old, the lonely and the housebound that through the monthly reception of the Eucharist on First Fridays they may participate in the Christ's body and be comforted and raised up.

For the dead that having shared in the banquet of eternal life here in communion they may enjoy it forever in heaven.

We ask all these prayers through the same Christ Our Lord here present with us as his holy Eucharistic people forever, amen.

### Reflection:

This week's Corpus Christi and Sacred Heart feasts make a similar point. Both remind us of Christ's Real Presence. For the Blessed Sacrament is his beating heart of love present to us forever. Lets ask Mary to keep us in that love - Hail Mary

# Second Sunday of Ordinary Time C

## Introduction

Our readings today deal with the union of the man and woman as God's plan. The first reading compares this to God's union with his people. And in the Gospel Christ stresses the importance of marriage by changing water into wine for relations celebrating their wedding. Lets confess ways we fail in married constancy.

## Homily

"Male and female he created them" (Gn. 1:27, JB). I often wondered how being male and female makes us like God? I think the answer is that man and woman united in body and soul in enduring love images the Trinity. With children they form a threesome of creative fruitful love such as the God is. For we now understand the Trinity as the force behind creative life in the world. The great plan of this one God is that every person born into the world should be born of love. That's why casual sex is wrong, it reduces the sacredness of loving sexual union to selfish passing pleasure. God's plan is for a constant union of the sexes to bring the unity of love and family togetherness to the world.

That's why we see Jesus in today's gospel beginning his ministry at a wedding. He came to restore in us the image of God which marriage symbolizes, and when he died he created a new marriage of God and humanity, the church. He is its bridegroom and we, his people, the church, are the bride. We constantly bear children for the increase of his family through Baptism. So we're the ever increasing family of God in Christ. Everywhere he went Christ turned life into love. The challenge for us in union with him as the church is to do the same.

One key way to do this is good Christian marriage. For at Cana Christ both blessed marriage and infused it with a new ideal of enduring faithfulness. Good Christian marriage is redemption for the world, provided it lasts. For most unions start off great but at some stage the wine runs low. Then comes the test, to keep the best wine to the end. To say then: "there's nothing more in it for me", is to reduce marriage to cynical worldly standards. But our vow at the altar is to go one loving no matter what. Christian love in marriage is a constant choice to go on loving even when the going gets tough. It involves a suffering self-giving like Christ on the cross, and he is lord of every good marriage.

And we also have a mother in our struggle to be faithful Christian husbands, wives and children. Mary's life of love began with her annunciation "I do"; we echo that "I do" in our marriage vows, to be the handmaid of each other. At Cana we see the sensitivity of Mary to the couples' needs. She notices the wine has run low, the occasion could be ruined for the young couple. So she begs Jesus to intervene, to begin his ministry by helping a marriage. Then again, in Nazareth, with Joseph and Jesus, she presided over the perfect family. She followed her child to the cross and waited in the sealed room with the apostles for his Spirit to come. The picture emerges of a person who loved in good times and bad, a great gentle faithful wife and mother, a model for each marriage.

Christian life and marriages are watched over by this heavenly trinity of Jesus Mary and Joseph still. Lets live our lives and marriages then in their light to transform the world into an image of the perfect home which is heaven. For this world passes but Christ is Lord of suffering, faithful, enduring love forever and ever, amen.

So as God own committed to marriage, true love, and faithfulness to Christ and his church, let's profess our faith.


## Prayers of the Faithful

As God's people lets pray for our needs, especially the needs of married people.

For the Holy Father and leaders in the church that they may continue to affirm the importance of Christian marriage.

For civil leaders that they may pass laws that support marriage and the family and so serve the good of society.

For our youth that they may see the importance of the sacrament of matrimony, that it gives the essential extra grace of God to maintain a union of true love between them and their beloved.

For the sick, the aged, and especially those who have lost beloved spouses that they may be consoled by our love and care until they are united with their beloved ones again forever.

For our dear departed that through our powerful communal and Eucharistic intercession for them they may reach their final rest in the lord and with those who have gone before them in faith.

And we ask all these prayers through Christ who is one with his holy people and intercedes for them forever and ever, amen.

## Reflection

There's a joke about a man who put an ad in the paper: "wife needed, donkey dead". Marriage today isn't donkey work but a joyful union of equals. This reminds me of another joke: the first year of marriage the wife speaks and the husband listens; the next year of marriage the husband speaks and the wife listens; the third year of marriage they both shout and neighbors listen. There's a point in the joke in that good marriage involves listening, sharing and respecting each other's feelings, and making up quickly when things go wrong. For when we realize the other person's not perfect, the challenge is to still love them warts and all. To hang in there when trials come so that the union will mature and produce the best wine at last. Lets ask Mary to help married couples do this. Hail Mary.

# Third Sunday of Ordinary Time C

## Introduction

Our readings for this week deal with charity. Christ was sent, as he says, quoting Isaiah, to bring the good news to **the poor**". Lets confess ways we fail in charity.

## Homily

There's a story told of a man coming before Peter for judgment. "I see you've many sins piled up against you", said Peter" have you done any good at all in life". "Well" he said "I did give a loaf of bread to a poor person some time ago". "OK" Peter said, "we'll put that in the scales". On one side of the scales he put the man's sins and on the other the loaf. Lo and behold the loaf outweighed all the rest; he was saved.

This is just a story but it shows how important helping the poor is in the lives of Christians; St. Peter says, "love covers over many a sin" (1 Pr. 4:8-9, JB). And Christ tells us that even a cup of cold water given in his name is rewarded. But apart from the fact that charity aids our salvation, we Christians should help others for another reason. Because they're children of God, our brothers and sisters in Christ, and because ordinary humanity dictates that we cannot be indifferent to human suffering.

For Christ commands us to love not just in a vague sense but in a real way. Yet too often we walk by brothers or sisters in the gutter, and I include myself in this. Every day on TV we've images of hurricane or earthquake victims or starving children in Africa and though many help, some also turn their eyes away. Are we responsible for righting such wrongs? Yes, because we're partly to blame and because we are our brother's keeper. When I was in the Philippines I saw how 60% of its GNP went to repay debt to western banks. We westerners can be blind to the fact that for every euro we give to poor countries we take 9 back in debt repayments. Bono went around trying to get rich nations to forgive some of the debts of poorer ones but didn't have much success.

But there are always charitable demands at home too, especially as the recession kicks in. The needy are all around us, if we open our eyes; I read in a Catholic newspaper recently that quite a lot of people go hungry now in Europe, with the cutbacks and widespread lack of work. Giving to Vincent De Paul is one way to help. But in whatever way we can we might give some of our surplus to the less well off. Its our duty to make the world God's more just world, and its good to start at home. Even people living with us can be needy. In our homes there may some who need a hug, or a pat on the back.

In this or in the wider field, we Christians are asked to love in action. Otherwise Christ may say at the end of time: "depart from me ye cursed into everlasting fire for I was hungry and you did not give me to eat" and so on. If Christ came to us for help we'd give freely; but the needy are always with us and they are Christ. "Give to anyone who asks", he says (Mt. 5:42, JB). I find it hard to do that myself, but if someone asks I always try to give something. I may be taken advantage of, but I can't deny the Gospel. Its better to err on the side of generosity than be mean.

For we're sons and daughters of a God who's so good to us. If Christ gave his last drop of blood for me, I know I should give freely until it hurts. And like the man who gave the loaf of bread, even the smallest act of generosity will be rewarded by Jesus, when he comes to judge the living and the dead. For riches and hoarding this world's goods are no use to us at last, we carry nothing with us into the grave. But Christ is lord of just and giving hearts for our happiness in this world and forever and ever, amen.

So as God's people committed to charity and a juster world, let's profess our faith.

## Prayers of the Faithful

And as the people of God lets pray for our own needs and the needs of all disadvantaged people in these difficult times.

For the Holy Father and all leaders of the church that they may remind the powers that be of their duty to bring justice and equality for all, equal sharing of earth's resources.

For civic leaders, may they not be so obsessed with economics as to the lose sight of their duty to help all people achieve a good standard of living, especially the poor and underprivileged.

For youth that in their rightful pursuit of the good life for themselves, they may not lose sight of their duty to practice charity, to make some contribution to a just world for all.

For ourselves in our homes that in these difficult times we may have plenty for our children and some left over to help others.

For the sick, the aged, the lonely and the oppressed that through our love and charity they may know the love of God.

For the dead whose deeds are know to God alone, that they may reach the reward of the blessed with the help of our prayers.

And we ask all these prayers through Christ the only lord of love forever and ever, amen.

## Reflection.

There's a story told of Mother Theresa when she was getting established in Calcutta. She acquired a derelict Hindu temple for her work, but the locals objected that the place of worship should not be desecrated by hobos. "Ah", she said, "God does not recognize whether the poor are Hindu or Christian or whatever, only that they need help". Its the same with us, we should not discriminate on grounds of race, color or creed, but help all who need our help, in whatever way we can. We pray to Mother Mary, mother of all people, to give us such generous hearts. Hail Mary

# Fourth Sunday of Ordinary Time C

## Introduction

Our scripture this week is about discrimination. Jeremiah faces rejection by his people but God takes his part. In the same way Christ, because he's just the carpenter's son, is cast out of the synagogue. Lets confess any areas of prejudice in our lives.

## Homily

You may know the story of Max Kolbe. Sent to Auschwitz because he opposed the Nazi regime he was especially badly treated there because he was a priest. Driven by secularist ideology, Fascists abhorred religion. They said, following Nietzsche, that we must get rid of God and pursue our own desire and power regardless of divine standards of right and wrong. So they crushed the weak and inferior races. In some ways that's still the creed of a secular age; recently, in Britain, a woman was sacked for wearing a cross to work. Kolbe died witnessing to universal charity and against all forms of discrimination.

After an attack on Auschwitz by the resistance the camp commandant retaliated by ordering 10 prisoners to be executed. Kolbe saw that one of those chosen was a family man. He asked the guards to take him instead. He was injected with poison and took 3 days to die. The guards finally beat him to death with rifle butts. On his cell wall they found a crucifix scratched by the nails of his hand. What a perfect illustration of faith as defined by St. Paul in our second reading, where he says the greatest of all virtues is love. Kolbe lived Christ's way, not that of the Nazis or other tyrants of our age, or that of the Pharisees in the Gospel. They saw poor inferior groups as unclean; even Christ to them was scum, a carpenters son. He died, like Kolbe, to witness that all are God's children.

As we approach racial justice Sunday we're asked to live that truth also. To see each person as an equal child of God and love them without prejudice. As Kolbe gave himself for the family man, we should love others even to extent of laying down our lives for them. Kolbe was just doing what Christ himself preached and did. Jesus gave to the last drop of his blood for everyone, especially the poor and oppressed. We're called do likewise. Not looking at skin, color or creed but loving without exception.

That's a huge challenge today, to hold to Christ's gentle values rather than those of the hard world. Its interesting that they cast Christ out of the synagogue after he preached from Isaiah that he was sent to set the downtrodden free. He asks us to carry on his work, to love God and others wholeheartedly, completely, unconditionally. We cant pass by on the other side of the road when we see a fellow human being suffering as the pharisees did. We can't say like Cain: "Am I my brother's guardian?" (Gn. 4:10, JB). We're responsible for each other's welfare. Indeed, we're asked to love the aids or famine victim or sick neighbor or immigrant as if they were Christ himself.

If we live up in even a small way to this Christian ideal the world will be a perfect place. And that's the world were called to build, the just Kingdom of Christ. We may not be called to sacrifice our lives like Kolbe. But as demanding are everyday acts of non-discriminatory kindness, that may cost us, but also bring rewards. For the world's hard values fade to ashes and leave us empty at last, but Christ is lord of love, peace and grace for this world and forever and ever, amen.

So as God's people called to build a just all-embracing society, here where we are, with Christ's help, lets profess our faith.

## Prayers of the Faithful

And as God's holy people lets pray for the things we need to our heavenly Father.

For church leaders, that they may reach out to all races with the all-embracing love and justice of Christ the Good Shepherd.

For civil leaders that their care and leadership may extend to all, especially those underprivileged or downtrodden in society.

For our youth that they may have open and unprejudiced minds and hearts and so shape a kind all-inclusive future society.

For ourselves in our homes that in that great tradition of Christian hospitality, they may be open houses for our neighbors.

For the immigrants, travelers and all who come to our shores that they may find welcome, succor and unqualified acceptance.

For the dead that through our prayers they may reach the home of the blessed.

And we ask all these prayers through Christ the lord of love forever, amen.

## Reflection

Catholics or other racial of religious emigrants were often discriminated against in America at one time. In the last century, signs in some shop windows said, "no Catholic or Irish need apply". But God always casts down the mighty and raises up the lowly. For example, perhaps the two greatest soccer clubs in the United Kingdom, Celtic in Scotland and Manchester United in England, were clubs originally set up to serve such excluded groups. The exclusion must have hurt a large number of people, but they triumphed in the long run. We should learn from that. not to discriminate against those who come to our countries for employment, or shelter from famine or war. Jesus, Mary and Joseph were such exiles in Egypt, and we pray to Mary to give us hearts to embrace all those who come to us in need, or just for a better job, or a better way of life. Hail Mary.

# Sixth Sunday of Ordinary Time C

## Introduction

Today we have the most beautiful of Christ's moral teachings, the Beatitudes. They are his commandments, yet they are not a list of laws, but ways to be blessed children of God. Lets heed these wonderful guides and confess any ways we fail to do so.

## Homily

"I have a dream", you may know the Martin Luther King speech and its importance for the human rights struggle of African Americans. Today's gospel is Christ's "I have a dream" speech, a charter for the just Kingdom of God on earth, he came to establish. Very simply, in the Beatitudes Christ puts purity of heart before the law. He puts the horse of a right inner spirituality before the cart of morality. In the old testament law was everything, as moral strictness was in a pre-Vatican 11 church. Christ's beatitudes are a necessary corrective to all that. Which is why people like Gandhi and Tolstoy found them so beautiful. Rather than "thou shalt nots", Christ lists the inner attitudes we must have to lead a good life, detachment, mercy, peace, thirst for right and so one.

As such the Beatitudes, so-called because of their first word "blessed", are a blueprint for the transformation of the world into a totally happy place. Luke in today's gospel has three, but they're extended in Matthew to eight. But even Luke's shortened list is powerful.

Take the first "How happy are the poor in spirit" (Mt. 5:3, JB). Christ isn't saying its good to be poor but that God takes the part of the poor, endorses their struggle, and ensures their place in heaven. But there is far more than that in Christ's words. He gives us the solution to poverty by asking all to be poor in spirit, detached from ruthless possessiveness within, the root of injustice. In effect, being satisfied with enough, and equal sharing of resources is the only sure and blessed way.

But there's more still to the beatitude; this detachment will free us within and so make us happier; like Scrooge, the unhappiest person of all is the slave of gold. Free from all that we have friends everywhere, even in low places. But he also warns that the corrupt world will hate us for showing how useless and unsatisfying materialistic obsessions are.

In a way, practicing this beatitude led to Christ's death. Though accused of many specious crimes his real mistake was showing up the Pharisees and Romans, the cruel and cynical exponents of this world's wealth and power politics. They couldn't stand him and thought they'd destroy his vision by killing him, to save their corrupt system.

That lesson is as urgent for us today. Despite opposition from the world we must continue to shun excessive greed and witness against it; in poverty of spirit, overflowing love, and inner freedom and generosity. For the resultant happiness and salvation for ourselves and the world will make it more that worthwhile. Even in this life we will be blessed, and in the world to come raised to the eternal bliss of the blessed. For we'll have helped in whatever small way to bring about the dream of Our Lord, a just world. Our life will be worth while, and we'll share in the glory of Our Lord, forever and ever, amen.

So as God's own called to the inner way of beatitudes such as peace, mercy, purity of heart and freedom from the tyranny of possessions, we profess our faith.


### Prayers of the Faithful

And as God's people lets pray for the things we really need.

For the Pope and bishops of the church that eschewing the pomp and ceremony of palaces and wealth they may be an example to the flock of freedom from possessiveness, and purity of heart in every way.

For civil leaders that they may not just serve their own power and wealth, but be humble servants of the common good, and work for all the people who elected them.

For our youth that they may not be enslaved by the pursuit of wealth and big houses, but nourish their souls also by simplicity, and share with those less well off.

For ourselves; in our homes, community and work place may we put love of our children, relatives, friends and work mates before the ruthless pursuit of wealth and the tyranny of keeping up with affluent neighbors.

For the sick, the aged, the lonely and the oppressed that through the time we make for them, and the care we give, they may know that they are loved by God for themselves.

For the dead that free from their mortal chains they may rise to the glory of heaven with the help of our generous prayers.

We ask all these things through Christ who though he had "nowhere to lay his head" is lord of all forever and ever, amen.

## Reflection

The great early Christian saint, Brigid, is know for her holiness and service of the poor, and her kindness even to animals. When young, she was working for a rich man, and one day she put three pieces of meat to cook for her three employers. But a poor starving dog came to the door and whined for help. So she took one of the pieces of meat and gave it to the dog. Now she was in trouble, how would she account for the lost meat. Lo and behold, when she prayed, and the men came back for dinner, when she looked in the pot there were three pieces of meat there. This is just a story of course but it illustrates the kindness of heart, to man and beast, that should characterize the Christian. Lets pray for that kindness to our tender Mother. Hail Mary

# Seventh Sunday of Ordinary Time C

## Introduction

Our readings this week continue themes of the Sermon on the Mount, notably the message of non-violence and love of enemies. Lets repent of violence or hate in our lives.

## Homily

There's a fine anecdote about Mahatma Gandhi. During his non-violent campaign for independence in India, a Christian adviser asked him to be more militant. "What about turning the other cheek as Christ teaches", Gandhi said. "Ah", the Christian said, "we don't take that literally". He found Christ's words too challenging, Gandhi didn't. During the India-Pakistan war Gandhi fasted until both sides ended the war. A non-Christian, yet he proved that Christ's way of non-violence can end vicious cycles of conflict. Violence begets more violence and the only sane way is to get off the wagon. We are called by Baptism to do just that, to love so-called enemies and spread peace by our lives. For world peace begins with peace in each human heart, replacing hatred with forbearance and love.

Gandhi found Christ's teachings in the Sermon on the Mount indescribably beautiful. Certainly, the value of non-violence is a universal truth; the human heart needs to be converted to peace. For that's the only way to transform the world into God's happy kingdom, to produce harmony on earth. Christ's, "happy are the peacemakers", is not a restrictive law but the way to universal happiness; humankind with a peaceful heart.

But this is more than a passive virtue; its related to active love in the image of God. Let me tell you of two people I knew who realized this.

First a young student doing theology. She told me that what changed her into a fervent follower of Christ and helped her bring her family to the church, was the gospel message of God's unconditional love. "Go out as a priest", she said, "with this message: tell young people, who are tempted to abandon the church because they sin and think God rejects them, tell them he doesn't, he loves them no matter what". Another example is my nephew's fiancee. I met them for a chat before the wedding. She told of a vision she had. God said, "tell people how special each of them is to God, he loves them regardless". Peace is living love, not hate.

And that's what Christ's Sermon is about, unconditional love and peace from the heart. Being blessed in acting like God whose sun shines on good and bad alike; loving one's enemies, turning the other cheek to end the cycle of violence, lending without hope of return, being compassionate rather than judgmental, forgiving freely and giving generously to all who ask. And we do this not just for a heavenly reward but to make us happy in this life too. Christ says that the love we give we'll more than get back: "a measure pressed down and running over will be poured into your lap" (Lk. 6:38, JB).

This is happiness for this world too, for the more we promote peace the more it will grow in our own hearts; we will we the blessed children of Christ's new kingdom and help redeem a violent world. For worldly greed and violence leave us empty, but he is lord of love, peace, grace and happiness both for this world and forever and ever, amen.

So as God's people called to live Christ's way of love, generosity, forgiveness and peace lets profess our faith.


## Prayers of the faithful

And as God's people we pray for the purity of heart that we need.

For our Holy Father and all church leaders, may they lead the world in the way of non-violence, peace and reconciliation.

For civil leaders that they may continue to promote and uphold the peace, and do their utmost to foster lasting reconciliation among all the warring communities on earth.

For our youth that they may recognize that God loves them no matter what they do; may they respond to his love by living their faith with peaceful generous hearts.

For ourselves, may we maintain an atmosphere of love and peace in our homes, with our children, spouse, relations and neighbors.

For the sick, especially those bed-ridden or in special need of our care, that we may reach out to them with our time and love.

For the dead that they may come to the everlasting peace and happiness of heaven with the help of our charitable prayers.

And we ask all these prayers through Christ, the Prince of Peace for this world and forever and ever, amen.

## *Reflection*

According to group of local children, Our Lady appeared recently in Medjugorje, part of a war-ravaged region of Europe. You do not have to believe in such private visions but certainly the message the children proclaim as coming from her is very Gospel based. She calls all the people of the world to pray and work for peace. And like Christ in our gospel she says that such peace must begin in each human heart. Lets pray for that peace in ourselves, our community, our country and in the world of today. Hail Mary

# Eight Sunday of Ordinary Time C

## Introduction

"A man's words flow out of what fills his heart" (Lk. 6:45. JB), Christ says, and urges us "not to praise a man before he has spoken" (prov. 8:22-31, JB). Christ asks us to avoid judgmental condemnation in our speech. Let confess ways we misuse the tongue.

## Homily

"Among all the parts of the body, the tongue is a whole wicked world in itself", St. James says (Jm. 3:8, JB). We sometimes don't realize how much we can hurt people by ill-spoken words. For we are sensitive beings whose feelings are easily hurt, and the harsh word can hurt more that physical abuse. In the home, we can't be too careful about what we say. Our children are like tender plants in our garden, easily damaged by the poison of bitter words. But this true in general. The catechism listed the sins of the tongue as lying, slander, backbiting, malicious gossip, perjury, swearing, false oaths, and so on.

I suppose deliberate lies is the most common way of misusing the tongue. It is a serious sin because people should be able to trust our words; the very integrity of our character and soul is at stake. So is community, for it must be based on the truth, not on lies. I am always annoyed by the reports in the media that do not exactly tell lies, but twist and misrepresent the truth to suit the ideology of the commentator. There should be total fairness in our media reports, and concern for absolute integrity. The Pharisees were constantly trying to catch Christ out in his speech and at his trial twisted what he said, by means of false witnesses before Pilate. This was a double blasphemy.

The same is true of our oaths and vows; if we don't really mean them we shouldn't take them at all; things like marriage vows, court oaths and swearing in public. Christ was so worried about them that he said it would be better not to swear at all: simple truthful forthrightness in speech is his advice: "All you need to say is 'Yes' if you mean yes, 'No' if you mean no" (Mt. 5:17, JB). He was especially concerned at how religious authorities used oaths, they invoked God as surety to underpin their devious practices; it was misuse of both the tongue and an insult to the God of truth.

Slander of course, telling an untruth about someone so as to undermine their character and moral credibility, is as destructive. And we must be careful also to avoid telling even the truth in an uncharitable way. There was much wisdom in the old saying, that if we couldn't say something good about someone we should say nothing at all. That's as it should be. If we want to even remotely come close to God, we must continually soften our words, for the bitter word can leave scars that are slow to heal, especially in our relations with loved ones. That's why James talks of the tongue as something nothing can tame; we can use it to bless the Lord, but also to curse men who are made in God's image. And in rhetoric it can be used to inflame people and make them do the most terrible things, as in Hitler's evil eloquence.

That's why scripture tells us today that words of generosity only should flow from the store of goodness in our hearts. And in our speech lets be especially sensitive to people's feelings, conscious of how harsh words can cut to the bone, and lead on to alienation and even lifelong conflict. There may be some we are "not speaking to", because of something said in the past; lets try to rectify that if possible. James says the tongue can be a wicked world in itself. But he also says that it can be a blessing if used to praise God and build up those around us. And even when pointing out the truth and correcting them, we should do so gently. For the evil one sows bitterness and division through wicked words, but Christ is Lord of love, gentle speech, truth, and goodness, for our happiness in this world and forever and ever, amen.

So as God's people, committed to open hearts and kind loving speech, that reflects truthful and integral hearts and builds up those around us, lets profess our faith.

## Prayers of the faithful

And as the people of God lets pray to Our gracious Father in heaven for the things that we truly need to be holy like he is.

For church leaders that in their gentle speeches and pastoral letters they may encourage and inspire the faithful, and indeed those of the wider world of good will, to follow the way of God, the way of building up and not that of divisive, slanderous or contentious words.

For civil leaders, may they not indulge in demagoguery but use words in their speeches that lead all to justice and truth.

For our youth, that they may always respect and speak the truth, and avoid anything that hurts others, or stirs up trouble by falsehood or misrepresentation.

For mothers and fathers in the home, that the words they use in the home may not beat their children down, or hurt them, but build them up with the peaceful message of open caring love, expressed in kindly words and actions only each day.

For the sick, the old and the lonely that we may come to speak with and heal them with our friendly chat and attentive care.

For the dead that through the kind prayers we speak on their behalf before God they may come safely home to heaven.

And we ask all these prayers through Christ who intercedes for us always before his Father in heaven, amen.

## *Reflection*

Words can inspire us, but can also do harm; like the words of the nagging wife or husband, or the over-strict parent. Scripture says we should say only words that build people up. Let's be careful of the words we use, for they can hurt. Lets ask Mother Mary to make us truthful, wise, tender and non-judgmental in our speech. Hail Mary

# Ninth Sunday of Ordinary Time C

## Introduction

Healing is the theme of scripture this week. We may not realize that we can all carry on the healing work of Christ. Lets confess ways we have done the opposite.

## Homily

No doubt some of you are familiar with Brid McKenna, the miracle-working nun. When she was a young sister, she suffered terribly from arthritis. That was not easy to bear, especially for a young person. One day she went to the chapel and implored God to help her. Suddenly a voice spoke to her: "Brid you are healed, now go and heal others". She got up from her knees free from pain. Now she goes around the world preaching and healing people. She wrote a best-selling book, *Miracles Do Happen*, because in her ministry she witnessed so many miracles of grace. She has a special mission to priests for she says that the devil is launching a special assault on them today; he knows they are in the firing line of God's great mission of spiritual healing. Her physical and spiritual miracles, hardened sinners coming back to the church and the sick restored to health, happen usually at mass when the people are blessed with the monstrance.

You may say why all this extraordinary activity, our faith by contrast is simple and ordinary. But in fact there is nothing extraordinary about Brid's ministry. All that she does was done by Christ before her, as today's Gospel makes clear. We see him healing the centurion's son in response to faith. Throughout his ministry Christ healed innumerable people. Then he went to pray in a place alone; he needed that contact with his Father to energize his preaching of the Gospel and his healing.

His are the three great things also practiced by Brid McKenna today, healing, preaching the gospel and prayer. All three must be part of our Christian life too, for they are our life.

Of course most of God's healing today is done through the miracle of medical science. So if sickness is part of all our lives, and we find suffering hard to explain, we also know that without it we wouldn't have the wonderful example of all the healing doctors, nurses and house carers. These are the modern hands of Christ. But with this we need the added power of prayer. For healing to be complete must minister to the whole suffering person, physical, mental and spiritual.

You may say this is a pious platitude. No! a modern study by secular psychologists have shown that those in hospital who have faith are much more likely to recover from sickness that those who do not. Moreover the scientific study found that they recover more quickly. We should not be surprised. Even non-believers see the need for faith and prayer in the face of sickness and suffering. For its close contact with God which heals us most. The closer we grow to him the more he enables us to bear with unavoidable suffering, and offer it up if it cannot be healed by the ordinary means he supplies.

Most of Christ's time was spent healing sinners and the sick, the two related types of illnesses, spiritual and physical. For sickness and suffering is not from God, its part of our fallen human condition. But in Christ it can be redeemed, turned into a source of immense spiritual wealth. Like Brid McKenna let us turn to God in our pain; he'll never let us down for his Christ is still with us as saving Lord forever and ever, amen.

So as his people sharing in his healing ministry to those in pain around us, lets profess our faith.


### Prayers of the Faithful

And as the people of God lets pray for the things that we need to be whole physically and spiritually.

For the church throughout the world that it may never fail to bring Christ's deep healing presence, in body and soul, to our needy world.

For civil leaders that they may prioritize the health of the nation by as generously funding the health system as possible.

For our youth that they may give of their time to be the healing presence of Christ to others, especially their old, sick or disadvantaged relatives, neighbors or friends.

For our homes that they may be places where healing faith, prayer and the presence of Christ, the healer in every way, is to be found.

For our sick in particular, especially the sick of our parish, (lets each of us now mention silently someone belonging to us who is sick) that through our prayers and caring outreach they may know the healing love of Christ.

For the dead that they may reach their final rest with the help of our prayers.

And we ask all these prayers through Christ who is healing lord of life forever and ever, amen.

## Reflection

Sr. Brid describes one wonderful healing that she witnessed at a healing mass. The priest was carrying around the Monstrance to bless the people. As it passed one mother with a sick child in her arms, the child looked at the Blessed Sacrament and cried out. Later, the mother brought the child to sister to show that he had been completely healed of the recurrent illness that had dogged his life. Not all healing is so dramatic; there are secret healings of the heart and soul that are known only to those who felt them. Lets pray for healing in our lives and that we will be part of that ministry through prayer, active charity and compassionate outreach to all around us who are suffering. Hail Mary

# Tenth Sunday of Ordinary Time C

## Introduction

Our readings this week carry on the theme of healing in God. In the first Elijah heals the widow's son and in the Gospel Christ restores the widow of Nain's son to life. Lets confess any ways we fail to respond to the sick who need us.

## Homily

There is a story told of Mother Theresa. One day, she was going along the street in Calcutta when she saw a poor man in the gutter; people were callously passing by, ignoring him. He was thin, sick, covered all over with flies and sores, dying. She lifted him up, though frail herself, and took him to her house. She washed and anointed his wounds, and gave him fresh clothes and food. Soon after he died. Her friends said what's the point, he died anyway. The point she said, was the smile on his face as he died. Yet the media gripe that she shouldn't be made saint due to doubts about one of the miracles.

But she's a saint not because she conformed to a self-centered world, but because she followed Christ heroically in compassion for the sick and dying. We see that in action in our gospel where he healed the widow's son. Like Theresa, he saw the need and acted to heal the hurt without prejudice. We'll all be judged at the end of our life and the end of the world by our degree of such caring love. God will say to us on that final day: "well done good and faithful servant" if we helped others, especially the sick. Excuses like "I minded my own business, did nobody any harm" won't do. Christ walks the earth in the form of our suffering neighbor; Theresa knew that we must help our brothers and sisters to live and die according to their human dignity. Otherwise how can we face Christ on the last day. The acts of mercy we performed will then be the measure of our reward.

That's why this gospel frightens me. I'm a priest, yet do I respond to the sick as Christ did? Safe in my fine parochial house do I even have an inkling of the suffering of the ordinary people during recession. Or wider afield, do I feel for starving millions in Africa, wells dried up, clothes falling from backs. Do I help in some way to change that?

Its the spirit of God that asks these questions. Ease and selfishness has not yet killed my conscience. As a Christian I still know I dare not be indifferent. I want to help Christ build the caring Kingdom of God, but the excess money I have, do I hoard it? The Gospel challenges us to pledge a generous portion of our surplus to help the needy.

We may not all be Mother Theresa. But we can all do our little bit. Not out of fear, God will judge us gently, but out of love for our servant King who had nowhere to lay his head. He said that the greatest among us must be like him, one who serves humanity. True, none of us can be as perfect as him, nor does God expect us to be. But we can do a lot during our lives to alleviate suffering. We can show more Love, reach out more to needy brothers and sisters in Christ. If we can't do it out of the best motives, love of God and concern that all live and die according to their human dignity, lets do it to avoid the great judgment, to ensure that our life in this world isn't wasted, that we will not be cast out on the last day. Mother Theresa saw that man in the gutter and did something; let the compassionate Christ be our model too. For all else fades to dust at last, but he is lord of caring love, for our happiness in the world and forever and ever, amen.

So as the people of God reaching out to those in need in whatever small or great way we can, lets profess our faith.

## Prayers of the faithful

For our Holy Father and the leaders of the church that they may be examples to the faithful and the whole world of concern for the poor and needy.

For leaders of our society that the poor, sick and needy may be their special concern and that they may allocate what funds they can, in difficult times, to help the underprivileged.

For our youth, especially those without employment, that they may find more prosperous times in the not so distant future.

For ourselves in our homes, community and country that no one may be in need of love or care in our environment.

For the sick, the old, the lonely and the oppressed that through our love and caring help they may know the love of God.

For the dear departed whose love is known to God alone that through our continuing loving remembrance and prayers, a great work of charity, they may come to fullness of life in the Lord.

And we ask all these prayers through our all-caring lord, amen.


## Reflection

For years I was a member of the De La Salle order and its founder is a great model of care for the needy. He was a rich man who lived in a fine house and served as a privileged canon of Rheims Cathedral. Yet he gave away all he owned to the poor and went to live among them, setting up schools for poor street children. He ate the rough food and wore the rough clothes of the poor like St.Francis, because as a Christian he could not stand idly by and see God's children suffering. Lets pray to Mary that we'll have similar concern for the sick and less well off, and help in whatever way we we can. Hail Mary

# Eleventh Sunday of Ordinary Time C

## Introduction

Our scripture this week features sin and forgiveness. David sins grievously and is forgiven but his sin has consequences. In the Gospel Christ's forgives the woman who anoints him. Lets seek forgiveness for our sins and their effects, trusting in God's mercy.

## Homily

Maybe some of you saw the film *The Scarlet And The Black*, about Fr.O'Flaherty, the priest who was called the Vatican Pimpernel. He used his Vatican diplomatic status to smuggle 1000s of prisoners and Jews out of Rome's Nazi torture-chambers during World War 11. We hear about *Schindler's List,* but O'Flaherty, a similar savior of Jews and prisoners-of-war, gets less press. Maybe this is because our secular age doesn't want to give credit to the church. In any case, O'Flaherty is a modern hero who not only helped escapees, but in a last amazing act of inclusive mercy smuggled the German commander's family out of Rome before it fell. And during the commander's imprisonment for war crimes his only visitor was O'Flaherty; he became a Catholic due to the priest's forgiveness.

Today's readings deal with God's similar all-forgiving mercy. The first reading tells how David sinned grievously, and yet when he repented he was forgiven by God. Then we've Christ's forgiveness of the notorious woman who washed his feet, a lesson for the hard-hearted Pharisees. Christ tells them, that harsh judgment awaits those who don't forgive others. God forgives us; we must forgive others to redeem a hate-filled world.

But even from a psychological viewpoint this makes sense. Psychologists, talking of recent abuse cases, have pointed that for the victims healing must include justice, but also eventual forgiveness of those who abused them. Otherwise their ordeal will never end. For nursing bitterness, we never find inner peace, hatred eats us up. But with the inner freedom to forgive, a great burden is lifted from our shoulders; we move on with our life.

Moreover, such forgiveness is necessary for our salvation. We can't go before God with hating hearts. At death we must have love and forgiveness in our hearts, for our eternal peace. Otherwise, we risk having only a narrow hating soul for all eternity. Moreover, the life and death of each of us shapes others. If we fail to forgive, we can leave that legacy to our children.

So Christ's request for forgiveness is also a recipe for society's health. But often today I'm shocked by how hard and unforgiving our so-called liberal press and society can be, totally ruthless in pursuing corrupt public offenders, not letting up until they are completely humiliated and destroyed. Is this unmerciful climate part of a materialistic hardness and cruelty creeping into society? I hope not. For its alien to the Christian mentality, which always tended to be tolerant and forgiving. Let he who is without sin cast the first stone.

As Shakespeare says the quality of mercy isn't strained, it blesses him who gives and him who receives. But many cling to grievances like dirty money. And the one we fail to forgive most is often ourselves. So lets forgive and move on, like Christ who readily forgave those who crucified him. For the world's harsh unforgiving ways are Satanic traps that contaminate the heart, but Christ shows us the way of mercy and compassion, both for our happiness in this world, and forever and ever, amen.

So as God's people called to have loving forgiving hearts for all, to redeem our world in God's image, lets profess our faith.

## Prayers of the Faithful

And as the generous people of God lets pray for our needs.

For the Holy Father and all leaders in the church, that they may be example of merciful forgiveness, and so point the way forward for those who would perpetuate vengeance and hatred between people and nations.

For civil leaders that the punishment of public criminals as part of the justice system, may be tempered by mercy, rehabilitation, and the outlawing of capital punishment.

For our youth that they may learn to forgive and show generous mercy, so that their lives may not be blighted by unrelenting hatred and ongoing resentments that embitter the soul.

For ourselves at home, may we be models of forgiveness for the failings of our spouses and children, and continue to love them "warts and all".

For the sick, the lonely, and the oppressed, that through our love and caring compassion, they may know the love of God in their lives.

For our dear departed that by our communal prayers and loving remembrance they may come safely to their heavenly home.

And we ask all these prayers through our all loving and forgiving Christ who is our gentle Lord forever and ever, amen.

## Reflection

Once a person came to me and said with great anger: "I'll never forgive the man who wronged me". I had given a homily such as I've just given. She was intransigent: "One should never forgive abuse. You should have said that in the homily". I could understand her deep hurt at being abused when young and the difficulty of letting go. But I also felt that she was clinging to that wrong in an unhealthy way. It would continue to do damage as long as she refused to forgive, she would be a victim forever. When deeply hurt of course, we have to wait until we're ready to forgive; and that can take time, but I think it should come at some stage, for our own good and freedom within. "Forgive us our trespasses as we forgive those who trespass against us". Lets ask our Mother Mary to give us the strength to be able to forgive eventually, even the deepest hurts. Hail Mary

# Twelfth Sunday of Ordinary Time C

## Introduction

Our gospel this week features the cross. Christ asks us to renounce ourselves, take up our cross, and follow him. There's no escape from life's crosses. But how we approach them makes a difference. They can embitter us, or bearing them in Christ, we can turn them to gold. Lets confess if we fail to bear unavoidable crosses with Christian fortitude.

## Homily

He who lives more lives than one, more deaths than one must die, a common saying says. Its true. When my brother was nineteen he decided to leave a secure job and start his own company. Everyone said he was mad to throw away a good job, going it alone was dangerous. He ignored them and took the risk. Shortly after, the firm he had been working for collapsed. He went on to establish a company that employs many still. His was a hard decision; he had to die to security and follow his deeper instinct.

Life's a series of risks and deaths. The womb was our first tomb. We emerged from it, crying, into a harsh world. Then there was death to childhood, painful coming of age. Then death to single comforts and multiple partner choice, to give all to spouse and children. Religious give up family, property and marriage for God. Celibate priests die to desire to serve Christ and the flock. All crucial bridges in life we must cross without a safety net.

Christ says we must take up our cross. As Christians we must die to self continually if we're to be holy, we must take the risk of giving all for God and others even unto death. Our gospel is a challenge to our modern ethos, which says, pamper self at all costs, shun sacrifice. You know that ad that used to be on TV; the child shouts at his mother "Where's my Liga". She answers apologetically: "children today, so demanding".

Yet a self-centered way doesn't give joy in the long run. There's more life in the faithful partner in marriage, the enclosed religious, the celibate priest, the lay person slaving for the Vincent De Paul. It doesn't bring instant gain or pleasure but deep down it satisfies the soul. Christ, the best of all, gave himself on the cross without reserve. But first he had to resist the lure of selfish wealth, pleasure, and glory, that Satan tempted him with. That's why Christ said to Peter who wanted to keep him from the cross, "get behind me Satan"(Mt. 16:23, JB). He had to die to self to bring all humanity to life.

So must we, his followers, for Christ says: "if anyone wants to be a follower of mine let him renounce himself and take up his cross and follow me" (Mt. 16:4-25, JB). Make no mistake, if we're really true to God we will suffer. We'll be attacked as Christ was, but we'll have more enduring happiness. In that sense every Christian is called to live the passion of Christ in his or her own life.

This Sunday we're challenged to do just that, to follow Christ in self-giving faith and love through all the trials and sufferings of life so as to turn them into gold. For that's the way to not only save our own souls but bring life to a spiritually dead world. Dying to baser selves, serving God and others on the cross of real love, we'll find fullness of life here, and with Christ and all other holy and selfless souls forever and ever, amen.

So as God's own, taking up the cross of loving service of God and others even unto death, bearing life's sufferings with Christian fortitude, we profess our faith.

### Prayers of the Faithful

And as God's holy people, lets pray to our heavenly father for all our needs.

For church leaders, that they may carry joyfully the cross of humble service of the faithful and be true suffering witnesses to truth before the world.

For civil leaders, may their leadership and service of the people be carried out in self-giving integrity and dedication.

For our youth that they may not be afraid to take up the crosses involved in dedicated service of God and others within the church, and its freeing moral code.

For parents and married couples, that they may bear the cross of loving service of their children, and be faithful in marriage through all trials and temptations the world throws at them.

For the sick and housebound that through our visits, company and caring help they may be consoled in their sufferings, and offer them up, if unavoidable, to redeem the world.

For the dead that through our prayers they may come to rest and peace from all suffering.

And we ask all these prayers through Christ who on the cross gave even his soul for the salvation of the world, amen.

## Reflection:

In that film, *The Last Temptation Of Christ*, he is tempted to get down from the cross, marry Mary Magdalene and forget about saving the world. In imagination he does so. He lives with her and their children as a carpenter. But years later, he sees his apostles coming to him and asking why he let them down so badly. Christ rejects the imaginary temptation then. It was the same temptation Satan offered in the desert, to put himself and his desires first. All of us, celibate priests or religious, those with marriage vows, those scrimping for their children's education, face a similar temptation, to give up, put self first. But that's an illusion. Lets be wise and see that the cross of doing what's right is more satisfying in the long run, despite temporary pain; for most things worth doing involve suffering. Lets ask Mary, who stood by her son's cross to help us in this. Hail Mary

# Thirteenth Sunday in Ordinary Time C

## Introduction

Scripture this week is about dedicated faith. Elisha leaves all to follow Elijah. Paul tells us to bear every trial for God; and Christ says that the man who puts his hand to the plow and turns back is not fit for his kingdom. Lets confess any wavering in our faith.

## Homily

Many of you may have read about Van Gogh, the painter. He sold only one work during his life. After his death, they found one of his paintings propping up the door of a chicken coop. Most laughed at his daubing and he lived in abject poverty, dependent on his brother Leo. Eventually dedication to art cost him his life. Yet he persevered to the end; he knew that what he was doing was worth the jibes of detractors.

The same is true of faith. We persevere in it for deep down we know its our lasting happiness. As Christ makes clear in our Gospel; once we put our hands to the plow at Baptism if we looks back we're not fit for the Kingdom of God. This warning is spot on for today when many abandon Christ for passing worldly values, or baulk at the effort involved in practicing the faith, or find Christian morality too challenging. Today's gospel challenges those who say, "serve self at all costs, don't let God or moral values get in the way".

Jesus warns us that hard self-centered worldly ways don't satisfy in the long run and can leave us empty and lost on the shore of eternity. For if we reject God in this world we may also do so at death and that's hell. Moreover when we abandon the faith we neglect the soul's deeper desires and needs. Even from a practical point of view, modern psychologists agree, faith is good for us. It helps our survival for it gives a depth and grace to our lives which nothing else can. And only faith can bring the life within us to full flower. That's why even scientists agree that evolution favors those of faith.

Its no wonder then that Christ says of the godless people of his day: "let the dead bury their dead". In effect, the faithless self-centered way is inner death. For what's the use of having all material things and pleasures if we're dead inside. Man doesn't live on bread alone. The world may mock married faithfulness or the religious who gives all for God and the church, or the priest who lives a celibate life for the safe of the Kingdom of God, or the devoted lay person who sacrifices his or her free time to go to mass on Sunday, or collect for Vincent De Paul. But for Christ such dedication is to be truly alive.

True, commitment to God and others in love may not bring wealth or instant pleasure, but deep in the heart it cleanses and frees us both for eternity and deeper happiness in this world. That's why Christ didn't just preach the urgency of faith and love, he lived them. Resisting the lure of godless wealth, pleasure and self-glory which is worship of the evil one, he left all to be a poor preacher and bring humanity to life on the cross.

We Christians must also give as much as we can: for Jesus says "anyone who wants to save his life will lose it; but anyone who loses his life for my sake will find it" (Mt. 16:25, JB). Make no mistake, like Christ, if we're true to God, faith and his church the world will hate us. But we'll have enduring happiness, Christ's glory in our lives. For by keeping the faith and living our Baptism commitment to be true to his values, when he comes again we'll go out to meet him with the saints and he'll say, well done good and faithful servant. For the world's values of which Satan is lord pass and leave us empty inside, but Christ is lord of life, goodness, truth and happiness both for our deep happiness in this world and forever and ever amen.

So as God's people setting our hand to the plow and continuing in living faith through every test and trial that comes our way, lets profess our faith.

## Prayers of the faithful

And as God's steadfast long-suffering faithful lets pray to God for our needs.

For church leaders throughout the world, especially our Holy Father, that they may persevere in proclaiming, living and witnessing to the faith, for the deeper life of the world.

For civil leaders, realizing that man does not live on bread alone, may they may help preserve the faith our ancestors suffered for.

For our marvelous youth that putting their hands to the plow at Baptism, Holy Communion and Confirmation, they may persevere in faith and worship unto death, for their deeper life here, and their happiness forever with their loving Lord.

For parents and children, may they, as Vatican 11 says, be the "domestic church", faithful to Christ and love of one another through thick and thin.

For the sick that through our love, care and prayers they may be strengthened, comforted, knowing God's love in their suffering.

For the dead that through our continuing prayers they may come to the final peace and happiness promised by Christ to the faithful.

And we ask these prayers through Christ who cares for his holy people forever and ever, amen.

## Reflection

That film *The Devil Wears Prada* makes a point like that of Christ in our gospel. It features a girl tempted to lose her soul to the ruthless world of fashion. Eventually, she realizes its empty show is not worth the losing of friends and deeper values. Many during the economc boom followed the way of fashionable clothes and vain shows of vulgar wealth. Of course we should enjoy the world's good things, but not to the extent of losing our true focus. There are more important things than keeping up with the devil who wears Prada, love, integrity, friendship, practice of the faith and so on. Lets pray that Mary will help us when tempted to abandon Christ and church practice for worldly vanity. Hail Mary

# Fourteenth Sunday of
# Ordinary Time C

## Introduction

Our readings this week feature God's love. The first reading depicts that love as an intimate one, like that of a mother suckling her child at her breast. The Gospel prays that all will come to those tender arms. Lets confess any failure to cling to God as his beloved.

## Homily

Sheep without a shepherd. In the Holy Land sheep that had no shepherd wandered aimlessly in the desert to be lost, starved to death, or eaten by wolves. The souls who are not safe in God's caring fold are often seen in scripture as metaphorically sharing that plight. That's why Christ came, to be God's good shepherd, bringing home all people on earth. And that's why he sent out the apostles after Pentecost. He ascended, not to abandon us, but in his risen state to lead all souls on earth to salvation. In the gospel we see him sending out seventy-two in that task. Today, active caring believers, people like you and me, are those he asks to help him bring lost wandering souls to God's safe fold.

The apostles began that work, but its survival depends on us. For if Christ's flock, which is all humankind, has been a prey to worldly wolves and philosophies in the past, that's still true today; human nature doesn't change. Our era also has ravenous wolves and spiritual deserts: materialism, militant atheism, moral decay, and so on. Our role in the church, one of God's key folds, is to protect the human flock from all that destroys it, especially our youth. For the evil one, a wolf of souls, targets the vulnerable.

"The harvest is rich but the labourers are few" Christ says (Lk 10:2-3, JB); how true that is today in affluent areas, where vocations to be shepherds of the flock, priests, religious and ardent lay people are few. Christ's heart burns to save his lambs. Let's pray for good priests, bishops and laity to help him revitalize the church and bring back the lost.

Sure, some shepherds have failed us in recent times, but there's nothing new in that either. Christ attacked the religious shepherds of his day for serving their own power and wealth and neglecting the flock. Criticism of bad shepherds today reminds us of what we should be. For the constant temptation of authorities in church and state is to serve their own interests and institutions rather than the needy flock. Recent clerical scandal are cases in point, but they only highlight how vital good pastors who imitate Christ are. He washed people's feet and said that leaders in church and state should serve humbly.

That's what we need today: good lay apostles, priests, bishops and even Popes who care for all the lambs of God diligently, humbly and selflessly. Of course, the church, like all institutions is human and will never be perfect. We need renewal now as never before, bringing to book bad shepherds who deter good ones. Through scandals God is doing that now, bringing down the corrupt, so that service of the vulnerable may be prioritized again. For exploitation of the innocent is a crime God never let's go unpunished. We priests need the present dose of humility as a wake up call.

Christ begged his shepherds not to lord it over people. But we mustn't use the fact that some shepherds failed, as an excuse to abandon the faith, throwing out the baby with the bath water. Rather lets back renewal. For a vast needy flock of lambs are out there crying for spiritual guidance in an increasingly violent, immoral desert world. And if our times prove anything its that spiritual and moral chaos serves no one. Amid the collapse of the family, drug killings and so on, the challenge for us is to be true shepherds again. With the good shepherd's help we can and must do that. For this world's values of which Satan is lord leave people empty for this world and the next, but Christ is lord of goodness and salvation for all the needy flock of the world, both for their deeper happiness and safety in this world, and forever and ever, amen.

As God's people called to be soul-nourishing shepherds for Christ in our world of today, lets profess our faith with new hope.

## Prayers of the Faithful

And as God's children held in his arms lets pray for what we need

For our Holy Father the Pope that he may be a true shepherd of the whole flock, and indeed the whole world, so that people everywhere may suck the milk of faith, wisdom and salvation from the loving breasts of God, Christ and mother church.

For civil leaders; may they be conscious of the needs of all the people in these difficult times and serve all as good shepherds.

For our wonderful generous youth that they may remain safe in the tender arms of the lord and his holy church.

For ourselves in our homes, communities and country that we may be true shepherds to our children and spouses. nurturing them with love and care as God nurtures us in Christ.

For the sick that through our care and love they may know the love of God in their lives.

For the dead that they may come to the loving arms of the Father with the help of our prayers.

And we ask all these prayers through Christ, the good shepherd who cares for us his flock tenderly forever and ever, amen.

## Reflection

One of the great stories of history is that Joan of Arc, the maid who shepherded a whole people to freedom and self-determination, inspired by the voice of God within. Of course she was burned at the stake for her pains. This a reminder to us that all great shepherds face potential persecution; Christ himself said to those he was sending out on mission that he was sending them like lambs among wolves. Lets persevere in our pastoral roles, regardless, and ask Mother Mary for fearless shepherds for the flock. Hail Mary.

# Fifteenth Sunday of Ordinary Time C

## Introduction

This is Good Samaritan Sunday, calling us to charitable love, especially towards those hurting by the waysides of our world. Lets confess any ways we fail to help fellow human beings fallen by side of life's road, and for whom no one cares.

## Homily

Mother Theresa was a good example of a Good Samaritan for our time. She lifted up many a man and woman from the gutter, in the slums of Calcutta, though she also had to encounter opposition from those who had passed by, pretended that those needy people didn't exist, or deliberately turned their faces away. Even recently I heard some criticism of her on the media, that her facilities weren't modern enough, though she was working on a tight budget, suffering constantly from lack of funds, which the very people who criticized her wouldn't provide. But, like the Good Samaritan she toiled on, and established other inns, and innkeepers, the nuns of her order, to carry on her work.

This Good Samaritan Sunday we are asked to reach out to the needy in this real way also. We're to be Good Samaritans in action, living the gospel now, as Theresa did. Not walking past those suffering in body, soul or mind, but lifting them up. We have mother's day at this time and Theresa was a mother to all without discrimination, especially the poor, her brothers and sisters in Christ that she found discarded by society.

Our charity must also start at home. Even in mansions, children or spouses may be in need of love, but we're too busy to give them a timely hug. Mother Theresa insisted that her helpers should not just feed and clothe the poor, but give them human love too. For we humans can live without many things, but not without love.

But what is love? The story of the Good Samaritan shows us what love means, caring in action at every level of human need. Whether with those around us or those wider afield, the church is really a family of prayerful active love, not law. As St. James say, its no use telling people to keep fed and warm, if we do nothing to meet their needs. We must walk the walk as well as talk the talk. Some say faith is enough, but its empty without charity. Christ says, "your light must shine in the sight of men, so that seeing your good works, they may give the praise to your Father in heaven" (Mt. 5:16, JB).

Another story of Mother Theresa shows up talk, as against action. One day she was going in to a major conference on world poverty in Calcutta, and as she went in she noticed a poor man outside the door of the big hotel begging. All the grand delegates walked past him without even a glance, like the priest and Levi in our gospel. He was just a statistic. They were talking about helping the world's poor, but let that man die in front of their very eyes. Talk is cheap, and sometimes its just a way of justifying ourselves; Bono, who does much good jetting round the world to champion the poor, keeps his billions.

Recent surveys have shown that its people on the ground that make a difference in famine-stricken areas. Much international aid lodges in stores or is siphoned off in corruption; and when the crisis blows over the people are as bad as ever. *Band Aid* may paper over the wound for while, but the long term disease must be tackled in a more real and persistent way. Those who make a difference are long term volunteers: digging a well to irrigate the land, giving a cow to feed them for the future, building schools and hospitals.

But even with our neighbors at home we can be Good Samaritans: providing a mourning neighbor with comforting shoulder to cry on; bearing with a difficult adolescent; offering a lift to school to the child of the single mother next door who needs to go to work. Like the Good Samaritan we should see the need, provide help, and care for long-term. Then we'll make a difference and pile up reward in heaven. For cold uncaring self-centeredness leaves us empty inside but Christ is lord of real active caring love, both for our real happiness in this world and forever and ever, amen.

So as such real caring people of God where we are, lets profess our faith.

## Prayers of the Faithful

And as the people of God lets pray for all our deepest needs and the needs of those struggling to live in times of recession, or global times of famine and war's ravages.

For church leaders throughout the world that like the present Holy Father they may be parents to the poor, caring tenderly, and confirming their faith by charitable giving.

We pray for the leaders of our country that they may lead us in true concern and real justice for all, especially the needy and most vulnerable in society.

For all those who have wandered from the fold today, lost by the spiritual wayside, especially young people, that they may return to the loving arms of their heavenly Father and Mother in their great spiritual need.

And we pray in silence for all our own intention and especially for neighborly love and caring homes in these difficult times.

We pray for our sick, that we may show to them the care and love of Christ, the all-caring and motherly Lord of all who suffer.

For our dead who have died in Christ and within the bosom of his holy church, that they may know the sure hope of the resurrection to eternal life that sustains us.

And we ask all these prayers through Christ to our heavenly Father who cares for us forever and ever, amen

## Reflection

Many, notably in South America, were was delighted when our present Pope was elected and he took the name Francis, after the saint who spent his life helping the needy. Indeed, even when archbishop, the present Pope lived in a simple apartment and went every week to the poorest parts of his parish. Lets imitate his love of the poor. Hail Mary.

# Sixteenth Sunday of Ordinary Time C

## Introduction

Our readings this week feature godly hospitality. Abraham's hospitality is rewarded by his wife's pregnancy. Martha feeds and cares for Christ and Mary cares more so by listening to him. Lets confess any failure to have open hearts and hospitable homes.

## Homily

We are all proud of our welcoming homes, but are they as open as they used to be? I think of a scene from Alice Taylor's *The Woman Of The House*. Kate returns from England to attend her parents' funeral to find her old home locked. She recalls when her parents were alive That house was always open, neighbors came freely for a chat or cup of tea. Now Martha is the woman of the house. Her door is closed, the door of her heart. God forbid we're like her. Security is vital today, but so is open hearts. Neighborliness is part of our Christian culture; let it be so now too. For no man or woman is an island; we're all in the human endeavor together, regardless of race, color, creed or social status. Hospitality is one way of showing that solidarity. There should be less room for heads in the air, despite our affluence, more room for simple humanity.

Yet community seems to be fading, notably in urban areas. Visiting in town parishes now, I'm shocked at the number of people who don't know their neighbors. Our generation seems to have seen a gradual narrowing of the family, from the extended family to the nuclear family, to the one-parent family, to the closed door family. Is all this due to arrogant affluence? People in big homes with electronic gates shutting neighbors out? Neighborliness does require humility, no "delusions of grandeur" as my mother said. And fading of community spirit is tragic, for when trouble comes we need others.

Our gospel shows us this in action. Martha and Mary were open house people; they received Jesus warmly. Calling to them, hot, dusty, and hungry from teaching and healing, he was washed and fed. Though a reasonably well off family, they have no delusions of grandeur. And with their hospitality went openness to God. Mother Theresa used to say that when we shut ourselves off from God we also close ourselves off from others. The Pope says when the light of faith dims, other lights dim as well. Martha can't be accused of that; but she's a fusser. She thinks like many today that material things are enough. But we don't live on bread alone. Mary sits and listens. As Jesus's neighbor she hears his human fears, for he is on the way to Calvary, and needs comforting.

That's the better part, our open listening humane heart. When I go to hospitals to visit, I see nurses and doctors bustling around efficiently, That's fine. But the more successful ones treat patients as persons. In a strange place, lonely, afraid, its vital to know someone cares and listens. Mary is such a one, she listens to Christ's god-given wisdom, but also to his needs as a troubled human being.

Like Mary, or Kate's parents, open to humanity, Christians need to be open and caring, with homes where both God and people are received and loved. And this applies within the home too. How many women tell me of husbands, he spends his time reading the paper, I can't talk to him. Or husbands say she's great around the house and with the kids, but I feel I'm living with a stranger. In the struggle to live, we mustn't forget the better part; culture, dreaming, God, prayer, wisdom, and above all love. A kiss, a shoulder to cry on, an ear to listen is as vital as food, clothes or shelter. With neighbor, work mates or at home, its our humane love which make us sons and daughters of God. Hard worldliness, isolating ourselves from God and others in material grandeur, makes us hard of heart, empty for this world and the next. But Christ is lord of caring love, both for happiness here below, and forever and ever, amen.

So as God's people, his caring listening presence to others in faith-filled, warm welcoming homes, lets profess our faith.

## Prayers of the Faithful

Lets petition the Father now for what we need as his open-hearted family.

For our Holy Father and the bishops of the church that they may be examples of parental care for the faithful, and lights of faith, humanity and love to the world.

For our civil leaders that the people they serve may be more that just numbers, may they serve the humane and spiritual needs of each citizen by means of caring and godly programs of government.

For youth, may they continue our great tradition of faith-filled and open-hearted hospitable homes, even in the busy world of today.

For ourselves in our homes that like Martha and Mary we may continue to make Christ part of our family and welcome with open generous hearts all those who come into our houses.

For the sick, the aged, the lonely and the poor that through our care and help they may know the love of God.

For the dead that our love and care for them may extend beyond the grave in prayer and remembrance until they may come safely to their heavenly home where we will be reunited one day.

And we ask these prayers through Christ, our loving Lord forever and ever, amen.

## Reflection:

I talked to a person who had worked with Mother Theresa once. She told me that Mother always stressed that as well as practical care her sisters should love the poor patients above all, take time to speak to and listen to them as precious children of God. She said that was God's approach, for he loves us intimately and individually. Lets pray that we'll try at least in some small way to be the same real, kind, and intimate presence to those around us. Hail Mary.

# Seventeenth Sunday Of Ordinary Time C

## Introduction

Scripture today features the greatest of all prayers, the Our Father. Christ only gave us one prayer because it says everything. Lets confess if we pray it mechanically.

## Homily

The Our Father is the gospel. The perfect prayer, it tells what we, his children, should ask of a loving Father God. And we must ask, for due to our free will God can't give is anything unless we ask. Even his kingdom can't come on earth unless we pray for it; that's the mystery of prayer. In it, by calling God Father, we recognize our dependance on him as a child depends on a parent. God is such a parent within our family, the church. For its "our" father we address not "my" father. This is both the personal plea of a child and the prayer of the world. Its because its such a prayer that all our liturgies end with it; as his gathered family we ask for what we need with confidence of a loving parent.

He is in heaven, majestic and holy, but not remote. No one can see God and live, so we don't see him. Yet in Christ he is as close to us as he could be, preparing a place for us in his own home; and sharing even in our worst sufferings. While on earth our role is to hallow his name. Like with our natural father we honor him, not dragging his name in the gutter. And in the family togetherness at the mass, we honor him in a special way. For we're on earth to know, love and serve him, and be with him forever in heaven.

Moreover, our task is to establish his holy kingdom on earth. The first words of Christ's public ministry was that the Kingdom of God had come. He started our Father's kingdom but needs us to build it and pray for its coming every day; for he handed its future over to us to build and keep it safe in the form of the church. It is its earthly form, though it also includes all good people on earth in its universal mystic aspect, for Christ saved all.

And the main way we build his kingdom of love is by doing his will as shown in the Gospel, the charter for God's world of truth, beauty, goodness, peace, and love. But we pray that that will come to pass in the church and be done everywhere on earth, for a heaven on earth. For only by putting his will before that of the world and secular power, can man achieve universal peace, love, truth and graceful living.

And justice. We pray also for our daily bread, for practical needs; the corporal works of mercy, to clothe the naked, to give drink to the thirsty etc. But we pray for vital spiritual bread too: the Eucharist, prayer, holiness, faith, wisdom, truth, grace; all that nurtures our souls unto life here and hereafter. We pray to forgive others as God forgives us freely; for he is a father of mercy. Finally we pray the most important prayer, to be safe from evil.

For here we need our Father's protection most of all, to be safe from all that destroys and oppresses us in body and soul. I shiver when I see youth leaving the church, they're left wide open to evil. We need God's protection against evil as much as life itself, for without it we can't achieve anything of lasting value, any real happiness or freedom. For this world's values of which Satan is lord pass and leave us empty inside, but Our Father is lord of goodness peace, truth and beauty both for this world and forever and ever, amen.

So in the light of the Our Father, our most complete prayer, lets profess our faith.

## Prayers of the Faithful

And lets pray confidently to our Father for our material and spiritual needs now.

For our Holy Father that like the heavenly Father he may give us and the world all the physical and spiritual nourishment needed to build the just Kingdom of God on earth.

For civil leaders that they may be fathers to all the citizens of our country and society in love, justice and integrity.

For our youth that they may love their Father in heaven, and his kingdom the church, and turn at all times to that Father to guide, protect them and lead them to his heavenly home.

For ourselves; in our homes may we be Fathers and Mothers of love to those in our care, imitating our heavenly Father and Mother.

For the sick, the aged, the lonely and the oppressed, that they may turn to their heavenly father at all times for comfort, and through our care know his enduring love.

For the dead that they may come safely to the home prepared for them by their heavenly father. with the help of our prayers.

And we ask all these our prayers of our heavenly father through Christ who intercedes for his people forever and ever, amen.

## Reflection

You may know that play, *All My Sons*, by Arthur Miller. Its about an plane maker who for profit allows some faulty planes to take to the skies during the war. His partner takes the blame, and one of his own sons dies in one of the planes. When his partner's son come back to expose him, he realizes at last the terrible crime he had committed, saying that for the first time he realizes that they were all his sons. He should take responsibility for all those killed due to his greed. All people are God's sons and we have to face his judgment if we wrong any of them. Lets pray that we will respect all people on earth as the saved and sacred children of God. Hail Mary

# Eighteenth Sunday of Ordinary Time C

## Introduction

"Vanity of vanities all is vanity". Wisdom says undue toil for this world's goods is foolishness. Paul also says to set our thoughts on heavenly things. And Christ says wealth will be useless when our soul is required of us. Lets confess sins of vain greed in our life.

## Homily

Once I bought a site for a house. Marking it for the fencer, I made sure I got every inch I was entitled to. Then the fencer sobered me by saying: "a few feet of earth is all we'll have in the end". He was teaching this Sunday's lesson, the foolishness of making a God of worldly possessions. Its a lesson important for today, when many unduly focus on fame and riches. Look how popular the series: "The Money Game" is. We've certainly bought into the dream whereby personal success is measured by our bank balance.

A luxury home, money in the bank and a new 4-by-4 jeep seemed the main measure of success during the boom. Often with this went binges on drugs, drink and casual sex. There's nothing wrong of course with enjoying ourselves, God gave us the world's good things to be enjoyed. Nor am I condemning a good standard of living, its what all in the world should have; the Pharisees called Christ a glutton and a wine-drinker. Its the way riches can take us over, make us hard of heart, that's dangerous.

That is, we can enjoy life, but also have our priorities right. Christ says that it profits a man or woman little if they gain the whole world but suffer the loss of their souls: "Fool! This very night the demand will be made for your soul, and this hoard of your's, whose will it be then" (Lk.

12:20-21, JB). In effect, once we have enough let's not become slaves of money-grubbing, neglecting more important things such as service of God and our family. This world is short-lived, and at death, and the end of time, its our souls that will be required of us, and we may have nothing to offer if we've sold it for passing dust. Life is short but the next one's forever, so its wise to build treasure in heaven. We carry nothing with us into the grave except our faith and the good we have done in life, the love we have shown. Like the man who built huge barns in the gospel, storing far more than he needed, we can only eat three meals a day or sleep in one bed at night.

People in every age fail to see this truth; the need for security becomes a passion of never enough. They focus on material wealth, greed and pleasure to the exclusion of God, others and more important things in life such as love and humanity; Scrooge is a good example. They sell their immortal souls like Judas for the world's thirty pieces of silver. They make money their God and greed their faith.

Our readings should challenge such futile philosophy. "Fool", the gospel says, "this night your soul may be required of you". We may be walking across the road and be knocked down, or suddenly get terminal cancer. What use will big cars and houses be then. We must have the wisdom to both enjoy life, and see, as my mother used to say, that we haven't here a lasting city. Someone said to me during the week, no removal van follows the coffin. On the last day Christ will ask about our charity, not our bank balance.

But even for our happiness is this world, making material things our all, is foolish. Wise couples soon find out that love is more important to their children than costly toys. Spending time with their children is more important than working day and night to give them Action Man. Nourishing their faith by practice is more important that sleeping in on Sunday because we're too tired from vain toil. That's why Jesus begs us to make ourself rich in the sight of God and all else will follow. These riches deepen our spiritual life, give wisdom and depth to our lives; and fill the void of emptiness and loneliness within. And when the things of this world fade to dust, they give lasting peace and happiness with the Lord forever and ever, amen.

So as God's people, enjoying life's good things but seeking also the treasures that will never decay, lets profess our faith.


## *Prayers of the Faithful*

And as the people of God lets pray for the riches of his kingdom.

For the Pope, while seeking a world where no one goes hungry, may he may also remind us that man doesn't live on bread alone.

For civil leaders that while fostering the material welfare of the people, they may also continue to leave the church free to cater for people's even more vital spiritual needs.

For youth that they may not be so caught up in the things of this world so as to neglect what's really important, love, faith, goodness and the salvation of their souls.

For ourselves in our home, community and country that we may not let the vanity of the world close us off from God and others behind electronic gates.

For the sick that their faith may enable them to bear all suffering and turn it into riches like Christ by offering it up for their own salvation and that of the whole world.

For the dead that they may come to the more lasting riches of heaven with the help of our powerful community prayers.

And we ask all these prayers through Christ who intercedes for us forever before the Father, amen.

## Reflection

"Vanity of Vanities and all is vanity", is one of the catch phrases from the Bible. It sums up a lot of our modern world. We're bombarded every day on TV with ads for cosmetics, shampoos, hair sprays. Hey presto, we're told, these will transform us into beautiful people. We should care for outward appearance, but not to the point of obsession, for real beauty is within. A fine appearance is important to attract, but it will not last if it isn't backed up by more lasting humane qualities. Lets seek more than empty vanity then and see and find lasting beauty in God, its source. Hail Mary

# Nineteenth Sunday of Ordinary Time C

## Introduction

Scripture this Sunday is a mixture of hope and warning. Christ says not be be afraid; we're part of his kingdom. Yet on the other hand he warns us not to be complacent, the Son of Man will come in Judgement. To be ready for his coming we must stay spiritually awake. Lets confess any temptations to sleep the sleep of the damned.

## Homily

Light is vital to us humans. Even our stone-age ancestors knew this. At Newgrange, at the heart of winter, the 21st of December, they'd a system rigged up so that the light came in and flooded the graves of the dead. It was a sign of hope for the new year, of the return of light-filled summer, a sign to those lost in death's darkness. Natural light signified spiritual light for the dead.

From now on days get shorter. There is no endless summer, darkness threatens to blot out the light, and unrelieved darkness is unthinkable. In the dark we're afraid, sensing a link with evil. No one wants to live in dark forever. When there is an electricity blackout we panic. Nowadays houses and driveways are radically lit up, as if to fend off all darkness.

Our Gospel today is about keeping God's light blazing in our souls so that we'll live in light forever. We're told not to let our light go out, for the master may come at any time to require our soul of us. God forbid that any of us should lapse into a pagan darkness without Christ, though that's an increasing risk today. Its easier now to let the lamp of faith and practice go out, to lapse into darkness, and so be excluded by the master from the eternal banquet. In that sense light has special meaning in Christian life. Christ is seen as the world's light. When we're baptized, we get a candle lit from the paschal candle. We're told to keep that light burning, until we go out with the saints to meet Christ at last.

But there is always the temptation to go asleep spiritually, to let that light go out, to forget to nourish the soul in life's hustle and bustle. We've no time for God, prayer, or the sacraments as we rush around frantically making money and enjoying ourselves, as if this life was forever. So the light of salvation in us can flicker and grow dim. There is even the danger that, through lack of the oil of practice and good works, it may go out altogether, quenched by the distractions and secularist trends of the modern world. So that when the lord comes at the end of time he wont recognize us. Our relationship with him will have gone out like the lamps of the watchers who fell asleep while waiting for their master to return from the wedding feast.

Knowing this danger, Jesus tells disciples to stand ready, for the Son of Man may come at any time. That's true of death or on the last day. We know not the day nor the hour and we don't want to share the fate of the unfaithful, though that's easier now when fewer people are faithful in carrying out their religious duties. Its easy to fall back into the sleep of spiritual death which Christ labored and died to deliver us from, the darkness of sin, the soul sickness of sad indifference. Yet its urgent that we don't do so. For in today's gospel were told that God at any time may require our soul. Its vital for us Christians not to let the light we received go out, but like the wise saints to be ready when Christ comes to lead the just into the banquet of eternal life. For all else fades and leaves us empty at last, but Christ is lord of light, truth, goodness, and happiness forever and ever, amen.

So as God's servants, keeping the light of faith alive through all the phases of life's night watch, lets profess our faith.

## Prayers of the Faithful

And as God's faithful servants lets pray for all we need.

For our Holy Father that his faith and energy may not fail him but that he may continue to lead all people to Christ's dawning light amid the difficult night watches of the modern world.

For civil leaders that they may not promote a lapse into pagan darkness, but help the church in its mission of saving light.

For our young people that they may keep the light of faith burning brightly in their hearts within his holy church, and so be ready to go out to meet him with all the saints when he comes, their souls aglow with the saving light of their eternal Lord.

For ourselves in our work places, communities, and homes that we may keep the light of Christ alive and pass it on to our children for their enduring welfare, the salvation of their eternal souls.

For the sick, the aged, the lonely and the poor, through our caring ministry God's light may shine in their lives.

For the dead that they may come into the eternal light of heaven.

We ask all these prayers through Christ, the light of the world. Amen.

## Reflection

The apostle's failure to watch with Christ is a warning for us. In Gethsemane when Christ wanted their support they slept. Three times he came to them for help and found them asleep. Lets not be so worn out by life's cares so as to neglect the Lord's service. Lets rise faithfully each Sunday to come, listen to his word, and receive his body. For the Eucharist is our life; Christ say he who eats his flesh and drinks his blood has eternal life and he will raise him up on the last day. Imagine that, we're already part of eternal life through regular Sunday Eucharist, sure to flower into glory at last. This banquet of light prepares us for the final banquet. Lets ask Mary to keep as part of a Eucharistic faithful walking in light to the end of time. Hail Mary

# Twentieth Sunday of Ordinary Time C

## Introduction

Scripture this Sunday warns that if we serve God we'll experience attack from the world. The prophet Jeremiah was thrown in the well; Christ was crucified for witnessing to God. Similarly, we must be prepared to suffer even attack from those in our own household for our beliefs. Lets confess any way in which we apologize for being Christian.

## Homily

During the Second world war, people rejoiced when the allies won the victory in Europe. For if Hitler had triumphed we cannot even imagine what our world would be like now. Though we deplore war, sometimes people have to fight for what is right. And its in that sense that we have Christ's strange words in today's gospel (strange for the whole trust of the gospel is that Christians should be peacemakers): "Do you suppose that I am here to bring peace on earth? No, I tell you, but rather division" (Lk. 12:51-52, JB). This seems a hard saying, yet it gets to the heart of faith. Christ is not talking of division in the sense of actual physical conflict, but rather in terms of the spiritual conflict between good and evil, belief and unbelief. If we follow him, he says, it may lead to division, even sometimes within our own family. But we must continue to do what's right all the same.

This interpretation is reinforced by the first reading (usually there is a close link between the first reading and the Gospel), where Jeremiah continued his fiery preaching though it led him into a major clash with the authorities, even to the extent of him being thrown into a well. What both reading say is that serving God always involves suffering, but, as Paul says in the second reading, we must keep on running the race through the pain, to gain the prize. For the war between good and evil takes no prisoners.

In these days of indifference, even opposition, to Christian faith, Christ's words ring a bell. There are always fresh dangers in being his followers, so we need to be united in the great struggle. For, as in Jeremiah or Christ's day, people whose evil are exposed won't tolerate our witness. They may even behave aggressively. A holy person said to me recently that the day may be coming when people will be persecuted, even killed, for the faith again, at home. Jesus makes no secret of the fact that bearers of God's Word may face rejection even from their own. But he says this to encourage us to remain faithful.

And not only faithful but proudly so. For the main obstacle to heroic faith is fear of standing out. This can hinder us from being the saints we want to be. I'm sure all of us can think of situations in our life when fear of being ridiculed or bullied prevented us from doing what we knew to be right. The Germans prosecuted for the Holocaust had that defense; they filled Hitler's gas chambers out of fear of superiors. But the war tribunal said that isn't a good defense. There's a higher law we must obey at whatever risk.

I think being Christian today means making a similar choice for God no matter what divisions it lands us in. Maybe in the company we keep, we'll lose friends if we insist on going to mass. Maybe we'll lose pals if we refuse to take part in idle gossip that drags others through the mud. Maybe we dare not say no to drink or drug culture. But remember for evil to triumph all that's needed is for good people to remain silent. Yeats says in one of his poems that in our age the best lack all conviction, while the worst are full of passionate intensity. Its easy to go with the tide. The smirks and sneers of unbelievers can con us into abandoning or watering down our witness. But Christ came so that the fire of God's salvation would burn away all evil. We can only help him in this work if we're confident and fearless in his service, remembering his words that he is with us always, even to the end of the world. In that surety lets stand up and be counted. So that when we've completed our earthly journey, he'll wont disown us, but claim us as one of his own before the father forever and ever, amen.

So as God's own, fighting the good fight through every suffering and opposition, let's profess our faith.

## Prayers of the Faithful

And as God's people lets pray for our and the world's peace.

For our Holy Father and the leaders of the church throughout the world that they may not be afraid to witness to God and what's right regardless of the consequences.

For civil leaders that they may not make it more difficult for the church to witness to the Lord and what's right.

For our youth that they may be prepared to stand up for Christ, as they promised at Confirmation, to be strong and perfect Christians, peaceful spiritual soldiers for Christ.

For ourselves that in our homes and work places, we may pass on the faith courageously, even in the face of opposition, ridicule and apostasy from some of our own.

For the sick, that through our care and love they may know the love of God in their lives and find healing and comfort.

For the dying, that through our great continuing charitable prayers on their behalf they may be freed from darkness and reach the light of Christ forever in heaven.

And we ask all these our prayers through Christ who suffered the cross for what was right and to set us free to do the same, amen.

## Reflection

You may have seen that film *The Agony And The Ecstasy* about Michelangelo. He spent endless hours on his back above the Sistine Chapel painting the famous frescoes, paint dripping on his face, aching with pain and constant criticism from enemies. Yet the result is stunning. It was restored recently and the brilliant colors shone like gems. Nothing great is ever achieved without suffering, and keeping the faith is a great struggle of art. But its worth it in the final ecstasy of union with God and the difference we'll have made by our lives. Lets pray we'll have the courage to persevere to the end. Hail Mary.

# Twenty-First Sunday of Ordinary Time C

## Introduction

Indifference to the salvation of one's soul is an evil prevalent in every age. Many wrap themselves up in the world, and little consider their larger purpose and destiny after death. The Gospel this Sunday warns us not to fall into that trap. Lets confess any ways we neglect the work of saving our soul, amid the hustle and bustle of modern life.

## Homily

"Many are called but few chosen". When I was young we'd say: "many are cold but few are frozen". The few who are frozen, doing little to fan the flame of God within, seem to have swelled today. Falling mass attendance, the rise of militant secularism, attacks on the church, the number of lapsed Catholics or other Christians rising. All point to a crisis among the redeemed. Hence the urgency of the question posed in our Gospel: "will there be only a few saved?". Jesus's answer is scant comfort for free-wheeling liberals: "try your best to enter by the narrow door" (Lk. 13:24, JB).

Here he identifies a key cause of falling from grace, affluent worldliness. For the narrow gate was for the poor in Jerusalem, the wider gate was for the rich. He might well be criticizing our nation, where as we get richer our moral gates seem to get wider and faith weaker. God forbid he'll say to our generation: "I do not know where you come from, away from me, all you wicked men!" (Lk. 13:27, JB). Yet the hopeful word in the Gospel is "try"; Christ knows we're weak, the least effort on our part is completed by his grace.

But the danger is that affluence breeds total hardness of heart. Visiting a hospital recently I tended to agreed with a patient who thought we'd gone mad with money, drink, cars, self. Our ancestors entered by the poor gate, yet were more chosen and faithful. But there's nothing new about the link between affluence and godlessness. Jesus had to warn the Pharisees, living in towers of arrogant wealth and power, that the poor that they looked down on, would enter the kingdom of heaven before them. They risked being cast out into dark after death, where there is "weeping and grinding of teeth" (Lk. 13:28, JB).

We dare not say rightly so, or be complacent; the warning is also addressed to us. The despised of the world may enter heaven before us too. We may wonder why Christ was so explicit, but it was out of love that he gave this admonition. He wants all to be saved, especially those at risk, those who, through greedy hardness of heart, risk exclusion from paradise. He warns that thieves and prostitutes may go into heaven before such people.

This warning holds good for today when many of our affluent generation, blinded by the world, think they don't need God anymore. But this Gospel is a warning not just to the arrogant rich, but a reminder to all that we shouldn't presume on heaven. As St. Paul says we must work out our salvation in fear and trembling. Christians are the chosen, but if much is given, much will be required. The banquet of the body of Christ is laid before us every Sunday, but are we too busy to come. Third-world poor flock to the church, while in "Christian" Europe many casually walk away from that heritage, and flaunt the fact.

True, the recent recession brought many down to earth. Christ's words should bring us to our senses spiritually, especially his warning that the last will be first and the first last. We cannot despise God, his church, and follow the world's corrupt ways, and yet presume on heaven. God is merciful but people now think that heaven is our choice; if we reject God in life, we may also do so at death. The way to ensure against that is to be faithful throughout life, keeping the white garment of our Baptism on, as we promised also at Confirmation. So that when Christ comes we'll go out gladly to meet him with all the saints. Mother Theresa says success in life is in being faithful. For the godless values of this world fade to dust at last leaving us empty; but Christ is lord of love, truth, and salvation for our happiness on earth, and forever and ever, amen.

So as God's own, staying faithful to him, despite the worldly pride of riches, and the evil one's wiles, let's profess our faith.

## Prayers of the faithful

For our Holy Father, may he continue to remind people to enter in by the narrow gate of inner life, not the wide one of outward spiritual death.

For civil leaders that they may serve the spiritual as well as the physical and social needs of all.

For our youth, that, amid the hustle and bustle of life, they may find time to also nourish their souls unto eternal life, for all else passes all to soon.

For ourselves, that in our homes and work places we may be lights of faith to our children and all those we meet.

For the sick, the old the lonely and the oppressed that they may remember that they are the chosen of God, and through our love experience his love in their lives.

For the dead, that they may come to the salvation promised by the help of our prayers, and we pray especially for.

And we ask all these through Christ who is infinitely merciful and strives to brings all to the salvation his death and resurrection made possible, amen.

## Reflection

The story of Macbeth, in Shakespeare, is a story of the mystery of damnation. Macbeth begins as a warrior hero who fights to save his country. Then pride and ambition takes him over and he kills his king to gain a bloody throne. Others murders follow and he says, at one point, that he is in blood, and its easier to continue in his bloody path than to turn back. Lets not let sin pile up on us like that until we cannot even hope for redemption, and lets ask mother Mary to help us turn from any path that is leading us astray, and into the grasp of the evil one. Hail Mary.

# Twenty-Second Sunday
# in Ordinary Time C

## Introduction

Our scripture this week is about Humility. The first reading says the greater we are the humbler we should be. For as Christ says in the Gospel, he who humbles himself will be exalted. Lets confess any ways we let false pride and arrogance rule our lives.

## Homily

Watching a TV program the other night, I was struck by what someone said, that the really good person doesn't draw attention to himself or herself; good people are usually surprised to be described as such. For example when I was young we'd an aunt, who was the soul of goodness. Always saying her beads and lavishing kindness on us – sweets for us every Sunday after mass. And it was the same with everyone, she couldn't do enough for them, from the wandering beggar, to the laborer who came to help out with the harvest, to the priest coming for the "stations". All were treated with equal kindness, yet if she heard us calling her a saint, she would get cross, "ah stop that nonsense". This is a living example of Christ's teaching in our Gospel that we should try to serve all humbly, without drawing attention to ourselves. This challenges us all. For most of us are in service jobs of some kind. Let's do these with Christian love and humility.

By contrast, "he's a legend in his own mind", people sometimes say ironically of the proud man. That's how Christ saw the haughty Pharisees. They were supposed to be simple religious pastors, but sought top places and being fawning on. More seriously, they only invited the rich and powerful to their banquets. We say bully for the Lord in exposing them as hypocrites. But that's a temptation we can all succumb to, self-centered ambition and pride. The Devil's fall began with a refusal to serve; he sought to exalt himself even to the extent of trying to subvert God. He led Adam and Eve into the same sin of pride.

Since the fall this is man's most persistent fault, his most incurable soul illness. As the first reading says, "there is no cure for the proud mans malady, for an evil growth has taken root in him" (Eccles. 3:17-20). Yet the cure is simple, as scripture says, the greater we are, the more humble we should be; giving the glory to our maker, not ourselves.

Lets pray to be such unpretentious servants of God and others; for that's the way we will be raised up to happiness in both this world and the next; for the arrogant man who lords it over lesser morals is loved by no one. And he certainly won't have the top place in the banquet of eternal life. So humility is good for us in every way, and in this too our example is Christ who became Lord of all through the humble self-emptying of the cross. He raised up a world fallen through pride, and bathed it in the true glory in God.

And that is the way we too will be raised up, like Mary who was exalted due to her humble self-knowledge. Like her, we should live out our Christian role of humble self-giving love and care in the ordinary duties of life. This means giving that bit extra in worshiping God and caring for the vulnerable. Then our lives will have made a difference on earth and we'll be storing up heavenly reward. That's our vocation, to make a difference by the simple humble kindness of our lives.

Then we will not only be happy in this life, and spread happiness around us, but we will also be raised up to the arms of God our Father forever. Indeed, the humbler our service is, the higher our throne. For the values of a hard self-serving world fade to ashes at last and leave us in the lowest place, even in hell, like Satan. But Christ, humble servant on the cross is lord of love, goodness, happiness, peace and beauty for this world and forever and ever, amen.

So as God's own, called to love humbly without prejudice, lets profess our faith.

## *Prayer of the faithful*

And as God's humble servants we bow and ask him for all that we need.

For Our Holy Father and all leaders of the churches, that they may not exalt themselves but lead the flock humbly in the truth, as servants of the servants of God.

For leaders and authorities in our society that they may carry out their roles with integrity, humility and fairness towards all, especially the poor.

For our youth, that they may put all their energies into humble service of God and others, so as to be exalted beyond measure forever at God's right hand, like Christ.

For ourselves that in our homes and vocations we may carry out our duties with integral and selfless service of God and those in our care, especially our children.

Knowing our need for God, we now pray in silence for our own special intentions.

For the weak, the vulnerable and the sick in our society that through our humble care they may experience the love of God.

For the dead, especially those who have died recently.

Heavenly Father we offer these prayers through the humble Christ, who reversed the sin of Adam and who lives and reigns with you and the Holy Spirit forever, amen.

## Reflection

A good example of someone who humbled himself and was exalted is John Paul 11. In early life he was a goalkeeper for a small soccer team, then he tried his hand as a starving actor. Finally he broke stones in a quarry for a living. It was down there among the people that he learned the wisdom that made him a great Pope. When he led the frail underground church under fascism and communism in Poland he was always with the people, and had innumerable Jewish as well as Christian friends. Likewise, we should never lose touch with the earth, for its the dust we'll return to. Let's earn a high throne by our humble love and faith, and ask the help of a humble village girl, who became the Mother of God, in this. Hail Mary

# Twenty-Third Sunday of Ordinary Time C.

## Introduction

"Anyone who does not carry his cross and come after me cannot be my disciple" (Lk. 14:27, JB). Scripture asks us to bear unavoidable crosses for Christ and the world's salvation, especially those that stem from keeping the faith, despite opposition, and giving to the poor. Lets confess ways worldliness hinder us from being heroic cross carriers.

## Homily

You may have heard of Padre Pio, the Italian mystic who is said to have borne the wounds of Christ in his body. We're not required to believe such things. But many feasts and scriptures remind us of the wisdom of the cross in Christian life. As Christ says in the Gospel: "anyone who does not carry his cross and come after me cannot be my disciple" At this time we've the feasts of the Sorrows of Mary, the Triumph of the Cross, and Padre Pio. I've no particular devotion to him, and some object to him being made a saint, saying he was a pious fraud. But in doing so they show that they haven't read the Gospel or taken to heart Christ's words that I quoted. For Pio's whole life centered on suffering with Christ for the world's salvation; that why he's a saint, not dubious wonders or stigmatas.

Indeed, as one person said, Padre Pio suffered during each holy mass as much as any person could suffer in a day. For from his youth he was dogged with ill-health; it almost prevented him from being ordained. But he offered up this suffering and turned it to gold. That and his intense love of the Eucharist, and the sacrament of reconciliation, were his paths to sainthood. His devout mass would last two hours. Thousands flocked to be present at it, and millions came to a confessional where he often spent seven hours a day despite his ill health. In all this he made a vital Christian point. Suffering is part of the human condition but if unavoidable, its not necessarily negative. Unavoidable suffering joined to Christ's can enrich the world immeasurably in a mysterious way. Everything medically possible was done for Padre Pio, as it should be, pain in itself is an evil and should be alleviated; but after everything is done if pain remains, it can be transcended.

Biographers wrote of Pio, that he lived in all its depth his mission of a crucified one with Christ, a martyr of the church who intercedes on behalf of all the faithful before the throne of God. Lets ask him to intercede for us and for people in particular who spurn the Lord's arms and his cross of selfless love. Let that prayer be strengthened by our unavoidable sufferings, part of the human condition, small or great, offered up with Christ's.

Like Padre Pio lets do so especially at the mass, which is the saving power of Christ's cross made present for us, with all its merits. As Pio says continually in his journals, we can unite our sufferings to Christ's, and so add to the saving efficacy of this great sacrament in some mysterious way. This is very scriptural. Paul says the same, that he makes up in his body's sufferings with Christ, to help him save the world.

The surest sign of human nobility is the capacity to endure suffering, even death, for the loved one. Christ showed that total love on the cross to the last drop of blood. So did Padre Pio at each mass. He used to say that suffering was his daily bread. That's why he's a great saint, not any supposed miracles he did, or his supposed capacity for bilocation. May we too appreciate how much Christ suffered for us and not be afraid to carry our cross with him.

Of course this does not mean that we should seek suffering. But the world provides plenty, and its unavoidable suffering can have a negative or positive effect. It can make us bitter, or deepen our soul. As the poet Keats says, its life's sufferings that makes this world a vale of soul-making. Let us ask for the grace to be Gods light to the world in suffering love, purifying our souls in the crucible of life, fit for glory. For the vain pride and pleasures of this world fade to dust at last, but the wisdom that lasts is that of suffering love and service of God and others like Christ, who was Lord of love, peace and deep happiness, even in pain, both for this world and forever and ever, amen.

So praying for ourselves and dear ones, that all may come to the Lord and find riches even in life's inevitable sufferings unto death in him, lets profess our faith.

## *Prayers of the faithful*

As the people of God lets pray for the things that we need.

For church leaders throughout the world that they may be brave, and preach Christ crucified, the infinite value of the cross of Christ, for the salvation of the world.

For youth, may they not be afraid to suffer in the heroic service of Christ and others, especially the poor and vulnerable.

For our civil leaders that they may rule us with justice, integrity, and with special concern for those in need.

For ourselves and the intentions that are in our hearts lets pray silently, especially for the grace and strength to carry our unavoidable crosses in following Our Lord.

For the sick in need of mental or spiritual healing that they may find it through prayer and our help.

For the dead, that their trials and sufferings over, they may come to heavenly happiness with the help of our prayers.

And we ask all these prayers through Christ whose wounds intercede for us forever before the Father in heaven, amen.

## Reflection

We know the Lourdes story of Bernadette. What most don't know about is the painful leg cancer she bore in later life; doctors did all they could but it was incurable. Confined to bed, she said she was as happy on her bed of pain with a crucifix as a queen on her throne. Lets pray for Christian fortitude faced with unavoidable suffering. Hail Mary

# Twenty-Fourth Sunday of Ordinary Time C

## Introduction

Scripture this week features mercy and forgiveness. In the first reading Moses prays for mercy for the people. And in the Gospel a kindly father, an image of God, readily forgives the prodigal son. Lets confess ways we may fail to forgive those who hurt us.

## Homily

One of the most inspiring films of recent times was *Schindler's List*. He saved thousands from the gas chambers. Similarly inspiring was the work of the Irish priest, Fr.O'Flaherty. Posted in the Vatican during the war, he smuggled 1000s of POWS and Jews out of Rome, using a network of helpers, under the noses of the occupiers. Though some helpers were captured, killed or tortured and he faced at least one assassination attempt, he continued the work. Why? When the Pope asks him this, he said that he knew nothing of politics, he was just a simple priest, who, when he saw people in need, just had to help them. In our mercy, he said, we must include all, for "God has no nation", his motto. Basically, he reflected Christ's boundless mercy, for "Happy the merciful, they shall have mercy shown them" (Mt. 5:7, JB), he even extended mercy to the enemy.

In the true film of his work, *The Scarlet And The Black*, at the war's end as Rome was about to fall, O'Flaherty is asked by the Nazi commander of the city to smuggle out his wife and child. O'Flaherty pointed out that the commander had tortured and killed the priest's friends and ruled Rome without mercy, yet now he expected mercy for himself. The commander replied that O'Flaherty was like all the rest of religious people, hypocrites, who preach universal mercy but do the opposite. The Nazi goes on to say that he represents the new Europe of power ethics without God or his moral code, which panders to the weak; he sees the future as rule without mercy by secular supermen.

But later, captured by the resistance, this commander, to his astonishment, is asked how he managed to smuggle his wife and children out of Rome. He realizes that O'Flaherty had been non-discriminatory in his mercy. He had got the commander's family out. Moreover, during the Nazi's stay in prison for war crimes the only one to visit him was O'Flaherty. He was so impressed by this forgiving kindness, he converted to Catholicism.

Christ asks us to be like that priest, loving and showing mercy even to our worst enemy. Like the father who receives the prodigal with open arms, our hearts must have compassion for all, even those who hurt us deeply. Sadly, we're more often like the older son. We judge others from hard self-righteous hearts, and shape God in that merciless image, like the revenge cult in modern films. But not just secularists, but also religious err in this regard. Jesus condemned the Pharisees who would stone the woman caught in adultery. Since we need mercy so much ourselves, we should extend it to others.

Yet our society relentlessly hounds errant politicians or clerics. Justice is seldom tempered with the mercy that Shakespeare commends; he says the quality of mercy is not strained, it honors both the giver and the receiver. We gain more from mercy than we give. By it, we free our heart from the bitterness and resentment; so our mercy becomes like a healing balm, that also heals our own souls.

That's why, though the younger son wastes his property on orgies and loose women, the father has none of the elder son's narrow jealousy, envy and self-righteous anger. Rather than celebrate his brother's safe return by merciful forgiveness, the eldest, like many strict religious, condemns him in a harsh unyielding way. But that is not God's way; his mercy is boundless. Lets have similar open hearts towards those we're tempted to cast out. Let's have Christ's forgiving heart on the cross. For this world's merciless spirit of which Satan is lord destroys all that's soft and humane in us. leaving us with hard hearts, desolate on the shore of eternity. But Christ's boundless love, goodness, and mercy leads to inner freedom and our happiness both for here below, and forever and ever, amen.

So God's own, living with generous, loving, forgiving and open merciful hearts like the Father in the gospel, lets profess our faith.

## Prayers of the Faithful

And as the people of God lets pray for the things we need.

For our Holy Father, that with the bishops of the church he may be an example of humble loving mercy and forgiveness to the world.

For civil leaders, may their jails temper justice with mercy and rehabilitation.

For our youth, may they stay safe in Christ and his church's joyful embrace.

For our homes, that divisions may be healed and black sheep welcomed home.

For the sick and those who need our special care, that through our love they may know God's love and healing in their lives.

For the dead that they may receive mercy and forgiveness for their sins in this world, and come to happiness in the arms of the Father, with the help of our prayers.

And we ask all these things through Christ, the only lord of all forgiving love and mercy forever and ever, amen.

## *Reflection:*

Shakespeare's play, *The Merchant Of Venice*, features mercy as one of its main themes. Shylock, the money lender, demands a pound of flesh as a payment, should his enemy fail to pay him the money he owes. Others try to persuade him to forget this harsh penalty, when the man cannot pay, but he is unrelenting. The people are shocked at this barbaric lack of mercy, and invoke a clause that sees the money lender's hardness of heart rebound on his own head. But the point made, is very much that of our gospel, that mercy and compassion is part of our humanity, and lack of it turns us into virtual inhuman monsters. Lets not fall into that trap of letting hatred, or revenge, or getting back at others, destroy our humanity and peace of mind, and lets ask Mary to give us Christ's compassion for all, and his gentle heart, which forgave even those who crucified him. Hail Mary.

# Twenty-Fifth Sunday of
# Ordinary Time C

## Introduction

The prophet Amos, in our first reading, condemns wealthy swindlers who prey on the poor. This links with the Gospel words, "you cannot be the slave both of God and money" (Lk. 16:13, JB). Lets confess ways we let lust for money unduly rule our lives.

## Homily

The story of the rich young man in the Bible is a salutary one. He came to Christ looking to be perfect. Christ tells him to keep the basic commandments, to love God and others. The young man says he has kept this commandment from his youth but wants more. So Christ said that if he wants to be truly perfect, he should give his wealth to the poor and follow him. The young man went away sad, for he had much riches.

In effect, these had more of a hold on him than God; he couldn't make the step that would set him free. An opposite story is that of St. Francis. Son of a rich merchant, in youth he lived it up. But suddenly God entered his life and he saw how empty his affluent lifestyle was. He gave away riches, and even clothes from his father's shop, to feed and clothe the poor. One Sunday in church his father asked him to return these. Francis took off his clothes, gave them to his father and walked naked from the church. He wore a rough robe, begged from the rich to help the poor, and lived a holy life. Yet he was joined by 10,000 rich young men who found joy in Christian poverty in order to serve humanity.

With Francis, free from slavery to possessions, they worked for a truer, juster world and church. For in his day even bishops served wealth and grand buildings rather than God's flock. For the temptation to serve power and wealth alone, is one that those in the church also fail. Indeed, its perhaps the key temptation each of us face; to slavishly serve gods of self, money, pleasure, fame and power, rather than the true God and humanity.

Even Christ resisted this lure in the desert, knowing the first commandment is the first for this reason, that so many put the idol of money before the true God; Judas even sold Christ for thirty pieces of silver. That selling of even our souls for money continues in every age. Christ's warning is just as apt for today, when individuals and faceless global companies shaft the environment, and the poor, for higher profit margins.

In a money-worshiping world our call is to be counterwitnesses, pointing souls to the riches of faith and sharing of earth's resources. Of course money isn't evil as such, a good standard of living and prosperity is God's will. But making riches one's whole focus, leaving no room for the things of the soul or humanity, is deadly. Its Satan promising to give all the world's riches to Christ if he's bow down and worship him. Making wealth and power into ruthless gods that trample on the true God and his people, is the same as worshiping Satan. Christ chose instead the cross of humble service of God and humanity.

To be truly Christians we must do the same. But strong faith is needed to do this now; economics is the new fetish. A politician interviewed recently about cutbacks was asked about how this might affect the poor, and he replied that helping the poor is OK but it doesn't make for good economics. Surely economics are for people not people for economics? That big money serves itself, is the perennial truth. Francis abandoned such folly, and our new Pope took his name and has a similar love of the poor. Both knew that hard money values fade to ashes at last, leaving us empty inside. But to Christ, a poor vagrant preacher, belongs the kingdom, the power and the glory forever and ever, amen.

So as God's people, avoiding the trap of making money our all, and dedicating ourselves to God and charitable sharing with the poor, we profess our faith.

## Prayers of the Faithful

And as the people of God lets pray for the things that we need.

For the Pope and bishops of the church; like Francis, may they convince people to share earth's resources, and lift up the poor.

For civil leaders, may they not put money and economic doctrine before the care of their citizens, especially those most in need.

For our youth, that like those young people who flocked to Francis, tired of the greedy godlessness of the age, they may serve God and the poor with generous hearts.

For ourselves, that we may not put money-making before our families, but give them our love and time, so that their nurture may not be neglected in any way.

For the sick, aged, lonely and poverty stricken; like Christ and Francis, may we find time for them, and build a just world.

For the dead, all their money and possessions of no more use in the grave, they may find a fuller life with God by the help of our prayers, a great work of charity.

And we ask all these prayers through Christ who'd nowhere to lay his head, amen.

## Reflection:

Avoiding excessive greed, also leaves us free to appreciate nature. St.Francis not only spurned riches, but also rediscovered nature's joys. He is usually depicted with a bird on his shoulder. Lets find time from the scrabble for riches for our children and feeling the good earth under our feet, lest, as the poet Wordworth says, "getting and spending", we "lay waste our powers". Lets ask Mary to help us find time for the things of the soul, and to build up our environment for our children's good and future, rather than continue to destroy nature to serve our greed. Hail Mary

# Twenty-Sixth Sunday in Ordinary Time C

## Introduction

This Sunday continues the theme of arrogant wealth as an enemy of godliness. Amos condemns the lavish sprawlers who are indifferent to the poor, and Christ's tale of Dives and Lazarus has the same message. Lets confess ways we succumb to that trap.

## Homily

Last week's gospel questions whether we can serve God and money. Today's gospel story of the Dives brothers carries the debate further. Let me tell a story that adds a modern perspective on this. A man parked a new Mercedes in a city. When he came back he found a poor boy examining it enviously. The boy asked if it was the man's car, said it was beautiful, and asked how much it cost. "To be honest I don't know", the man said, "I got it from my brother". "You mean your brother gave it to you and it didn't cost a penny", the boy said. "I wish that I …" The man was sure the boy would say, "I wish I'd a brother like that". But he said, "I wish I could **be** a brother like that". The man concluded: "There was I with a new Mercedes and there was the boy in rags. Yet he'd more love in his heart than I". Mother Theresa also says that we get more from the poor than we give.

In an increasingly affluent world, more and more risk becoming less like that boy and more like the Dives brothers, too busy planning the next big booze-up to even see the needy at their gate. Only now its an electronic gate, built to exclude the riff raff. Even when Lazarus died and was taken away like a piece of refuse, it made no difference to the Dives. Lets enjoy affluence, there's no virtue in poverty, but beware lest it make us hard of heart. Mother Theresa said that the terrible evil in the world today is lack of love - the indifference towards one's neighbor which is so widespread, especially in big cities.

A story she tells makes the point well. Once in Bombay there was a big conference on poverty. Outside the door where hundreds of delegates were "solving" the hunger problem, she found a dying man. She took him to her home for the dying. He died of hunger while the people inside were talking about how in fifteen years we'd have so much food, so much of this, so much of that. The lesson's clear. Sending a few pounds to Sudan is good, but it won't help the old person next door, dying of loneliness.

Charity at a distance is easy. Our western world salves its conscience with occasional aid to poor nations, but in reality we bleed them dry, with debt repayments to our banks. But that's the way of the world; the rich get richer and the poor poorer. I'm sure the Dives brothers solved all the world's problems over their lavish meals, while their brother at the gate wanted just crumbs to stay alive.

That is, we must walk the walk as well as talk the talk: help the single mother next door who needs someone trustworthy to care for the baby while she's at work; or the relative with a big family struggling with a mortgage; or the refugee next door who needs acceptance. Acts of kindness cost little, but they make a huge difference to the excluded.

And we cannot really call ourselves Christian, if we fail to see beyond our own affluence to needy around us. I say we, for we priests are no different; we can close our hearts to the people who are not "respectable", or part of our faith or congregation. Christ reminds us too, that at last we'll be judged by our indiscriminate charity. I hope he'll be able to say to me: "come possess the kingdom ... for I was hungry and you gave me food; I was thirsty and you gave me drink; I was a stranger and you made me welcome; naked and you clothed me; sick and you visited me etc" (Mt. 25: 35-37, JB).

He says that as long as we did it to the least of his brethren, whoever they are, and whatever their faith or social status, or color of skin, we did it to him. Lets not walk by him in the gutter, where he suffers today. For only open hearts make us citizens of heaven on earth. And the world adores the rich, famous and powerful but Christ is lord of love, and charitable sharing with all, for happiness in this world, and forever and ever, amen.

So as God's hands, committed to helping the needy of our world, our brothers and sisters of whatever creed or nation or social status, as the presence of the Lord himself among us, let's profess our faith.

## Prayers of the Faithful

And as the people of God lets pray for our own needs and those of others.

For the Pope and the bishops of the various churches, that abandoning their palaces, they may get down among the needy, as examples of real Christian care.

For civil leaders that in their concern for economics they may not lose sight of their larger duty to improve the lot of all the people of the nation.

For our youth that many may be inspired to give some of their time serving such as the Vincent De Paul or as volunteers to serve the poor in famine stricken areas abroad.

For ourselves in our homes, communities and areas that we may have some time for some charitable work with the needy.

For the sick, the aged, the lonely and the oppressed in body, mind or soul that through our love and care they may know God's love.

For the dead that our charity towards them may continue in our prayers and ongoing remembrance.

And we ask all these prayers through Christ Our Lord of overflowing love forever and ever, amen.

### Reflection:

I was chaplain once to the Bons hospital in Tralee and I was impressed by their motto. To minister to the sick, the poor, and the dying regardless of creed, race or social standing. In 1978 the sisters celebrated 100 years of service to the town. A newspaper editorial noted that the sisters came to a poverty stricken town to move among the sick, and serve the community well with their nursing skills and with a sympathy engendered by the holy life they led. The sisters are few now, but lay people can step into the breach. Lets do so, lets reach out to the Lazaruses among us today. Hail Mary

# Twenty-Seventh Sunday
# in Ordinary Time C

## Introduction

"The upright man will live by faith", the prophet says (Hab. 1:2, JB). The apostles ask Christ to increase their faith. Lets confess where our faith commitment is weak.

## Homily

"Increase our faith". This prayer should be constantly on our lips today when many abandoning faith, are rudderless amid life's storms. They live, as a recent newspaper survey noted, in the here and now. But we need God, we need soul salvation, we need an inner life, and since faith supplies all that its as necessary for us as the air we breathe. It adds fullness and depth to our lives, and enables us to flower into eternity at death.

Sheamus heaney, the Nobel laureate poet, said in an interview before his death that we should keep the faith that has been handed down to us for our welfare in this world, if for nothing else. Psychologists echo this view. And so does scripture. It says in our first reading: "see how he flags whose soul is not at rights", and the prophet goes on, "but the upright man will live by his faithfulness" (Hab. 2:4, JB). Christ adds his voice to this chorus: "Were your faith the size of a mustard seed you could say to this mulberry tree, 'be uprooted and planted in the sea', and it would obey you" (Lk. 17:5, JB).

To restore flagging souls to full confident faith is the Christian challenge today, when even priests seem to be catching the worldly malaise. Scandals and cover-ups show them living a long way from Christ's vision; for if they really believed they would live that belief.

The church hierarchy needs to be like you believers who come here to mass as naturally as breathing; you know faith is life, and you vote by your feet.

And that's the way to noble uprightness and integrity; as scripture says, "the **upright man** will live by his faithfulness". When we trust in God, and pray, then his holiness rubs off on us; grace enables us to do easily the good we cannot achieve on our own. And that is redemption. For to do good we must know the right way, and that's freely available to us through the Word and the following of Christ within mother church, and especially in our local faith community. For we need the community dimension of faith; without the church community perspective, guidance and support, we grope in a less supported individualism.

For faith must both take us into our deepest self, and yet open us up to the larger world of which our souls are a part. Those who don't believe are like those locked in a confined space, who think that's all there is, while out there is a vast world of God that expands our horizons to infinity. The terrible thing about much of modern life, in my view, is the narrowing and vulgarization of the human soul, the lack of nourishment for the inner person. Without that larger spiritual dimension, we always risk reverting to the animal state.

That is, people need faith to be raised up to their full human dignity. As Pope Francis says, when the light of faith dims, all other lights dim as well. And the motivational basis for right living is taken away. A scene in Camus's *The Stranger* makes the point well. A man commits a murder and they take him in, and ask him if he feels any remorse. He says no, he just felt like it, and if God doesn't exist and there is no reward or punishment why should one not kill, its all the same in the end what we do. Life is absurd, meaningless, and there is no higher reason why we should do good rather than evil.

To build faith communities where our children don't succumb to such amoral traps, is the challenge. For without supportive communal faith and the grace that communal worship brings, people are easy prey to forces of evil. So let's pray then that church structures will rebuild faith in a new flowering of the Spirit. All else is dust and ashes, but the body of Christ, the church, our mother in faith, is a light for us forever.

For worldly values pass and leave us empty before eternity but Christ is lord of love, goodness, truth, peace, and happiness for life in this world and forever and ever, amen.

So as God's people, growing in saving and enriching faith, hope and charity as Christ's living body, lets profess the faith we share as the enlightened people of God.

## *Prayers of the Faithful*

As the people of God gathered here lets pray our faith wont fail.

For our Holy Father and all leaders of the churches, may they be strong in faith so as to light up the world in Christ.

For civil leaders; may they foster a faith handed down with great sacrifice by our ancestors.

For our youth that clinging to the faith and its practice within the church, for without community support faith is empty, they may come to inner happiness and bring that light to the world.

For us in our homes, may we be diligent in increasing our own faith by practice, and pass on a living faith to our children.

For the sick in mind, body or soul that through their faith and our care for them they find comfort and peace.

For the dead whose faith is known to God alone that through our prayers they may come to their eternal rest.

And we ask all these our prayers through Christ who is lord of life forever and ever, amen.

## Reflection:

There's a story told of an person visiting a monastery. There were many monks bustling around and the person said to the abbot: " this is a thriving religious place. How many disciples do you have?". "One or two", the abbot replied. Sometimes our faith can be like that, vague mediocre following of Christ. So we need always to pray in the Spirit, "increase our faith", so that we may be true and fervent disciples of the Lord. Lets pray to Mother Mary for life-long faith, and well-tempered zeal in God's service. Hail Mary.

# Twenty-Eight Sunday of Ordinary time C

## Introduction

Our scripture continues the theme of faith and associates it with healing and giving thanks. Naaman is healed by Elisha's faith. Christ heals the lepers, though only one came back to thank him. Lets confess ways we fail to give thanks for healing faith in our lives.

## Homily

Let me tell today's Gospel as seen by one of the lepers. I am a deformed leper shunned by everyone. People run into houses when they see me. I've to shout that I'm unclean. My life is one of endless pain, suffering, loneliness, dirt and poverty; I wish I were dead. Someone please help. Wait! The healer I've heard about, Jesus, is coming. "Holy one of God, have pity on me", I shout. "Shut up", his disciples say, "get away from the master, you foul thing". I'm desperate, I don't care, I shout louder. Then wonder of wonders, Jesus comes. I say, "please heal me". He touches me, the first time anyone has done so in 20 years. I feel my flesh revive. I can't believe it, the sores are gone, I'm well. Thank God. Now I can go home to my family and live a normal life. Thank you, Lord.

Who in our day has the same story; a person infected by aids? An old person shut up in a home, out of sight and out of mind? The street children excluded from our cozy middle-class world. But that world has lepers too, spiritual lepers insulated in big houses from neighbors, ignoring God, too lazy to get up for mass, like Naaman before he met Elisha, caught in the clutches of useless plastic gods of aspiritual affluence. To these Christ brings another deeper healing message today, repent and believe.

For in some ways the sickness of the soul is more serious, and more close themselves off from healing now. Encased in make-believe TV worlds we don't want to hear about challenging realities: death, sin, disease, suffering, judgment, God. Once, asked about hell in school, I explained what it was. Later parents complained that I frightened the children. We want to be safe in an escapist TV world from all that challenges us spiritually; heeding only sanitized "nice" aspects of the gospel. We cast out those who would remind us of evil and mortality. Or we turn our face from God and support the secularists who'd exclude Christ's challenging message altogether. The affluent like Dives shun the beggar at their gate. Yet when in hell, Dives pleaded for the beggar's help in vain; it was too late.

Now is always the acceptable time, the time to embrace and live healing faith. Lest spiritual and physical lepers around us cry out in vain. St. Theresa of Avila says: "Christ has no body now on earth but ours". As his healing hands to a broken world, we dare not fail. For so many need his healing presence, from the tramp to the abandoned street child, to wealthy fat cats. To all children of God of whatever ilk, we are our brother's keeper.

That is, we cant pursue ruthless self-interest like Dives regardless of our neighbor suffering or their need for salvation. For to us no one is a leper. Our Christian family includes the homeless, the refugee, the addict. It includes the agnostic who should be reminded that lack of faith is bad for life, let alone the soul. A retired person told me recently that in a course with psychologists to prepare for retirement they were told to keep the faith as vital for their general well-being. And a wise man told me, we should live our life here on earth as we would like to live it for all eternity with God.

For final glory belongs not the self-serving world but Jesus who, as the song says, has friends in low places. Lets enjoy this world but with eyes wide open also to the needs of others and our souls. For hard worldly values fade to ashes at last, leaving us empty before eternity but Christ is lord of healing love, peace, beauty and happiness for this world and forever and ever, amen.

So as God's own, called to steadfast faith and charity towards the spiritual and physical needy around us, we profess our faith.

## Prayers of the faithful

And as the people of God in need of God's healing in every way and giving thanks for his loving care, we pray for what we need.

For the Pope and bishops of the church; may they be examples of heroic healing faith and of constant thanks to God for his love.

For civil leaders that in they may allocate generously to the HSE and always provide free medical care and support for the poor.

For our youth that they may be conscious of those sick and needy around them and not just their own concerns and ambitions.

For ourselves at home, may we be especially helpful towards sick relatives and neighbors; and always give thanks for our families.

For the dead that their sickness and suffering over they may come to heavenly home of the blessed, helped by our prayers.

And we ask all these prayers through Christ who is lord of healing love and thankful hearts forever and ever, amen.

## Reflection:

A modern day version of the gospel is the story of St. Damian and the Lepers. He ministered as a priest in a leper colony, when no one else would work there. One day before mass, while bathing his feet he found that he could feel nothing, a sure sign that he had got the disease. When he went out onto the altar, instead of his usual address, he said "we lepers". They realized he was now truly one of them. We may not be called to such heroism, but we all have sick or aged family members who need our simple care. Lets find time for them, and for spiritual ministry to them too. Hail Mary

# Twenty-Ninth Sunday of Ordinary Time C

## Introduction

"Pray continually, and never lose heart" (LK. 18:1, JB), Christ tells us in our gospel. We may not realize what a great glory prayer is. It heals the world, nourishes our inner life and unites us with God; lets confess any neglect of prayer in our Christian life.

## Homily

I read once about an Orthodox saint in Russia. He traveled all over Europe asking people how to pray all the time, even when asleep. Eventually an abbot in a monastery told him that if he went to bed at night praying, he'd carry that on through sleep. We may not pray all the time, but to pray well is the best thing we can do. Our Lady speaking to visionaries, stresses prayer as the heart of Christian life. In Medjugorje her message is: "Pray! Pray my little children", for peace especially, and that all humankind will come back to God's healing arms. This may be Satan's age, with the holocaust and so on, but prayer can defeat him, and in a mysterious way transform our world into God's paradise.

If we don't believe private visions that say this, believe the Gospel. It tells us unequivocally that if we pray always and never lose faith, good things will happen. True, sometimes particular petitions aren't answered, God doesn't work wonders to order, that would negate the normal functioning of the world; and we don't want to be puppets of an all-controlling God. But he promises that prayer is always heard in some way if we ask in the right Spirit. But the real importance of prayer is that it builds a relationship with God.

Sometimes, as in communion we don't even need words for this. Prayer at its best is a heart to heart meeting with God. St. Theresa of Avila tells us that silent prayer and meditation can brings us so close to God, he can seem but a breath away. And that's the aim of faith, to draw us ever closer to Our Lord. For its not an ideology; it can only be experienced in the mystery of a faithful and worshiping context. Our Christian life stems from reflecting on scripture, mass, communion, personal prayer, meditation in the church before the Blessed Sacrament, and prayer as God's gathered family. For we're saved and experience God best, as part of the body of Christ. Thereby we're united with God and our inner life flowers. And what we need to nourish most is our inner life in God.

I always marvel at the radiant peace and happiness of holy people. Union with God raises them up to the highest heaven, and makes their life on earth a vale of joy. For once we're one with God through prayer, everything else falls into place. Like a child in mother's arms, or a flower in the sun, we blossom. Our humanity is fulfilled in the divinity.

Even petition prayers help in this. One might respond, why ask for things at all, God knows our needs? The answer is our freedom. He can't give us anything unless we ask, and, a good dad, he only gives what's good for us. That answers those who say I prayed to win the lotto yet didn't get it. Prayer isn't pagan magic; as Christ, says we shouldn't put God to the test. But all prayer is valuable and answered in some way.

I'm sure whatever peace there is in our world is a result of the prayers for peace we said down the years. Because God always grants good petitions, if they are possible, given our freedom. So lets not get discouraged in prayer. Keep on storming heaven as my mother used to say. For it also gives us inner depth and great inner strength during hard times. In hospitals, people constantly say to me without prayer I'd never have got through illness.

That is, the cure for most world ills is prayer. Thereby we grow in dignity, wholeness and freedom within. The world would be Satan's long ago, only for the prayers of the faithful. For all else eventually fades to dust and ashes at last and leaves us empty before eternity, but if we ask in prayer Christ will give us love, truth, goodness, and happiness for overflowing life in this world, and happiness forever and ever, amen.

So as God's own, deepening a relationship with him in personal and communal worship, lets profess our faith.

## Prayers of the Faithful

As God's own, gathered at the most fruitful form of prayer and union with Christ, lets ask for our material and spiritual needs.

For our Holy Father and all leaders of the church, that they may be lights of faith and prayerful healing for the whole world.

For civil leaders, may they have God's guidance and blessing in their work for the people, especially those most in need, and foster not stifle prayer in public life.

For our youth that they may return to the lord and the church if they have strayed and find in prayer their true selves.

For our parents, homes and children that the lord may guide and protect them always and that they may pray and stay together.

For the sick that through our prayers and care, the healing strength, grace and love of God may ease their suffering.

For the dead that through our continuing charitable prayers and remembrance they may enjoy the Communion of the Saints.

And we ask all these our prayers through Christ who intercedes forever for us before Our Father in heaven, amen.

## Reflection

There's a story told of St Theresa of Avila. Once, she prayed constantly for an notorious felon about to be hanged, that he would come to the lord and salvation, for he was a militant unbeliever. Lo and behold on the scaffold, he surprised everyone by kissing the crucifix. Theresa saw that as the fruit of her prayer. Lets all have the same trust in the power of prayer, which, in some mysterious way, brings the world to its true destiny, harmony, love and peace. Hail Mary

# Thirtieth Sunday of Ordinary Time C

## Introduction

Our Scripture praised the humble tax collector's confession of sin, as against the Pharisee's proud self-righteousness. Lets confess any refusal to acknowledge sin.

## Homily

Why does God hate sin? Obviously he is holy and abhors any thing unholy, but its also because he loves us and knows it is bad for us; the commandments were given to the Jews as part of their liberation from slavery. For sin is always a rejection of God or our neighbor in selfish pride that hurts us, others, and society. Our first parents' fall happens in us every day. By sin we abandon his paradisaical way, further world corruption, and destroy our inner happiness for this world and the next.

Yet sin is rooted in our freedom, our choice to do evil rather than good. The fall story is ongoing; with every sin, suffering, death, disease, and cold enter the world against God's will. Significantly, after the first sin came the first murder; Cain's killing of Abel. So sin also begets violence, war and death. That's the answer to those who say sin on, and feel no guilt. Why then have laws to curb its excesses, so society can at least function?

But our faith wants more than a world where evil is barely kept in check. We work for a full free life in God, to counteract man's fall and free us from slavery to sin. For in every age, choosing godless Satanic pride, lets untold evil into the world. We reject God's loving guidance for our good, again and again, at personal and societal level.

Too often we think of sin as individual, but forget its main source, social structures of sin. In our societies, structures of sin often underlie individual sin; patterns of abortion, injustice, and war for example. Personal sin is blameless in that sense; sin to be culpable must be a free choice; imposed social structures of sin make such choice difficult.

Thus, the Pharisee in our Gospel was part of a religious structure that blinded him to sin. Full of self-righteousness, despite his ill-gotten wealth and power he says: "I'm all right, Jack". In overweening pride he's blind to the need to repent. Contrast that with the the tax-collector. He's a sinner too, but he knows it, and seeks redemption. He admits his fallen state and seeks forgiveness from God. And Jesus accepts him rather the arrogant sin-hardened Pharisee who ignores all efforts to open his heart to repentance.

That's the other mystery of sin, the accumulation of guilt and the need for healing forgiveness best gained from a divine source. For without that the weakness of sin can harden into the obstinacy of damnation. Recent scandals show that even church leaders can fall into that trap. They allowed sinful power and self-preserving structures to blind them to the greatest evil, abuse of the innocent. This reminds us that the church, even at the highest level, is made up of sinners; and can become a structure of sin. Now its shocked back to sense, repentance and reparation. So should we. For prideful blindness to sin, a destructive slavery of body and soul, can shut out God's light in our souls.

"He who exalts himself will be humbled", Christ reminds us, and the self-righteous Pharisees. Its not high rank that make us God's people, but innocent sinless hearts. And when we sin through human weakness, due to our fallen nature, the key is to repent and come humbly back to God. Indeed, in this, paradoxically, sin can do us good, if it forces us to accept our limiting sinfulness and need for God's healing grace, like it did the tax collector, beating his breast at the back of the church. For only Godless sinful arrogance destroys the soul and makes the world a hell, but Christ is lord of love, peace, goodness, and forgiveness of guilt, for our happiness in this world and forever and ever, amen.

So as God's own, shunning sinful pride, lets profess our faith.

## *Prayers of the faithful*

And recognizing our deep need for God, lets pray for what we need.

For the Holy Father that God may inspire him in his work for the church and the world and keep him as a humble servant of God, bringing the world his vital forgiveness.

For civil leaders that they serve the people, and not just their own interests.

For youth; avoiding sinful pride may they know their need for God and his church, and serve both humbly and faithfully in the joy of the Spirit, as promised at Confirmation.

For ourselves, like the tax-collector may we recognize our areas of sinfulness and confess them humbly, so as to be acceptable to God, and save our souls.

For the sick, that through our care they may know the love and care of God.

For the dead that their sins washed away, they may come to their heavenly home with the help of our prayers.

And we ask all these prayers humbly and contritely coming before God, who is our Father of loving care forever and ever, amen.

## *Reflection:*

When I think about repentance and humble acceptance of God into one's life I think of Johnny Cash. At one stage in his life he reached the end of his tether, drugs reduced him to despair. He crawled into a cave in the wilderness to die. But there face to face with himself, God spoke to him. When he crawled out, he was a different man; as he said, God brought him from darkness into light. Afterward he always included Gospel songs in his concerts, and made a recording of all the Gospels. We all need to find God personally like that in humble acceptance born of fallen need. Lets pray to Mother Mary, that God may keep us safe from the pit where the evil one would keep us in darkness forever. Hail Mary

# Thirty-First Sunday of Ordinary Time C

## *Introduction*

Scripture this Sunday continues the theme of sin and humble repentance. We have the beautiful story of Zacchaeus, who finds joy by the entrance of Christ into his house. Lets confess ways we refuse to let Christ into our homes, to change our lives for good.

## *Homily.*

"Will the circle be unbroken by and by, Lord, by and by/There's a better world awaiting, in the sky, Lord, in the sky". You know the common popular hymn, made famous by Johnny Cash. Its message is that life's a circle that's complete only when we blend earth and heaven, God and our souls, in one eternal harmonious whole.

During the boom, an ad showed luxury cars circling a town center; this is the better world it said. Much modern life is summed up in that; all we need is sex, big cars, mansions, drink, drugs, holidays abroad. Many buy the illusion that money is happiness and the world enough. But what about the riches of our inner life? And the fact that this world ends all too soon, and may leave us high and dry before eternity.

That's what Zacchaeus realized when Christ entered his house. He'd lived all his life as a cheat, money his god. He'd raised the taxes on the poor and kept the extra money for himself. He'd lived as if this world's wealth, gained by foul means, was all he needed. But when Christ entered his house, the eyes of his soul were opened, he repented, and began a more just life, even compensating those he'd cheated.

Christ needs to enter many houses in the same way now. Rich people for example, who gain riches by selling drugs that destroy our youth and spawn gun wars. All who repent and make reparation for crimes, like Zacchaeus, should be saved. The church paying compensation and providing counseling for abused, is a good example.

Such examples show that Zacchaeus's story is still relevant. Today too people can pursue wealth and pleasure regardless of the cost to others and their souls. But as the first reading reminds us, they'll have to face God's judgment if unrepentant. And there's nothing new about this, remember the flood. They were eating, drinking, swapping wives, living immorally right up until Noah went into the ark, and the flood swept them away.

In every age, caught up in this world and its values of which Satan's lord, we can lose sight of higher values and our soul's salvation; we can become blind to God and judgment. Not that we shouldn't enjoy the world, it was given to us by God to be enjoyed; but its no use if we're unhappy inside due to unrepentant sin; as the popular saying goes, there's no rest for the wicked. I often think those drug lords, with pads in Spain, don't really enjoy themselves, their consciences must be at them all the time.

Zacchaeus was such a gangster of his day who found salvation in Christ. We should learn that lesson; that we shouldn't inhabit a half circle of clay-bound moral and spiritual death, but complete it by living in the circle of the soul's fullness in God and right. Otherwise, we may have no content in this life, and face an even bleaker eternity.

That's why as the year ends, the church reminds us of Christ's Second Coming in judgment; she says that at any time our souls may be required of us, to wake us up spiritually, like Zacchaeus was woken up. For what we do on earth echoes through all eternity; and if our souls are empty here they may be so forever. So its vital to repent like Zacchaeus, if we need to change our lives. Then when Christ comes at last he'll say well done good and faithful servant. Having joined the circle of heaven and earth in integral lives of faith and righteousness we'll go to meet him with all the saints. For all else is shadows and dust but he is lord of happiness for this world, and forever and ever, amen.

So as God's own, uniting the spiritual and material circles in a perfect harmony of Christian grace and peace and inner completeness, we profess our faith.

## Prayers of the faithful

And as God's people, lets pray for our happiness in this world and forever.

For the Pope that he may continue to remind the world that our life in this world must be part of the circle of eternal values.

For our civil leaders that they may not try to divorce society from their spiritual welfare in a half-circle of futility.

For youth, like Zacchaeus may they invite Christ and his church into their soul's houses and so complete the circle of life and eternity.

For ourselves that we may not be so caught up in the world of money making that we neglect to care for our own and our children's soul needs.

For the sick, the aged, the lonely and the oppressed that Christ may enter their homes to bring God's love and peace through us.

For the dead that through our continuing charitable prayers for them they may complete the circle of earth and eternity forever.

And we ask all these prayers through Christ who is lord of saving grace, integral living, and inner peace forever and ever, amen.


## Reflection:

Christmas is coming and Zacchaeus's story reminds me of the King Wenceslaus carol. He too lived off taxes wrung from the people, but gave back some of that to the poor so that they could survive. Taking steps to right wrongs we help to create, is vital for our salvation, not to mention peace of mind. Like Zacchaeus, lets humbly confess sinful mistakes and try to right them as best we can. Hail Mary

# Thirty-Second Sunday of Ordinary Time C

## Introduction

"For you there can be no resurrection", brothers being martyred say to the cruel pagan king. Similarly, Christ points out in the Gospel, that God is lord of the living, not the dead. Lets confess ways we fail to appreciate the importance of faith, unto resurrection.

## Homily

Light is precious this time of the year when days are short and dark. Hence the Christmas lights. We celebrate delivery from darkness by Christ's birth. Even our pagan ancestors knew we needed such light. In the megalithic tombs, on the 21st of December they'd a system rigged up so that light came in and flooded the graves of their dead. It was a sign of hope for those lost in death. Given the winter weather, clocks going back and dark days, we too need this hope. That's why the church, at the year's end, asks us to reflect on the end things, death, the end of the world, judgment. But she also tells us not to despair. Christ delivered us from darkness; he's lord of the living, not the dead.

For like a child is the dark we can be afraid, sensing the link between darkness and evil. None of us wants to live in darkness forever. That's also why we have two great feasts at this time; All Saints and All Souls. We're asked to imitate those saints who light us to heaven. We also remember those who need our prayers to come to eternal light.

The Gospel gives us infinite hope in this context; in God all are in fact alive. All we need do to avoid the fate of eternal darkness, is to faithfully walk in the Savior's light. That's what Christ tried to tell the Pharisees. But they were too concerned with power and greed to accept the life he offered. The stupid story of the man marrying seven wives proves this. Christ tells them that at the resurrection we'll be like angels, worldly vanity left behind. But first we must follow his radiant way here below. For at any times we too in darkness of heart are tempted to reject Jesus. And that's more probable now, when pagan forces today would lure us back into the darkness from which Christ freed us.

We lit a candle of faith from the Pascal Candle at Baptism and promised to keep that flame of faith alive in our hearts until we went to meet the Lord with all the saints. But we're tempted today to renege on those promises, to go asleep spiritually. In the bustle of money-making and worldly care the light of faith lit at Baptism can flicker and go out.

Don't let that happen! Deluded by worldly propaganda lets not lapse back into the hopeless darkness that reigned before Christ. Lets not make unbelief and immorality our gods instead of his faith and goodness. For in the unredeemed world, people glory in their shame. They would persuade us that darkness is light and light darkness. Lets not be fooled by the father of lies but cling to God until, in his light, our souls flower into eternity.

Lets be like the brothers in the first reading. They defied the pagan king even unto death. Similarly, new pagan powers-that-be may pressure us into abandoning God today. Powerful forces such as the media can be harbingers of spiritual death. The brothers said to the pagan king: "for you there can be no resurrection, no new life" (2 Macc. 7:14, JB). It would be awful if, having neglected our faith here, we choose the way of darkness and death for eternity too. For people can die within as well as physically. Theologians now say that hell isn't God punishing us but people refusing to accept God after a life of doing so. He can't force us into heaven. Its vital for our choice of it at death, to constantly keep our light of faith burning on earth. For worldly godless values pass and leave us in the dark, but Christ is lord of light, glory and salvation for this world and forever and ever, amen.

As God's own, living in his light all life long and so being part of the saintly throng when he comes again to raise us up body and soul to heaven, we profess our faith.

## Prayers of the Faithful

And as as Christ's living light of the world lets pray for what we need.

For the church throughout the world and its leaders that it may be the light of Christ to all willing to receive his grace.

For civil leaders that they may be enlightened enough to support the various faiths of their people and our main tradition, the light we've followed through history.

For our youth that they may walk always in the light of Christ as practicing members of his light-filled holy church.

For parents and homes, the domestic church, that they may be places where the faith is passed on intact, for the good of all.

For the sick that they may find in faith, prayer and our help the consolation, strength and healing that they need.

For the dead that our powerful communal prayers here may light them home to their heavenly home.

And we ask all these prayers through Christ, the eternal light of the world, amen.

## Reflection

Maybe we'll find in the next world what we believe in here. An experience of my own seems to bear this out. I talked to a woman who had gone through a near-death experience and come back to life. "There I was" she said, "bathed in wonderful light and the Sacred Heart was coming towards me with open arms. I was so happy, and then they brought me back". A life-long devotee of the Sacred Heart, she was deeply disappointed to be brought back to the world. God came to receive her in the form she knew and loved. Our resurrection will be glorious and a source of greater joy that we could ever experience in on earth. Lets ask Mary to keep us on the glorious road to that haven. Hail Mary

# Thirty-Third Sunday of
# Ordinary Time C

## Introduction

Fittingly, scripture on the last Sunday feature the apocalypse, the end of the world and Christ's Second Coming. The first reading talks of evil-doers being burnt like stubble then, but also the sun of righteousness shining out with healing in its rays. Christ says to endure in faith to the end whatever it brings. Lets confess, prepare now for our final hour.

## Homily

This is a dark time of year and there's darkness around us also: violence, war, unbelief, injustice, hunger and recession. But scripture tells us not to despair. Even if the end of the world comes with fearful sights our perseverance in faith, hope and charity will save us. We face winter now. Cold is setting in, and the hours of daylight are short. We hate the dark, and an eternal winter of the soul is unthinkable. It won't happen if through faith and prayer we keep God's light burning in your hearts. With that assurance, the church reminds us now of the end things - death, judgment and Christ's Second Coming when he'll judge the world by fire, and gather his faithful from all times and nations.

But that won't so much an end as a new beginning, the completion of God's plan of salvation. Our sure hope is that we, if faithful, will be part of that great gathering in light? Though we live in an increasingly irreligious world our endurance through it all will be our reward, hence Christ's advice in our gospel, to persevere in faith no matter what.

But such endurance isn't easy. A headline in a newspaper recently said: "10 years ago we thought we'd killed God but now he seems to be alive again". Why are we so anxious to kill God again and again?

Didn't we do enough by crucifying him once? Yet our world seems bent on returning to the darkness from which his suffering delivered us. Why? It makes no sense. Even psychologists agree that faith is vital for our general well-being; Jung the great psychiatrist said that the "death of God is the death of man". We need him to reach our full humanity and even to survive; evolution favors those of faith. Why destroy what's salvation for this world and the next? Its just stupid human perversity and arrogance? Or do we reject him because he condemns our selfish immoral ways.

Perhaps some of you saw the film *The Omen*? Its about the anti-Christ who's to come before the world's end to lead even good people astray. The film is a distortion of the message in the Book Of Revelation, which says the end will really be our final joyful liberation from evil. But its interesting that in the film the anti-Christ is from a rich family with global business power. He kills his parents and uses that power to promote his anti-God message. Some say the anti-Christ's already with us in this way, in a host of anti-God forces: materialism, secularism, militant media atheism, libertarianism, uncaring capitalism; the horns of the beast that would root up God on earth, as the Bible warns.

Be that as it may, let's be strong enough to resist such forces, for the first reading warns: "the day is coming now, burning like a furnace, and all the arrogant and the evil-doers will be like stubble" (Mal. 3:19, JB). But for those who continue in faith, "the sun of righteousness will shine out with healing in its rays" (Mal. 3:20, JB). Christ says the same in the gospel: "You'll be hated by all men on account of my name, but not a hair of your head will be lost. Your endurance will win you your lives" (Lk. 21:18-19, JB).

The key then is to keep faith, whatever the envious world throws at us, however it assails us, so we'll be gathered at last into his heavenly mansions. For worldly values pass and leave us empty on the shore of eternity but Christ's lord of life, light, truth, beauty and salvation both for our happiness while here on earth, and forever and ever, amen.

So as God's own, faithful amid all attacks and sufferings, and so joining his saints in glory on the last day, when he will judge the world by fire, we profess our faith.

## Prayers of the Faithful

And as God's faithful lets pray for the gifts only he can give.

For our Pope and all church leaders, that they may persevere in the faith and in the proclamation of God's Word in season and out of season, and so redeem the times.

For civil leaders that they may facilitate the church and the people's learning and practice of their faith.

For youth that wisely reflecting on the end things, they may persevere in the faith that is life for this world, and forever.

For our homes, may parents nurture love, faith, grace and peace for happiness for themselves and their family now and to the end.

For the sick, the old, the lonely and the poor that through our care for them in body and soul they may know God's love.

For the dead that through our continuing remembrance and prayers they may join the saints in glory when Christ comes at last; and we pray in particular for those on the list of the dead.

And we ask this through Christ who intercedes for us before the Father as Our Lord of life and love forever and ever, amen.

## Reflection

During the millennium some proclaimed the world's end, but this is unscriptural. Even Christ didn't know the time nor the hour, he said its known only to the Father. What is sure, however, is that the world will end some time. Like everything else, scientists agree, its finite. But that end's probably a long way away. For each of us, however, its quite near, our death is our own particular apocalypse. Let pray we'll be ready when the end comes, having kept hope and faith alive in our hearts. Hail Mary

# Christ the King C

## Introduction

We call Jesus Lord or King because at his resurrection God gave him all power in heaven and earth. But our gospel reminds us that Christ is not a worldly king, lording it over people, but a king of love on the cross. Lets confess if we offend our gentle King.

## Homily

Do you remember the old stations of the cross. They were full of sweat and blood and a sorrowful Savior rebuking us for our sins. They were partly right, Christ's suffering were real and a result of our sins. But they missed the fact that Christ also became king and lord of the world on the cross. There he revealed a God who triumphs through infinite suffering love. That's why our gospel for the feast of Christ the King features him not on a heavenly throne, but on the cross. It shows him as a king of love on Calvary.

He made that choice at the beginning of his ministry when, in the desert, Satan tempted him to be a corrupt power-loving earthly king. He chose instead to be scripture's suffering Messiah. And he resisted the apostles also in this. They too wanted him to be a political Messiah and themselves sitting at his right hand in power. Christ had to say to Peter to get behind him, Satan, when Peter wanted to stop him going to Jerusalem to die. Only at Pentecost did the apostles understand the wisdom of the cross.

Its the lesson we must learn too. If we want to be like Christ, his follower, we too must be kings of love, humble servants of God and others. Christ was that to the last drop of his blood and he passed the chalice on to us, to love one another as he loved us. He loved us to the extent of giving up everything, even his very soul at last, not only to save the world but to be an example to humanity of a selfless love that's the way to Eden.

For perhaps the main temptation each person faces is to pursue one's own power, wealth and glory at the expense of God, what's right, and the poor. Is it because the church teaches Christ's law of selfless love that many abandon God and the church today? The world tells them to serve self and desire regardless, to avoid the cross of doing what's right, of worshiping God in spirit and truth, of giving until it hurts. Just as the world would have priests avoid the cross of celibacy, and religious the crosses of obedience, chastity and poverty. They laugh at the lay person who sacrifices time in church ministries or charitable works, or give short shift to couples who insist on difficult marriage faithfulness.

Yet to be such kings of love like Christ is our true nobility. The other is the way of the world of which Satan is king: living it up regardless of who we hurt, greedily getting as much money as we can at whatever the cost to our souls or others, being totally ruthless and selfish, dumping God if his worship is inconvenient or challenges our immoral living. All this leaves us empty at last before eternity and spawns a hell on earth. By contrast Christ's way of love, of weekly worship and daily charity may involve some suffering but it builds up our souls in deeper joy and peace. Moreover, we thereby make a difference for good by our lives and help to make the world a better place for all. And having built treasure in heaven we flower at last into eternal life. For the world's ruthless values pass and leave us empty at last but Christ is king of life, love, freedom and peace both for our happiness in this world and forever and ever, amen.

As God's own, adoring Our King and imitating his self-giving faith, love and gentle goodness to save the world, we profess our faith.

## Prayers of the Faithful

For the leaders of the church throughout the world that they may serve the Kingdom of God and bring all to kingly fullness in Christ.

For civil leaders that in serving their own kingdom of earthly power and glory they may not put any obstacles in the way of the growth of the Kingdom of God in the world.

For youth, may they see beyond the cruel passing kingdoms of this world of which Satan is lord to the deeper and more enduring Kingdom of God in Christ, and remain true and practicing members of the holy church, his flawed but essential human instrument.

For ourselves in our homes, work places and communities that we may be witnesses to the gentle loving Kingdom of God, and bring its eternal riches to our children and all we come into contact with.

For the sick, the aged, and the lonely that through our love and care they may know the consolations of the Kingdom of God, which is a kingdom of real love.

For the dead that they may come to the final kingdom prepared for them since the foundation of the world, helped by our powerful communal prayers as the body of Christ.

And we ask these prayers through Christ Our Lord, to whom belongs the Kingdom, the power and the glory forever and ever, amen.

## Reflection

Kerry is called *The Kingdom*. Apparently it belonged to a ancient kingdom that centered in the Southern area of Ireland. When Kerry played Cork recently in Gaelic football I marveled at the fervor of its supporters. The same is true of the devotees of English soccer clubs. They wear the jerseys with pride, and wave banners that say "keep the faith". The same is true of American football or baseball supporters. We should be as fervent in serving God's Kingdom, and wear our Baptismal garments as proudly for Christ our King. We pray to Mother Mary the mother of the church to make us true in this, unto the great eternal All Ireland or Premiership Cup or Superbowl prize in heaven. Hail Mary

# PART IV

# Homilies For
# Special Feasts

# All Saints

## Introduction

Today we remember not only the canonized saints, but all the ordinary saints we have all known. It is a reminder to us that our central Christian call is to be holy as our heavenly Father is holy. Let's confess any ways we fail in this witness.

## Homily

This time of year, as the days grow short and dark and the weather cold and wet, the Church wisely asks us to reflect on the end things. It does so not to frighten us, but to keep us awake spiritually. A child in the dark is often afraid, sensing the link between darkness and evil. No one wants to live in darkness forever. That's also why we have two great feasts this week—All Saints and All Souls. We remember those who kept the faith and reached eternal light, and also those in darkness, who need our prayers to be free.

In today's scripture the Church tells us how to avoid that fate, and how to be part of the vast throng of white-robed saints Christ will lead to eternity on the last day. We're to go through life free from worthless desires. We're to keep our hearts as pure as Christ's. He lists the virtues the saints should have: they should be free from greed, loving and gentle, bearing sorrow bravely, courageously following what's right; merciful, pure in heart, peaceful, ready to suffer in keeping the faith, people of verbal integrity and so on.

These are some of the main paths to sainthood. They are also ways to happiness here below, to knowing God, to being his true sons and daughters, to being authentic members of his holy kingdom, the church. They are a charter for our happiness and for the world's salvation. And they are the main vocation we received at Baptism. Then we were given a candle lit from the Paschal candle, and told to keep the flame of God burning in our hearts, until we went out with all the saints to meet Christ at last.

Today we celebrate those saints who've gone before us on that road to glory, many of them ordinary people we knew. People like our mothers or grandmothers always saying their beads, who kept the faith in difficult times and had kind, gentle hearts. It's not that they were perfect—who is? Holiness is the constant struggle to do our best, despite our human faults; and most of us have plenty of those. Christ puts the ideal before us, but knows that we're sinners. That's also why we have masses said for our departed during November. Christ not only showed us the way to God, but bore our sins on the cross, and every mass is an enactment of that sacrifice.

That is, every mass ensures that darkness is washed from our souls, and if offered for our departed, from their souls. Indeed, scripture says its a good and holy thing to pray for the dead "so that they may be released from their sin" (2 Mcs. 12:45, JB). The basis for this is our creed belief, the Communion of Saints. In that timeless communion, the dead, still part of the church, can be helped by our prayers, and their prayers can help us.

At this dark time of the year, we're not only called to be part of the heavenly saints in light, but also to follow their example, lest we be plunged into darkness forever. That's certainly where none of us want to be. To inspire us the church puts the saints before us as example of heroic faith and virtue. For that's how saints are defined; they practiced shining heroic faith and virtue. The more recent saints put before us as such – Pope John the XX111, and Pope John Paul the 11 – certainly did that. But, we also know ordinary unheralded saints from our own background who also inspired us; we celebrate them too.

The feast of all saints today! All souls tomorrow! Throughout the book of Revelation, which deals with the world's end, we're us asked to be worthy of our calling as the saints of God in light. Lights in the winter of a hard, unbelieving world, and to those stilled trapped in the lower regions of the other world. We're to be saints for today, imitating our Risen Lord, Jesus Christ, who is Lord of love, life, truth, beauty, and salvation for our happiness in this world and our glory as his saints forever in heavenly bliss. Amen.

So as God's own, called to be one with the saints in light and offering our powerful prayers for those still in darkness, let's profess our faith.

## Prayers of the Faithful

And as his people, let's offer our prayers for ourselves and those still in darkness.

We pray for the Church throughout the world and especially the Church in our country, that through the prayers of all the saints it may be renewed in faith and holiness.

We pray for civil leaders, that they may put no obstacles in the path of the saints of God within his holy Church.

We pray for ourselves, that we may keep on the path of holiness and join all the saints we knew who have gone before in faith.

We pray for all those who are still immersed in the darkness of this world's unbelief and sin, that through our prayers they may come into the light of Christ and lasting peace.

For deceased relatives who have passed away, in this month of the holy souls, that they may reach their heavenly home.

For all our own special intentions, worries, troubles, sickness, or whatever that the Lord and all the saints may lead us to light peace and consolation.

And we ask all these things through Christ Our Lord, from whom all good things come, for he is Lord of Love forever. Amen.

## *Reflection*

Great saints inspire us and aid our spiritual journey. Saints like Peter and Paul, Francis, Anthony, Kevin. We pray to them in the truth of the living "Communion of Saints." In the light of this truth, we can also pray to ordinary saints we knew in our lives—good people who kept the faith in every adversity, who lived good lives, and are still part of a family that includes the living and dead in the Communion that is the timeless Church. Let's us ask Mary to make us like them, and join them one day. Hail Mary.

# Corpus Christi

## Introduction

My parents often talked of the famous fifties Eucharistic Congress, which celebrated our legendary devotion to the mass. We have been so wise in this devotion. For as the first reading reminds us, Communion is as essential for our Christian journey as manna was for the People of God in the desert. Thereby we grow in God's life here and are sure to be raised up on the last day. Let's confess any failure to appreciate this great gift.

## Homily

Corpus Christ, the Body of Christ. Today's feast stresses the bodily as well as spiritual presence of Christ in the Eucharist, and what a presence! When great people enter a room, there's a buzz. It was like that with Christ. His powerful yet gentle presence made people flock to him. You may say, "I wish I'd been there." But we are there in every Sunday Communion. At each mass, bread and wine changes into his real presence; a flesh and blood Christ infolds us, as he did his beloved while on earth.

Not like a person talking to you from miles away, Jesus comes to us in the host in a close personal union. He nourishes our faith and charity and makes us Christian to the core. He keeps our souls healthy like good eating does our bodies. He sustains us for life's journey and enables us to grow in God's life. He binds us closely to the Church. He makes us strong to witness to him in the world. He enables us to defeat sin, suffering and death. We become what we eat, and what we eat here is the glorious Risen Lord.

But priceless blessings come to us also from visits to his sacramental presence in each church, signified by the red light. Even our genuflection before that presence is a wonderful prayer, recalling the early church exhortation that every knee should bow, every tongue confess that Jesus Christ is Lord. If you knew Jesus was visiting your area in the flesh, you'd rush to meet him. But he's in the Church all the time. Benediction, exposition and processions are other public ways of celebrating and honoring that Presence. The procession especially says that we're proud to affirm his presence before the whole world.

All in all, then, we can't overemphasize how precious a gift of God the Eucharist is. Our wise forefathers knew this as they braved death at mass rocks and private houses during times of religious prosecution. Jesus had been there for them; they wanted to be there for him. Let's continue to let this great gift mold and transform our lives in graceful living. For from the beginning, it was the life of the Christian community. The Acts of the Apostles tells how Christians met for prayers, scripture reading and "breaking of bread", the early name for the Eucharist (Acts. 2:42-47). It was what made them Christian. It's still the most essential way in which we draw close to Christ, the Church, and each other.

But it is not only our essential spiritual food for life's journey, the essence of our unity and worship as God's people; it's also the door to a happy eternity. For when we see Our Lord face to face, we won't be strangers: "anyone who does eat my flesh and drink my blood has eternal life, and I shall raise him up at the last day" (John 6:54, JB), Christ says. If we commune with our great Lord here, and confidently honor him before the world in devotions, then he'll honor us before the Father at death. Indeed, we already anticipate that in every mass and Communion. For this world and its godless values fade to dust and ashes at last, but Christ in the host is Lord of life, love, beauty, truth, life, and salvation both for our happiness in this world and forever and ever. Amen. So, conscious that we are an infinitely blessed Eucharistic People, let's profess our faith with new enthusiasm and witness to it before the world by our special devotions today.

## Prayers of the Faithful

As God's people in Communion with Christ, presence to and for us here in body and soul, let's pray confidently for what we need.

For Church pastors throughout the world, especially our Holy Father the Pope. May they always enthusiastically encourage the people of the world to receive and be the living Body of Christ and thereby flower into eternal grace, beauty, and truth.

For our regular Eucharistic meetings here in Church, may they bring us to an ever-deeper appreciation, pride in, and living union with Christ's Real Presence in the Eucharist.

For ourselves, that we may never fail to come every Sunday to be nourished at the table of the Lord and then spread his loving and healing presence to the world around us by charitable living.

For the sick, the old, the lonely, and the housebound, that through monthly reception of the Eucharist on First Fridays, they may participate in the body of Christ and be raised up.

For the dead, that having had a taste of the banquet of eternal life already in this world at the table of the Lord, they may enjoy it fully in the eternal feast of heaven.

And we ask all these prayers through Christ Our Lord who is here present with us his great and glorious Eucharistic people. Amen.

## Reflection

This week we also have the Sacred heart feast. The usual depictions of the Sacred heart, are not very artistically inspiring to say the least. But this is an important devotion. For in all iconography, the heart symbolizes love. The Sacred Heart symbolizes the infinite love of Christ, which he proved on the cross when his heart was pierced for us. It reminds us also that Jesus, in his human nature, has a real heart. He is not some remote God, spiritually divorced from humanity. The greatest things one could say of a person who had passed away, when I was young, was that they'd a "great heart". Lets pray that in our everyday lives we may imitate the great heart of Christ, in the human warmth of our love. Hail Mary.

# The Assumption of Mary

## Introduction

The Assumption of the Blessed Virgin Mary's body and soul into heaven was the only doctrine of the Church proclaimed by the unanimous voice of the faithful, *vox populi*. So it is important. Why? Because it confirmed Christ's resurrection, and prefigured our's, body and soul, at last. So let's confess any failure to appreciate this key belief.

## Homily

When I was lecturing in Palestine, I often visited the holy places—the nativity Church in Bethlehem, Calvary, the tomb of Christ in Jerusalem. One thing struck me; nowhere could I find Mary's tomb. She was with the early Church. They revered her; why didn't they keep her tomb? The answer, of course, is that there's no tomb, because of her assumption, body and soul, into heaven. Her body never rotted to dust, due to her sinlessness and, since her body was God's dwelling place, he couldn't let it decay.

But there are other reasons. Because she shared her son's suffering, it was right that she should share his bodily resurrection. Her assumption was the first fruit of that resurrection, an image of our resurrection at last. Her assumption highlights a key aspect of faith—bodily resurrection. Mary was taken body and soul to heaven. This prefigures how, on the last day, our bodies will be joined to our souls and be one with God forever.

But there is still more to this great feast. It highlights her continuing role in the Church and our lives. Raised up to her son's side, she understands, loves, and helps us from heaven because she's bodily human as we are. Moreover, her bodily assumption shows that all material things are holy; our bodies as well as our souls are sacred. Mary's a real in-the-flesh human mother in heaven. There have been visions lately of her crying blood. Of course she cries over her children's pain, because she loves each of us more than any earthly mother. She shudders to see any of her young ones, especially, destroying themselves physically and spiritually. For as a real, caring mother of the Church and world, she walks with us in suffering. And her prayers lead us home and enable our final triumph over evil. There's no final tomb for Mary; there won't be for us.

But there's one further great lesson of the Assumption—its social message. Mary tells us that she was raised up because God regarded her lowly state. These words should send a shiver down the spine of corrupt fat cats. For she tells us that God is on the side of those they crush; he casts down the mighty from their thrones and lifts up the lowly. He fills the hungry with good things and sends the rich away, empty. By choosing Mary, a village maid, and raising her up to glory as a paragon of our species, God shows he doesn't judge as the world does, but takes the part of the poor. So must we. Mary's Magnificat is a plea to all of us to help in the struggle for justice (Lk. 1:46-55). Mary, no paper saint, was really a social revolutionary, though we don't usually see her as such.

So, all in all, we've so much to give thanks for on this feast. In its light let's pray that Mary will continue to reign in our hearts, and that, as God's own, we'll be faithful to Christ and his Church through every suffering as she was, so that, like her, we'll be raised body and soul to glory with Christ the only Lord of love peace and happiness in body and soul for now and forever and ever. Amen.

So as God's people anticipating our final resurrection to eternal life, body, and soul like Mary, our mother in faith and glory, let's profess our faith.

### Prayers of the Faithful

As the people of God gathered on this glorious feast of our holy Mother, let's pray to God and her for what we need.

For the Church throughout the world and its leaders, that they may help raise all people up to God, and to their heavenly dignity.

For civil leaders, that they may raise all people, especially the poor and underprivileged, to a standard of living in keeping with their heavenly origin, dignity, and destiny.

For our young people, that they may cling to the faith like Mary through every joy and trail, and so be raised up to glory in body and soul, both in this world and forever more.

For ourselves in our homes, communities, and workplaces, that, imitating Mary, we, our children, and our neighbors may be raised up in body and soul to the glory of God when Christ comes again.

For the sick, that through our love and care they may know the love of God and his Holy Mother and be raised up above their suffering.

For the dead, that they may, like Christ and his mother, be raised up to glory with the help of our prayers.

And we ask all these prayers through Christ and his Holy Mother who, raised up to glory, looks after us all from her heavenly throne.


## Reflection

Michael Joncas's song *On Eagles' Wings* tells us, "he will raise you up on eagles' wings." Brendan Graham wrote the lyrics to a song called *You Raise Me Up* in which we hear the words, "You raise me up to more than I can be." That's what God did for Mary and what he'll do for each of us if we remain faithful through all the trials and suffering of life. We pray to Mother Mary, assumed into heaven as the first fruits of the resurrection that we too will be raised up body and soul, when our vital work in this world is done, and done well. Hail Mary.

# Saint Patrick's Day

## *Introduction*

This weekend we celebrate the great and joyful feast of Saint Patrick, the Irish national patron. He was and is still a great light of faith to all Christians and indeed the whole world. Let's confess any ways we fail in following him in faith and love and goodness.

## *Homily*

Why is Saint Patrick the national icon of Ireland? Maybe because down the years he's symbolized various aspects of the Irish identity. Our rich spiritual faith and all the great saints its produced. Our artistic tradition. Our struggle for freedom and nationhood. Yeats said early in the twentieth century that the task of our new state was to recreate the Irish soul lost through eras of occupation. Saint Patrick had a huge role in that recreation, coming to sum up our pride in the cultural, historical, and spiritual riches we inherited.

Some may laugh at the practice of dying rivers green on Patrick's day, but that shows ignorance of how huge the "wearing of the green" was in our struggle for identity at home and abroad. Immigrants in the USA marched and wore the shamrock to assert their rights when job signs read, "No Irish need apply." And gallant patriots, who struggled for the freedom and social equality of an oppressed race, were once hanged for wearing the green. So the shamrock came to stand for cultural, spiritual, and social freedom. And, as such, it reflects a universal human struggle for rights in the face of political and cultural repression. So our pride in Saint Patrick's Day is as vital to others as it is to us.

So why is it mocked today? I cringe when presenters on TV with fake foreign tones mock Irish accents and call for the scrapping of the Irish language in public life, or for a new manufactured national anthem. They'd make us third-class citizens again, cut off from all our ancestors fought for. And with this often goes an imported anti-religious ideology that ignores our rich religious heritage. A day that should celebrate our joy and pride in being Irish and our hard-won religious freedom is often trivialized into a booze-up. But maybe it's inevitable that today's real patron saints—money and economics—should squash the things of the souls we once cherished, and the transcendent freedoms we espoused.

Saint Patrick used the shamrock to teach the Trinity. Since, as a historian said, the Irish have had one foot in this world and one in the next, without Saint Patrick's legacy we would have little lasting to celebrate. The island of saints and scholars after him produced learning and art that was the envy of the world—round towers, high crosses, illuminated manuscripts. The Irish went out, in his vision, to dazzle the world. Thomas Cahill's book, *How the Irish Saved Civilization: The Untold Story of Ireland's heroic Role From the Fall of Rome to the Rise of Medieval Europe*, tells how Irish monks brought culture back to Europe in the dark ages. That legacy is continued by Irish-Americans and others of Irish origin who march proudly to honor him today.

For Patrick straddles the earth as well as the Irish landscape from Croagh Patrick (Patrick's Mountain) to Gallarus Oratory, an early Christian church in County Kerry, to St.Patrick's cathedral in New York. Yet we see him in his confessions as a very down-to-earth man. He was brought to Ireland from Wales as a slave, and Ireland became his home. It is even possible he was partly Irish, as some Irish people had settled in the Welsh area he came from. This explains how he could blend Christianity with pagan Celtic lore. His was never a sectarian faith; faith, learning, art, music, and poetry were one in his vision. So his followers ornamented life with rich imagination and spiritual depth.

On the mountain known as Sliabh Mish, Patrick prayed one hundred times a day and one hundred times at night, for freedom. We should pray for that today, for he represents all free souls. As such, Irish people, and all people, can celebrate this day, wear the shamrock, and sing with pride in his heritage; "Dóchas linn Naomh Pádraig, aspal mór na hÉireann" (Bring hope to us, St Patrick, great Apostle of Ireland).

So, as God's people, spiritual and cultural children of Patrick and the worldwide scholars, artists, and poets who have flourished under his tradition since, let's profess our faith.

## Prayers of the Faithful

And we pray to the father with the help of the prayers of Patrick for our needs.

For our Pope, that like Patrick, he may bring Christ's light to all. We pray for the Irish Church that in the all-embracing spirit of Patrick, it may thrive now as in his day.

For Irish people at home and abroad on this national holiday, especially youth forced to migrate to find work, that they may know our care and treasure along with us our land's great spiritual and cultural heritage.

For Irish missionaries abroad, that God may sustain them in their work and that they find in Saint Patrick a guide and inspiration.

For peace and reconciliation in Northern Ireland and throughout the world through the prayers and inspiration of Patrick.

For our sick, that they may know the love of the Lord through our care and love and that of Patrick and all the saints.

For our dead, especially those who've died recently, may they be helped by the prayers of Saint Patrick and all the Irish saints who have gone before them to eternal life.

And we ask all these our prayers through Christ Our Lord, who lives and reigns through his saints everywhere forever and ever. Amen.

## Reflection

Pope Francis said recently that he wanted a poor Church for the poor. He had no palace in Rio De Janeiro where he was archbishop, but an apartment where he cooked for himself and took the public bus to help the poor. Patrick was like that. His book, *The Confessions Of Saint Patrick* doesn't confess sin, but all that God did for him. He attributes nothing to himself—all to God. Simple love of, and reliance on, Christ enabled a holiness that lives on after 1500 years. Let's ask Mary to help us imitate him. Hail Mary.

# The Immaculate Conception

## *Introduction*

This great feast, one of the few left in the Church, reminds us of the dignity of the sinless one, our Holy Mother. For, since Christ was like us in all things but sin, so it was with his mother. Conscious of our efforts to overcome evil in our lives, let us call to mind our sins.

## *Homily*

"He has pulled down princes from their thrones and exalted the lowly" (Luke 1:52, JB). Mary's words say that the important people in God's world are not wealthy egotists, but innocent people who spend themselves doing good, though they seldom get worldly praise: pious nuns, kind carers, selfless fathers and mothers, faithful parishioners, and so on They're the ones we celebrate on this feast. At Mary's conception there were plenty of rich, self-serving people God could have chosen. Yet he went to Anna in a small village, and made her daughter free from sin so that she could bear his Christ for our salvation.

The message for us is to rediscover our innocence in a world where sin is almost the norm, where even Christmas innocence is secularized and commercialized into profits and New Year sales. By contrast, a Mary-like Christmas is twelve days of joyful family gatherings, midnight mass, visiting the crib, reaching out to all in love.

That is, this feast tells us to uphold God's gentle innocent values against the hard world, as Mary did, so that like her we will be raised up to the great heights too. Let's commit ourselves to such values, raise others up this Christmas, and help change the world and our Church to original innocence. For by choosing Mary, God called the world back to that innocence, as he calls each of us by this feast.

At Baptism, we put on a white garment, were freed from sin, and made God's sinless children; we were told to keep that white garment on until we went out with the saints to meet Christ at last. Lets do that against every structures of sin in the world, Of course we'll never be as perfect as Mary. But she understands that and loves us still, as a mother loves her baby through every misbehavior.

We'll never be fully perfect like Mary, but we can be holy, which is mainly a constant struggle to be as good as we can as mothers, fathers, sons, daughters, workers, priests, religious, whatever. Despite inadequacies and failures, we carry on, knowing God's overflowing grace in Christ can enable us to do great things, overcome evil, keep our Baptismal garment stainless, and free our souls from worldly corruption. This feast is a call to make straight a way for the Lord in our lives if we've drifted from that original vision.

Look at the difference the act of God on Mary's behalf made. And he constantly does the same for each of us, restores our innocence every day. Through prayer, confession, Advent, and Lenten renewal, he purifies a people fit for himself. And that's how his kingdom will come—through ordinary good people like ourselves, trying our best to bring the world back to an innocent original Eden. For the values of the sinful, cruel, violent world of which Satan is lord leave us empty and destroyed in soul on the edge of eternity; but Christ, born of a sinless mother, is Lord of life, love, goodness, beauty, and truth for our soul's happiness in this world and forever and ever. Amen.

So as God's people with an Immaculate Mother as our model, struggling to live up to our vocation to holiness, despite our recurrent sins, we profess our faith.

## Prayers of the Faithful

And as God's people let's pray for all our needs.

For our Holy Father the Pope and all the leaders of the Church, that they may continue to challenge the world with the sinless message of the gospel, of Christ, and of his holy mother.

For civil leaders, that they may do all they can to protect the innocents in society from injustice, crime, and evil.

For young people, that they may recommit themselves at each stage of their lives to the white Church garment put on at Baptism and Confirmation and never give up believing in God's love and grace.

For ourselves, that we may inspire our children, relatives, and friends with the quality of our lives as dedicated Christian people.

For the sick, the aged, the lonely, and the oppressed, that they may take courage from Mary's words, "he has pulled down princes from their thrones and raised up the lowly." Through our care may they know the care of God and his Holy Mother.

For the dead, that they may be freed from all sin, and restored to an immaculate state of soul as they enter heaven with the help of our prayers and continuing love and remembrance.

And we ask all these prayers through Christ, and the intercession before him by the immaculate Mother of us all.

## Reflection

The most amazing aspect of Bernadette and Lourdes is the reply of Mary to her, when she asked the lady, "Who are you?" "I am the Immaculate Conception," the lady said. And immediately she asked for Bernadette to help her heal the world in body and soul; to set up a church for spiritual healing, and a hospital for bodily healing. So this feast also links with social justice and healing in the world. Let us all pray for that too, for healing in our own lives, and for the innocent restoration of the world in the image of the simple, just, and Immaculate Mother of God, as we say, Hail Mary.

# The Sacred Heart

## Introduction

At a funeral I attended a person told me a story about the woman who had died. A few weeks before, she had almost died. Later she complained: "I was almost there. The Sacred heart was coming toward me with outstretched arms, and I was so happy. But they brought me back." Conscious of the importance of the Sacred heart devotion in the lives of many, let's confess any lack faith in his heart of love that is ever beating for us.

## Homily

This feast represents, as that woman rightly saw, the deep love of Christ for each of us. This sense of rest in the heart of Christ at last—the delights of the world multiplied a hundred fold—was such that the woman I mentioned didn't want to come back.

That total love in the heart of God is typified on the cross, as we see in our gospel. There we see his heart being pierced with a lance for us. He gave everything to the last drop of his blood, so that when he was pierced for our sake there came out blood and water. So that woman rightly saw that the Christ who died for us will not fail to give us every blessing on earth and unbelievable happiness in heaven if we only let him. And there's the rub. Christ can't force us to accept his love and grace. His heart burns to save, heal, and bring us every blessing, but we are free. He cannot help us unless we ask.

This is the story of the two thieves. One, hardened by the world, mocked Christ and refused his saving grace. The other, knowing his need for God, for his saving presence in his life, called out to Christ and was instantly brought to paradise. We should be like that thief, for no matter what our lives have been like, Christ is always there for us. All we have to do is to reach out and take his hand, and he'll lead us to every delight.

That boundless love of God for us in Christ is beautifully expressed in our first reading. There, God's love is represented as a father or mother's tender love for their child. God takes us in his arms, leads us with leading strings of love. He lifts us up like a mother feeding her child at the breast. He is like a mother lifting her little boy or girl to her cheek. And that's only a faint reflection of the love of God for us in Christ.

Saint Paul fills out that love further in our second reading. He prays that Christ may live in our hearts, so that planted in love and built on love, we may grasp the breadth and the length, the height and the depth, until knowing the love of Christ, which is beyond all knowledge, we are filled with the utter fullness of God. What can beat that description?

And its what we celebrate in this feast, the infinite riches of Christ's heart of love for us, which is beyond human understanding. How privileged we are through the practice of our faith, the Word, Holy Communion, and prayer to experience and grow in that love, until we go at last to meet him, like that woman, to rest in his outstretched arms. May our final glory be like that of the woman who saw the sacred heart coming to meet her; and may the immense joy she felt be our joy too, as we go out with all the saints at last to meet Our Lord. For the trials and sufferings of this world will be no more, as we rest in his heart, the Lord of all joy and peace and love to whom belongs the kingdom, the power, and the glory forever and ever. For all else passes, but his tender heart waiting to receive us is the end of all our journeying in this world, the end of all pain and frustration in our hearts too, made for love in his image. So as the people of God glorying in the immense love of his sacred heart for each of us, let's profess our joyful faith.

## Prayers of the Faithful

And as people with a special place in the heart of Christ, let us ask for the things that we need.

For our present gentle Pope, that, like the tender-hearted Christ, he may reflect the infinite love of God to the whole world.

For civic leaders, that they may govern the people with a special regard for each citizen's unique dignity as a child of God, especially those vulnerable and poor among us.

For our youth, that no matter what they do, they may never lose faith in the infinite love of Christ for them, and rest always in his sacred heart, beating ever with unconditional love for them.

For ourselves, that in our homes we may love our spouses and children with the same tender love that God has for us.

For the sick, the aged, and those suffering in body, mind, or soul in any way, that they may find in our care and the heart of Christ the healing and peace that they crave.

For the dead, that trusting in the mercy of Christ's loving heart they may walk confidently into the heavenly home he had ready for them from their first moment of life.

And we ask all these prayers through the same loving Lord, who is with us forever in love. Amen.

## Reflection

The heart is the emblem of love in society from Valentine hearts, to jewelry hearts, to heart-shaped wedding motifs. The heart is more than an organ that pumps blood around the body, it's a symbol of our deepest selves, our deepest loves, our deepest aspirations; it is the center of our feelings and our souls. It is there also where we meet the beating heart of the universe, which is God, a God of creative beauty and love, who descended to us to love us in Christ. "You must love the Lord your God with all your heart" (Luke 10:27, JB). Let's ask Mary to help us to return the love of God that created us, with all the love our heart is capable of, until we are one with his heart of love forever. Hail Mary.

# Acknowledgments

I want to thank all those who helped me in preparing this book and gave me such encouragement. First of all my family: Jerry and Dan; Mary: Frank and Joan; Johnny and Margaret and family, and Maureen and David and family; Pat and family; Michael and Joan and family; Mary and Denis. Also my nephews and nieces, especially Liam, for his computer help, and Deirdre and the kids; Francis and Theresa and the kids; Ger and Francesca in Italy; Marion and Tom; Philippa and family in England. Indeed I want to mention also my beloved niece Suzanne and her family in Canada whose encouraging emails has kept me going; Ann Marie and family in New Zealand; Evelyn and Paul and family; Louise, and Gina; Mairead and Michelle; Timmy and Anna in Australia; also my cousin Fiona who has been so encouraging for my literary endeavours.

I am especially grateful to my Nephew Dan and Mairead for their help and advice. Dan has labored beyond the call of duty to post my homilies on the internet and create a web page. This was and still is much appreciated. I also thank in particular my good fiend and patron, Pat Culhane and his family. Our mutual good friend in Dublin, Noel Murphy and all his kind contacts there; especially Johnathan Edwards, the literary agent. Also my close Dublin friend from Maynooth days, Aine Cassidy, who has been so encouraging

I thank Bishop Bill Murphy for giving me sabbatical time off from parish work to complete this project; also Bishop Ray Brown, for his continuing support and encouragement. Also my diocesan colleagues for their forbearance; after I completed and published my book of poems, they must have thought I was batty to take on another large project. I thank them for their support.

I want to list a few acknowledgements for some material in the text. I am indebted to Bishop Joseph Cassidy's book, These Might Help (Dublin, Veritas Press, 2000), for the little girl story at the beginning of my Homily for the Fourth Sunday of Advent A. Also I am indebted to Fr. Flor McCarthy's book, New Sunday & Holy Day Homilies (Dublin: Dominican Publications, 2002), for the poor boy and the man with the Mercedes story in my homily for the Twenty-sixth Sunday in Ordinary Time B.

Finally I thank Kim Cavannah and all those who helped in my publishers in Authorhouse, for bearing with me and producing such a fine final product.

Lightning Source UK Ltd.
Milton Keynes UK
UKOW04f1943010315

247061UK00002B/55/P

9 781496 9841